MW00780322

MONEY,
LIES,
AND
GOD

MONEY, LIES, AND GOD

INSIDE THE MOVEMENT TO DESTROY
AMERICAN DEMOCRACY

KATHERINE STEWART

BLOOMSBURY PUBLISHING
NEW YORK · LONDON · OXFORD · NEW DELHI · SYDNEY

BLOOMSBURY PUBLISHING
Bloomsbury Publishing Inc.
1385 Broadway, New York, NY 10018, USA

BLOOMSBURY, BLOOMSBURY PUBLISHING, and the Diana logo are trademarks
of Bloomsbury Publishing Plc

First published in the United States 2025

Bloomsbury Publishing Plc does not have any control over, or responsibility for, any
third-party websites referred to or in this book. All internet addresses given in this book
were correct at the time of going to press. The author and publisher regret any inconvenience
caused if addresses have changed or sites have ceased to exist, but can accept no
responsibility for any such changes.

ISBN: HB: 978-1-63557-854-6; EBOOK: 978-1-63557-855-3

LIBRARY OF CONGRESS CATALOGING-IN-PUBLICATION DATA IS AVAILABLE

2 4 6 8 10 9 7 5 3 1

Typeset by Westchester Publishing Services
Printed and bound in the U.S.A.

To find out more about our authors and books visit www.bloomsbury.com and sign up
for our newsletters.

Bloomsbury books may be purchased for business or promotional use. For information on
bulk purchases please contact Macmillan Corporate and Premium Sales Department at
specialmarkets@macmillan.com.

TABLE OF CONTENTS

Introduction 1

PART I. MONEY

1. California Dreaming 17
2. A Tale of Two Busches 38
3. School's Out Forever 59
4. The Room Where It Happens 82

PART II. LIES

5. The Permanent Emergency 97
6. The Resentment of the Campus Misfits 120
7. Smashing the Administrative State 144

PART III. DEMONS

8. The Rise of the Spirit Warriors 159
9. God and Man in Las Vegas 181
10. No Exit 195
11. Exporting the Counterrevolution 213

Conclusion: The Way Forward? 235

Acknowledgments 247
Notes 249
Index 319

AUTHOR'S NOTE

All references to arrests, indictments, convictions, and other legal proceedings were accurate and complete to the best of my knowledge at the time of writing. The reader is encouraged to monitor the current status of the proceedings.

INTRODUCTION

The man in the MAGA cap and the SIZE MATTERS T-shirt allowed me to take his picture. The "size" in question had to do with bullets, which were represented on the shirt in a line from what looked like pistol- to bazooka-grade. He warned me not to use the picture to humiliate my husband and exhorted me to "serve him well." It sounded like a joke, but the expression on his face was hard and angry. Not far from us stood a man in a T-shirt that read MAKE MEN MEN AGAIN. He glared at the crowd like he wanted to punch someone in the face. Women walked past us in red-white-and-blue outfits. Many had Bible verse numbers or slogans on their T-shirts, though quite a few sported images of guns, some of them aimed at "RINOs." At one of the booths nearby a group of women was raising money for the "patriots" of January 6, now incarcerated in "the DC gulag."

It was a hot summer day in 2023, and there was little new for me at this gathering of right-wing activists in Las Vegas, apart from the fact that the T-shirts seemed nastier than I had previously seen in fifteen years of reporting on such events. Yet as I took in the January 6 memorabilia, I couldn't help thinking back on another, very different event four years earlier. In 2019, I found myself in a seventeenth-century palazzo in Verona, Italy, for a gathering of the World Congress of Families, where I sat in on speeches and discussions with American, Russian, and European political activists on "the LGBT totalitarians" and the evils of "global liberalism." The message was in some sense the same as the one in Las Vegas, but it is safe to say that among the well-heeled, stylishly dressed, highly educated, and well-traveled participants there, members of the Nevada T-shirt crowd would have stuck out like a platter of corn dogs at a fine Italian trattoria.

The last of the speakers in Verona was a diminutive white-haired academic in a nondescript jacket and tie, the dean of a small law school in California, and his brief tirade about "gender confusion" among the "radical left" did not leave much of an impression on me. I did, however, take note of his name: John Eastman. The same Eastman would later show up at the podium on the White House lawn on the morning of January 6. He would then turn up as "Co-Conspirator 2" in the federal indictment of Donald Trump for conspiring to overturn the 2020 election, and he himself would be indicted in Georgia for the same conspiracy and disbarred in his home state of California.[1] (He has pled not guilty to conspiracy fraud and forgery charges.)[2]

It's a long way from the palazzo populists of Verona to the RINO hunters of Las Vegas, but they are clearly part of the same story. And who knows—maybe some of the dollar bills collected from the crowd in Nevada will end up in the pockets of John Eastman's legal defense team. Yet the same narrative must encompass a still more far-flung cast of characters and chain of events. The big story of our time is the rise of an antidemocratic political movement in the United States. Like any such movement, this one is diverse and complicated. It brings together a collection of people and ideas that in ordinary circumstances would not dream of sharing a bed. It is united in its profound rejection of the Enlightenment ideals on which the American republic was founded, and it represents the most serious threat to American democracy since the Civil War. It is best described as a new and distinctly American variant of authoritarianism or fascism. This movement—or more precisely, my investigation into this movement from a wide but necessarily limited range of experiences and perspectives—is the subject of this book.

ABRAHAM LINCOLN HAD it right when he said that the United States is dedicated to a proposition. The American idea, as he saw it, is the familiar one articulated in the preamble to the Declaration of Independence. It says that all people are created equal; that a free people in a pluralistic society may govern themselves; that they do so through laws deliberated in public, grounded in appeals to reason, and applied equally to all; and that they establish these laws through democratic representation in government. In the centuries after 1776, in its better moments, the United States exported this revolutionary creed and inspired people around the world to embrace their freedom.

But in recent years a political movement has emerged that fundamentally does not believe in the American idea. It claims that America is dedicated not to a proposition but to a particular religion and culture. It asserts that an insidious and alien elite has betrayed and abandoned the nation's sacred heritage. It proposes to "redeem" America, and it acts on the extreme conviction that any means are justified in such a momentous project. It takes for granted that certain kinds of Americans have a right to rule, and that the rest have a duty to obey. No longer casting the United States as a beacon of freedom, it exports this counterrevolutionary creed through alliances with leaders and activists who are themselves hostile to democracy. This movement has captured one of the nation's two major political parties, and some of its leading thinkers explicitly model their ambitions on corrupt and illiberal regimes abroad that render education, the media, and the corporate sector subservient to a one-party authoritarian state.

How did such an anti-American movement take root in America? That is the question I aim to address in this book.

As a reporter, I like to look first and theorize later. I am interested in facts, not polemics—though I won't stand in the way of facts when they lead to pointed conclusions. This book is therefore a collection of dispatches from the front lines of the current assault on American democracy. My goal has been to record what I have seen and heard from the leaders and supporters of the antidemocratic movement in the auditoriums and breakout rooms at national conferences, around the table at informal gatherings of activists, in the living rooms of the rank and file, and in the pews of hard-line churches. The story features a rowdy mix of personalities: "apostles" of Jesus, atheistic billionaires, reactionary Catholic theologians, pseudo-Platonic intellectuals, woman-hating opponents of "the gynocracy," high-powered evangelical networkers, Jewish devotees of Ayn Rand, pronatalists preoccupied with a dearth of (white) babies, COVID truthers, and battalions of "spirit warriors" who appear to be inventing a new style of religion even as they set about undermining democracy at its foundations.

I don't pretend to cover all the angles. Others have found new and important ways to report on the subject, and I reference or cite the work of as many as I can throughout the book in the hopes that it will inspire further study. Even so, I think I have scouted enough of the territory to say something about the origins and nature of the antidemocratic movement in America. In this preface—the last of the pages to be written for this book—I will offer a handful of principal findings.

Let me begin by repeating the obvious: this movement represents a serious threat to the survival of American democracy. Even at this late date, I continue to hear feel-good suggestions that the political conflicts of the moment are the result of incivility, tribalism, "affective partisanship," or some other unfortunate trend in manners that affects every side of the political debates equally. All will be well, the thinking goes, if the red people and the blue people would just sit down for some talk therapy and give a little to the other side. In earlier times this may have been sage advice. Today it is a delusion. American democracy is failing because it is under direct attack, and the attack is not coming equally from both sides. The movement described in this book isn't looking for a seat at the noisy table of American democracy; it wants to burn down the house. It isn't the product of misunderstandings; it advances its antidemocratic agenda by actively promoting division and disinformation. In the pages that follow, I will bring the receipts to support these uncomfortable facts. For now, I will venture that few who have familiarized themselves with this movement will be tempted to minimize the danger it represents to our collective well-being.

What are the root causes of this development? There is no simple answer. But I will get the ball rolling with an observation about time frames. It can sometimes seem that the antidemocratic reaction snuck up on us and suddenly exploded in our living rooms. I confess that when I look back over the decade and a half that I have spent reporting on the subject, the escalation of the threat appears breathtaking. In 2009, I was reporting on an antidemocratic ideology focused on hostility to public education that appeared to be gaining influence on the right. By 2021, I was writing about an antidemocratic movement whose members had stormed the Capitol—and about a Republican Party whose leadership disgracefully acquiesced in the attempted overthrow of American democracy. In the 2024 election, that party was rewarded for its betrayal of American values. Yet the swiftness of the fall should not distract from the long duration of the underlying causes. The present crisis is deeply rooted in material changes in American life over the past half century. The antidemocratic movement came together long before Donald Trump descended on a golden escalator in 2015 to announce his candidacy for president. The outcome of the 2024 election only confirms the fundamental calculus described in this book. The forces hurling against American democracy will long outlive the current political moment, and they will continue to feast on the carcass of the Republican Party. Their various elements have emerged along the fissures in American society, and they continue to thrive on our growing educational, cultural, regional, racial, religious, and informational divides.

Of particular note, the antidemocratic reaction draws much of its energy from the massive increase in economic inequality and resulting economic dislocations over the past five decades. In the middle of the twentieth century, capitalist America was home to the most powerful and prosperous middle class the world had hitherto seen. By the second decade of the twenty-first century, capitalism had yielded in many respects to a form of oligarchy, and the nation had been divided into very different strata. At the very top of the wealth distribution arose a sector whose aggregate net worth makes the rich men of earlier decades look like amateurs. Between 1970 and 2020, the top 0.1 percent doubled its share of the nation's wealth. The bottom 90 percent, meanwhile, lost a corresponding share.[3]

For the large majority of Americans, the new era brought wage stagnation and even, within certain groups in recent years, declining life expectancy. In the happy handful of percentiles located just beneath the 0.1 percent, on the other hand, a hyper-competitive group has managed to hold on to its share of the pie even as it remains fearful of falling behind.

I do not mean to suggest that the political conflicts of the present can be easily reduced to economic conflicts. Far from it. My point is that the great disparity in wealth distribution is a significant contributor to the wave of unreason that has swept our politics and our culture. It has fractured our faith in the common good, unleased an epidemic of status anxiety, and made a significant subset of the population susceptible to conspiracism and disinformation.

Different groups, of course, have responded differently. The antidemocratic movement is not the work of any one social group but of several working together. It relies in part on the narcissism and paranoia of the subset of the super-rich who fund this movement, having decided to invest their fortunes in the destruction of democracy. They appear to operate on the cynical belief that manipulation of the masses through disinformation will enhance their own prosperity. The movement also draws in a sector of the professional class that has largely abdicated its social responsibility. Much of the energy of the movement, too, comes from below, from the anger and resentment that characterizes life among those who perceive, more or less accurately, that they are falling behind.

As these groups jockey for status in a fast-changing world, they give rise to a politics of rage and grievance. The reaction may be understandable. But it is not, on that account, reasonable or constructive. Although the antidemocratic movement emerged, in part, out of massive structural conflicts in the American political economy, along with investment, by antidemocratic forces, in the infrastructure of their movement, it does not represent a genuine attempt to address the problems from which it arose. The new politics aims for results that few people actually want and that ultimately harm everybody. Grounded in resentment and unreason, the new American fascism is more a political pathology than a political program.

What are the main features of this pathology? In America, just as in unstable political economies of the past, the grievances to which the daily injustices of an unequal system give rise inevitably vent on some putatively alien "other" supposedly responsible for all our ills. America's demagogues, however, have a special advantage. They can draw on the nation's barbarous history of racism and the fear that the "American way of life" is slipping away, abetted by an out-of-touch elite. The story of this movement cannot be told apart from the racial and ethnic divisions that it continuously exploits and exacerbates. The psychic payoff that the new, antidemocratic religious and right-wing nationalism offers its adherents is the promise of membership in a privileged "in-group" previously associated with being a white Christian conservative, a supposed "real American," with the twist that those privileges may now be claimed even by those who are not white, provided they worship and vote the "right" way. At the same time, I will also show the movement is the result of the concerted cultivation of a range of anxieties that draw from deep and wide roots.

Another glaring and related attribute of this pathology is perhaps already in evidence in the description above of the man with the SIZE MATTERS T-shirt. Anxiety about traditional gender roles and hierarchies is the rocket fuel of the new American authoritarianism. Among the bearded young men of the New Right, it shows up in social media feeds bursting with rank misogyny. In the theocratic wing of the movement, it puts on the tattered robes of patriarchy, with calls for "male headship" and female subordination, and relentlessly demonizes LGBT people. On the political stage, it has centered around the long-running effort to strip women of their reproductive health rights and, in essence, make their bodies the property of the state. That effort has had significant consequences at the ballot box—which is why a sector of movement leadership is starting to speak openly about stripping women of the right to vote. The tragedy of American politics is that the same forces that have damaged so many personal lives have been weaponized and enlisted in the service of a political movement that is sure to make the situation worse.

This movement rejects the primacy of reason in the modern world at the same time that it rejects democracy. This is the darkest aspect of the phenomenon, and I describe it only after having grimly ruled out more charitable explanations. The bulk of this movement is best understood in terms of what it wishes to destroy rather than what it proposes to create. Fear and grievance, not hope, are the moving parts of its story. Its members resemble the revolutionaries of the past in their drive to overthrow "the regime"—but many are revolutionaries without a cause.

To be sure, movement leaders do float visions of what they take to be a better future, which typically aims for a fictitious version of the past: a nation united under "biblical law"; a people liberated from the tyranny of the "administrative state"; or just a place somehow made "great again." But in conversations with movement participants, I have found, these visions quickly dissipate into insubstantial generalizations or unrealizable fantasy. There is no world in which America will become the "Christian nation" that it never actually was; there is only a world in which a theocratic oligarchy imposes a corrupt and despotic order in the name of sectarian values.

These visions turn out to be thin cover for an unfocused rage against the diverse and unequal America that actually exists. They are the means whereby one type of underclass can be falsely convinced that its disempowerment is the work of another kind of underclass. They are expressions of pain, not plans for the future. Perhaps for the same reason, some of the movement's political projects often have a strangely performative character. Fantasy, cosplay, snark, the validation of heroic self-images, and the ritual infliction of pain on their political opponents—not changes in policy or material conditions—seem to be the point.

The best label I can find for the phenomenon—and I do not pretend it is a fully satisfactory label—is "reactionary nihilism." It is reactionary in the sense that it expresses itself as mortal opposition to a perceived catastrophic change in the political order; it is nihilistic because its deepest premise is that the actual world is devoid of value, impervious to reason, and governable only through brutal acts of will. It stands for a kind of unraveling of the American political mind—a madness that now afflicts one side of nearly every political debate.

Though this be madness, to borrow from Shakespeare, yet there is method in it. Too often, the analysis of the antidemocratic movement comes to an end with psychological and sociological observations about the voters who lend support to it. But what I have found in my reporting is that this is a leadership-driven movement, not merely a social phenomenon. A central finding in this book is that the direction and success of the antidemocratic movement depends on its access to immense resources, a powerful web of organizations, and a highly self-interested group of movers and backers. It has bank accounts that are always thirsty for more money, networks that hunger for ever more connections, religious demagogues intent on exploiting the faithful, communicators eager to spread propaganda and disinformation, and powerful leaders who want more power. It takes time, organizational energy, and above all, money to weaponize grievances and hurl them against an established democracy—and this movement has it all.

To be clear, there is no single headquarters for the reaction. There are, however, powerful networks of leaders, strategists, and donors, as well as interlocking organizations, fellow travelers, and affirmative action programs for the ideologically pure. That matrix is far more densely connected, well-financed, and influential at all levels of government and society than most Americans appreciate.

History shows, however, that better organization does not always flatten the contradictions. On the contrary, it can sometimes amplify the conflicts. This is perhaps the most difficult aspect of the antidemocratic movement to appreciate and the source of both its weakness and its strength. This movement is at war with itself even as it wages war on the rest of us. It consists of a variety of groups and organizations, each pursing its own agendas, each in thrall to a distinct set of assumptions. Viewed as a whole, it seems to want things that cannot go together—like "small government" and also a government big enough to control the most private acts in which people engage; like the total deregulation of corporate monopolies and also a better deal for the workforce; like "the rule of law" and also the lawlessness of a dictator and his cronies who may pilfer the public treasury; like a "Christian nation" that excludes many American Christians from the ranks of the supposedly righteous. It pursues this bundle of contradictions not merely out of hypocrisy and cynicism but because the task of tearing down the status quo brings together groups that want very different things and are even at odds with one another.

To sort a complex grouping of people into admittedly simplistic categories in the interest of making this project manageable, I have divided the principal actors of the antidemocratic reaction into five main categories: the Funders, the Thinkers, the Sergeants, the Infantry, and the Power Players. It is the interactions and tensions among these groups, I have come to think, that are key to understanding the origins and evolutions of the American crisis. Before getting on with the reporting I will therefore say a few more things about each of these groups.

The Funders come from the minute ranks of beneficiaries of the massive concentration in wealth over the past five decades. Some of the Funders you will meet here are already quite famous: former secretary of education Betsy DeVos, the Wilks brothers, Rebekah Mercer, Tim Dunn, and the Koch brothers among them. Others are less well known, and quite a few make a point of hiding in the rooms where dark money lives. There you will find the secretive Chicago billionaire who likes to go by the pseudonym Elbert Howell (a mash-up of references to the Midwestern anarchist Elbert Hubbard and the millionaire from *Gilligan's Island*?); a minor-league California real estate scion who has taken it upon himself to join in the destruction of the system of public education in the name of Jesus; his neighbor, the wife of a Pepsi heir, who helps fund election disinformation operations; a Wall Street hedge funder whose think tank sustains ideological extremists caught up in the January 6 coup attempt; a number of energy tycoons; some tech bros; and a surprisingly diverse cast of eccentrics that are transforming our country in ways you likely never thought possible.

The distinguishing feature of the Funders is that they have chosen to invest their fortunes in the subversion of democracy. Given their successes in business and the cultural power of money in America, they are often pictured, even by their critics, as masterminds overseeing an intricate and well-conceived plan to rule the world. I regret to report that they do not appear to be, on balance, geniuses. Too often, they operate on the basis of remarkably simplistic, reactionary ideas about politics and society. And they are dangerously wrong in their biggest idea—that destroying democracy is a means of creating wealth.

Apart from the cognitive and emotional limitations that at times accumulate alongside unmerited wealth, the main reason why the Funders are confused about their own genuine interests is that they have outsourced much of their thinking—just as they have outsourced so much else—to other people. The Thinkers are a subset of the increasingly insular professional elite that has emerged in the modern American economy. They spend much of their time shuttling around a number of densely connected institutions with anodyne names, often drawn from grand figures or moments in history: the Federalist Society, the Heritage Foundation, the James Madison Center, and so on. Many of the Thinkers can boast of credentials from the nation's elite educational institutions, though they may consciously have set themselves against their former teachers. They are the "anti-intellectual intellectuals," as it were.

Quite a few are amphibious; they travel freely between the genteel world of reactionary think tanks and the alt-right spaces where young men who deploy the "Pepe the Frog" emoji in their social media monikers trade misogynist, racist, and anti-Semitic aperçus. In revealing moments—like when the academically well-polished leader of the Heritage Foundation declared that the "second American Revolution" that he and his fellow Trump supporters are leading "will remain bloodless if the left allows it to be"[4]—it becomes clear that the Thinkers' credentials are often thin cover for ferocious levels of aggression and insecurity. I will pay special attention here to the men of the Claremont Institute—they are almost all men—whose erstwhile reverence for America's founders has been transfigured, with the help of political theorists purloined from Germany's fascist period, into material support for Donald Trump's attempted coup against the United States.

Many of the Thinkers subscribe to an ideology that now fits mainly under the label of "the New Right"—even though it is neither new nor conservative. Their core doctrine isn't so much a political theory as an unwavering conviction about the root of all evil in modern society. That root, they say, is a supposedly all-controlling "woke" elite that cancels right-wing speakers at campus events and controls the rest of the nation from the back rooms of diversity offices. In the real world, the Thinkers themselves represent a far more powerful professional elite, sustained in a lavish welfare system at a network of think tanks and advocacy groups, and serving at the pleasure of the billionaires who pay their salaries. When you peel back their intellectual claims and political programs, or so I have found, it becomes clear that many of these Thinkers are primarily engaged in an intra-elite struggle with their real nemesis: the group at the other end of the faculty lounge. The Funders and Infantry are, for them, useful fodder in a psychic conflict driven by a highbrow form of reactionary nihilism.

The Infantry are drawn mostly from the millions of Americans in the middle and lower-middle sections of the nation's widening economic, educational, and regional divides. This group is large and diverse, and includes many different identities, ideas, and agendas. You will meet some of the Infantry in these pages at school board meetings, where they hope to save the nation by banning books with LGBT or sex-related themes from school libraries (even when such books are nowhere to be found), or by suppressing instruction on the brutal history of slavery and segregation in America. You'll come across others on the ReAwaken America Tour—a traveling Christian nationalist series of events that offers to prepare American patriots in "fifth generation warfare" so that they can take on an ever-rotating cycle of conspiracies. You will find many of them in the pews of America's hard-line churches, where radicalized pastors nurture a cohort of "spirit warriors" intent on waging battle with the moderate-liberal-left "demons" that have purportedly commandeered the culture. The Infantry includes many of those that the knowledge economy left behind, the people who get riled up with rhetoric about "elites." Satisfying the economic and emotional needs of this group is always the ostensible source of legitimacy of the antidemocratic movement, but it is never the actual goal. The real role is to supply the Funders, Thinkers, and key players with enough votes to win (or, as we saw in 2020, enough to pretend to win) power.

Within the Infantry there's a special group of unit leaders, or "Sergeants," that turn the movement's money and messages into votes and political action at the local level. This group includes culture warriors moonlighting as school board members and "moms" who think "liberty" means banning books they don't like. But the least appreciated subset consists of the tens of thousands of pastors at America's conservative churches. Many belong to groups with militant names like the Black Robe Regiment, Watchmen on the Wall, Faith Wins, and Pastors for Trump, and some number encouraged or defended the attack on the U.S. Capitol on January 6. But not all Sergeants are evangelical. Indeed, they are not all Christian; among the Sergeant cohort you will find some people who are not religious at all.

Stitching the movement together is a tiny elite I will call the Power Players—leaders of the Christian nationalist movement's policy and networking groups, legal advocacy organizations, messaging initiatives, and other features—who amass tremendous personal power by mobilizing others around their agendas. Some are celebrity preachers that outgrew their local congregations and took on a national profile, on the model of Jerry Falwell of the Moral Majority or D. James Kennedy of Coral Ridge Ministries. Others are super-lobbyists with tremendous influence on elections and elected politicians, like Ralph Reed of the Faith and Freedom Coalition and Tony Perkins of the Family Research Council. Many of them get together at Council for National Policy or Ziklag gatherings, or at the National Prayer Breakfast, where they trade favors on the path to still greater power. Most sit astride organizations with budgets in the tens and hundreds of millions of dollars, command media and pastoral ministries that reach tens or hundreds of millions of Infantry, and have the ear of presidents and other political leaders. They are the operational masterminds of the antidemocratic movement, and their organizations turn the Funders' money and the Infantry's votes into political power.

The dominant ideology they cultivate among the rank and file of America's antidemocratic movement is Christian nationalism. But this label can be misleading. Christian nationalism is not a religion. It is not Christianity. It is a political identity with a corresponding political ideology, and the ideology in question doesn't have a lot to do with the way many if not most Americans understand Christianity. You don't have to be a Christian to be a Christian nationalist, and plenty of patriotic Christians want nothing to do with Christian nationalism. "White evangelical," as I will show, should no longer be regarded as interchangeable with "Christian nationalist." Sectors of other varieties of Christianity and other religions, along with members of other racial and ethnic groups, are moving in, while at least some of the old members are moving out. More importantly, what matters is not formal or denominational religious identity but partisan political identity—and this partisan identity has in turn become something like a substitute religion. Christian nationalism does not just draw on old strands of a diverse religion but has also fabricated a radically new, intensely politicized religion centered on a newly concocted "pro-life" theology and—among a large number—the idea of "spiritual warfare."

Although it is at bottom a political ideology, moreover, Christian nationalism is not merely a policy program; it is perhaps best understood as a political mindset. That mindset, as I explain in further detail below, includes four basic dispositions: catastrophism; a persecution complex; identitarianism; and an authoritarian reflex. Catastrophism in this context is the foreboding conviction that the nation is doomed and that the blame falls squarely on the faithless. The persecution complex rests on the belief that conservative Christians are the principal victims of discrimination in America. Identitarianism is the belief that a "real" or "authentic" subset of Americans are entitled to rule over the rest. And the authoritarian reflex always calls for a strongman savior, on the grim assumption that only the cruel and lawless survive in a cruel and lawless world.

The chief limitation of the label "Christian nationalism," however is that it represents only one end of the antidemocratic movement. It is a tool for mobilizing the grievances of the people; but a stadium crowded with resentments would not add up to a political program without a tremendous amount of financial and organizational support. This is where the Funders and the Thinkers come in.

The Funders might share the Christian nationalist mindset with their followers but they certainly don't have to, and many do not. Some identify with other religious traditions, and some appear to have confessed to no religion more than the worship of money. The core of their belief system is that democracy in its current configuration threatens their power and privilege—as well as freedom and prosperity for all, or so they like to add.

Some of the Thinkers are even less committed to specific faith traditions than their rich patrons. One branch is essentially atheistic, another espouses hard-line Catholicism; some are Jewish, and many don't appear to have much personal interest in religion. They leave the Christian nationalism and all that for the little people whom they half-heartedly pretend to care about. They may be against the "woke" elite, but they aren't against elites as such. Indeed they see themselves as members of a new elite, destined to rule over a population that can never be brought to virtue on its own.

In brief, what the Funders are buying is not always what the Thinkers and Sergeants are selling or what the Infantry is hearing. Each gains power by deceiving the others. Inevitably, they attempt to deceive the rest of us, too, and then they begin to deceive themselves. The interactions among the elements of the antidemocratic reaction bring out the worst in each, as it were, and ensure that the whole will be worse than the sum of its parts. It would be nice to think that the movement will crumble under the weight of its internal contradictions, but that may be wishful thinking. Many such movements throughout history have destroyed the nations from which they arise before getting around to destroying themselves.

The chief threat to American democracy comes from a kind of collective psychosis. The age of economic and cultural fracture has yielded a politics of unreason. But the politics of unreason is not a random walk. It unravels in a particular direction. Unreason is the first and last resort of the enemies of democracy. In the final analysis, the antidemocratic movement is a symptom, not a cause, of the American crises.

This fact, as I will lay out in a brief afterword, can be a source of hope for the future. It can serve as a guidepost for the deep structural and organizational solutions that this crisis demands. In the meantime, I invite you to leave behind the land of political theory, buckle up, and join me on a journey through the madness and the beauty of the American political landscape.

PART I

Money

CHAPTER I

California Dreaming

M ontecito is a more complicated place than it looks. This sunny spot on the central coast of California is famous now as a playground for A-list celebrities and exiled royals. But it is also home to Westmont College, a private evangelical college that bills itself as the number one Christian liberal arts school in the western United States. And down among the foothills, scattered mostly in the lanes without views, you will find, inhabited by mere mortals, some rather modest homes, nothing like the eighteen-thousand-square-foot spread that Prince Harry and Meghan Markle purchased from a villainous Russian oligarch in 2020.[1] It was from our rental house, down in the foothills, fifteen years ago as of this writing, that I took my daughter to the local public elementary school, Cold Spring School, a picturesque jumble of one-story buildings in the SoCal Spanish style with a view of the mountains. And it was at that school that I first came across the Good News Club, an adult-led after-school Bible study group whose purpose is to convince children as young as five that their local public school endorses a fundamentalist variety of evangelical Christianity.

The beginnings of the investigative journey that began with that experience are recorded in my first book on Christian nationalism, *The Good News Club: The Christian Right's Stealth Assault on America's Children* (PublicAffairs, 2012). As I recount there, I wondered at first if the arrival of the club could be traced to some of the many families at the school who were associated with

Westmont College. But this hunch turned out to be incorrect. The Westmont parents in my circle were as surprised and alarmed by the arrival of the club as I was. The Good News Club was the work of outsiders. They were part of a national operation intended to erode the separation of church and state and to undermine public education at the same time. The organizers and funders of this agenda had no connection with our local community.

Or so I thought for some years.

On the stretch of verdant land just north of Sycamore Canyon Road, just a few hundred yards from Cold Spring School, the homes of the merely rich give way to the estates of the truly rich. There, just a tiara's toss or two from Meghan and Harry,[2] lies another one of the homes you can't see from the road. It is the residence of Joan Holt Lindsey and her husband, James B. Lindsey, an heir to a Pepsi fortune.[3] "It's part private park, part sanctuary," a write-up in *Forbes* pants.[4] "Altogether, it's a compound for the ages." Mira Vista—a home of this caliber naturally has a name—was in recent years listed for sale at $72.5 million. (As of this writing it appears to have been taken off the market. Perhaps it can be yours for a price cut; Zillow estimates the value at a mere $46 million.)[5]

But Mira Vista is something more than a private residence. It is also listed as the address of the James and Joan Lindsey Family Foundation.[6] A search of the foundation's public reports turns up, proportionally speaking, little of the kind of community-centered philanthropy characteristic of other wealthy locals. Instead, the records show a vast and steady flow of contributions to leading organizations in America's Christian nationalist movement. Every year over the past decade, the Lindsey Foundation has donated seven-figure sums in total to organizations such as the Family Research Council, Focus on the Family, Advancing American Freedom, American Values, WallBuilders Presentation, and evangelistic media and entertainment-focused organizations Mastermedia International and the Hollywood Prayer Network. Other grantees include the conservative think tank the National Center for Public Policy Research, known for promoting climate denial and other reactionary causes, and the Council for National Policy (CNP), a networking group for movement leadership and funders.[7]

"We are a Christian country. And the Founders were—definitely—and our founding documents were written under prayer each day of the writing," Joan Lindsey has said.[8] A vocal Trump booster, she announced on the eve of the

2020 election that "this election will either preserve faith's sacred place in our country or destroy it."[9]

From 2019 to 2022, the Lindsey Foundation funneled well over $1 million to a new organization, Faith Wins, intended to mobilize pastors at conservative churches in swing states to bring out the pro-Trump Republican vote. Faith Wins is part of a Lindsey-backed coalition called The Church Finds Its Voice.[10] In many respects, the Lindseys' investment in Faith Wins and The Church Finds Its Voice follows a long-standing pattern in the Christian nationalist movement of backing projects to turn America's networks of many thousands of conservative churches into a powerful partisan political machine.

But there is also something novel in the Faith Wins project, and it sheds light on the direction of the antidemocratic reaction in the aftermath of Trump's attempted coup. Unlike pre-Trump get-out-the-pastors projects, Faith Wins has made concerns about "elections integrity" a central part of the message for its target audience. These days, it isn't merely mixing its religion with democratic political campaigns; it is mixing its religion with a campaign against democracy. And Faith Wins is hardly alone. A number of other pastor-focused initiatives are working from the same playbook. Ken Blackwell, who serves as a senior fellow for the Family Research Council, a right-wing policy group that is affiliated with Watchmen on the Wall, a pastor-focused organization that has held many dozens of gatherings in swing states around the country as well as online, posted an article titled "Election Integrity Reform Is Key to Preventing a Socialist Takeover of America."[11] Tulsa, Oklahoma–based preacher Jackson Lahmeyer, who leads Pastors for Trump, which claims to have a chapter in every state, routinely lies about widespread voter trickery. Claiming without evidence that there has been "tremendous fraud," Lahmeyer has said, "The 2020 presidential election, that was a stolen election, and it can never, ever happen again."[12]

The pretense is that this is intended to shore up public confidence in elections. The reality is that the groups involved are consciously helping to lay the foundations for an antidemocratic future. The desired end state of Christian nationalism today is neither to win a majority nor to secure a seat at the table in a pluralistic democracy but to entrench minority rule under the facade of democracy.

Promoting the Big Lie about the (supposedly) stolen 2020 election is simply the way that movement leaders planned to undermine the legitimacy of all elections in preparation for legislation intended to tilt elections indelibly in their favor. The lesson from Montecito, as I will further explain in subsequent chapters, is that there appears to be no shortage of superwealthy individuals like Joan Lindsey eager to spring for the big bills required to spread the Big Lie. When exactly did so many rich people give up democracy?

CHANTILLY, VIRGINIA, SITS on the edge of Fairfax County, a prosperous D.C.-adjacent region pocketed with residential subdivisions. On a Thursday morning in late September 2021, at the Community Baptist Church, a midsize church built in the 1990s, a crowd of about fifty individuals, mostly pastors, most of them men, breakfasts on Chick-Fil-A sandwiches. A Republican candidate for the Virginia House of Delegates is there to work the room, as is a representative of the campaign of Glenn Youngkin, the ex-McKinsey private equity fund manager who deployed culture war tactics to upset Terry McAuliffe in the 2021 Virginia gubernatorial election.

I am there with my friend Steven Baines, at the time the executive pastor of National City Christian Church, the "national cathedral" of the Christian Church (Disciples of Christ), a social-justice-oriented congregation. Today he is serving as my "beard," as it were. Groups like Faith Wins work with "complementarian" churches that exclude women from leadership positions, and I asked him to join me because I was concerned that my presence in a room full of male pastors might seem anomalous.

With his open, friendly smile and modest demeanor, Baines has the intuitive ability to gain the trust of diverse congregations—a skill he uses in his work as an interfaith organizer. Raised in a conservative religious household, he counted himself a religious conservative until the day he came out as gay and embraced equality-focused forms of the faith. His former employer has supported a number of social justice campaigns. One such effort, the Poor People's Campaign: A National Call for Moral Revival, which draws on the social gospel movement that seeks to apply Christian ethics to a range of social challenges, calls for living-wage jobs and voter protections and is currently cochaired by Rev. William Barber II and Rev. Dr. Liz Theoharis. Baines also worked for several years as a field director for religious outreach at Americans United for Separation of Church and State, a national advocacy organization that seeks to protect First Amendment freedoms.

When I meet Baines in advance of the gathering at his home in the suburbs of D.C., which he shares with his husband and collection of pets, he seems game, if slightly apprehensive. As he prepares me a cup of tea, he relates a story from his childhood. "I shared a bedroom with my older brother who loved to terrorize me with stories about 'the bogeyman' who would attack me in the middle of the night." He laughs at the memory. "And I think it's very interesting that there are political and religious forces in America that want to make this debate about religious freedom or religious liberty the new bogeyman in American politics. What they are trying to do with their scare tactics is create a myth they can hold up and say, 'This bogeyman is coming after your religious freedoms, and pretty soon we're going to be communist Russia or communist China or communist Cuba, where faith is exiled.'"

We bundle into Baines's car, and after a short drive we arrive at the sanctuary of the Community Baptist Church. We pick up our Chick-Fil-A breakfast sandwiches and take our seats. I am one of only four or five women in the room, and I feel relieved to be Baines's plus-one. He is the official attendee; I am just there to smile and nod affirmatively. While I am putting on my best smile, however, he is fidgeting. He seemed comfortable enough on the ride over, but this setting seems to trigger something in him.

"Just a little PTSD," he whispers. He grins bravely, but I can see that the wounds from a childhood lived in shame for who he is are still tender. Then the meeting comes to order, and an organizer calls on the first speaker.

Chad Connelly bounds onto the stage bursting with energy. "We are in the middle of doing over forty cities, just like this, in sixteen states between Labor Day and Thanksgiving," he says breathlessly. He rattles off some statistics from an earlier leg of his "American Restoration Tour": eighty-nine meetings with 2,965 pastors across the country who command flocks totaling 741,000 potential voters.

A former chair of the South Carolina Republican Party and director of faith engagement under Reince Priebus at the Republican National Committee for four years, Connelly is both a political veteran and a key player in the Christian nationalist movement. In 2017 he appeared on a membership list of the United States Coalition of Apostolic Leaders (USCAL), a group associated with a religious movement that argues that conservative Christians should control all aspects of government and society.[13] Notably, Connelly serves on the CNP, where he sits on the board of governors. (Joan Lindsey, presumably by virtue of her open pocketbook, is a Gold Circle Member.)[14] The council was founded by Paul Weyrich, Tim LaHaye, and others at the dawn of the Reagan era. Today it is one of the movement's key networking operations, the apparatus that connects the "doers and the donors," as Rich DeVos, Betsy DeVos's father-in-law, put it, of Christian nationalism and the conservative political machine.[15]

"You're about to hear a presentation that's going to elevate your ability to understand what's going on, and it's also going to inspire you to say, 'I'm not doing enough,'" Connelly says, his voice cheerful but firm. "Everybody you know needs to have voted. Everybody you know needs to go vote early. Every church you know needs to do voter registration. Every pastor you know needs to make sure one hundred percent of the people in their pews are voting, and voting biblical values." As in most Christian nationalist gatherings, "voting biblical values" is a transparent euphemism for voting Republican.

Connelly happily makes clear that his work owes everything to the generosity of Joan Lindsey and her family foundation. "Joan Lindsey just started talking to me about this," Connelly tells the crowd. "So a couple years ago we really started this thing called The Church Finds Its Voice." He nods. "If y'all have ever seen Christian leaders on television, Joan Lindsey's likely trained 'em. She's a media guru. An expert."

THERE IS A part of Connelly's message, both here and in his social media presence, that will be familiar to anyone who has taken in a minimum dose of Christian nationalist rhetoric. But it's worth paying attention to the language because it reveals something about what Christian nationalism is and is not. There is a tendency on the outside to characterize the movement in terms of faith identities ("the evangelicals"), political doctrines ("America is a Christian nation"), and policies (like abortion bans). But on the inside, it looks more like a specific collection of feelings. What unites its varied constituencies is a certain mindset, or a common way of reacting to specific features of the outside world. And the first element of this mindset, as Connelly understands intuitively, is that America is going to hell real fast. A refrain heard across the movement, in various forms, is a hyped-up fear of the modern world meant to get people to the barricades, even if the enemy is illusory.

"This is a crucial time in our nation's history," Connelly says. "Is this our 1776 moment? Or is it 1944?" He adds, "I've never voted for a pro-death person. Never voted for anybody of any stripe that was okay with killing a baby in a mommy's tummy." In Christian nationalist circles today, every election is a contest against absolute evil, and the consequences of failure almost too dire to imagine. Only radical action can stop the apocalypse just around the corner.

A second element of the mindset is the conviction that we face the immediate reality of persecution. The "we" here refers to conservative Christians— and mostly to white conservative Christians. A 2023 survey, conducted by the Public Religion Research Institute (PRRI), which conducts research at the intersection of faith, culture, and public policy, shows that 85 percent of people who subscribe to Christian nationalist ideas also agree with the proposition that "discrimination against white people is at least as big a problem as discrimination against minorities."[16] An earlier report, this one a partnership between PRRI and the Brookings Institution, shows that three-quarters of Republicans and Trump supporters and nearly eight in ten white evangelical Protestants believe that discrimination against Christians is as big of a problem as discrimination against other groups.[17] Indeed, as PRRI founder Robert P. Jones, author of *The Hidden Roots of White Supremacy and the Path to a Shared American Future* (Simon & Schuster, 2023), tells me, "The protection of white Christian dominance, rather than the advancement of policy priorities, is the animating force among the political conservative movement today." In essence, as he notes, it's identity and not policy that drives divisions—and creates opportunities for movement funders and strategists to curate identitarian grievance and then exploit it on a wave of cash.

It is important to add that, whatever their ultimate causes, both the catastrophism and the persecution complex find expressions more frequently in status or cultural anxieties than in economic anxieties. "Compared to cultural factors, economic factors were significantly less strong predictors of support for Trump" in 2016, according to Jones. "Trump's 'Make American Great Again!' slogan tapped anxieties that were less about jobs and economic mobility but more about a deep sense of protecting a white Christian America from what they perceive to be a foreign and corrupting influence."[18]

A 2018 study from the National Academy of Sciences agreed that fear of status loss was a major driver of support for Trump. "It's not a threat to their own economic well-being; it's a threat to their group's dominance in our country overall," said Diana C. Mutz, the author of the study and a political science and communications professor at the University of Pennsylvania.[19] While political uprisings are often about downtrodden groups rising up to assert their right to better treatment and more equal life conditions relative to high-status groups, she said, "the 2016 election, in contrast, was an effort by members of already dominant groups to assure their continued dominance and by those in an already powerful and wealthy country to assure its continued dominance . . . Those who felt that the hierarchy was being upended—with whites discriminated against more than blacks, Christians discriminated against more than Muslims, and men discriminated against more than women—were most likely to support Trump."[20]

CONNELLY CERTAINLY APPEARS to feel the threat. At the height of the COVID-19 pandemic, he wrote that "government leaders decided—in their flawed wisdom—that church gatherings were not *essential* to society. You heard that right."[21] In religious right circles, the pandemic was a radicalizing event. It confirmed many Christian conservatives in their conviction that they are the most persecuted group in American society. It made many feel that they would soon be arrested, injected, and/or poisoned on account of their beliefs— that the tyrannical, Orwellian government long familiar to them from their bedtime stories suddenly had a very real face, and it looked a lot like Dr. Fauci.

A third element of the Christian nationalist mindset is the conviction that "we" have a unique and privileged connection to this land. The "we" here, again, is not "the people" mentioned in the Constitution; "we" are conservative Christians, mostly white, the supposedly original and authentic population of the land. It all starts, as Connelly understands, with the belief in a golden age of yore. "This place has been ordained by God," he said in a September 2020 podcast episode. "When the founders determined that, of course they were reading the Bible, and they were believers of the word of God," he explained. "And so America became unique and special because the founders understood that the founding had to tie in to God."[22] The idea that conservative Christians therefore have the right and the duty to rule the nation and impose their values on others, by force if necessary—all this follows closely upon this mindset.

A fourth and final piece of the mindset of Christian nationalism involves a rather dark picture of the nature of the world: Jesus may have great plans for us, but the reality is that this is a cruel place in which only the cruel survive. In the more self-conscious exercises of Christian nationalist thought, this perspective expresses itself in explicit critiques of the social gospel, or the idea that Christianity has something to do with cultivating empathy, loving thy neighbor, and caring for the least of these. Nineteenth-century versions of populism sometimes made use of social gospel Christianity, typically as a prelude to wealth redistribution programs, and progressive Christians today continue to draw on scripture in their pursuit of a more just society. But today's Christian nationalists have no time for the Jesus-is-love crowd. They want their Jesus to lift weights and carry a sword, and they are counting on Him to come down hard on the moochers and layabouts and those who challenge supposedly righteous hierarchies. The belief in cruelty in a cruel world finds expression in radical economic doctrines that embody a cold and punitive spirit, favoring total deregulation of exploitative monopolies and the elimination of the social safety net.

As Connelly puts it, the other reason for America's uniqueness and specialness—apart from the fact that it was ordained by God—"is the free-market system, which of course is God's biblical economy." Exactly where in Deuteronomy one is to find the commandments of hypercapitalist orthodoxy, he does not say. No matter—next comes the fear and loathing. "There's a far left now that doesn't believe in God, they're godless completely. They believe the state is the supreme being," Connelly says on the podcast. "It's actually a godless, communistic, Marxist style of government."[23]

It would be hard to find a mindset more at odds with the spirit of the American founding and the actual foundations of the American republic. Andrew Seidel, a constitutional attorney and author whose books include *The Founding Myth: Why Christian Nationalism Is Un-American* (Sterling, 2019), told me bluntly: "America was not built on the Bible, and that book had little to no influence on the creation of the American Constitution. The framers almost never referenced the Bible when they were debating the Constitution in Philadelphia in 1787. The separation of church and state, on the other hand, is an American original—that idea was born in the Enlightenment and first implemented in the American experiment. That separation ensures that we all have freedom without favor, and equality without exception."

There is no room in Christian nationalism for the separation of church and state encoded in the Constitution, however, no recognition of the pluralism that characterized the American experiment from the start, no interest in the rationalist, scientific spirit of America's founders. But there is also relatively little self-awareness, and if there is a heavy irony hanging over Connelly's bombastic claims about America's uniqueness and specialness and his defense of Donald Trump's effort to subvert the "sacred" Constitution, no one in Chantilly—perhaps with the exception of Steve Baines—appears to detect it.

THE BOTTOM LINE for Connelly—hardly surprising, given his past as a Republican Party operative—is to harvest votes. More precisely, his goal is to get the pastors present to harvest the votes. The Faith Wins website encourages event attendees to help lead voter registration in their churches with the help of a "Pastors Tool Kit," become poll watchers, and assist "with Voter Integrity Efforts" and other actions.

"Every Christian in every church in America needs to be registered to vote—and then needs to SHOW UP and vote Biblical values on Election day," the website reads.[24] Pastors are given a QR code, along with an online form, which leads to a suite of tools and messaging materials, including voter guides, voter registration resources, and videos they can use to activate their congregations.

There isn't the slightest doubt in Connelly's mind or the rest of the room about which party those congregations are expected to support. Within the Christian nationalist movement in general, there is little curiosity about the political opposition, and still less effort to understand it on its own terms. Democrats are simply—and sometimes literally—represented as demonic. "You are losing freedoms every day in this nation. They're being taken away like crazy," Connelly tells the Chantilly crowd. "The Constitution has been discarded and tossed aside very quickly. And when you lose the little freedoms, you already lost the big ones and didn't even recognize it. And it's happening at a record pace."

The demonization of the political opposition has always been a leitmotif of the Christian nationalist movement, but in Chantilly it has taken an explicitly antidemocratic turn. Running through Connelly's Chantilly presentation and his media appearances is the new defining theme in the Trump era:

"election integrity." The point, of course, is to convey the frightening but entirely unsubstantiated belief that vast plots are afoot to steal Republican votes. The same theme is also showing up at the State Policy Network, which serves as a networking hub for state-policy-focused think tanks. Election integrity is also a keynote theme of some of the newer state-level conservative organizations, such as the Virginia Project, which describes its mission as "leading the charge to uncover evidence of election manipulation, irregularities, and voter fraud in Virginia," and has referred to Democrats as "rats." Vote early, the group's mailings insist—because that way "your name is marked as voted and <u>no one can claim to be you and steal your vote</u>."[25]

Connelly hits all the key message points in Chantilly. "We cannot sit on the sidelines and let ourselves get kicked in the teeth, and guess what, it's happening. Like November the fourth," he says, alluding to the 2020 election. By "kicked in the teeth," it is clear from his expression that he doesn't mean that Trump was defeated; he means that Trump was cheated.

FOLLOWING CONNELLY AT the podium is Tim Barton, son of David Barton, founder of the WallBuilders organization and one of the Christian nationalist movement's most influential activists. WallBuilders presents itself as "dedicated to presenting America's forgotten history and heroes, with an emphasis on the moral, religious, and constitutional foundation on which America was built—a foundation which, in recent years, has been seriously attacked and undermined."[26]

In Chantilly, we are told that David Barton has taken ill. But Tim disposes himself in a manner that would make his father proud, offering a rapid-fire litany of Bartonesque half-truths and distortions of American history. America's founders were one and all "believers," according to Tim Barton, and the Constitution comes straight from the Bible. And an Advanced Placement U.S. history course for high school students, Barton adds for good measure, is just liberal propaganda aiming to undermine America's godly heritage.

Tim Barton has delivered versions of this talk at numerous events, such the 2023 Moms for Liberty Conference in Philadelphia, Pennsylvania, which I report on in a later chapter. Like his father, he poses as a "nonpartisan" historian. But nobody can take the pretense seriously, not even himself. There is no way to separate his pseudohistorical narratives about the nature of

George Washington's faith from his argument that voting Republican today is exactly what George Washington wants us to do.

Barton's presence here underscores a fact about the Christian nationalist movement that those who are not close to it often fail to appreciate. From the outside one sees a collection of seemingly independent organizations pursuing distinct projects. From the inside, the movement looks much more like a hive, with individuals and groups reassembling themselves in ever-changing configurations, but always around the same purpose.

Faith Wins is in many ways a reincarnation of prior groups; among the most prominent of these was United in Purpose. A data, networking, and messaging organization, UiP played a vital role in fostering evangelical and conservative Christian unity in the run-up to the 2016 election.[27] David Barton was a key figure in that group and many others with overlapping agendas. According to movement research and data guru George Barna, as of 2016, "there were roughly 75 faith-oriented non-profit organizations, along with a few thousand conservative churches in the nation, who strategically cultivated support for a variety of pro-life, pro-family, limited government candidates in swing states." United in Purpose, Barna said, pulled them together. "The glue that bound together the entities in the United in Purpose partnership was their faith in Jesus Christ, their conservative Bible-based theology, and the shared notion that politics was one of the life spheres in which their faith should have influence."[28]

Faith Wins and The Church Finds Its Voice draw from Barna's work, too. "We had Barna do that data for us," Connelly says in Chantilly. In its background materials, The Church Finds Its Voice claims that it consists of a coalition of four groups (of which Faith Wins is one), which are "backed by 75 others."[29]

Tim Barton is unnervingly keen to emphasize a certain rather violent type of imagery embedded in Christian nationalist mythology. His father, David, has long been obsessed with old stories about America's colonial-era priests tearing off their robes, becoming soldiers, and leading their congregations out into military battle. He and WallBuilders created a group of activist conservative clergy called the Black Robe Regiment[30] in remembrance of the colonial-era ministers who argued for the cause of independence from the pulpit. "I can go down the list of dozens of pastors who led their congregations to oppose the British because they open fired on us, they declared war on us," Tim Barton says. Referring to the battles of Lexington, Bunker Hill, and Concord, he adds, "Almost every one of these early battles it was nothing more than pastors leading their churches in the battle."

The concern with masculine military virtue, though always a part of the movement, has become a signature feature of Christian nationalism (and its adjacent ideologies on the New Right) in the Trump era. For example, Tony Perkins, head of the Family Research Council, has in recent years formed a partnership with Lt. Gen. (Ret.) William Boykin, who formerly served at the Central Intelligence Agency and has played a role in nurturing Christian nationalist networks in the military and among "disaster relief" NGOs abroad. The pair have helped lead a men's ministry called Stand Courageous to help men "make commitments that will move men closer to God's good purpose and design—men who will Stand Courageous!"[31] At Stand Courageous gatherings across the country, masculinity, patriarchy, and militarism are the name of religion itself. "We need men to be men, tough with compassionate strength, bent toward justice without compromise, locking arms and standing," the group's materials declare. "We need to be the men God created us to be; warriors for all that is right, true, and just."[32]

Other men's ministries are humming the same tune. Video from the first day of the 2023 Emerge Men's Conference at Awaken Church, a church network with eight locations in three southwestern states, shows a mini-drama staged for the purpose: A helicopter lands and armed men cosplaying in military gear kick the bad guys to the side and rappel onto the stage to "rescue" a damsel in distress.[33] As a male vocalist sings "Freedom! Freedom!" in a triumphant mode, the word VALOR is superimposed over the action and a cheering crowd.

In the pre-Trump era, reporting on this kind of militaristic rhetoric was inevitably greeted with a shrug and the excuse that it was, after all, merely rhetoric. But on January 6, 2021, a number of pastors aligned with the Black Robe movement urged their flocks to participate in the attack on the U.S. Capitol in support of Donald Trump's effort to steal the 2020 election.[34]

BEFORE INTRODUCING THE next speaker, Connelly exhorts members to steep themselves in Barton's work and ideas, "So you can erase this nonsense we're hearing out there from school boards, that nobody wants God to be involved. That's insane." He continues: "This time we cannot sit back. I know y'all are doing a phenomenal job in Loudoun County of saying to the school board 'Enough is enough.'" No doubt, Connelly is referring to the aggression and chaos that right-wing activists have brought to school board meetings in Loudoun County, Virginia, and beyond—a continuation of the right's long-standing effort to undermine public education. "If you have not been to a school board meeting, you should be," Connelly says.

Hogan Gidley, who worked as the deputy press secretary in the Trump White House and is billed as an "elections expert," is the final featured speaker of today's presentation. It is his presence on the agenda that makes the subtext of the meeting the text. "The Center for Election Integrity that Chad mentioned, it's nonpartisan," Gidley announces. Then he promptly offers the kind of misinformation that passes for wisdom in the Trumpist incarnation of the Republican Party: "You saw the stuff in Arizona, you're going to see more stuff in Wisconsin, these are significant issues, and they can't be dismissed out of hand anymore, the facts are too glaring."

Remarkably, he is referring to the circuslike GOP-backed "Cyber Ninjas" audit of votes in Arizona's largest county—which, after discrediting itself with its bizarre antics, managed only to confirm that Biden won Arizona by slightly more votes than previously thought.[35] But the narrative of persecution is too valuable in activating the base to discard simply because it's not true. "Any officeholder who allows it to happen should be held accountable, not to mention the fact that if we find someone committing fraud, they've broken the law, and they have to face a penalty as well," says Gidley. In time, he launches into a well-worn conspiracy about the so-called cemetery vote: "About two million dead people are listed on voter rolls right now! We saw something new in this last election. Dead people didn't just vote. They requested mail-in ballots, filled them out, and somehow got them into the drop box."

Perhaps the most alarming aspect of the Chantilly experience is the crowd's response. Murmurs of outrage punctuate the proceedings as listeners take on board the disinformation. "This last year was rough . . . if you're not at the table, you're on the menu. You've gotta be in the room," Gidley says, wrapping up his talk. The crowd nods and huffs in approval. On the way out he takes a swing at other targets of right-wing grievance and ties them to the election fraud myth. "We've seen this with critical race theory." He nods back sagely. We are given to understand that perverting the minds of schoolchildren comes just as naturally to Democrats as stealing elections. A grim "Amen" rings out. But Gidley chooses to end on a high note: "I have never seen people more engaged than they are right now."

DURING THE WATERGATE crisis, the leadership of both major parties ultimately united against a president whose alleged crimes would have disappeared from memory before cocktail hour in recent years. Yet in the summer of 2020, President Trump laid the foundations for an attempted coup by refusing in advance to accept the legitimacy of an election in which he would lose. Upon losing the election, he did indeed attempt to overturn the results of the election in an effort that culminated in a violent attack on the Capitol by his supporters. At Trump's second impeachment trial, Republican senators went on to exonerate an attack that was not only instigated to subvert the electoral process but also put some of their own lives in danger. The question that Trump's attempted coup raises is how such a disgraceful and seemingly improbable event was not only possible but ultimately assimilated into narratives that framed it as an extension of "politics as usual." There is no answer that does not place Christian nationalism and variant forms of reactionary nihilism front and center.

There are of course many overlapping explanations for the recent transformation of American political life. Perhaps the most important fact to acknowledge is that it did not come from nowhere. While much of the commentary continues to focus on the economic anxieties and cultural commitments of the Trumpian base, events such as the one in Chantilly should make clear that a considerable amount of organizational work, propaganda, and money went into preparing the ground for an antidemocratic politics. The essential precondition for the kind of coup that Trump attempted is the existence of a substantial base of supporters primed to embrace the Big Lie. It isn't enough simply to have a population of disempowered and aggrieved people. Without coordinated efforts to indoctrinate such a base, no lie can take hold. To create such a base, four key steps are necessary.

The first step is to build an information bubble within which supporters may be maintained in a state of fact-denial. Much attention has rightly been placed on right-wing media in creating such a safe space for conservatives. Detailed studies have shown that a right-wing media sphere centered on groups like Breitbart News, the Daily Signal, and Newsmax have been extremely successful in skewing coverage in both mainstream and right-wing propaganda networks alike. It is by now well established that both Fox News and conventional mainstream media tend to favor right-wing agendas in the framing of the issues—for example, by implicitly accepting the view that Hillary Clinton's email troubles, Joe Biden's age, and Kamala Harris's alleged leftism were the most important issues at stake in the 2016 and 2024 elections. But more attention should be paid to the conservative networks that supply the backbone of the Christian nationalist movement. Pastors of the sort who attended the event in Chantilly have millions of churchgoers at their disposal every Sunday, and many of them use that time to pound home the antidemocratic movement's political talking points. Organizations like Faith Wins, Pastors for Trump, Watchmen on the Wall, and many others, some targeting specific communities such as the Asociación de Ministros Hispanos del Sur de la Florida and the Coalition of African American Pastors, aim at faith leaders because they know that for their target voters, pastors and religious communities are often the most trusted sources of information.

Step two is that this base must be conditioned to expect an imminent, cataclysmic event that will threaten its identity and everything it values. Christian nationalism almost universally comes with apocalyptic visions and persecution narratives, as do many other elements of the antidemocratic reaction. In a sense, it doesn't matter how you think the world will end or who you think is coming after you; the important thing to believe is that the end is nigh and that the bad guys always look like liberals.

A third step is to transfer the perceived source of political legitimacy from democratic processes like elections and law enforcement mechanisms to "higher" authorities that allegedly represent the "true" spirit of the nation. This, of course, is the device through which a minority of the country can come to believe that it has a providential role in ruling the whole. As Steve Bannon said at a rally held on October 13, 2021, in Richmond, Virginia, in support of Glenn Youngkin, "We're putting together a coalition that's gonna govern for 100 years."[36]

The final step is to do what President Trump did starting before the 2020 election: undermine at every opportunity public confidence in the democratic process. Arguably, the coup attempt began on national television during the first 2020 presidential debate, when Trump made clear that he would not accept the results of the election if he lost.[37] Or maybe it began much earlier, in 2016, when Trump let it be known that he would not necessarily endorse the result if he didn't win. At an October 2021 rally for Glenn Youngkin, Trump called in. "We won in 2016. We won in 2020—the most corrupt election in the history of our country, probably one of the most corrupt anywhere," he said. "But we're gonna win it again."[38]

The most insidious aspect of this program to sow distrust is that it is aimed squarely at those parts of the population that already have some reason to distrust the system. Glenn Youngkin made his fortune in management consulting and private equity, where the pursuit of short-term profits tend to be more important than crushed wages and churned-through communities. Now, alongside his hero Trump, he hopes to exploit the resulting alienation. What could be better for the Funder class he represents than a population that no longer believes in democratic government as a means to constrain the oligarchy?

IN THE IMMEDIATE aftermath of the coup attempt that began with Trump's refusal to accept defeat in November 2020, it appeared to many outside observers that the Christian nationalist movement faced a quandary. If they recognized the actual results of the election and supported the orderly transfer of power in our constitutional democracy, they would also have to acknowledge that "God's President" was a liar and a seditionist.

This proved to be a tough decision for just a tiny handful of prominent religious right leaders, and only for a nanosecond. The eminent evangelical pastor Robert Jeffress, for instance, acknowledged in an opinion piece for Fox News that it appeared Joe Biden would become the forty-sixth president of the United States and urged his followers to pray for him.[39] A larger number, however, played along with the Big Lie. Very quickly, the waffling ended, and everyone that really mattered in Christian nationalist circles got back on the bus.

Mat Staver, chairman and founder of Liberty Counsel, a well-funded legal advocacy group advancing a Christian nationalist agenda, said, "What we are witnessing only happens in communist or repressive regimes. We must not allow this fraud to happen in America."[40] Michele Bachmann called Biden's win a "delusion";[41] and Richard Antall, writing for *Crisis Magazine*, an ultraconservative Catholic publication, likened reporting on Biden's win to a "coup d'etat."[42] In response to news of the election outcome,

Kenneth Copeland, a preacher known for his private jet, multiple luxurious homes, limousines, and other lavish assets, laughed derisively. "Yeah, he's going to be president, and Mickey Mouse is going to be king," he said.[43]

President Trump's attempt to subvert the certification of the Electoral College results by inciting an attack on the U.S. Capitol on January 6 at first seemed to amplify the quandary. Far-right extremist preachers, such as Greg Locke and Ken Peters, played a significant role in riling up the crowd in the days and hours preceding the riot, and Christian nationalist symbolism was all over the event.[44] Movement leaders now had to decide whether their cause would get behind an armed attempt to overthrow the U.S. government.

In retrospect, though, it has become clear that the apparent moral quandary was a mirage. Christian nationalist leaders became even more committed to Trumpist politics than they were in January. My Faith Votes, a faith-based voter mobilization organization, launched its new initiative, Election Integrity Now. The group issued a prayer guide with a seven-point plan for asking God "to protect American elections and deliver trustworthy results."[45]

To be sure, some voices in the leadership of the Christian nationalist movement preferred a strategy of obfuscation. There was no Big Lie, they said; there was only honest concern for elections integrity misrepresented by the liberal media. This denialism, however, has proven to be merely a cover for the endorsement of Trump's coup attempt and a commitment to antidemocratic politics. The more blunt-spoken leaders of the movement have not hesitated to make the position clear.

At the June 2021 Road to Majority conference, an annual gathering of the movement's key activists, strategists, and politicians, Eric Metaxas, a thought leader of the Christian right, let it be known that the real victims of the January 6 event were the good people who ransacked the Capitol. He fired "an arrow across their bow" (his words) to Republican leaders: "Any Republican that has not spoken in defense of the January 6 people to me is dead. They're dead."

The right-wing political commentator and activist Dinesh D'Souza echoed the sentiment. "The people who are really getting shafted right now are the January 6 protesters," he said in conversation with veteran religious right strategist Ralph Reed. "We won't defend our guys even when they're good guys."[46]

At the Conservative Political Action Conference (CPAC) in Dallas in July 2021, January 6 was even reconceived as a possible Democratic plot. "[The

Biden] administration is about tyrannical rule. They don't want to follow the constitution," said Texas congressman Louis Gohmert, before he recast events driven by far-right extremists as bizarre and possibly Democratic conspiracies. "On January 6 the Sergeant-at-Arms had turned down, on behalf of the Speaker, having the National Guard there to help protect the Capitol. Why did that happen? You think they were setting things up? Well I do."[47]

As of this writing, there is no indication of any letup in the antidemocratic politics of election denialism which continued to raise the specter of voter fraud in the run-up to the 2024 election. Christian nationalist leaders continue to prime the base for the next Big Lie. As in Chantilly and the many dozens of cities on the Faith Wins tour, they continue to retool the nation's networks of thousands of conservative churches into partisan political cells on behalf of a party that does not believe in democracy. Working through pastoral networks; through militant, often hypermasculine groups like Stand Courageous; through "parent activist" groups that appeal to right-wing women such as Moms for Liberty, Moms for America, and Parents Defending Education;[48] and through political action committees such as Patriot Mobile Action and Heritage Action, among many others, they are cultivating a cadre of activists—a national team of Sergeants, as it were—engaged at the local level, and prepared to use the threat of disruption, chaos, and perhaps even violence to "protect" the "true" results of any election. Because if God tells you in advance who is supposed to win every election—and then the other candidate wins—the only acceptable explanation is that the election was stolen against the wishes of God. And that means war.

As I sit in the Community Baptist Church with Steve Baines, he leans over and reminds me of the myth, remarkably still echoed in some segments of the media, that the religious right is headed toward irrelevance. "They're not paying attention," he says. "Fundamentalist religious organizations are pouring a ton of money into what are essentially political campaigns."

As the event in Chantilly winds down, Byron Foxx, one of the evangelists touring with Chad Connelly, takes to the stage. "It is not time to be complacent," he instructs the crowd. "The church is not a cruise ship. The church is a battleship."[49]

ON A RECENT visit to old haunts in Santa Barbara, I hike past the Cold Spring elementary school, where I can still see my daughter's second-grade classroom and some new construction. Just down the road I strain to catch a glimpse of the home of the James and Joan Lindsey Foundation, but it remains hidden. Since Joan does not give interviews to people like me, as I have discovered, the clues to what goes on behind the impenetrable thickets of greenery have to be gleaned mainly from public sources.

As far as can be determined from her sporadic posts and the letters she signs as a member of the CNP, Joan Lindsey is proud of the movement she is helping to finance. Some of the donors who back Christian nationalist projects appear to be nonbelievers or members of the self-congratulatory church of libertarianism. But Lindsey seems to be a true believer, at least on the surface. Her political fantasy looks more like a Puritan theocracy than something taken out of the pages of *Atlas Shrugged*. Conservative pastors, she wrote on the website for The Church Finds Its Voice, are "already leading the way back to God's way for us. A tremendous number of you have led voter registrations and are speaking truth about our duty as men and women of faith to support Godly governance."[50]

She may also draw comfort from the fact that she doesn't have to look far to find an heir to take over her mission. Her daughter, Kielle Horton, a graduate of Pepperdine University, vice president of Lindsey Communications, and president of the James and Joan Lindsey Family Foundation, seems equally invested in her parents' agenda. In addition to her work with Faith Wins and her position on the CNP, she offers support to the Child Evangelism Fellowship of Southern California, which sponsors Good News Clubs, like the one that showed up at Cold Spring School. She even seems to have figured out which secular, Santa Barbara–based nonprofits to support in order to credibly blend in with those Montecito ladies who host some of the town's best fancy-dress parties. At a February 2023 fundraiser held at her parents' home for an antitrafficking organization she is spearheading, Strategic Alliance to Fight Human Trafficking (SAFE-SBC), Kielle and her cohosts directed the well-heeled guests not to donate directly to SAFE-SBC but rather to register their donations, through a QR code, with the National Christian Foundation, a donor-advised fund that disburses over $1 billion annually to a variety of right-wing and religious causes.[51] SAFE-SBC appears to be partnered with an organization whose name might have predicted the unorthodox donation instructions: Kingdom Causes Inc.

As of this writing, Kielle is also launching a new podcast, *Politically Basic*. "We're focusing on Millennials, Gen Z, and breaking down the basics of every political issue, making it okay to talk about politics again," according to the website.[52] On a January 2024 episode of *Washington Watch*, the TV show hosted by Family Research Council president Tony Perkins, Kielle said, "I think we have tremendous opportunity right now, particularly in the church, but with our political parties as well, in reaching them, because they are seeking."[53]

Kielle, who has adopted the name Kyle Campbell for her new venture, appears to be going through an extraordinarily messy divorce. Nevertheless the Christian nationalist agenda and its supposed reverence for "family values" remain ever-present. A blog post co-written by mother and daughter in August 2020 warned that "the opposition desires to rewrite our nation's entire founding and purpose" and "has plans to destroy what we hold most sacred . . . the attempted eradication of the Church as we know it, likely replaced by the state."[54]

Joan's son Patrick may be in line to carry the mission forward as well, though he seems preoccupied. In his Twitter (since rebranded as X; for clarity this book uses the name Twitter) feed, he describes himself as "Trader turned driver turned pilot." Responding to news of the iconic New York City restaurant 21 Club's pandemic-related financial woes, he tweeted, "Daaaaaaannng!!! This place was so awesome. De Blasio & Cuomo can sukkit long and hard. #reopenNOW."[55]

With multiple holdings in addition to the proceeds from their $46 (if not $72) million home, including Cal-Pepsi Inc. and the Pepsi Cola Bottling Co. of Bakersfield Inc., the Lindseys are not likely to run out of the money they need to promote "Godly governance" in the United States anytime soon. Whether American democracy can outlast their good fortune remains to be seen.

CHAPTER 2

A Tale of Two Busches

his is what they have done," Robert Busch writes to me with weary
outrage as he forwards a photograph of a group of nuns, one of them
wearing a STOP THE STEAL button, cheerfully joining President Trump's rally
outside the White House on the morning of January 6, 2021.[1] Busch, who
lives in Redwood City, California, recently formed a study group on economic
justice within the Thomas Merton Center, which is affiliated with the
St. Thomas Aquinas Parish in Palo Alto.[2] Like most of his fellow study group
members, he calls himself a Francis Catholic, in deference to Pope Francis.
You could also call him a Nuns on the Bus Catholic, after the progressive
Catholic group, which he supports, that advocates for a range of social justice
issues. He is as earnest in person as he is passionate in his emails. He usually
has at the tip of his tongue or typewriter a citation from any number of writings in the long tradition of Catholic social teachings. He remains personally
opposed to abortion but rejects its political use as a wedge issue.

Robert Busch reached out to me online just as I was returning from the
March for Life, an annual gathering of antiabortion activists and their
supporters that takes place every year on the National Mall in Washington,
D.C. While the march draws in a religiously diverse crowd, it is heavily Catholic and includes hundreds of busloads of kids from Catholic schools, for
many of whom attendance is all but mandatory. But many other Catholics are
morally opposed to the politicization of the abortion issue and are horrified
by the takeover of the Supreme Court. Busch and members of his study group

are among them. They were determined not just to go on record with their opposition but also to do something to get their message and their vision of Catholicism out.

Robert Busch works as an administrator in a development office at Stanford University. Edna Jamati, one more of the dozen-odd members of the Thomas Merton study group, is a retired nurse. Another member, Vicky Sullivan, is a grandmother who attends mass several times a week. Shannon Griscom is a retired teacher. Their group represents a cross section of the Catholic laity in their community, says Busch, which is to say that they are mostly middle-class, if rather whiter, older, and more educated than the median resident.

Just a few miles up the road, in the bucolic wine country of Napa, is one of the luxury hotels managed by a company whose founder and CEO is a man named Timothy Busch—no relation to Robert. Timothy Busch is also a Californian who identifies as a devout Catholic. But he is manifestly not what Robert would describe as a Francis Catholic. According to Timothy Busch, Catholic doctrine takes a dim view of labor unions and raising the minimum wage; it favors right-to-work laws; and it absolutely rejects political leaders who fail to be antiabortion absolutists. He appears to have no room for Catholic social teachings and little awareness of the long and deep tradition of Catholic support for labor rights.[3] "Capitalism and Catholicism," he has said, "can work hand in hand."[4] In 2017, he greeted the inauguration of President Trump by declaring that a "time of light" was now at hand, which he contrasted with "a time of darkness," by which he apparently meant the Obama presidency.[5]

Both Robert and Timothy are very active in promoting their very different views about the place of Catholicism in the American political economy. In this sense, they are representative of a growing division among Catholics in the United States. Although American Catholics are culturally and theologically diverse, they are increasingly split into two blocs along political lines. They are the "jump ball" of American politics, in the words of right-wing political operative Ralph Reed.[6] They are divided over the teachings of Pope Francis, over America's culture wars, over the right way to realize their faith in public life. In the 2020 election they split 52 to 48 percent, narrowly in favor of Joe Biden.[7]

The divided response to the election of President Joe Biden illustrates the schism well. A lifelong practicing Catholic, President Biden tapped the Jesuit priest Father Leo O'Donovan to deliver the invocation at his inauguration, and millions of Catholics hailed the president as one of their own. The other side, however, castigated him as a "fake Catholic."[8] José H. Gómez, then president of the U.S. Conference of Catholic Bishops (USCCB), warned that Biden "would advance moral evils" with his support for birth control and other reproductive rights and his approval of marriage equality.[9] The same split characterizes American Catholics' attitudes toward Pope Francis—as the pope himself knows well. In August 2023, in a private meeting in Lisbon with members of the Jesuit community of which he is a member, the pope warned of the growth of "a very strong reactionary attitude" within a sector of the Catholic hierarchy in the United States, in comments that were certain to antagonize the USCCB conservatives.[10]

Political positions aside, there is one other difference between Robert and Timothy Busch, and it may be the one that matters most in the struggle that troubles the future of Catholicism in America. It comes down to the fact that Timothy is rich—very rich. And, like the other members of the class he represents, he has been getting richer much faster than the economy is growing. He inherited part of an upscale Midwestern grocery store chain founded by his father. He is also the founder and owner of an estate planning firm for wealthy people, in addition to serving as CEO of a firm that has ownership in and operates a collection of hotels and luxury resorts.[11] And he does not hesitate to use his money to advance his version of the faith—and to smash that of his Catholic rivals. "The evangelization of our country is being done by private foundations, Catholic NGOs, like Napa Institute and Legatus," he has said. "They have access to capital that the church doesn't."[12]

Together with Charles Koch—whom he has praised[13] as "the re-founder of America"—Timothy provided the seed money for the Busch School of Business at the Catholic University of America in Washington, D.C. The idea, he promised, was to create a "teaching pulpit" for Catholic bishops and the Vatican, "especially on the issue and topics of business."[14] He is the cofounder of the Napa Institute, a foundation that hosts $2,900-a-head gatherings bringing together free-market fundamentalists from Washington, D.C., think tanks, Republican politicians like Senator Lindsey Graham and former Wisconsin governor Scott Walker, and conservative Catholic clerics with business leaders and other well-heeled members of the laity. He is an active member of Legatus, a Catholic lay organization founded in 1987 by Domino's Pizza titan Thomas Monaghan that strictly limits membership to extremely wealthy business leaders. He also sits on the board of Eternal Word Television Network (EWTN), a Catholic media empire that claims to reach an audience of 250 million worldwide and that preaches a political religion very much in line with Timothy's brand of Catholicism.[15]

According to Robert Busch, it's all rather unfair. "When a small cadre of the superwealthy has undue influence, where is the will of the pope and the people in the pews?" he asks. "They think that because they have money in their pockets, they should have the church in their pockets, too." If the study group at the Thomas Merton Center were engaged in a battle of ideas with the Napa Institute, Robert figures, "I would like our odds." But this isn't a battle of ideas, he says ruefully. "It is a battle between ideas and money."

A GOOD YEAR to begin the tale of the two Busches is 1986, when America's National Conference of Catholic Bishops issued a pastoral letter calling on Catholics to pursue "economic justice for all."[16] This sweet sentiment was interpreted—correctly—as a challenge to President Ronald Reagan's trickle-down economic ideology. It cited the gospel of Matthew 5:5, "Blessed are the meek"—and it set off five-alarm fire bells among Catholic conservatives. It sounded like the reprise of the dreaded social gospel—the heretical doctrine that Jesus wants us to help "the least of these" at the possible expense of corporate profits. In the event, it proved to be something more like a last hurrah.

Even before the bishops got their letter into print, the influential conservative theologian Michael Novak published a lengthy refutation from his perch at the American Enterprise Institute.[17] The true meaning of the gospel of Matthew, Novak argued, was not to pursue social justice but to promote the capitalist institutions of property, markets, and free enterprise.[18] To be fair, Matthew 25:29 does indeed tell us that "For whoever has will be given more" and "whoever does not have, even what they have will be taken away from them";[19] as ever, what the Bible means depends on just who is doing the interpreting. Over subsequent decades, a significant number of ultrawealthy Catholics heard the call of the gospel as Novak interpreted it, and they poured their energy and money into the defense of capitalism against the alleged heresy of the social gospel.

Among the leaders of the reaction were pizza billionaire Thomas Monaghan, subprime credit card mogul Frank Hanna, private equity hero Sean Fieler (described by the *Chronicle of Philanthropy* in 2023 as "one of the most powerful yet little-known philanthropists driving the cultural conservative movement," who has devoted "at least $40 million to nonprofits and $6.3 million to candidates and political groups"), and of course Timothy Busch.[20] Helping them spend that money were political operatives like Leonard Leo, the powerhouse behind the Federalist Society, currently serving as cochairman of its board of directors and current chair of CRC Advisors, which directs over $1 billion in right-wing funding toward reactionary causes. Carl Anderson, the leader of the Knights of Columbus who once worked for Jesse Helms and Ronald Reagan, is another substantial contributor, "underwriting think tanks and news outlets while gaining entrée into some of the highest levels of decision-making in the church," according to Tom Roberts at the *National Catholic Reporter* (NCR).[21] Founded in the nineteenth century to assist Irish immigrants, the Knights of Columbus, under Anderson's leadership, has retooled itself as a defender of the conservative ecclesial and political ideologies that buttress great wealth and privilege at the expense of labor.

Working toward the same end is the secretive, ultraconservative Catholic group Opus Dei, founded in fascist Spain and aimed squarely at cultivating wealth and power. In his 2024 book *Opus: The Cult of Dark Money, Human Trafficking, and Right Wing Conspiracy Inside the Catholic Church*,[22] the financial journalist Gareth Gore details allegations of malfeasance alongside the push for a reactionary version of Catholicism around the globe. Though Opus Dei's founder, Josemaria Escriva, secured a unique dispensation to operate largely free from supervision from the Vatican, the group appears to lean decidedly against the present pope, who has issued documents that seek to make changes to its leadership and oversight.[23] The organization appears to have taken an interest in U.S. politics, and there is little mystery about which side of the partisan divide it seems to think has God on its side.

"Right from the beginning, Opus Dei has actively encouraged its members to consider themselves above the law in their mission to Christianize the world—what the founder called 'holy intransigence, holy coercion, and holy shamelessness,'" says Gore. "Over the years, many of its members have taken this message to the extreme." Project 2025, he says, "promises to turbocharge the influence of Opus Dei and catapult many of its followers right into the heart of government."

Opus Dei does not disclose its membership, but Leonard Leo has a listed entry on the website of the Catholic Information Center in Washington, D.C., which is operated by Opus Dei, according to the *Catholic World Report*.[24] A large portrait of Jesus laying hands on Leo's daughter Margaret, who was born with spina bifida and is now deceased, sat for a time at the organization's entrance. As the money from these donors and operatives flooded in, the American cultural landscape blossomed with a range of ultraconservative think tanks, legal advocacy groups, media organizations, and policy and other activist groups, many aimed at transforming the courts.

Cathleen Kaveny, a theologian and legal scholar at Boston College and the author of *Ethics at the Edges of Law: Christian Moralists and American Legal Thought* (Oxford University Press, 2017), has tracked the rise of this new, hyper-conservative Catholic ecosystem. "Where conservative Catholics have the edge on more progressive Catholics is that they have set up networks and institutions that allow them to get together," she told Tom Gjelten on National Public Radio (NPR). Those institutions include CatholicVote, the National Catholic Prayer Breakfast, the Catholic League, and many others. Conservative Catholic media platforms have included *EWTN News*, *Crisis Magazine*, and the now-defunct *Church Militant*, which fell apart in 2024 in the wake of morality clause violations on the part of its leadership. "My impression is that they've got quite a lot of money. Liberal Catholics tend not to have that amount of money," Kaveny added, in an epic understatement. Indeed, the rapid escalation of wealth inequality over the past half century has been a force multiplier of historic proportions for the right-wing side of the Catholic schisms.[25]

At the very same time that big right-wing Catholic money was helping to remake the conservative world, the power of the Catholic hierarchy was on the wane. The horrendous crimes of abuse against children committed by thousands of church leaders and officials, compounded by the church's reprehensible response to the revelations, replete with denials, evasions, and cover-ups, delegitimized the church hierarchy in the eyes of many Catholics and former Catholics. But bad news for the church turned out to be good news for the wealthiest of its parishioners. As Stephen Schneck, then executive director of Franciscan Action Network has explained to me, the consequence of the rise of the wealthy and the fall of the church has been "a transfer of power from church hierarchy to wealthy laity, who are in a sense developing a parallel establishment to the official church, an alternate magisterium, because their resources are so tremendous."

Particularly significant is the way in which the institutions of the new Catholic right work outside and alongside the traditional hierarchy rather than within and through it.

"What is relatively new is they have established parallel institutions, unconnected to the overarching institutions," John Carr, the director of the Initiative on Catholic Social Thought and Public Life at Georgetown University, told Tom Gjelten, adding his commentary to Gjelten's piece on NPR.[26] The U.S. Conference of Catholic Bishops, Carr explained, is supposed to serve as the main policy and advocacy arm of the U.S. Catholic Church. But because the conference cannot endorse political candidates, it tends to refrain from intervening aggressively in political debates. During his two decades working for the conference, Carr looked on as leaders of the new Catholic right bypassed the conference and other traditional church power centers. They were determined to consolidate conservative Catholic constituencies for Trump, and they did so by creating parallel institutions. Of this new, parallel establishment of political Catholicism, Carr told NPR, "Key parts of it are very narrow, very elite and very substantial."[27]

The institutional networks of the new Catholic right are also far more committed to an explicit political ideology than the traditional hierarchy ever was. "The Catholic church is big enough for those who like traditionalist devotions and those who prefer a guitar mass; for those for whom abortion and same-sex marriage are primary social issues and those for whom hunger or homelessness are the most important issues," Heidi Schumpf, a senior correspondent at *NCR* who has been working at progressive Catholic publications for thirty years, tells me. "But this is much deeper than those surface differences. These right-wing Catholic groups have conflated their faith with economic libertarianism and Republican politics, so much so that some of it is barely recognizable as 'Catholic' anymore."

Schlumpf, along with her colleagues at *NCR*, Tom Roberts and Michael Sean Winters among them, have carefully detailed the fruits of this new dispensation of Catholic power in a series of articles.[28] The beneficiaries of plutocratic largesse include the Becket Fund for Religious Liberty, which was instrumental in extending religious privileges to corporations in the *Burwell v. Hobby Lobby Stores* case; the Federalist Society, which has successfully stocked the federal judiciary all the way up to the Supreme Court with right-wing partisans; *First Things*, the journal founded by ultra-right-wing convert Richard John Neuhaus and that, under its new leader, R. R. Reno, appears to have reinvented itself as a center for pro-Trump theology; Courage International, an organization that encourages gay Catholics to remain celibate; FOCUS, a group that targets college students with conservative messaging; the Witherspoon Institute, cofounded by Princeton University–based professor and political activist Robert P. George; and the Acton Institute, a Michigan-based think tank cofounded and headed by a priest, the Rev. Robert A. Sirico, who champions the union of libertarian ideology and "the Judeo-Christian tradition" and frequently appears on Fox News.[29]

The jewel in the crown of the plutocratic wing of the Catholic church is EWTN Global Media, on whose board Timothy Busch sits. Just prior to the 2020 election, President Trump's approval rating among Catholics, which was about 44 percent, was not distinguishable from that of the general population.[30] But you wouldn't know that if you watched only EWTN, which Schlumpf characterized as "the 'Fox News' of religious broadcasting."[31] In advance of the 2020 election, Michael Warsaw, CEO of EWTN and chairman of the board, endorsed Trump in a column titled "Voting for a Vision, Not a Person."[32] The choice, he wrote, "isn't really between Donald Trump and Joe Biden. It is a choice between two completely different views of America." When Biden stepped aside, Warsaw attacked Harris for standing "diametrically opposed to the Catholic conception of true freedom."[33] Warsaw also denounced the "protesters and rioters" and "anti-Christian direction" that Joe Biden and Kamala Harris allegedly represent.[34] Host of ETWN's *The World Over* Raymond Arroyo, who also frequently appears on Fox News, spends much of his program attacking supposedly "woke" elites and Democrats.[35] The network offers scant mention if any of poverty, inequality, and climate issues, treating viewers instead to endless coverage of abortion and the debate over transgender competitors in women's sports. Robert Busch draws a straight line connecting EWTN's wealthy backers and the stop-the-steal nuns. "The wealthy right-wing activists who sit on the board of EWTN and have remade it into their media mouthpiece," he told me, are "complicit in fueling the flames over many years, which led to the violence and death of January 6."

With the emergence of EWTN and other high-volume mouthpieces, Robert Busch observes, the worst features of the radio age have reemerged in the internet age. "One bishop suddenly has a megaphone for the entire country, much like Father Coughlin did back in the 1930s, with his anti-Semitic broadcast from Michigan," he notes. "He used the power of modern radio back then to do what he did, and sure enough, here in 2020, we have the power of modern internet being used by these conservative bishops."

The Catholic left, to be sure, did not shrivel in the face of the well-funded onslaught from right-wing Catholic money. A collection of progressive Catholic groups that emerged in the wake of the Vatican II reforms of the early 1960s have continued their work to the present. Among them are NETWORK Lobby for Catholic Social Justice (the sponsors of Nuns on the Bus), DignityUSA, Call to Action, and Catholics for Choice. When a group of left-leaning Catholic theologians called Catholic Scholars for Worker Justice learned of the Koch brothers' involvement in Timothy Busch's libertarian business school project at Catholic University, they issued a stern letter of protest.[36]

The Thomas Merton group fits squarely within this Catholic liberal tradition, and it is determined to push back on efforts to drag the faith to the right. With modest support from members of his parish and the Thomas Merton group, Busch has experimented with a virtual gathering spot for socially progressive Catholics. The aim is to offer highly interactive worship services—in the church of Zoom, as it were—as well as breakout sessions, forums on themes from racial justice to voting rights to food security, and suggestions for social engagement and volunteerism. "This platform will give tangibility to what our Thomas Merton group is working on," Robert Busch told me. "A social justice clearinghouse and rallying point for Pope Francis Catholics to unabashedly present the social gospel as part and parcel of our faith."

But the Catholic left is not the equal and opposite of the Catholic right, and there is nothing fair and balanced about their conflict. While the two sides jostle as notional equals on theological grounds and popular appeal, there is no comparison in terms of funding, organization, and political impact. Relative to the Catholic right, the left can effectively be regarded as having little real money or central organization, and no dominant media. It tends to favor the politics of declarations, volunteerism, and protest activities. Even as many if not most American Catholics skew moderate or liberal in their theology and politics, as well as in their social attitudes based upon lived experience, their perspectives are often dwarfed by the political influence operations of the Catholic right.

"There are wealthy liberal Catholics too!" Schlumpf tells me. "But many progressive Catholics work in ministry, social service, or other fields that do not result in massive wealth accumulation. And progressives also tend to give money to organizations that do direct service"—such as feeding the poor and providing health care—"and perhaps are less strategic in funding organizations that have broader influence, such as lobbying, activism, and media."

The easiest way to read the results of the contest between the Catholic left and right is to examine the religious composition of the U.S. Supreme Court. There are six Catholics on the Supreme Court as of this writing. Only one, Sonya Sotomayor, can be associated with liberal Catholicism, and she has characterized herself as a "lapsed Catholic." The rest are without question representatives of right-wing Catholicism. All (plus Gorsuch) have strong ties with the Federalist Society; all showed their secret colors when they overturned precedent and stripped women of rights over their own bodies in the *Dobbs v. Jackson Women's Health* decision; and all benefited from right-wing money in advancing their careers. Amy Coney Barrett alone sailed through her confirmation hearings with $30 million at her back, much of it funneled from anonymous donors through Leonard Leo's various Federalist Society–adjacent organizations.[37]

The triumph of Timothy Busch and his people, however, goes well beyond stacking the federal judiciary. They were prime movers in the creation of the antidemocratic reaction that now dominates the political right. It is easy to forget that a defining public policy goal of the Christian nationalist movement over the past four-plus decades—to expunge women's rights over their own reproductive health—was once widely believed, by many Republican leaders, to be an exclusively Catholic concern. Although Christian nationalism today is often conflated with conservative evangelical Protestantism or "white evangelicals," the Catholic right's contribution was indispensable to the creation of the movement—revealing a significant gap between the popular narratives about the movement and the way it actually works.

It is worth stepping back in history to see just how significant and paradoxical the Catholic contribution to Christian nationalism is. No one in the nineteenth century would have imagined that American Catholics would find themselves at the forefront of a religious nationalist movement in the United States. At the time, the champions of Christian America identified the great threat to the nation as immigrant Catholic populations. In editorial cartoons,

Protestant nativists depicted Catholic bishops drawn to look like alligators crawling up from the beaches to attack America's children and families.[38] In the infamous Philadelphia riots of 1844, Protestant nationalists violently assaulted Catholics, torching churches and dozens of homes. By the time it was over, at least twenty residents of the City of Brotherly Love lay dead in the streets, and over a hundred were wounded.[39]

And yet, at the exalted levels of high-finance Christian nationalism today, it is as if centuries of Protestant-Catholic conflict never happened. The funders of the hard-right Acton Institute, which was founded by a Catholic priest, for example, include not just Timothy Busch but also members of the Prince/DeVos family, who are vocal members of the hyper-Protestant Christian Reformed tradition. Acton also received support from the beneficent Koch brothers as well as the Bradley Foundation, DonorsTrust and Donors Capital Fund, the Sarah Scaife Foundation, and other big funders of right-wing causes.[40]

A case in point in the blending of Catholicism and Protestantism on the extreme right can be found in the career of Supreme Court justice Neil Gorsuch. Gorsuch undertook intensive, advanced study of "natural law" under his mentor, John Finnis, former professor of law and legal philosophy at the University of Oxford, who has also taught at the University of Notre Dame Law School and whose spiritual journey is Gorsuch's in the mirror: Gorsuch was raised Catholic and now attends an Episcopalian (Anglican) church, while Finnis was raised Anglican and converted to Catholicism.

To study with Finnis is to study Finnis's philosophy of law, which he laid out in *Natural Law and Natural Rights* (1980). Finnis maintains that there are certain "basic human goods," built into the nature of reality, and our moral and political life consists of reasoning our way toward them. These basic goods, he says, are "irreducible," "non-instrumental," and "incommensurable."[41] That is, we pursue them for their own sake, we must respect them in all our actions, and they cannot be measured against one another.

There are exactly seven such basic goods, and the first is "life." But it seems that only certain kinds of lives are worthy of Finnis's blessing. "A life involving homosexual conduct is bad even for anyone unfortunate enough to have innate or quasi-innate homosexual inclinations," he writes.[42]

Finnis has also condemned "non-marital intercourse" as "unacceptable," and he has argued that "there is no important distinction in essential moral worthlessness" between masturbation and prostitution.[43] Finnis thinks that even married sex is morally suspect, if it has "gone so far that one's sex acts, even if they are in fact with one's spouse, are a kind of adultery."[44] But his real obsession is with same-sex intimacy, a topic he has written about volubly and voluminously, assigning to it blame for all kinds of social ills. Comparing homosexuality with bestiality, Finnis claims that those who endorse same-sex marriage "have no principled moral case to offer against (prudent and moderate) promiscuity, indeed the getting of orgasmic pleasure in whatever friendly touch or welcoming orifice (human or otherwise) one may opportunely find it."[45]

Gorsuch's 2006 book, *The Future of Assisted Suicide and Euthanasia* (Princeton University Press), which appears to have originated out of academic work performed under Finnis's supervision, showcases his mentor's influence. The argument for aid in dying fails, in part, he says, because it does not recognize that certain goods are "incommensurable." Legal aid in dying will send us down some horrifying slippery slopes, and he offers no shortage of hypotheticals. By the end of the book, the theory standing at the altar looks very much like the one that the author first met in school. "There are certain irreducible and non-instrumental goods," Gorsuch concludes; life is one of these basic human goods; and respect for life necessarily prohibits giving aid to or respecting the wishes of some people facing the prospect of a painful death.[46]

This is not just an argument in the style of Finnis. It is the argument that Finnis actually makes in a 1998 article about euthanasia. But Gorsuch is a conscientious scholar, and he footnotes Finnis appropriately when declaring his own position. The future justice articulates it in such a way as to make the antiabortion implications crystal clear. Gorsuch thanks Finnis in the first line of his acknowledgments for having "provided thoughtful comments on, and kind support through, draft after draft."[47]

Like his hero Antonin Scalia and other conservative stalwarts of the court, Gorsuch describes himself at times as an "originalist." But he appears to dispense with the founders whenever their legacy conflicts with the wishes of the funders who backed him in the Senate campaign for his Supreme Court nomination. As he made clear in the *Dobbs* decision, he won't let precedent get in the way of the beliefs he articulated while a student at Oxford. As he further made clear in the 2024 decision granting Trump a novel form of presidential immunity, he also won't let precedent, history, or the plain meaning of texts in any period get in the way of critical partisan goals.

This remarkable convergence between the Catholic right and the Protestant right was a long time in the making. The evolution of the term *Judeo-Christian* tracks the story well. That term first came into use in the 1920s as a way to extend a friendly hand to Catholics and Jews in the face of nativism and anti-Semitism coming from the KKK and America's surging fascist movement. In the Cold War era, *Judeo-Christian* was reappropriated as a means of building national identity around an abstract "civil religion."

In those years, the main motivator behind the term's usage was to draw a new line of division between "us" and "them." "Them" were the communists of the USSR. "Them" were godless, too—that was the main point of the term *Judeo-Christian*, which often amounted to a statement of the cultural superiority of monotheism. Notably, "us" did not include Islam, notwithstanding the fact that Islam is included with Christianity and Judaism in the category of Abrahamic religions. With the rise of the religious right in the 1970s, however, the term *Judeo-Christian* morphed again, this time becoming a way of distinguishing between righteously religious Americans and their bad internal enemies—the secularists, humanists, relativists, and liberal Christians who allegedly no longer believed in family values. In a sense, the Judeo-Christian idea did what snowboarders would call a frontside alley-oop—a 180-degree rotation—from a defense against anti-Semitism in the 1920s to a new, more generalized form of demonization of the shadowy internal enemy in the present era.

The reunion of the (right-wing) churches really took off with the consolidation of the religious right against its perceived enemies in the 1970s and early 1980s. Conservative Catholics and conservative Protestants realized that they were on the same side in the battle over the future of American culture. At the top of the list of enemies were the advocates of women's equality, who had allegedly set about to destroy the traditional family and the natural order of the genders. For a time it appeared that the Catholic activist Phyllis Schlafly might unify the right around opposition to feminism and the Equal Rights Amendment. Next on the list of hot-button issues was the supposedly unfair tax treatment of segregated religious academies. Outraged that the IRS had deemed whites-only private religious schools potentially liable for taxes, conservative leaders toyed with the idea of unifying the country around a program of tax breaks for racist educators. By the late 1970s, however, New Right operatives like Paul Weyrich, who cherished the same libertarian economic vision that has motivated people like Timothy Busch and the Kochs, grasped that the right needed a starkly binary issue to rally religious conservatives around the free-market flag. That is when he and his fellows on the New Right discovered a new passion for abortion politics.

Contrary to the contemporary origin myth of Christian nationalism, the evangelical wing of the movement did not rise as one in rebellion against the Supreme Court's 1973 decision in *Roe v. Wade*. Leaders of the Southern Baptist Convention spoke for many Protestants when they welcomed the decision that recognized a right to abortion, endorsing a 1971 resolution for the legalization of abortion to preserve the "emotional, mental, and physical health of the mother" as well as in cases of rape, incest and "deformity."[48] Abortion had hitherto been seen as a Catholic issue, for the most part, although at times it had been tied to various eugenics and Protestant nativist ideologies. The idea generally was that white women needed to be prevented from having abortions so they could keep up with immigrants and other undesirables. While evangelical leaders such as Francis Schaeffer worked with clergy to politicize them and turn them against abortion, there was no broadly accepted school of "pro-life" theology among Protestants, in the sense now understood—that is, as the theological claim that the human soul exists from the moment a male gamete and a female gamete unite in a diploid zygote—and the further claim that the preservation of the earthly life of the soul from this putative moment of inception is the one moral duty that trumps all others.

When Weyrich and his fellow operatives went down the list of issues that might unite the right, nonetheless, they realized that abortion was political gold. If they framed the abortion issue as one of taming sexual license and restoring the gender order, they could bring along evangelical clergy and all the antifeminists as well as any who felt uncomfortable with the various liberation movements of the 1960s and 1970s. Since the (false) perception among their target base of white voters was that sexual license was a particular problem for Black people, they could even use abortion to call in the racists. Sure, they would have to do something about the theology—but that was an easy fix. All that was needed was a few tweaks that, practically undetected, would change the very nature of American religion.

Many Catholic leaders, by virtue of being antiabortion, were already halfway there. For them, it was just a matter of reconfiguring what had previously been thought of mainly as a subset of family planning concerns into a claim about the moral status of the fetus. And the Protestant theology around pregnancy was a thinly populated field at the time. It proved easier than anticipated to concoct a new theology that would construe opposing abortion rights as an unconditional religious duty.

The process took about two decades, and the success was near total for the New Right. Theologians who took issue with the new doctrine on the genesis of the soul were sidelined and silenced, just as pro-choice political leaders were pushed out of the Republican Party. Right-wing Catholics, right-wing Protestants, right-wing preachers, and right-wing politicians—all were swiftly united around the plan to deprive women of control over their own bodies and families of their most intimate and impactful decisions.

A landmark in the process of unification came in 1994 with the publication of the manifesto "Evangelicals and Catholics Together," an essay that declares that "abortion is the leading edge of an encroaching culture of death."[49] The lead authors were Watergate felon Charles Colson, who found evangelical religion in prison, and Richard John Neuhaus, a Lutheran minister who converted to Catholicism at the age of fifty-four. Neuhaus was the editor of *First Things*, the magazine launched by Michael Novak, and his highly influential career is emblematic of the higher union between two main sides of the western Christian church. In 2005, *Time* magazine anointed him one of most influential "evangelicals" in an article titled "Bushism Made Catholic."[50] He was instrumental in lining up religious conservatives behind Bush's war in Iraq, and for a time it appeared that his so-called theocon vision would unite the old religious right with the neoconservative movement.

Further declarations of amity across the denominational divides soon followed. A notable instance is the 2009 Manhattan Declaration ("A Call of Christian Conscience"). A principal mover behind the declaration was Professor Robert P. George, the reactionary Catholic activist who runs an affirmative action project for conservative students and lecturers at the James Madison Program in American Ideals and Institutions at Princeton University.[51] In addition to the prestige it derives from a Princeton affiliation— an irony given George's frequent potshots at "elite institutions"—George's operation benefits from big-dollar donations from notable funders of religious right causes, including the Bradley Foundation and the John M. Olin Foundation.[52] Though the program does not currently provide information about its donors in annual reports, its list of advisers includes Harlan Crow, who has given multiple donations, free trips, and other gifts to Supreme

Court justice Clarence Thomas; Crow's wife, Katherine; and hedge funder and fellow Supreme Court justice care provider Paul Singer, who has been represented in cases before the very Supreme Court whose justices' careers he has helped to fund.[53] From the Manhattan Declaration we learn that conservative Christians of all denominations are to be united around their desire to deprive gay people of the right to marry, and women of the right to control their bodies and futures.

Notwithstanding the outsize role that Catholic and Catholic-funded intellectuals play in supplying its ideological rhetoric, the rank and file of the Christian nationalist movement remains on balance evangelical Protestant, including many who describe themselves as nondenominational or who adhere to right-wing Pentecostal and charismatic forms of faith. This paradox tells us something—not about Catholicism or Protestantism per se, but about the structure of the movement. Specifically, it tells us something about a division of labor that has emerged to serve the movement's very different constituencies.

At the risk of generalizing too much over a highly varied reality: the evangelical style of leadership tends to be rather identitarian or personality driven. Congregants attach themselves to a particular leader or a particular group. This style of direct appeal is especially effective among the rank and file of the Christian nationalist movement. The kind of leadership offered on the Catholic vanguard, however, is very different. The Catholic intellectuals who play an outsize role in the Christian nationalist movement aren't offering personal allure, necessarily, but academically tested ideology. This kind of ideological leadership is something on which the Catholic church can bring millennia of experience to bear. The ideology can cut left or right, of course, but it often finds its warmest reception among those with the privilege and power to defend it. Ideology is the way that plutocrats explain to other people why everyone needs to obey the rules that let them hold on to their money. In the Catholic intellectuals who helped to script the Christian nationalist movement, the rich men must think, they certainly got their money's worth.

IN THE AGE of reactionary nihilism, the hard-right edge of the intellectual world found new ways to align itself with the powers that be. R. R. "Rusty" Reno, Neuhaus's successor at *First Things*, called in his book *Return of the Strong Gods: Nationalism, Populism, and the Future of the West* (Regnery, 2019) for the "return of the strong gods" to save the West. By "strong gods," he evidently meant nationalism, illiberalism, authoritarianism, and Donald Trump. Former attorney general for the first Trump administration William Barr appears to have had roughly the same idea in mind. According to David Rohde, writing for the *New Yorker*, Barr served on the board of the Opus Dei–affiliated Catholic Information Center along with Leonard Leo.[54] In June 2018, Barr submitted an unsolicited memo[55] to the Justice Department critiquing special counsel Robert Mueller's investigation into Russian interference in the 2016 election and arguing that Mueller should not be permitted to question Trump about possible obstruction of justice. Critics denounced Barr's theory that the president has "all-encompassing" and "absolute" constitutional authority over actions by executive branch officers in carrying out law enforcement powers given to them by Congress.[56]

Barr's letter may have served as something of a job application, and it worked. Shortly afterward, in December 2018, Trump announced that Barr would succeed Jeff Sessions as his first administration's attorney general.[57]

Barr articulated his doctrines in a pair of speeches, delivered in 2019 at Notre Dame Law School and before the Federalist Society in Washington, D.C. In his October speech at Notre Dame, he argued that "secularism" is to blame for "virtually every social pathology," from suicide rates to "the wreckage of the family," and described legal appeals to Establishment Clause concerns as "a battering ram to break down traditional moral values and to establish moral relativism as a new orthodoxy."[58] A month later, at the Federalist Society's National Lawyers Convention in Washington, D.C., he accused Trump's political opponents of "unprecedented" abuse, said they were "engaged in the systematic shredding of norms and undermining of the rule of law," and defended the former president's imperial ambitions by decrying the "steady grinding down of the executive branch's authority."[59] (In the period following his departure from the Justice Department, Barr offered without apology views on his former boss's attitude toward the rule of law entirely inconsistent with such claims.)[60]

Barr found a warm welcome from at least one professor at Notre Dame, Patrick Deneen, who hailed the former attorney general's speech at that school as "masterful, learned, and extremely important."[61] Deneen has argued that "liberalism has failed" and must be replaced with something else.[62] What he means by "liberalism" is pretty much everything that has happened in the political world over the past two centuries (the reactionary brush here sweeps the libertarian right into the same trash can as the New Dealers). All of it, says Deneen, is horribly selfish and has wrought unimaginable suffering on Americans. The details of what he means by "something else" are hard to discern through the portentous prose, though they appear to involve a world where the genders are placed in their "natural" and hierarchical arrangement, clerical leaders collaborate with the state in imposing reactionary values on a community, and all modern ills have been thus resolved.

In her critique of Deneen's book *Why Liberalism Failed* (Yale University Press, 2018), Kristin Kobes Du Mez, author of *Jesus and John Wayne: How White Evangelicals Corrupted a Faith and Fractured a Nation* (Liveright, 2021), writes, "Let's look briefly at who gets things right, according to Deneen. The Amish. At times it seems that Deneen's enthusiasm for the Amish rivals that of the Christian romance industry." The reason for Deneen's admiration? Du Mez dryly notes, "The Amish 'community' is a patriarchal one with direct and almost unbending exercise of authority."[63]

Joining Deneen in the burn-the-modern-world-down-and-bring-back the-ever-righteous-feudal-priesthood bunker is a new line of intellectuals like Sohrab Ahmari, an Iranian American convert from atheism to Catholicism who abhors political liberalism and counts no-fault divorce and pornography among the "forces arrayed against" the family; J. D. Vance, who has characterized his political opponents as "childless cat ladies" and "neurotic lunatics" who wish to "replace" real American voters; and Rod Dreher, a Vance fan who, when not promoting a retreat from an ungrateful modern world in the style of Saint Benedict, champions installing illiberal, corrupt, and Putin-friendly authoritarian regimes around the world on the model of Viktor Orban's Hungary.[64]

A version of the same illiberal extremism dressed up in scholarly rhetoric comes from Adrian Vermeule, a professor at Harvard Law School who appears convinced that he and his fellow travelers are so persecuted that they may soon be rounded up and put in liberal gulags. Vermeule argues for "common good Constitutionalism," by which he means a system that has nothing to do with the U.S. Constitution but rather invites a priestly and political elite to determine the common good for everyone else.[65]

Notwithstanding his academic pedigree and verbiage, Vermeule has provided a window into this new elite's idea of "the common good" by descending into right-wing trolling. In 2021, he appeared to make fun of the disappearance of Chinese tennis star Peng Shuai on his Twitter feed and "liked" a post by a pro-China account that said, "We know for certain by now US MSM has no journalistic integrity, let alone *self-respect,* when it comes to reporting on China."[66] Vermeule has also engaged on Twitter with accounts that disparage "'Uighur genocide' propaganda."[67] In an article for the *Atlantic*, he wrote that in the States the reigning conservative legal theory had "outlived its utility."[68] In an interview he gave to the Chinese Communist Party–owned *Beijing Review*, he cast the "liberal-democratic view" of governance as "institutionally imperialist." "Rights are themselves justified not on the liberal ground of individual autonomy, but insofar as recognizing such rights benefits the community," he noted.[69] And of course, he and his priestly allies wish to be the ones to decide what "the community" wants. Rather than opposing a more authoritarian governance, he appears to admire it, and perhaps wishes to learn from it. In doing so, he joined a crowded echo chamber of authoritarianism-friendly fellow reactionaries such as Michael Anton, who argued in the *Federalist* that the U.S. should allow China to seize control of Taiwan.[70]

To be sure, some of these members of the New Right make anticapitalist noises—an indication of just how far things have moved from the days of Michael Novak. Deneen seems think that the capitalists are just as liberal as the liberals;[71] Vermeule sweetens up the "common good" package with what look like social welfare programs operated out of convents and church basements. It is hard to know whether such gestures are merely naive or outright insincere. Paul Singer, Harlan Crow, Timothy Busch, and the rest of the economic elite that hopes to capitalize upon New Right screeds against secular liberalism represents the same sector that pays for their sinecures and think tanks. J. D. Vance wasn't in the Senate to serve the people whose grievances he exploited; he was there to serve Peter Thiel and the other superwealthy people who backed his entire political career. The same may be said of William Barr, Adrian Vermeule, and Leonard Leo. In the end, they answer to Timothy Busch or someone very much like him, and the Timothys just don't do anticapitalism.

Much more detail could be supplied on the figures and arguments of the Catholic right, but the big picture should already be clear. Considered in the broad sweep of several decades' worth of political history, the thinkers of the hard Catholic right are the ultimate snowflakes. They support international adventures when the neocons are in charge, and they flip to nationalism and isolationism when the weather shifts in favor of nativists. They claim to represent the forgotten *populus* against a depraved elite of cosmopolitan liberals—and then they announce that they themselves are the core of a spiritual elite destined to rule.

When politics and theology collide, the Catholic right's sacred task is to fabricate whole-cloth new theologies to make a political point. Their greatest metaphysical creation is the theology of "life"—a creed intended to unify conservative religionists of every denomination around the single commandment that abortion, along with some popular and effective forms of birth control, must be completely abolished. There are only two constants in the intellectual world of reactionary Catholicism today: in the end, the ideas always blow in the direction that big money favors, and what big money wants more than anything is obedience.

AND YET—FOR Timothy Busch, is it really about the money? On the one hand, the perfect convergence between his financial interests and the market-fundamentalist theology he promotes would suggest that his investment in the political radicalization of the Catholic church is purely transactional. On the other hand, if you listen to what Busch has to say about his ultimate ends, the connection between money and religion seems at least a little more complicated—and much more perverse.

"The focus of my life is getting myself to heaven and to help others get there too," says Timothy Busch.[72] Heaven, he seems to imply, is for those who lead a life that is both pure and productive. It's a special place for the kind of people who stop other people from doing bad things, like having abortions, and who do good things, like pay for church establishments. And it offers quite some reward for those who follow this plan. Heaven, he seems to suggest, is the ultimate luxury vacation and the perfect reward for a hardworking businessman, for the job creator at the center of the American universe. It is an exclusive resort where the best people have the best of times—kind of like the posh hotels in his upmarket collection, or luxury vacation tours that the Napa Institute organizes. In short, Timothy appears to believe in a rich man's heaven, a place where rich men get what rich men want, only more of it.

Which raises the question: Does he control the money, or does the money control him? He is using money to get what he wants, but it seems like what he wants are only the things that money can buy: a turbo-charged variety of capitalism, a neo-Darwinian world where only the rich and "elect" thrive, unburdened by concern for the common good that, it would appear, extends all the way up through heaven.

ROBERT BUSCH, AT least, is in no doubt about the root of all evil. When I discuss the money-strewn fault line in American Catholicism with him, his words tumble out in an avalanche of frustration. "You know, it's one-percenters who own the society, if you will," he says. "They have the money in their pocket to control our economy, and our society. And they want to now buy the church." But what really galls him is the kind of religion they want to buy—and the kind they want to throw away. "They make fun of us as 'social justice warriors,' tree-hugging types. What a thing to have in a church—thinking there is fun to be made of people who are out there running food pantries and helping the homeless!" People in the pews are interested in the social justice aspects of the faith, he tells me, "but the conservative seminary system, under very conservative leadership, has led to a conservative hierarchy infrastructure. For them it's all about personal morality and holiness, with never a word about social justice. What a diminishment of the church!"

For Robert Busch, the story in its outlines is as familiar as a morning in Sunday school. He points to the parable of the Good Samaritan who stopped on the road to rescue a stranger attacked by thieves. In a country where the top 1 percent have now amassed more than $34 trillion in wealth,[73] leaving a mere $2 trillion for the bottom 50 percent to share among themselves, he suggests, this seems like a Bible story worth remembering.

CHAPTER 3

School's Out Forever

I t's the late spring of 2023, I'm relaxing in Santa Barbara, and I can hear the rumble of the school board wars like distant thunder across the landscape. Books are tumbling off shelves, librarians are running scared, and a tiny population of kids who identify as nonbinary are being told they represent the greatest threat to civilization. At the center of the conflicts is a group that grandly calls itself Moms for Liberty. I learn that the Moms are planning a National Summit in Philadelphia for July. I immediately buy a ticket and pack my suitcase.

Outside the Philadelphia hotel, small clumps of protesters clog the sidewalk. It's the tail end of the Pride festival, and the brand-name stores lining the streets of City Center are still festooned with colorful flags and glitter. A number of homeless people rest on the edges of the festive sidewalks, like extras from the wrong film set. The air, hazy from the Canadian wildfire plumes raging a thousand-plus miles away, parches the throat; overhead the sun appears orange. Donald Trump has just been indicted on seven counts in the classified documents probe regarding alleged mishandling of classified material. The vibe is slightly apocalyptic.

The first event at the Moms for Liberty conference is an evening tour of the Museum of the American Revolution. To my astonishment, a police escort accompanies the bus that takes us there. A small but noisy group of protestors have gathered outside the museum; presumably the police and event organizers are taking no chances. The police form a protective corridor from the bus to the museum. The organizers appear to welcome the security theater. "Thank the police officers for protecting us, okay?" says a staffer as we stream inside.

The Joyful Warriors National Summit, as it is billed, properly begins the following morning in the conference center. Joining me is my friend and fellow journalist Annika Brockschmidt, the German author of *Die Brand-Stifter* (*The Arsonists*) and *Amerikas Gottes-Krieger* (*America's Godly Warriors*). A historian by training, she is tall, blond, and stylishly attired in a pale-green suit.

The atmosphere in the lobby is militantly cheerful. Groups of women in four or five chat excitedly and compare notes. Every fingernail looks carefully polished, every cheek is bronzed. Dressed in flowing trouser suits or dresses with stylish heels, the women look well prepared to take on the photographers who roam the event in search of promotional material for social media channels.

The origin myth of Moms for Liberty says that it all started in sun-dappled Florida during the pandemic, when three conventional suburban moms bonded over complaints about mask mandates and school closures. The reality is that the Moms had high-level connections to the Florida GOP from the beginning, and "conventional" is not always the best way to describe them. Cofounder Bridget Ziegler is married to Christian Ziegler, the former chairman of the Republican Party of Florida, and a few months after the Philadelphia conference, it was revealed that the couple engaged in three-way sexual adventures with other women[1]—one of whom accused Christian of rape in another incident.[2] (In January 2024 police cleared Christian of the rape allegation[3] but asked prosecutors to charge him with illegally recording a sexual encounter. The state attorney general declined to pursue video voyeurism charges.[4]) In any event, the group appears more focused on money than sex. It reported $2.1 million in total revenue in 2022, including hundreds of thousands from Publix supermarket chain heiress Julie Fancelli and the George Jenkins Foundation, of which Fancelli is the president and sole funder.[5] (The George Jenkins Foundation also contributes substantially to reactionary and Christian nationalist groups such as Judicial Watch, Patriot Academy, and Moms for America; Fancelli was a prominent financial backer of the January 6 rally that preceded the attack on the Capitol.) The Moms funneled a portion of that rich haul to a company funded and operated by Christian Ziegler. His firm, Microtargeted Media, specializes in targeted text messages and takes in hundreds of thousands of dollars from right-wing political campaigns. Their motto: "We do digital & go after people on their phones."[6] (Christian Ziegler has applied a digital strategy to his own legal defense; he used a phone video he made of himself engaging with his accuser to argue that the sex was consensual.)

The framing of the Moms' activism has all the hallmarks of what author Michelle Nickerson calls "housewife populism."[7] In *Mothers of Conservatism: Women and the Postwar Right* (Princeton University Press, 2012), Nickerson points out that conservative women's political engagement in the postwar era was a powerful tool in the battle against communism and moral degeneracy. "Capitalizing upon cultural assumptions about women and motherhood, they put themselves forward as representatives of local interests who battled bureaucrats for the sake of family, community, and God," she writes.[8] The challenge to public school policies and curricula here is based on the idea that the Moms have a unique moral authority—superior to that of professional educators and administrators (whom the Moms often deride as the "K-12 mafia").[9]

The photographers begin circling my friend Brockschmidt, having apparently mistaken her for a populist übermom. She ducks a bit, and they move on. The social media feeds begin to fill with images of mama-bear solidarity. The smiles are those of sisterhood and sacrifice: We're just in it for the kids.

Tickets start at $249 for the three-day event, excluding transportation and lodging. All meals are catered, and several trips by bus to museums and other local attractions are included. I dip into the spread of fancy appetizers that greets us at the Museum of the American Revolution, and it is delicious. I have been attending right-wing conferences for about fifteen years, and this one is among the most lavish. These are moms with deep-pocketed sponsors.

To be fair, it is very hard to know where the proselytizing ends and the profit making begins. One speaker at the event turns out to be Erika Donalds—the Florida-based education entrepreneur who happens to be the wife of Republican congressman Byron Donalds, from Florida's nineteenth congressional district. A close ally of Florida governor Ron DeSantis and Donald Trump, Byron Donalds frequently speaks at right-wing conferences and events touting privatization as the cure for the nation's woes. Privatization certainly appears to enhance his own household. His wife is the founder of two for-profit companies that are sure to stand first in line for the school privatization gravy train. Her for-profit company OptimaEd is explicitly dedicated to expanding the network of schools associated with Hillsdale College, the Christian nationalist Michigan school that members of the DeSantis administration have richly praised. She has also founded Classical Schools Network Inc., a charter management company, which is poised to cash in on the Hillsdale expansion. Erika Donalds was also savvy enough to set up a nonprofit, the Optima Foundation, which, as the journalist Keira Butler reported in *Mother Jones*, fundraises for the same academies that her companies help manage.[10]

While approximately 17 percent of charter schools nationwide are run by for-profit companies, according to a report by the Network for Public Education, the number in Florida is close to 50 percent. Noting that the number of Florida students enrolled in charter schools has jumped from 200,000 in 2013 to nearly 362,000 just nine years later, Butler writes, "Donalds' companies are among those cashing in on the Florida charter school boom."[11] One faculty member, she reports, "noted that OptimaEd 'seems dedicated to profit sometimes to the detriment of the school itself.'"[12]

But the profit making is frequently ignored when packaged in a protective layer of sanctimony, and from the podium at Moms for Liberty, Erika Donalds delivers it sweetly. "Lord, you have elevated this organization to do your good work in this country," she preaches. "We're grateful that the truth is being exposed, that parents are being able to see what's *really* going on in education in our country."

A LARGE SECTION of the conference area is given over to lively booths from an extraordinarily large number of right-wing organizations—significantly more than the two or three dozen that I saw at the Road to Majority conference the previous month. I wander through and pick up a few of the resources on offer. Parents Defending Education offers free booklets and other materials with tendentious allegations about the content of public school curricula and instructions for parents on how to root it out. EpochTV, a division of the conspiracist right-wing media company the Epoch Times, which is associated with the Falun Gong religious movement, is promoting a documentary titled *Gender Transformation: The Untold Realities*.[13] The Pennsylvania Family Institute is hosting a "biblical" leadership conference for teens that promises a "unique experience of using the political process as a means of cultivating leadership skills."[14] The Alliance Defending Freedom (ADF) and the Southeastern Legal Foundation are giving away guidebooks and other tools for "saving America's Public Schools."[15] The California-based organization

Protect Our Kids, which adheres to the "biblical truth which teaches that God created mankind in His image, male and female," offers detailed instruction on how to force schools to allow parents to "observe and volunteer" in classrooms, examine curriculum materials, and access student records and policy materials, as well as opt out of "anti-bullying" lessons.[16] Everywhere, parents are urged to submit open records requests, inspect instructional materials for any hint of critical race theory (CRT), complain volubly and disruptively if schools take issue with any of their findings, and threaten legal action. In short, it's a school administrator's nightmare.

I enter the enormous ballroom and take a seat at one of the round tables, where I fall into conversation with a woman outfitted in tasteful shades of beige. While a waiter serves us each an omelet, sausages, grits, toast with preserves, fruit salad, and a selection of pastries, she tells me her story.

About a year ago, she discovered that her local public school library was carrying *The Diary of a Young Girl*, often referred to as *The Diary of Anne Frank*. It wasn't the story that bothered her, she assures me; it was "the homosexual content." I struggle to recall any such content in the diary of the young teenager who documented her two years hiding from the Nazis in a secret annex before perishing in a concentration camp. I remember in some detail her fraught relationship with fellow teen Peter van Pels, with whom she fell in and out of love. Later, when I look it up, I read that Anne asked one of her best friends, Jacqueline, if they could touch each other's breasts as proof of their friendship. (Jacqueline, who managed to survive the war, declined, and later chalked up the experience to adolescent curiosity rather than sexual attraction.)

It was this brief, ambiguous passage in a 384-page book about the Holocaust that sent my tastefully dressed seatmate over the edge. Already involved with an anti-abortion organization, she supported a variety of conservative Christian causes. Now, she resolved to join the school board wars. In preparation for her new education mission, she went through a few trainings, in which she was urged to scour the library. To her disgust, she discovered a few books with gay characters. She also found what she described as "CRT."

Such "discoveries" don't happen by accident. In fact, they are the work of reactionary activist leaders like Karen England, executive director of the National Christian Foundation–funded Capitol Resource Institute and a member of the Council for National Policy's board of governors. England, whose "Housewife Populist"–style website is titled "The Kitchen Table

Activist," systematically trains conservative activists how to identify books they label as pornography and get them banned from their school district.[17] Those initiatives also encourage parents to "opt out" of their school district and, like England, homeschool their children. Her work has helped spawn a nationwide network of local activists; one woman from a South Carolina–based organization calling itself Concerned Citizens for Education challenged over 150 books in a South Carolina school district in spite of not having a child in the system.[18]

My well-dressed seatmate asks me who I intend to vote for in the Republican primary. I let slide her assumption that I plan to vote in the Republican primary and reply, "Well, I just can't see myself voting for Trump." She fixes her gaze on me intently and grasps my arm. "We *have* to vote for him," she says. "We need Trump. He's the only one that can win. Don't believe anything you read about him. None of that is true."

After breakfast, I chat with a bright and determined woman who wears a tailored jacket over her cocktail dress. With her youthful face, I am surprised to hear she's already a grandmother. "You must have been a child bride," I tell her, and this time I really mean it. She tells me her story. Her son, a divorced father, lost custody of his child when he failed to affirm the child's chosen identity. At least that's how she tells it. "We're in a war for our kids," she said. "When that happened, I knew I had to do something." So she translated her anger and frustration at her son's custody dispute into aggression toward public education.

Planned Parenthood appears to be a special target of her ire, and the theme of gender identity is the primary focus of the entire weekend. I am familiar, both as a reporter and a parent, with the Planned Parenthood health curriculum. In my own children's public school, one very brief section of a single lesson covered the gender issues that she describes.

In the main conference room at the Philadelphia Marriott Downtown, the speakers begin beating their drums. Public schools have become gender distortion academies, or so everyone here seems to believe. They exist to turn girls into boys and boys into freaks, all for the pleasure of a sick, woke elite.

Another repeated talking point, it soon becomes clear, is that we are all supposed to be joyful. The people out there—the speakers keep gesturing toward the streets, which are presumably crawling with leftover Pride marchers—may think that we are angry, bigoted fanatics. But we are joyful! So keep smiling.

Another theme that immediately comes to the fore is Christian nationalism. The summit's opening reception at the Museum of the American Revolution features a presentation by WallBuilders president Tim Barton, he of the Faith Wins crew, who appears to be vying to outdo his dad, David Barton, in promoting bogus Christian nationalist history to conservative audiences.[19] Tim calls out his quotes and factoids in Dadaesque rapid-fire. The firehose of half-truths seems intended to make us think he is oh so smart—how else could he have memorized so many facts?

Tim Barton's presence at this conference is no accident. Years ago, his father explained everything worth knowing about America's system of public education in a couple of graphs. SAT scores, he showed, were on a steady climb until around 1962 or 1963, when they suddenly began to plummet. Other educational markers, such as literacy and mathematical achievement, followed the same ominous track. How to explain this mysterious and unfortunate development? Barton had a ready answer: the Supreme Court banned school prayer in a pair of decisions in 1962 and 1963, thereby separating forever the schooling of children from the religion of their forefathers. There, he claimed, was the explanation for the collapse of public education in America!

No credible researcher into public education has yet taken seriously Barton's analysis. After all, one could take the evidence he cites and blame it all on the Beach Boys, who also happened to make it big in 1962. One would also have to ignore, as Barton does, the many other dramatic changes in the school systems and the country in general that were taking place at the same time. And yet the underlying story he tells about the trajectory of religion in public education has long been accepted as an article of faith among the rank and file of the religious right.

In the absence of God, according to this narrative, schools became temples of secular humanism, indoctrinating children in a warped philosophy of moral relativism. The inevitable consequence is rising divorce rates, child abuse, drug addiction, gangs, nose rings, and whatever else they can throw at the schools. This is the narrative religious right leaders lean on as they seek to force their religion into public schools through various means—mandating Bibles and Ten Commandments in public school classrooms, placing religious "chaplains" in public schools, establishing fundamentalist "clubs" that confuse elementary-age children into thinking that their school endorses a deeply hyperconservative form of Christianity, devising sectarian "Bible curricula" aimed at public schools, and others that I describe in my 2012 book, *The Good News Club*. The same groups defending these initiatives in schools promote the type of anti-public-school activism that Moms for Liberty represents.

Outside observers might imagine that reforming the public schools is their main goal, or that such groups are simply defending their "free speech" rights or pursuing a seat at the table in the noisy forum of American democracy. But the story is more complicated. In a society as diverse as ours, the attempt to turn America's public schools into right-wing and religious academies is bound to fail, after all, except in sowing divisions within communities and undermining support for public education. Why pursue a policy that is bound to fail? Maybe failure is the point.

In failing, the plan weakens the schools, diverting school personnel's energy from the task of educating students and compromising a sense of loyalty to the schools among the communities they serve. It also allows religious conservatives to use public education as a scapegoat for all the failings and complexities of a modern society—and to reap the profits when education budgets are rejiggered to fund "schools of choice." In fact, the national groups supporting initiatives to increase involvement with the public schools are the same ones behind initiatives to defund and ultimately eliminate those schools.

If you can't own it, break it.

During a talk at Hillsdale College, the far-right institution that operates as a gathering spot for thinkers of the antidemocratic reaction, Christopher Rufo, the right-wing activist best known for pumping up critical race theory hysteria, advised the audience to create a narrative around public education and supposedly woke corporations that is "ruthless and brutal." The reason was clear: "To get to universal school choice, you really need to operate from a premise of universal public school distrust."[20]

The religious right's long-standing hostility to public education has roots in Reconstruction-era hostility to emancipation, along with mid-century opposition to desegregation and pluralism, as I will explain in the following chapter. In our time this hostility has persisted like a lingering viral infection. In March 2024, E. Roy Moore, the cofounder of Exodus Mandate and Public School Exit, groups that exist to persuade people to pull their children out of public schools, held an event at Donald Trump's Mar-a-Lago property in Palm Beach, Florida, to highlight the message "on how the nation's K-12 public education system is failing our students." Public schools, according to a press release for the event, "are destroying American children physically, academically, morally, and spiritually."[21] Moore was joined by Dran Reese, the CEO of Salt & Light Council and Biblical Voter, organizations that conduct presentations at churches and mobilize pastors and congregations to support far-right candidates for public office.

Reese often works with Mat Staver, president and cofounder of Liberty Counsel, one of the more vocal legal advocacy groups of the religious right. In 2010, when I attended the national convention of the Child Evangelism Fellowship in Talladega, Alabama, Staver's own views on public education were abundantly clear. Echoing David Barton's talking points, he said, "When you remove Christ as the foundation of education, that which was intended for good ultimately becomes a consequence of evil." Staver clearly shared Barton's view of public education as a fervent struggle with demonic forces for possession of children. "Often we drive by public schools and the tanks are there on the playground," he said. "Bullets are being hurled over their heads as they are in the classrooms. The mushroom clouds are billowing." As he wound up his speech, he shouted encouragement to the crowd: "Knock down all of the doors, all of the barriers, to all of the sixty-five thousand plus elementary schools in the country and take the gospel to this open mission field now!"

AT THE PHILADELPHIA conference, subsequent speakers demand school-sponsored prayer (they always mean Christian prayer, though they don't always say it) and Bible readings at school. They insist that the nation's public schools are the scene of spiritual warfare, and the bad guys are the ones who believe in diversity, inclusion, and the separation of church and school.[22]

The Christian nationalist rhetoric at the conference isn't for the faint of heart. It is of the militant variety that one hears among militia groups and other extremists—and this is no accident. Teddy Wilson, a journalist who covers far-right movements and publishes the newsletter *Radical Reports*, has documented at least nine county chapters of Moms for Liberty with connections to extremist groups, including the Proud Boys.[23] They and other "so-called parents' rights groups are ideologically aligned with far right extremist groups," he notes, "and have often appeared alongside each other at events such as protests of mask mandates and school board meetings." A significant number, he tells me, "are adherents to conspiracy theories including QAnon."

The Moms for Liberty do have a catchall slogan for their program, and it is "parents' rights." After taking in the rhetoric in Philadelphia, it becomes clear to me that the Moms' idea of parents' rights is ripped straight out of the right-wing homeschooling movement playbook. While homeschooling in America is a big tent, drawing in an extraordinarily diverse mix of families, the home-schooling *movement* is a much more focused entity, with advocacy disproportionately in the hands of a small but belligerent minority who believe that parents have absolute rights over their children and that any form of regulation at all—even a requirement that parents inform the state of their plan to homeschool—amounts, in the words of some homeschooling advocates, to "tyranny."[24] Leading the effort to eliminate any form of accountability in homeschooling is Michael P. Farris, founder of the Home School Legal Defense Association and the former president and CEO of the ADF. (The ADF in turn represents Moms for Liberty in court.)

Curiously, on their one major theme, Moms for Liberty contradicts itself by casting aside any concern with parents' rights in favor of the state's right to decide medical questions. The conference keeps circling back to the greatest evil of our age, which, to judge from what these speakers have to say, is the existence of transgender people and the provision of related treatment, even with parental consent, to minors. Medical gender transition for minors is banned or restricted in the UK and a number of European countries, and in the U.S. it remains rare. According to Komodo Health Inc., there were fifty-six genital surgeries among children aged thirteen to seventeen from 2019 to 2021.[25] In 2021, a further 1,390 minors initiated puberty blocker treatment. (In June 2024 the Biden administration issued a statement opposing gender surgery for minors.) For comparison, about six hundred thousand children are abused by their families every year; over seven thousand youths and young adults commit suicide; about two thousand children die from abuse and neglect; and gun deaths, having risen by 50 percent between 2019 and 2021, are now the leading cause of death among American children.[26] Moreover, while the scourge of child abuse exists across all sectors of society, including among the nonreligious, the scale of the problem in faith-based organizations around the world is extraordinary, and public awareness is growing. At this conference, however, there appears to be little interest in children's welfare unless it involves transgender identity, deployed as a form of outrage politics. The only kind of child molestation or pedophilia that comes up for discussion with the Moms is that which, in their minds, is associated with trans people and alleged LGBT "groomers."[27]

"My pronouns are Bible believer, Jesus lover, gun carrier, and mama bear," thunders Leigh Wambsganss from the main stage. She is the chief communications officer of Patriot Mobile, a conference sponsor that is dedicated to organizing right-wing school board takeovers across the country. "This is a spiritual war, not a political war," she declaims.

Tina Descovich and Tiffany Justice (cofounders of Moms for Liberty along with Bridget Ziegler) take the stage to praise the Leadership Institute, a right-wing training powerhouse with revenue close to $40 million per year that has nurtured the careers of hundreds of thousands of right-wing activists. An introductory video explains that the institute has "trained thousands of joyful warriors to save our school boards" and that both groups are "rapidly growing to meet the challenges and opportunity of this unique moment in history." The Moms then present Leadership Institute founder and president Morton Blackwell with a "Liberty Sword Award"—a trophy shaped like a large blade. (The previous year, the award went to Ron DeSantis.) As the investigative outlet Right Wing Watch reported in August 2021, the Leadership Institute, Family Research Council, and other right-wing political groups are focusing on school board takeovers as a strategy for activating a new grassroots movement in local communities and thus building political power. The Leadership Institute offers a twenty-hour online course to train conservatives to run for school boards and "stop the teaching of Critical Race Theory before it destroys the fabric of our nation."[28]

In a breakout session titled "More Than Victims," the people who turn out to be more than victims are Black Americans. Attendees are urged to "counter the divisive and manipulative distortions that have attempted to sever Black Americans' attachment to their own nation." The man leading the sessions, a pastor named J. C. Hall, is married to the fiery antigovernment activist KrisAnne Hall, whose work focuses on pushing David Barton–esque myths about the supposedly biblical underpinnings of the Constitution, and who preaches her ideas to churches and far-right "constitutional sheriff" groups.

Hall's participation in this event follows a certain stratagem in Christian nationalist circles to elevate Black conservatives who offer critiques of the left laced with coded forms of racism. Kyle Spencer illustrated this gambit well in her book, *Raising Them Right: The Untold Story of America's Ultraconservative Youth Movement and Its Plot for Power* (HarperCollins, 2022). Onstage with Charlie Kirk at Turning Point USA's Black Leadership Summit, Candace Owens said she was "sick of the Left's obsession with 'victimization'" and added that Andrew Gillum, who earlier that week was defeated in his bid for the Florida governorship by Ron DeSantis, had just had his "Black card denied on a national level!"

"'You are allowed to say that,' Charlie said, suggesting that as a white male, he could not in fact say that. Then he grinned mischievously, as if to say: *Can you believe I found her?*"

According to Spencer, "The mostly white audience roared with glee."[29]

When author James Lindsay takes the podium, the audience grows truly excited. "He's amazing," my seatmate enthuses, grabbing my arm. "You need to listen to his podcast." Lindsay is a convert—from New Atheism to right-wing conspiracism—and his tale of taking the red pill seems to be at the core of his appeal to this group. In 2012, while wearing a secularist hat, Lindsay self-published a book titled *God Doesn't; We Do: Only Humans Can Solve Human Challenges.* For a time he was popular on the New Atheism circuit. But then, after cowriting a series of hoax papers and submitting them to obscure journals in remote corners of academia,[30] he decided that the great evil facing all of humankind is not religion after all, but "wokeness."[31] His work now focuses on the phantasma of the right—gender issues, critical race theory—and he is frequently invited to speak on right-wing platforms. From a business perspective, it was certainly a judicious flip. His book sales appear to have improved considerably, with titles including the self-published *Race Marxism* and *The Marxification of Education* (both 2022) and *Cynical Theories: How Activist Scholarship Made Everything About Race, Gender, and Identity—and Why This Harms Everybody* (Pitchstone, 2020). A *Daily Telegraph* reviewer, Tim Smith-Laing, was probably being kind when he charged Lindsay with "leaping from history to hysteria."[32] In Philadelphia, Lindsay is introduced as a kind of guru, "a decoder, I guess, helping us to be able to connect what's happened in the past to what's happening right now."

Like many of the other speakers, Lindsay starts off on a defensive note. "You got this southern poverty thing calling you names, saying that you're something, domestic [terrorists], awful people," he says, referring to the Southern Poverty Law Center, which tracks right-wing extremism and militia group activity.

"The reason that you are under these crazy attacks, the reason the Department of Justice is naming you as domestic extremists and terrorists, the reason the FBI is calling some of you when you go to school board meetings, the reason that they are trying to smear you so desperately before this beautiful summit is that [you] are mothers trying to protect [your] kids," says Lindsay.

Lindsay's trademark trope can be summed up under the attack label "Cultural Marxism." The idea, in a very nutty shell, is that the culture wars in America are the moral equivalent of Chairman Mao's murderous cultural revolution in China in the 1960s, in which as many as two million may have died (estimates vary significantly). In his Philadelphia diatribe, Lindsay sticks with his story about the China connection. "Mao Zedong launched a cultural revolution in 1966 to regain power" and "fired every teacher in China and sent them to reeducation, so there would be Socialist education only in China," he intones. "Does that sound familiar? . . . What is happening in America and throughout the West, right now, is the Western cultural revolution."

He glares at the audience in a vaguely menacing way before continuing with the potted history. "And so, in 1957 . . . Mao's at the top of his game, and he launches a program that if we had anti-Communist education in this country, which every one of you should be advocating for, all fifty states, you would know, it's called the Great Leap Forward. We have a great leap backwards today called the Great Reset, which is a little ominous."

The audience seems to be humming along happily. "So, if you've been to a DEI training at your workplace or your school, that's what you got put through," Lindsay concludes. If there is something outrageous and frankly immoral about his comparisons between Mao's murderous atrocities and American school board skirmishes over race and gender, no one here seems to notice.

For his finale, Lindsay returns to the gritted smile that represents the dominant mood of the gathering in Philadelphia. "And this is why it's so important that we're joyful warriors," he says. "I want to convince you, also, that this is what we're going through in America, but it's so important that we keep this joyful warrior attitude, that we keep this poise, that we keep the dignity that we're showing." As he belabors the talking point, I get the sense that he really doesn't trust this well-dressed audience to not screw up. "They want you to get mad. They want you to flip out. They want you to be a PR nightmare for yourselves. Don't worry about making mistakes. Worry about jumping into the hole that they're digging for you. If you just keep telling the truth, and you don't give up, we are going to transform this country."

IT IS ONLY when the politicians take the stage that the real agenda of the conference becomes clear. Donald Trump, Nikki Haley, Ron DeSantis, and Vivek Ramaswamy—the leading contenders at this point in the race for the Republican nomination for the 2024 presidential election—have all come to curry favor with the Moms for Liberty. Each delivers a pitch for their candidacy, and each promises to outdo the others in taking on the woke menace at public schools. If that means throwing kids and families who don't conform under the bus, the candidates are all for more buses. "I will also take historic action to defeat the toxic poison of gender ideology to restore the timeless truth that God created two genders, male and female," Trump says in his disjointed talk.

Not a single conference-goer appears to find it strange that no Democratic candidate for office is expected anywhere in the vicinity. The "Joyful Warriors Conference" is a Republican Party outreach effort. The immediate goal of Moms for Liberty is to deliver voters and activists to the GOP.

The high-level partisan-political nature of the Moms' operation helps answer the money question that hangs over this conference. Two hundred forty-nine dollars is a lot for a three-day event, but my back-of-the-envelope says it cannot come close to covering the costs of the speakers, the outside events, the luxe venue, the swag, and all those lavishly catered meals. In fact, as one would expect from organizers reared in the moneyed gardens of the Florida political machine, Moms for Liberty has scored funding and other forms of support from many of the wealthy powerhouses of the religious right, including the Bradley Foundation, the Heritage Foundation, the Family Research Council, and the Leadership Institute. The Leadership Institute began advising the group from the start, and before her spectacular fall from grace, before she was met with DON'T SAY THREE-WAY signs at her public events,[33] the Leadership Institute hired Mom Ziegler as the vice president of the Leadership Institute's School Board Programs and national director of School Board Leaders Programs.

As I leave the Philadelphia conference, eager to return to the tranquil world of Santa Barbara, I learn about an upcoming gathering of educators in

Washington, D.C. I realize that it's time to hear from the other moms and dads, the ones who are presumably against "liberty."

JENNIFER JENKINS DOESN'T look like a woke warrior. Her sleek dresses and stylish heels, her cheerful suburban demeanor, her neatly feminine coif and statement jewelry, all say something like "soccer mom who lunches." An early childhood educator who lives in Brevard County, Florida, with her husband and eight-year-old daughter, she looks like she would be at home on the golf course, or maybe at the clubhouse. It's hard to understand how anyone could imagine that she is the leader of a Maoist-style insurgency intended to round up conservative Christians and promote pedophilia.

"I've always dressed like this," she tells me when I meet her at the Network for Public Education conference in Washington, D.C., in October 2023. In the large ballroom of the Capitol Hilton Hotel, surrounded by administrators and librarians in sensible shoes and demure cardigans, Jenkins stands out in a stylish pink dress, coordinating heels, and pearl drop earrings. "I think that's how I was able to win over the majority of the constituency with bipartisan support," she confides.

In 2020, Jenkins ran for the deep-red District 3 school board seat in Brevard County. With her unexpected win, she welcomed the chance to represent all her constituents. In retrospect, she realizes, she didn't have a clue. "I didn't understand that I was walking into a war zone."

Her moderate views on issues like COVID-19 mitigation efforts and support for antibullying programs were like gasoline poured on the raging local culture war. Hostile activists staged hours-long protests in front of her house. They tracked the whereabouts of her then five-year-old daughter, photographed her repeatedly, and posted the pictures to social media. The plants in her garden were destroyed, and someone burned F* YOU in three-foot letters into the grass of her yard, which the many children who pass her home on their way to school were bound to see. A state representative harassed her, saying there was "a special place in hell" for her in a public forum.

It didn't stop here; Jenkins was doxed. A website sprang up to say that she was having an affair. Next came accusations of child abuse. Then the death threats started coming in.[34]

Jenkins is not in much doubt about the origins of the harassment campaign she experienced. She won her board seat on the Brevard school board by defeating incumbent Tina Descovich, one of the three cofounders of Moms for Liberty. The hate, she maintains, was payback.

"I cried every single day for a year and a half of my life," she tells me. But she didn't give up. "I continue to fight for my daughter. Because I don't have a choice. I am the only member of my five-member board who is always looking out for students and staff."

Eager to prove his dictatorial bona fides, Florida governor Ron DeSantis waded in with his trademark rubber boots. He put out a "target list" of supposedly liberal-leaning members of school boards around the state.[35] The list actually included some registered Republicans, along with independents and Democrats, and Jenkins was on it. But by this point she had toughened up. She fired back at the governor: "For you to spend your time, energy, and resources in a super majority Republican district against a member who is on a super majority Republican board already, it tells me you're intimidated by me, so I guess I should be flattered," she wrote. Still, DeSantis's cruel indifference to her situation stung. She, her child, and her family had been threatened. How could a governor be so irresponsible?

The real losers, Jenkins feels, are students and families in the district. The other board members, she says, were all culture war all the time. They kicked out the superintendent for specious reasons and eliminated social and emotional learning (SEL) programs. "We are number one in staff vacancies," she tells me, her voice tinged with sarcasm. "But rather than propose policies to improve the education children receive and remedy the district's poor record in testing, the board members spend their time debating book bans and discussing terrifying plans to distribute firearms to teachers. I don't know the last time we talked about anything positive for our kids."

ANOTHER INDIVIDUAL ON DeSantis's ill-considered "hit list" was Tom Edwards, who sits on the board of Sarasota County Schools. Six years earlier, Edwards thought he would cap a successful business career with service to his community. "I really did this because I had an incredible foundation in public education, and I believe I was able to leverage myself forward and persevere, in spite of the challenges I faced, with the tools that my education gave me," he tells me when I corner him for a chat at the Washington, D.C., event. "So I wanted to give back." He thought the position would involve about twenty hours a week. And as someone who comes from a fairly centrist perspective, or, as he describes it, "the philosophy that most of America lives between the forty-yard lines on both the right and the left, and that's where our most important values are," he didn't anticipate much difficulty in collaborating with a Republican-majority board. But he, too, suddenly found himself in a cultural and political battlefield. "I suppose I was naive," he says.

When the Republican majority wished to eliminate a character education program, he objected. When they sought to suppress curricula about the role of slavery in American history, falsely labeling it CRT, he objected again. When they decided to terminate the superintendent—a self-described "conservative Republican" who had consistently received A ratings from the state and had previously received positive ratings from the school board—for allegedly bringing "wokeism" to the district, he objected again.[36] In retrospect, he admits, he didn't have a chance.

Like Jenkins, Edwards had inadvertently stepped into the middle of the right-wing outrage machine. People called him names when he was walking down the street. He received a significant volume of hate mail. Over two consecutive school board meeting, Moms for Liberty members and their allies called Edwards, who is gay, a "pedophile" and a "groomer."[37] A woman named Sally Nista, who was at that time a member of Moms for Liberty and had an association with the Proud Boys, implied that Edwards wanted to harm children. "The room was emotionally violent," Edwards recalls of the school board meetings. When Bridget Ziegler, the chairwoman of Edwards's school board—soon to be famous for her sexcapades—ignored his request to object to the slander, Edwards walked out in protest.

"I didn't do it because I felt personally attacked," Edwards told me. "I really did it because I was protecting my students and my community from the bullying and hate and ugly rhetoric. It was the only thing I could do to shut it down."

Edwards became convinced that his services were more needed than ever. Though he had originally planned to serve only one term, he decided to run again in 2024. "All this politics is such a shame," he says, "because it does nothing to help our kids or improve education. And that's really what we should be focusing on. They are not all moms, and they don't care about liberty. It's a political activist group that wants to tear down public schools for the privatization of your tax dollars." He added, "This is all about the destruction of public education, period. The culture wars in Florida are there to create mistrust."

In the wake of the sex scandal that appears to have ended the Zieglers' rise within the Republican Party, Edwards has more to say. "The hypocrisy of what Mrs. Ziegler has done is the low-hanging fruit," he told CNN's Michael Smerconish.[38] "What really happened is that students' self-esteem and their mental health has been seriously wounded and damaged. Because while they are in their formative years, they've heard 'Don't say gay.' And so when you're discovering your identity in the world, you're attacked . . . And by the way, that happened to Black children. Whitewashing Black history. 'Stop woke.' 'The benefits of slavery.' And if you're Black and gay, you have it to the third power."

Christian Ziegler, he of the alternating two-way and three-way sexual encounters, called Edwards a "phony, radical, and self-admitted WOKE Liberal Activist School Board [sic]."[39]

Edwards soon came to understand that his experience was not unique. At the Network for Public Education conference in Washington, D.C., he joined Jennifer Jenkins and Lucia Baez-Geller, who spent fifteen years as an English teacher before running for the board in 2020. During her tenure, Baez-Geller was often the sole vote on a host of issues associated with liberal values. She also happened to have made the DeSantis hit list.

"They are going after AP psychology, African American history, and every marginalized person," Geller tells me, explaining her recent decision to run for a congressional seat in Miami. "They're not doing anything to actually help kids in schools. I remain committed to protecting our public education system and defending our democracy."

IN THE AFTERMATH of the pandemic, the school board wars spread far beyond the Sunshine State. In Colorado, school board races in multiple districts brought forth candidates promising to ban books and restore "parental rights." In Georgia, Katherine Rinderle, a fifth-grade teacher, was fired for reading to her class a book about a child who enjoys playing with toys marketed for both girls and boys. Music venues and bookstores hosting drag performers received bomb threats. Groups of Proud Boys disrupted Drag Queen Story Hours at public libraries. In San Francisco, one protestor was photographed in a T-shirt that read KILL YOUR LOCAL PEDOPHILE.[40]

According to a 2022 survey by the National Education Association, while strong majorities of voters have favorable attitudes toward their local public schools, almost half of public schools reported challenges to teaching about issues related to race, racism, and LGBT rights. Right-wing media stoked the frenzy, using trans issues in particular as a kind of laser-pointer cat toy to distract the public from their real agenda: undermining faith in public education in order to soften the ground for a wholescale assault, pushing for privatization and the appropriation of public funds for religious schools. An April 2022 report from Media Matters revealed that over a three-week period as it covered Florida's "Don't Say Gay" bill, Fox News hosted 170 segments focusing on transgender people.[41]

In the suburbs of Cincinnati, I locate Melissa Weiss, a mother of two and president of her local public school board. The pandemic years were challenging, she recounts, but this year has proven even more difficult. "Not only do we have to continue pursuing safety precautions and offer multiple options," she says, "but we also have this added element of politicization." At crowded school board meetings, as Weiss tells it, some attendees have taken to yelling out pro-Trump slogans such as "We're going to make America great again" or bursting forth with vaccine and virus misinformation.

When the tensions first emerged, Weiss was perplexed. She had served for years on the school board, and most of the meetings had been somewhat tedious affairs, devoted to budget and instructional issues or planning details for events such as the annual science fair. Why had school board meetings become so loaded? Then the threatening messages started to roll in: "We're watching you," "You better be careful."

"They come in as direct emails to the school board," Weiss tells me. "We pass them on to the local police. This summer, when it was pretty bad, we had a uniformed officer assigned to our meetings. That is not typical at all. After one school board meeting, I had the officer walk me to my car," she adds. "Because I wasn't sure my tires would not be slashed."

In Weiss's district, much of the anger has shifted from the pandemic response to "critical race theory." (When it comes to the right's war on public education, it doesn't matter who the enemy is, you just need one.) "People will send us links to articles and say, 'We better not be doing this in Sycamore schools.'" The reality, Weiss adds dryly, "is that critical race theory is not a K-12 subject."

Local school boards are far from the only battlefields in the culture wars over public education. The rise of public charter schools has opened a whole new front, and Christian nationalists have been quick to seize the opportunity. One strategy is to smuggle a crypto-religious school into a district under the cover of the charter system. In Oklahoma, to the astonishment of most observers, the Catholic archdiocese dispensed with smuggling anything, crypto style; they sought—and received—approval for an explicitly religious charter school.[42]

Over the objections of Oklahoma attorney general Gentner Drummond, Oklahoma's Statewide Virtual Charter School Board voted in favor of this wildly unconstitutional plan. "It's extremely disappointing that board members violated their oath in order to fund religious schools with our tax dollars. In doing so, these members have exposed themselves and the state to potential legal action that could be costly," said Drummond.[43] The plan, he noted, violates not only the U.S. Constitution but Oklahoma state law, which specifically prohibits sectarian charter schools. Rachel Laser, president and CEO of Americans United for Separation of Church and State, added: "It's hard to think of a clearer violation of the religious freedom of Oklahoma taxpayers and public-school families than the state establishing the nation's first religious public charter school. This is a sea change for American democracy."[44]

The plan was put on hold in June 2024 when the state supreme court deemed it a violation of the Oklahoma and U.S. constitutions, as well as a breach of state law. In response, the Diocese of Tulsa and the Archdiocese of Oklahoma City issued a statement that they would "consider all legal options." Given that they and their allies on the state's virtual charter board have friends in high places, it would not be terribly surprising if the case makes its way to the U.S. Supreme Court. Supporting the effort to funnel Oklahoma taxpayer dollars to the Catholic church is the Notre Dame Religious Liberty Clinic at Notre Dame Law School. Formed in 2020, the clinic has deep ties to the Federalist Society.[45] The clinic's director, Stephanie Barclay, clerked for Justice Neil Gorsuch and litigated cases for the Becket Fund for Religious Liberty. An associate dean, Nicole Stelle Garnett, clerked for Justice Clarence Thomas and has written approvingly of the Supreme Court's decision last year in *Carson v. Makin*, which expanded taxpayer funding for religious schools in Maine, and for which the clinic submitted an amicus brief.[46] Given the Supreme Court's penchant in recent decisions for granting special privileges and access to public money to religious groups in the name of "religious liberty," the plan to take money from Oklahoma's public school system and turn it over the Catholic church for religious instruction has a reasonable prospect of success down the line.

One may suppose that the Oklahoma archdiocese is pursuing its culture war on public education primarily for cultural purposes. Over in North Carolina, the case of the Roger Bacon Academy illustrates how culture wars in the charter world can be used to advance rather more material purposes. The Roger Bacon Academy is a four-school charter network. It is the creation of Baker Mitchell Jr., a North Carolina businessman, friend of right-wing political funder Art Pope, and a staunch advocate of "free markets," "deregulation," and school privatization. Mitchell's chain of charter schools has taken in tens of millions of dollars in taxpayer funding; the Charter Day School, one of four schools in his network funded with taxpayer money, receives 95 percent of its funding from federal, state, and local governmental authorities.[47] As ProPublica has detailed, Mitchell also owns and operates the companies that supply these schools with just about everything they buy or lease: the buildings, the computers, the desks, the educational training programs, and more.[48] Mitchell has declined to make his own salary public.

How does he get away with this type of self-dealing? Well, Mitchell has a strategy for demonstrating that he is on the side of the angels, and it has to do with girls' skirts.

The dress code at the Charter Day School requires that female students wear skirts, jumpers, or "skorts." Mitchell has justified the dress code by explaining that girls are "fragile vessels."[49] These schools can't be bad, we are encouraged to believe, because they teach "traditional values."[50] What are these values? The pledge that students at the Roger Bacon Academy are required to adhere to includes the stipulation that they will guard against "the stains of falsehood from the fascination with experts" and "overreliance on rational argument," along with a promise to "obey authority" and be "morally straight."[51]

In 2016, the family of a kindergartner complained that the dress code violated their daughter's civil liberties. A federal appeals court, in *Charter Day School v. Peltier*, had no trouble agreeing that the requirement was "based on blatant gender stereotypes" and a "clear violation of the Equal Protection Clause."[52] Mitchell, however, understood well the uses of a culture war: he claimed to be a victim of antireligious bias. He pulled in amicus briefs from Catholic Charities of the Diocese of Arlington, Virginia; the Jewish Coalition for Religious Liberty; the Religious Freedom Institute; and the Notre Dame Religious Liberty Clinic, the legal group that is representing the Catholic archdiocese in Oklahoma.[53] Given the understanding of "religious liberty" that prevails on the U.S. Supreme Court, charter operators of the future may very well want to get some religion as a means to secure their stream of profits from the public treasury.

WHEN I FIRST started covering the religious right's war on public education back in 2009, the preferred narratives often focused on individual districts and represented events as the spontaneous work of parents with certain ideological predilections. But the reality then, as even more today, is that the school wars are largely the work of well-funded national groups.

There are two basic types of groups working to undermine public education in America, and you can call them the Proselytizers and the Privatizers. On the one hand, a who's who of Christian nationalist groups is lining up against public education. In late 2021, the Family Research Council, a Washington, D.C.–based Christian-right policy group, held an online School Board Boot Camp, a four-hour training session.[54] Among the leaders of the boot camp was Gen. (Ret.) Jerry Boykin, who brought a militaristic framing to instructions on how to run for school boards and against the imagined threat of critical race theory and recruit others to do so. Another group that is active in promoting this transformation in American education is the Truth & Liberty Coalition. Evangelist Andrew Wommack, the organization's Colorado-based founder and president, boasts of using "materials prepared by preeminent historian David Barton," who sits on their board. As Frederick Clarkson, senior research analyst at Political Research Associates, noted in *Religion Dispatches*, the organization distributed voter guides that rated candidates on just five issues: "Critical Race Theory," "Parental Rights," "Boys Playing Girl's Sports," "Sex Education," and "Gender Identity Pronouns." The guide, Clarkson wrote, is "intended for distribution in churches on the Sunday before Tuesday elections."[55]

On Team Money, an equally powerful array of advocacy groups has taken aim at public education. The Bradley Foundation, Heritage Action for America, the Leadership Institute, and the Manhattan Institute are among those providing support for groups on the forefront of the latest public school culture wars. All are on record promoting voucher schemes and other privatization initiatives intended to turn public schools over to right-thinking individuals and private or religious entities.

Why do they want to destroy public education? The agenda that unifies the anti-public-school movement now is hardly limited to banning a few books gathering dust on library shelves or canceling nonexistent CRT courses. In most cases the goal is to undermine public education as it currently exists and replace it with publicly funded private academies (along with taxpayer-subsidized homeschooling). The immediate objective for religious partisans is to nab a flow of public money for their religious organizations. For fiscal conservatives, the aim is to indoctrinate children in their preferred economic ideology. More broadly, the agenda is of a piece with the antidemocratic goals of the new American fascism. Movement leaders understand that public education was at the center of progressive reforms that built the American middle class and sustained American democracy. In an increasingly stratified age, with a new oligarchy arising out of growing economic and political equality, public education must yield to private systems capable of producing a compliant citizenry—and steady profits for the righteous and rich.

Tom Edwards puts his finger on the larger agenda. "The real game is HB 1," he says. That is the legislation, recently passed, allowing the largest expansion of school vouchers in Florida history. Right-wing politicians banging on the school-choice drum, as Edwards well knows, have plenty of skin in that game. The payoff from the culture wars consists of taxpayer money flowing freely into the pockets of right-wing power players in Florida and beyond.

Back home after my tour of the school board wars, it is the profiteering that disturbs me the most, perhaps even more than the demonization of LGBT Americans or Lindsay invoking Mao's murderous regime or book banners trumping the Holocaust with homophobia. I decide that, once again, it's time to follow the money.

CHAPTER 4

The Room Where It Happens

B arre Seid was born to Russian Jewish immigrants in Chicago around the start of the Great Depression and attended the University of Chicago. He would later identify with "basic libertarianism."[1] He went into business in the unglamorous end of electronics parts—power strips, cables—and established a reputation as a consummate micromanager. Even as his company grew, he was known for tweaking prices for each of its hundreds of products. When the personal computer boom arrived, generating an almost insatiable demand for those power strips, he hit the jackpot. He would eventually dispose of his main company, TrippLite, for $1.65 billion.

Seid has no children, but he has expressed a desire to "steer history," or so says his adviser and apparent confidant Steven Baer.[2] Seid wants to change the lives of millions of people, to shape the climate in which they live and the nature of the schools they attend, says Baer. But he does not believe that those millions deserve to know his name or anything about him. By his own admission, he is prone to "anonymity paranoia"—that is, he is a privacy nut.[3] Sometimes he goes by the pseudonym Ebert, perhaps a reference to the Illinois-born anarchist philosopher Elbert Hubbard, or by Elbert Howell, a possible nod to Thurston Howell III, otherwise known as the millionaire on the TV show *Gilligan's Island*.

Seid achieved fame, or at least notoriety, in 2022 when he made a $1.6 billion donation to a trust controlled by Leonard Leo, the right-wing moneyman best known for his role in stacking the Supreme Court with conservative ideologues drawn from the Federalist Society.[4] Leo sits at the center of the large and well-funded right-wing legal ecosystem and plays a vital role in coordinating a network of dark money groups that aim to impose a Christian nationalist and right-wing economic agenda through the law. According to Alex Aronson, executive director of the advocacy group Court Accountability, "Leonard Leo has been the driving figure of the conservative movement's decades-long effort to reshape the Supreme Court's composition and outcomes."[5]

Seid's donation took the form of the equity in his firm, and it was structured so as to claim as much as a $400 million tax reduction. (Seid and his fellow libertarians hate the way government appropriates their money through taxes, but they seem quite happy to appropriate money from other taxpayers for their favorite projects.) The donation is believed to be the largest in American political history, and Leo is sure to use it to continue to advance his antidemocratic project.[6]

Seid's blockbuster gift wasn't about turning over a new leaf; it came after two decades of support for right-wing causes behind the scenes. According to tax records obtained by ProPublica, Seid gave out at least $775 million between 1996 and 2018.[7] Some of the giving followed predictable libertarian orthodoxy. A major beneficiary was the State Policy Network, a network of state-focused think tanks that push tax cuts for the wealthy, deregulation of sometimes polluting, often market-destroying industry sectors, cuts in safety-net programs, reductions in public health-care programs, and other initiatives that warm the hearts of Chicago School of Economics–style professors.

Another cause that appears to warm Seid's heart is climate denialism. Seid had long been opposed to bans on DDT, and when he heard about theories of anthropogenic climate change, he smelled a rat there too. He was certain that leading climate scientists are wrong when they blame global warming on human-generated carbon emissions. Baer—who seems strangely ubiquitous in channeling both Seid's money and his mind—introduced the billionaire to Joseph Bast, then the head of the Heartland Institute. A conservative think tank that got its start defending tobacco companies, Heartland found a bigger revenue stream pushing climate denialism on behalf of fossil fuel companies. Heartland's climate denial is an open secret. In their book *The Republican Reversal: Conservatives and the Environment from Nixon to Trump* (Harvard University Press, 2018), authors Jay Turner and Andrew Isenberg characterized Heartland Institute as leaders of "the scientific misinformation campaign," with an annual conference featuring "fringe scientists."[8] Heartland welcomed Seid as "a major patron," and Seid supplied the think tank with both money and personnel. The late Chuck Lang (d. 2018) served as both the chairman of the board of Heartland and chief financial officer of Seid's electronic parts company.

Seid's experience as an electronic parts magnate also appears to have imbued him with the conviction that he knows how to fix not just the climate but also what's wrong with higher education in America. One major beneficiary of his educational wisdom is the Antonin Scalia Law School at George Mason University. Six Supreme Court justices—all from the Leonard Leo wing of the court—attended the inauguration of the school in 2016, and three—Thomas, Kavanaugh, and Gorsuch—have been members of the faculty. True to its namesake, the Antonin Scalia Law School has established a reputation as a hotbed of reactionary legal theory. It's the kind of place where conservative jurists can augment government salaries with well-compensated, all-expenses-paid teaching gigs, seminars, and lectures in picturesque European cities and spa resorts. It's also the go-to place for legal opinions in defense of presidents impeached for attempting to overthrow the U.S. government.[9] Helping the Scalia law school get off the ground was $20 million from a donor who insisted on remaining anonymous. That donor was Barre Seid.

Hillsdale College in Michigan, too, is a beneficiary of Seid's effort to steer history. Hillsdale is perhaps best known for its efforts to inculcate hard-right thinking in its students and to feed the Trump administration with staffers. But it deserves more attention for its work in public education. The college presides over a growing network of over seventy affiliated charter schools that use public money to pay for right-wing public schooling. It extends its influence by allowing other charter networks to utilize Hillsdale material or curricula. Individuals associated with Hillsdale have been instrumental in prosecuting Florida governor Ron DeSantis's war on woke in the public schools of the Sunshine State.

Does Barre Seid really care about public education? Is he really committed to Leonard Leo's program to instigate an ultratraditionalist vision of a religious America? Does he really believe that "Jesus Was an Anarchist," as the late Elbert Hubbard titled his manifesto?[10]

Seid doesn't talk, so we will probably never know for sure. Steven Baer, on the other hand, seems to know what's on his mind. Asked by ProPublica about

Seid's motivations, Baer explained that, "like the billionaire donor Charles Koch," Seid "understands the need to unite the conservative movement to change the direction of the country."[11] The best guess is that Seid simply believes the libertarian fairy tales he may have learned at school. He appears to have concluded that democracy will fail to deliver on those fantasies. If he needs to work with antiabortion fanatics and the public school demolition crew to keep the dream alive, he will do it. Presumably he imagines that maybe one day the millions who will never know his name will thank him.

TO UNDERSTAND THE impact that people like Seid have on our world, it is helpful to revisit the long history of the campaign against public education. The roots of the anti-public-school frenzy on the right go back at least as far as Reconstruction. When victorious Yankees introduced the idea of public education in the defeated territories of the Confederacy, the leaders of the redemption discovered one of their most enduring objects of contempt. Robert Lewis Dabney, a hard-line leader of the Southern Presbyterian Church who ardently defended slavery before the war and segregation afterward, thought it a moral outrage that white citizens should have to pay for the schooling of "the brats of black paupers."[12] A. A. Hodge, a conservative Presbyterian theologian from Princeton Seminary, added in 1890 that a system of public education would become an "efficient and wide instrument for the propagation of atheism."[13] As if anticipating a later trend in right-wing polemics, he referred to these allegedly nightmarish reeducation centers as "government schools."

"I am as sure as I am of Christ's reign," he said in a lecture that was published in 1887, after his death, "that a comprehensive and centralized system of national education, as is now commonly proposed, will prove the most appalling enginery for the propagation of anti-Christian and atheistic unbelief, and of anti-social nihilistic ethic, individual, social, and political, which this sin-rent world has ever seen."[14] The union of this kind of fanaticism with the financial needs of the (formerly) slaveholding oligarchy of that time set the pattern for the anti-public-education crusades to come.

The reaction of white southern communities in the aftermath of the Supreme Court's 1954 decision in *Brown v. Board* requiring the desegregation of schools largely followed that nineteenth-century precedent. Determined to maintain segregation in schooling, the white supremacists in control of the South advanced voucher schemes. The idea was that white families could take a slice of public money and use it to pay tuition at private, racist religious academies. At the same time, conservative Christians increasingly portrayed public schools as the devil's playground. Rousas J. Rushdoony, the Christian Reconstructionist theologian who became in some sense the godfather of today's religious right, argued that the goal of "statist" education is "chaos," "primitivism," and "a vast integration into the void," and claimed that public schools "train women to become men."[15] In 1979, Jerry Falwell Jr., founder of the hopelessly misnamed Moral Majority, announced, "I hope to see the day when there are no more public schools; churches will have taken them over and Christians will be running them."[16]

Not to be outdone, in 1986, the influential preacher D. James Kennedy, who received at least $5.5 million from the family of former secretary of education Betsy DeVos, said that "the infusion of an atheistic, amoral, evolutionary, socialistic, one-world anti-American system of education in our public schools has indeed become such that if it had been done by an enemy, it would be considered an act of war."[17] In 2009, Dr. Morris H. Chapman, president and chief executive officer of the Southern Baptist Convention's executive committee, put the same message in front of America's largest evangelical denomination. Public school children, he claimed, are "bombarded with secular reasoning, situational ethics, and moral erosion."[18]

In the 1960s, moneyed interests with libertarian economic leanings acquired a new and powerful ally in the assault on public education. Armed with a seminal 1955 paper by economist Milton Friedman, they put forward a battery of economic arguments against it. Education is not a public good, they said; it's a consumer item that should be traded on an open market in which parents look for the best deal, and those who cannot afford any of the schooling options for their children will just have to suck it up. Bringing government into schooling can only introduce waste, inefficiency, and political agendas to the process. Right-wing think tanks got in on the action, publishing screeds denouncing the "command and control mentality" of the "government school," which "robs teachers and administrators of the joy and professionalism of their important work."[19] In an Acton Institute review of the book *Public Education: An Autopsy* by the libertarian author Myron Lieberman, William B. Allen praised the author's prescription for replacing public education with a for-profit model. "As public education fails and dies, it carries along the ghosts of natural abilities atrophied in young children who could not escape in time," Allen wrote. The solutions to America's educational challenges, he asserted, "must derive from the 'death of public education.'"[20]

Soon, the anti-government-school rhetoric coming from religious conservatives became almost indistinguishable from the libertarian attacks on public education. At the Family Research Council, a reactionary and Christian nationalist policy group, senior vice president Rob Schwarzwalder wrote in 2010 that "the Department (of ed) is unconstitutional, ineffective, and wasteful. In short, it should be abolished . . . Aim carefully and slay the dragon for once and for all."[21]

While voucher and charter proponents have tended to couch their rhetoric in secular language, large numbers are animated by the same hostilities that drove the religious right's war on public education. The late Mae Duggan, who founded the DeVos-funded voucher front group Citizens for Educational Freedom, said disparagingly, "We don't want people teaching humanism. Secular humanism is the basis of the public schools."

FROM THE BEGINNING, the profit motive was hard at work in the assault on public education. Some of the most passionate advocates of voucher systems in the postsegregation era were the leaders of the same private schools that stood to collect taxpayer funds through those vouchers. As privatization plans grew bigger and bolder, the attacks on public education escalated. They also began to extend up the educational ladder. Not just primary and secondary schools but institutes of higher education, too, were allegedly irredeemably infected with secularism, wokeism, gender ideology, and every other object of reactionary anxiety. To be sure, extreme versions of such ideologies may be counted within the diverse philosophical assemblages that exist in university settings. But according to the right-wing narratives, such institutions are no longer to be trusted because they are corrupted through and through.

The decisive development in the first decades of the twenty-first century was not the alliance between Team Money and Team God but the simple fact that, thanks to escalating inequality, the big money got a lot bigger. What was new was the number of zeroes in the checks—and the extremism of the thinking guiding the money people. To understand the war unfolding on school boards across the country, it turns out, you need to know something about the education of a sector of America's billionaire class, including reclusive Houston-based software magnates, paper products bigwigs, Texas fracking kings, the descendants of a Michigan-based multilevel marketing scheme, and other Americans of extraordinary fortune. Rarely have so few done so much so thoughtlessly to undermine the educational resources on which democracy depends.

BARRE SEID IS far from the only billionaire who wants to play history maker. Many others have joined him in the dark-money room. Although each pursues his or her own dream, the lion's share of the big ideology money has ended up on the side that wants to demolish the existing system of public education. The DeVos-Prince family, for example, has spent vast sums pushing school privatization schemes in Michigan and elsewhere. The Bradley Foundation and the Scaife Foundation are also taking aim at public education and litigating the culture wars, along with the Freedom Foundation, an organization dedicated to breaking unions and undermining their push for better wages and benefits for the workforce. Tim Dunn, who sold his private Midland, Texas–based oil company CrownQuest Operating LLC to Occidental for $10 billion, and the Wilks brothers, who also owe their billions to the oil fields of Texas, are with Seid on climate denialism and education denialism, and they add to the mix an evangelical version of the Christian nationalism that Leo favors. Dunn is the vice board chair of the Texas Public Policy Foundation, which in November 2021 sent out a fundraising letter announcing that "the time is ripe to set Texas children free from enforced indoctrination and Big Government cronyism in our public schools."[22] The time has come, one presumes, for enforced indoctrination in the belief systems of fossil-fuel cronies, with a big assist from the public treasury.

Pennsylvania's answer to Texas is Jeff Yass, a mathematician who struck gold in the fine arts of high-speed securities trading. With a net worth of $28.5 billion, Yass is an admirer of Milton Friedman and funder of the Club for Growth, which pursues the predictable antitax, antiregulatory agenda. The other major funder of the Club for Growth is Richard Uihlein, a Midwestern packaging and shipping magnate and beer-family scion. He and his wife Liz devote tens of millions of dollars to political action committees that support far-right candidates across the country.[23] They devote further millions to funding far-right propaganda networks masquerading as local news. The Uihleins also contribute handsomely to causes dear to the right, such as the Ohio referendum intended to overturn an earlier referendum supporting abortion rights. Yass, Uihlein, and their Club for Growth, predictably, advocate for "school choice" and are eager to fund antiabortion judges to get there.

Joining them in the pro-theocracy movement are Ann and Neil Corkery. The Corkerys have funded a vast array of right-wing organizations, including the Judicial Crisis Network, which campaigns to get conservative justices confirmed to the U.S. Supreme Court. They also help fund CRC Advisors, chaired by Leonard Leo, the go-to public relations firm and networking outfit for right-wing reactionaries. Back in Texas, Mike Rydin, the Houston-based software entrepreneur, has contributed $25 million to the Conservative Action Project, the MAGA-aligned organization crafting America First political infrastructure that promotes lies about the 2020 election. Meanwhile, according to *Politico*, Rebekah Mercer, who manages political giving underwritten by her hedge fund billionaire father, Robert Mercer, "has supplanted the Koch brothers as the right's most important megadonor—expanding the scope of what constitutes political spending along the way."[24] Rebekah Mercer had a heavy hand in Trump's first administration, having been at one time a close associate of Steve Bannon; she also supported Mike Flynn as Trump's national security adviser. Her father endorses a mix of reactionary social ideas, fringe scientific claims, and extreme economic libertarianism. According to investigative journalist Vicky Ward, a former colleague "recalls him saying, in front of coworkers, words to the effect that 'your value as a human being is equivalent to what you are paid.'"[25]

These are just a few of such donors—and donations—on record. A glance at the leaked membership lists of the secretive Council for National Policy (CNP) will turn up any number of deep-pocketed movement funders, from dairy magnate Robert Hilarides to CNP vice president William L. Walton to charter school kingpin and Betsy DeVos contemporary J. C. Huizenga. But for those who prefer to hide their giving through intermediaries, such as donor-advised funds and private foundations, there's the National Christian Foundation (NCF), the largest U.S. charity for Christian and Christian nationalist causes, which disbursed $2.1 billion in grants in 2022.[26] Other donor-advised funds include the Servant Foundation, once an affiliate of the NCF but now a separate organization, which received more than $1 billion, much of it from the NCF, after the split.

Among other beneficiaries of money that cycles through the National Christian Foundation and the Servant Foundation are multiple U.S. organizations pushing a broad religious supremacist agenda. They include the American Center for Law and Justice, the Family Research Council, the Heritage Foundation, the Fellowship Foundation, and the ADF, which received $65.9 million from the Servant Foundation between 2018 and 2021. The ADF and its related foundation received additional funds from the National Christian Foundation and the donor-advised fund DonorsTrust as well as the Signatry, another donor-advised fund that has disbursed over $4 billion in grants since 2000.[27]

The list of significant donors and donor-advised funds, as well as their linkages, is too long to include here, but the staggering sums involved tells us something about why the movement has been such a success. There is no shortage of superwealthy people who identify as liberal or progressive, and they too engage in political giving. But the nature of that giving is different. "Donors on the right are much better at building values-based political movements and funding multi-issue organizations and networks that advance an overall narrative about what's gone wrong with American life—and then tell us how to fix it," David Callahan, founder and editor of Inside Philanthropy, a digital media site, told me. "Liberal funders in contrast tend to give to the DNC or to the politicians whose names they recognize, even though those politicians may be in safe seats or may not need the money. Also, the issues and organizations that they do support have tended to work in silos."

As awareness of the Christian nationalist movement's aims and modes of operation has grown, more of Blue America's money is finding its way to the grassroots. The coalition partners of the Leadership Conference on Civil and Human Rights includes hundreds of groups engaged in the defense of our freedoms and democracy. But such groups often end up competing for funding from the same relatively limited set of known givers. Too many liberal-leaning donors, as Callahan notes, fail to understand or support the type of organizational infrastructure building and relationship building that's required to forge a broad political movement. "Liberal donors can be a bit technocratic and think you make social change by coming up with solutions that are evidence-based.

And that's not really how politics works," Callahan says. "People are less rational than a lot of liberal funders would like to believe."

And what about the reactionary funders; how rational are they? A curious fact about big right-wing money is that those who dole it out are apparently only in control of the platitudes behind it. Like Seid, they may be "basic libertarians," who believe firmly in the doctrine of government bad, private sector good. But if we want to understand the mechanics, or how their streams of money get sluiced into a Christian nationalist charter group in Florida, for example, or into an effort to license the Catholic diocese covering Oklahoma to build a Catholic religious school with public money, we must turn to the people who appear to have the billionaires' ears. In the room where it happens, big money typically sits opposite a well-dressed professional. And it is the courtier who explains just why a donation to this think tank or that policy group will advance the dream. Unfortunately, the meetings that matter are almost always behind closed doors. That's why it's called dark money.

Ensconced in my Santa Barbara retreat, as I pondered this matter, the investigative watchdog and journalism project Documented got its hands on some tapes that take us, at least for a moment, into that dark money room.

IN MAY 2021, former attorney general William Barr—who, as mentioned earlier, submitted a memo to the Justice Department critiquing the special counsel's investigation into Russian interference in the 2016 election—delivered a speech to the ADF. In that speech, which was given in thanks for an ADF award, Barr made the case against public education. "I think we have to confront the reality that it may no longer be fair, practical, or even constitutional to provide publicly funded education solely through the vehicle of state-operated schools," he said.[28] Barr's point resonated with ADF leaders. They, too, believed that moral corruption in America had reached such a point that the public schools could no longer be trusted. For decades they had backed Christian fundamentalist groups that sought to promote sectarian prayer and indoctrination in public schools. The final solution would be to use public money to fund private schools that could be counted on to teach children the truth: that America is a Christian nation, whose laws should be based on their interpretation of the Bible.

The ADF leaders swiftly organized secret meetings with wealthy Christian-right donors to discuss the future of the public education system. Central to the fundraising plan was the Ziklag Group, a secretive organization for "high net-worth families" that vacuums in funding for the ADF and its allies.

The name of the group tells you something about its ideology. In the Old Testament book of Samuel, references to the town of Ziklag appear in several places. At the beginning of 1 Samuel 27, King David vows to flee to the land of the Philistines and is granted the town of Ziklag. In another passage, Ziklag is plundered by the Amalekites, who represent the pinnacle of evil because they rebelled against God. (According to the curriculum promoted by the Good News Club, a program developed by the Child Evangelism Fellowship and spoon-fed to elementary-age children in public schools nationwide, Amalekites deserved mass slaughter for having committed the "sin of unbelief.")[29] King David and his men mount a battle and defeat the Amalekites, saving all of their own people. (The tale of the Amalekites is one of the Bible's many inconsistencies; in an earlier passage, Samuel 15, God orders Saul to murder all of the Amalekites—the women, the children, the babies, the animals; "every living thing"—and he kills them all, with the exception of the king.)

The Ziklag Group today clearly sees itself as the center of a reconquest, too. In this context, Ziklag appears to be a refuge of last resort, a safe place to retreat to until forces of evil (Saul, secularism, whatever) are vanquished and the forces of righteousness can prevail. In fact, a description of the Ziklag Group by United in Purpose decries "the 'raid' that's taking place on our country."[30] In biblical translations, Amalekites are referred to as "raiders" and Ziklag as a "last refuge."

The Ziklag Group met in June 2021. The recording that Documented managed to obtain gives us at least a glimpse into the thought processes of education-denying wealthy donors. One of the leaders on the high-net-worth side of the table was a man named Peter Bohlinger, who as of 2020 was a member of the CNP. After a discussion of legal challenges to secular public education across the country, Bohlinger seized upon what he evidently took to be the grand strategy of the movement: "Our goal is not to just throw stones. Our goal is to take down the education system as we know it today."[31]

I recall feeling a certain gratification on reading this little statement of grandiose nihilism. It was not that the sledgehammer of ignorant money seemed any less terrifying; it was just that the secret part had at least been said out loud. Too many Americans have trouble acknowledging the extremism that has sprung up in our midst. And here was one of America's self-appointed holy rich men making clear that yes, indeed, the goal is to demolish the system of public education that powered America's rise to middle-class prosperity beginning in the nineteenth century and to replace it with an eminently corruptible network of privatized religious and right-wing academies operating with public funds for the ultimate benefit of a sanctimonious oligarchy.

The sense of satisfaction, however, yielded to unease when I took a closer look at Peter Bohlinger. It turns out that he is a California real estate investor and developer. He appears to have inherited a family business, and he makes handsome profits by buying up properties and then jacking up the rents. That in itself was no surprise—the people who want to steer history, as the case of Barre Seid illustrates, develop their delusions of expertise in public education through all sorts of happy business experiences. The thing that drew my attention is that Peter Bohlinger is based in Santa Barbara. The house in which he appears to live is just a tiara's toss or two from James and Joan Lindsey's Montecito mansion. I often pass it on my daily strolls through the neighborhood. In fact, Bohlinger plays tennis from time to time at a local club with people I happen to know.

When I left my Santa Barbara base and toured the country in search of the ultimate source of the conflicts raging on America's school boards, I had failed to appreciate that, owing to quirks in the way that big money moves around the country, it was coming out of a game being played in my own backyard.

PART II

Lies

CHAPTER 5

The Permanent Emergency

I n 2019, I attended the annual gathering of the World Congress of Families (WCF) in Verona, Italy. Founded in 1997 by an alliance of post–Cold War American and Russian academics and activists, the WCF describes itself as "pro-family"—which essentially means that it blames liberals, feminists, and gay people for the impending collapse of Western civilization. In a seventeenth-century palazzo that looked like the perfect setting for Shakespeare's *Romeo and Juliet*, I listened to speakers such as WCF president and cofounder of the National Organization for Marriage Brian S. Brown, Italy's deputy prime minister, Matteo Salvini, Russian Orthodox archpriest Dmitri Smirnov, and Vladimir Putin ally Alexey Komov offer their calls for war on "global liberalism," feminism, and "the LGBT totalitarians." In between tirades, I chatted with an American homeschool activist who informed me that the secular left was now so radicalized that it would shortly begin a program of shutting down churches and arresting conservatives. In the break rooms I caught glimpses of Ignacio Arsuaga, founder of the far-right activist groups HazteOir and CitizenGO, and Giorgia Meloni, who has since gone on to become prime minister of Italy.

At the time I did not pay much attention to the small, white-haired American academic who was invited to deliver the conference's closing talk, a professor and former dean of California's Chapman University School of Law named John Eastman. I have more recently taken the time to listen to my audio recordings of the event.

In his talk to the Verona crowd, Eastman retailed the same story about how secularism, liberalism, and gender confusion are destroying everything good in the world. "You know the other side is getting more and more radical," he said. "But I am old enough to know that life is a pendulum. And the further they push the pendulum in one way, the harder and faster it will swing back in the direction of truth." He praised the conference logo for suggesting "a longing to live according to the dictates of God, whether revealed to us by reason, or nature, or by revelation. And it also suggests a longing for the moral clarity that must be brought to bear by our clergy, our shepherds," he added. "When the church is awakened, great things can happen."

Eastman was not at the 2019 WCF by accident. He was chairman of the board of the National Organization for Marriage and a signatory to the manifesto in which WCF leader Brian S. Brown articulated a set of reactionary doctrines, and he has made clear in subsequent work that he is deeply hostile to gay marriage, reproductive rights, and other targets of the WCF crowd. But in retrospect I can see why his speech did not leave much of a mark on me. He did not appear to be quite one of them. The true believers don't offer shout-outs to "reason" and "nature" as possible alternatives to "revelation" for knowing the "dictates of God." They tend to take for granted that the Bible is all you need. They also tend to speak of priests as inspired bearers of the Word, not as mere functionaries working the flock for moral clarity. Eastman in Verona was a committed ally of the theocrats, to be sure. But his talk hinted at some foundation other than biblical literalism.

Looking back over Eastman's academic work, one can find traces of the same sensibility: a belief in the immense utility of religion—and the absence of much concern about belief in a particular religion. Eastman clerked for Supreme Court justice Clarence Thomas and remains on friendly terms with him.[1] He also corresponds with Thomas's wife, Ginni.[2] In a lengthy 2014 essay in the *Claremont Review of Books*, he sets out to push his friends on the court as far as possible to eviscerate the Establishment Clause of the First Amendment.[3] The argument will be familiar to anyone acquainted with Christian nationalism today. Eastman strings together a series of decontextualized quotes from America's founders, the gist of which is ostensibly that the founders never really intended to separate church and state. They loved religion and wanted everybody to have some. How else to inculcate virtue among the *populus*? Sure, they wanted to be careful not to favor any one particular

Christian sect over any other. But they definitely wanted some religion over none, which is to say, they wanted to rid the world of those woke secularists, the great scourge of their age and ours.

The curious fact, however, is that in Eastman's theoretical musings about the social value of religion and the urgent need to impose it on the population according to the founders' (supposed) wishes, he speaks of God yet says little about Christianity or any other faith. Any religion will do, he seems to suggest; and it probably doesn't matter whether you actually believe in it. It appears that the important thing is to make sure that other people believe—or at least that they conform.

These nuances in Eastman's reactionary thought-world became much more interesting in July 2023, when he was outed as "Co-Conspirator 2" in the Department of Justice's indictment of Donald Trump in connection with the plot to overturn the 2020 election. The interest grew further in the following month, when he was criminally indicted in the state of Georgia for his role in the same conspiracy.[4] (A judge ruled that he should be disbarred.[5] Eastman, who has pled not guilty, plans to appeal.)

IN MAY 2023, shortly before Eastman was charged on nine counts, I attended the National Conservatism Conference in London. About one thousand supporters of that movement gathered in the semicircular auditorium of the Emmanuel Centre, a couple blocks south of Westminster Abbey, to hear from a range of scholars, commentators, politicians, and public servants. NatCon conferences, as they are often called, have been held in Italy, Belgium, and Florida and are associated with what is increasingly called the New Right. According to author and investigative journalist Kathryn Joyce, the New Right comprises "a highbrow gathering of right-wing academics, writers, and think tankers who, for the last several years, have argued that the old Reaganite coalition uniting religious conservatives, anti-Communists, and free-market libertarians is over, and some new shared vision must take its place."[6] What this new vision involves is very hard to specify with precision, but it generally includes a mix of nationalist rhetoric (in whichever nation the conversation happens to be taking place); vague (and typically insincere) gestures toward economic populism; and copious amounts of hate for liberals and, worst of all, "the woke."

The London event, like those elsewhere, was lined with booths from organizations such as the Danube Institute, a Hungarian group associated with Viktor Orban's cronies; the Bow Group, a UK-based conservative think tank; the Heritage Foundation, the reactionary American think tank that has veered into New Right territory; and the Alliance Defending Freedom, the massive legal advocacy group that seeks to impose religion on the population in the name of religious freedom and which now has offices in a half-dozen European cities.

There is a story you hear from the podiums at NatCon conferences, and if you go to enough of them, it will sound as familiar as a classic rock song. It goes something like this: The sum of all our problems—and the greatest threat that the United States and its sister republics around the world have ever faced—is the rise of the "woke" elite. Cosmopolitan, overeducated, gender-fluid, parasitic, anti-Christian idolaters who worship at the shrine of diversity, equity, and inclusion, the leaders of this progressive cabal are bent on elevating undeserving people of color while crushing hardworking "real" Americans (or real Britons, or whoever is in the audience). They control "the regime," or so the song tells us: "the administrative state," the institutions of culture, law enforcement, even the military. Their singular, defining gesture is to "cancel" right-thinking people, which they do all day long everywhere just for spite. Any and all means to annihilate the power of the woke, up to and including political violence and overturning elections, must be seriously considered if we (right-thinking nationalists) are to "save our country."[7]

The funding for the NatCon shows appears to come mainly from the Edmund Burke Foundation, which was founded in 2019 with the aim of strengthening national conservatism, and the money behind that group comes in large measure from a New York private equity investor named Thomas D. Klingenstein. In a series of recorded speeches with a distinct refrain, Klingenstein has made clear that he is all in on the NatCon song. The totalitarian evil of our time, he warns us, is "woke communism."[8]

The tune is so popular that it has spread far and wide on the right. In the run-up to the 2023 Road to Majority conference in Washington, D.C., an annual gathering of religious right activists, strategists, and politicians, seasoned Christian-right operative Ralph Reed sent out a fundraising email asserting that "woke culture and anti-Christian, anti-American radicals drive our public life further and further from the Light of God's Word."[9] From the main stage of the conference, Ron DeSantis railed against the "woke mind virus";[10] Vivek Ramaswamy took swipes at both the woke thing and the "administrative state";[11] and Josh Hawley asserted that "woke corporations" and "Marxists in the C-suite" are "pushing relentlessly this Marxist agenda, pushing relentlessly this religion of woke."[12] At the gala dinner, Trump delivered a rambling attack on his political opponents in the Democratic Party, whom he accused of "trying to impose their blasphemous creed of woke communism."[13]

At the NatCon conference in London, no one sings the antiwoke anthem more insistently than Michael Anton, who served as a national security spokesman in the first Trump administration. A former private equity investor with a taste for fine suits as well as political polemics—he worked as a speechwriter for Rupert Murdoch and Rudy Giuliani and published a book about men's style—Anton shot to fame in 2016 with his infamous essay "The Flight 93 Election," which was said to make the "intellectual case" for Trump.[14] Anton argued that the election of Hillary Clinton would be the equivalent of a mass terrorist attack on the United States. (He also compared it to Russian roulette; with a seemingly unquenchable thirst for metaphors, he added it would be "pedal-to-the-metal on the entire Progressive-Left agenda.") Published under the byline Publius Decius Mus (a Roman consul who nobly sacrificed himself for his country—how grand!) but later attributed to Anton, "The Flight 93 Election" argued that conservatives had no choice but to rush the cockpit.[15] All those weak-kneed RINOs had better join the rebel team—or face "certain death."

As I settle into the wooden pews at the Emmanuel Centre for Anton's presentation at NatCon London, he starts off with what he seems to think is the intellectual case for Brexit. In a speech titled "Britain's Grand Strategy for the 21st Century," he hails Brexit as "Britain standing up for herself against the globalist Borg." And he takes a swipe at American and British support for Ukraine. "A Russia that has difficulty reaching, much less crossing, the Dnieper does not seem much like a threat to cross the channel," he says. No matter, he goes on; the real threat to the West doesn't come from without but from within. "There are more ways to dominate, exploit, bully and enervate than military conquest," he says. "It is tempting to want to think of foreign policy in the traditional way, as threats from predatory empires and nation states. But that is not the threat that we face today, not the main one." The great nemesis, he reveals, is not rogue nuclear states or climate change, not economic stagnation or corruption, not declining health indicators or crime—but wokeism. It is an alien phenomenon, he insists, yet it has insidiously infiltrated the weak-minded here at home. "This ideology was not born in our countries" but "has taken root here and in America. It has captured our elites and our institutions. And I am sorry to say we are partly to blame because so far, at any rate, we have failed to stop it."[16]

"What I consider to be the real threat," Anton tells the audience, "may consume the West and even potentially the whole entire developed world." He raises his eyes and looks around the room as if chewing on a mighty idea. "Is it wokeism, is it the media, is it the administrative state, is it the university NGO international busybody complex?" Brief but pregnant pause. "I would say it is all of the above, broadly understood under the rubric of 'the regime,' a transnational regime or movement or web of peoples and institutions that seeks to control both our countries, plus many besides, and that, if we are to be honest, already does to an extent."[17]

How sinister. There is something particularly detached from reality in Anton's narrative of imminent doom at the hands of a shadowy global enemy. As I survey the auditorium here in central London, the enemy starts to come into focus. The crowd here is united in their opposition to an evil elite. They righteously claim to stand for the hardworking people of the nations, the salt-of-the-earth types from the English countryside who demanded to get out of the European Union and/or the small-town heartlanders who elevated Trump. But in fact, they hardly look like the "real" Americans (or salty Englishmen) they are meant to represent. This is after all a conference in swankiest London that draws in jet-setting populists from around the world. Educated, urbane, stylishly if conservatively attired, eminently professional—they look much more like the villains in the tale than the people who are supposed to be rising up against the regime. The great war on the woke, I'm starting to think, isn't between "the people" and the "elites." It's about how one part of the upper middle class deeply resents and fears another part of the upper middle class.

IN 2022, THE war on woke came to New College, a part of the state university system in Florida. Known as a haven for a diverse and eclectic mix of students and teachers, New College combined a reputation for respectable academic performance with an openness to students and perspectives outside the mainstream of the rest of the state university system. But Florida governor Ron DeSantis, in hopes of burnishing his credentials as a stiff-necked culture warrior in his spectacularly unsuccessful run for the presidency, decided to eviscerate this beast of wokeness and replace its innards with some NatCon-style righteousness. The stated plan was to model the new New College on Hillsdale College, the private Christian nationalist college in Michigan that has served as a feeder for the Trump administration and hard-right causes everywhere.

To the new board of the college, DeSantis appointed reactionary henchman Christopher Rufo. As Rufo helpfully explained in a tweet, "The goal is to have the public read something crazy in the newspaper and immediately think 'critical race theory.' We have decodified the term and will recodify it to annex the entire range of cultural constructions that are unpopular with Americans."[18] In other words, the point was to demagogue a nonexistent threat to K-12 students from theories that they weren't taught, all to mobilize moms and dads in support of right-wing authoritarianism. In speeches and more recently a book,[19] Rufo has argued that the nation's universities—pretty much all of them—have been captured by remnants of the violent leftist movements of the 1960s and turned into factories of wokeness. The upshot is that it's only fair for conservatives to retake the universities and cleanse them of the woke. Joining Rufo on the board was, among others, Charles Kesler, a conservative academic perhaps best known to the public for his work on the 1776 Commission. Conceived as the Trump administration's answer to the *New York Times*'s 1619 Project, the 1776 Commission garnered so many poor reviews from the academic community that even many in the Trump administration thought it best to forget the experience.[20]

As of this writing, about 40 percent of New College faculty had left in response to the reactionary makeover. Nearly half of the student body at that time applied to other schools, too.[21] The new administration, however, viewed these developments as a useful purge, and it set about recruiting new students, including a disproportionate number of athletes. Apparently determined to recruit manly young men, it admitted a large number of baseball players—even though the college did not at the time have a baseball team or sufficient athletic facilities, and had not yet been accepted to the National Association of Inter-collegiate Athletics. Administrators were quoted as saying that the athletes were there to offset the old, woke student culture—though they conceded that the recruits drove down the school's previous average grade point average, along with its average SAT and ACT scores.[22] The new recruits were given prime dormitory housing, while some returning students were packed off into hotels far from campus. Meanwhile, at Rufo's suggestion, the academic courses were divided into "technos" and "logos."[23] Nobody could quite make sense of what this meant, but it sounded learned in a classicsy way. Whether the new team will succeed in turning the place into a feeder for the national conservative administrations of the future remains to be seen. As long as DeSantis remains governor, however, it is a safe bet that the leaders of the new New College will receive enough funding to pursue their regressive dreams for some time.

BY 2024, IT was clear to me that the alliance I had glimpsed from a balcony in Verona had blossomed into a very serious relationship. Christian nationalism and the New Right are the power couple of American fascism. If there is one document that cements the vows of this new union, it would have to be the Heritage Foundation's Project 2025, a voluminous plan, published in 2023, for how the next conservative president would save the country.[24]

On the one hand, Project 2025 unambiguously sings from the old Christian nationalist hymnal. Heritage's would-be secretary of labor opens his contribution with this claim: "The Judeo-Christian tradition, stretching back to Genesis, has always recognized fruitful work as integral to human dignity, as service to God, neighbor, and family."[25] Rather than emphasize ways to strengthen the rights of the workforce or seek to revive America's tottering labor unions, he thinks that the top priorities of the next secretary of labor are to "Reverse the DEI Revolution in Labor Policy" and eliminate "Critical Race Theory Trainings," whatever those may be, to rescind laws prohibiting discrimination on the basis of sexual orientation, to promote "pro-life measures" and "Keep anti-life benefits out of 'benefit' plans" to ensure that corporations like Hobby Lobby enjoy full religious freedom to deprive female employees of contraception coverage. He is also determined to enact policies based on the supposedly demonstrable fact that "God ordained the Sabbath as a day of rest." Heritage's plan for the Department of the Interior is likewise on America's right to exploit its fossil fuel reserves to the max, squaring neatly with its determination to eviscerate climate change legislation intended to promote renewable energy, which is characterized as "Biden's war on Fossil fuels" and a "radical climate change agenda."[26] The incoming head of Health and Human Services likewise sets as his "Goal #1" "to protect the fundamental right to life, protect conscience rights, and uphold bodily integrity rooted in biological realities, not ideology."[27]

It's clear that Project 2025's obsession with "gender ideology" is just the tip of a much larger iceberg. In May 2023, the Heritage Foundation tweeted, "Conservatives have to lead the way in restoring sex to its true purpose & ending recreational sex & senseless use of birth control pills."[28] Several months later, in December, William Wolfe, a Heritage Action for America alum and former Trump appointee who is part of the Project 2025 consortium, tweeted, "Want to restore the American family?" In addition to a ban on abortion, his solutions include "an end to no-fault divorce"; "reduced access to contraception"; and "overturn Obergefell," among other measures. (The tweet appears to have been subsequently deleted, but not before being captured and extensively covered.)[29] The Center for Renewing America has stated, in a document drafted by CRA staff and fellows, that one of their top priorities for a second Trump term is "Invoking the Insurrection Act on Day One" to suppress protests, and included "Christian nationalism" as an affirmative bullet point.[30]

Yet Project 2025 frames this transparently identitarian, theocratic agenda as merely one aspect of a total war on woke. In his introduction to the work, Heritage president Kevin Roberts identifies "the Great Awokening" as a form of totalitarianism and *the* existential threat to the American republic: "The entire Project 2025 is a plan to unite the conservative movement and American people against elite rule and woke culture warriors," he writes.[31] The contributors corresponding to each department rush to join in this denunciation. "America cannot be saved unless the current grip of woke and weaponized government is broken," writes Project 2025 contributor Russ Vought, president for the Center for Renewing America, who served as Trump's director of the Office of Management and Budget.[32]

To be sure, the sensibility of the antiwoke warriors even seems to shape the tone of the reaction in ways that veer from the traditional Christian nationalist script. The authors of Project 2025 clearly don't see *LGBT* and especially *trans* as terms to describe individual human beings; they use them as dehumanizing labels for ideologies and pathologies. There is little room for the old "Love the sinner, hate the sin" trope here. According to Roberts in his introduction, "transgender ideology" is ubiquitous on the liberal left; it is simply pornography. Teachers and public librarians who "purvey" anything classified as pornography "should be classified as registered sex offenders," and anybody caught up in its production or distribution needs to be in jail.[33] Here, as ever, the obsession with a minute number of trans people serves as a shiny bauble to distract from the larger project of dismantling our rights and our democracy.

The union of Christian nationalism and the New Right reveals something essential about both sides. I now think it represents one of the most significant developments in the antidemocratic reaction in the past two decades. It marks the moment where whatever was left of the social conservatism of the old religious right passed away, to be replaced with authoritarianism, or fascism.

WHERE DID THE one-note tune of the antiwoke anthem come from? There is no simple way to connect the dots, but there is one place on the map that happens to link together the educational carnage in Florida, the surrealism of NatCon, and the repressive projects of Verona. If the war on woke has a headquarters, it is surely located in southern California, in the offices of the Claremont Institute.

John Eastman sits on the board of the Claremont Institute (as of this writing). NatCon star Michael Anton published his Flight 93 rant in the *Claremont Review of Books* (at first pseudonymously, but later officially acknowledged) and continues to contribute regularly. Thomas Klingenstein, the principal backer of the NatCon show, is also the principal funder of the Claremont Institute. The Claremont Institute has other funders, too; the Sarah Scaife Foundation, the Bradley Foundation, Donors Trust and the Donors Capital Fund, the Dick and Betsy DeVos Family Foundation—all have chipped in.

The new New College is in essence a brainchild of the Claremont Institute. Board member Charles Kesler is the longtime editor of the *Claremont Review of Books*. His ideological mate on the board, Rufo, is a former fellow at the institute. The president of Hillsdale College, which supplies the model of Trumpist higher education to which Florida now aspires, is Larry Arnn, a founder and former president of the Claremont Institute who remains on the board of directors as vice chairman.

Founded in 1979 in the city of Claremont, California (but not associated in an official way with any of the five colleges there), the institute has always been on the right, but in its first decades it was not widely thought to have gone off the rails. It was probably best known for publishing the *Claremont Review*, which was sized and laid out to resemble the *New York Review of Books*, as if to suggest that it was in direct competition with its more established and exalted Manhattan counterpart. The institute also hosts a variety of fellowship programs, aimed mainly at boosting the careers of young conservatives. The house style traditionally centers on high-toned discourses on America's incomparable founders and how we have sadly fallen short of their ideals today. The men of the Claremont Institute (they are almost all men; more on that in a moment) have long idolized Washington, Madison, Hamilton, and Lincoln; they champion seminar-flavored words like *prudence, virtue*,[34] and *statesmanship*; and they speak of Plato and Aristotle as if they are esteemed colleagues in the office down the hall.[35]

In the 2016 presidential campaign, notwithstanding its long celebration of prudence, virtue, and statesmanship, the Claremont Institute threw its support behind the man who descended that golden escalator with a mouthful of hateful rhetoric.[36] Through every imprudent, unstatesmanlike, and unvirtuous act of the Trump administration, they doubled down on their endorsement. Their attachment appeared to climax in John Eastman's involvement in Trump's attempt to overthrow the government of the United States in 2020–21. But then they doubled down again. Claremont Board member Christopher Flannery called Eastman a "hero" for his work promoting Trump's Big Lie and has asked us instead to condemn "the Stalinist machine" (meaning U.S. federal law enforcement) for persecuting him.[37] In fundraising memos as recently as 2021, the institute lauds this hero of the coup attempt as the "point of the spear" in their legal efforts.

In 2021, the men of the Claremont Institute honored Florida governor Ron DeSantis with their coveted "Statesmanship Award."[38] The governor returned the favor by organizing a discussion with a "brain trust" that included figures associated with the Claremont Institute.[39] But even as DeSantis's presidential endeavors petered out, Claremont and its associates have remained integral to the "brain trust" of any new Republican administration. Indeed, some of them are certain to become appointees in the administrative state that they wish (or so they say) to destroy.

The Claremont Institute's appearance of remarkable tolerance for the harder forms of political opposition to the government of the United States[40] is not limited to Eastman's efforts to whip up the mob that gathered at the Ellipse in preparation for the assault on the Capitol, nor can it be excused as mere metaphorical excess in the war of ideas. Here is one example of the kind of thinking that makes it onto the pages of the *American Mind*, the institute's online magazine: "Given the promise of tyranny, conservative intellectuals must openly ally with the AR-15 crowd . . . Able-bodied men, no longer isolated, are returning to republican manliness in a culture of physical fitness and responsible weaponry. They are buying AR-15s and Glock 17s and training with their friends, not FBI-infiltrated militias or online strangers but trustworthy lifelong friends to build a community alongside."[41]

The author of this bloodthirsty bit of prose, Kevin Slack, is not some rando teenage social media poster. He is a professor at Hillsdale College, and this passage comes from a lengthy book excerpt that the men of Claremont chose to publish.

Even as their politics turned grotesque, the men of Claremont appeared to lose whatever scholarly bearings they once possessed. In an earlier time, they defended intellectual rigor against the alleged relativism of contemporary academic culture. But now the champions of Plato and Aristotle provide a platform for misogynists, racist "replacement" theorists, and conspiracists such as Jack Posobiec, who works with extreme far-right and pro-authoritarian figures, has extensive ties to white supremacists, promoted the debunked white genocide and Pizzagate conspiracy theories, and hailed "the end of democracy" at the Conservative Political Action Conference (CPAC), bellowing, "We didn't get all the way there on January 6th, but we will endeavor to get rid of it. Amen!"[42] The men of Claremont once hailed the United States as "the best regime" in Western civilization.[43] Now they feature contributions and podcasts from people like Charles Haywood, the founder of a secretive network of far-right, all-male fraternal lodges, who openly fantasizes about becoming a "warlord" at the head of an "armed patronage network" in a post-new-civil-war America.[44]

The saga of the Claremont Institute in the Trump years is readily told as one of moral collapse. "What the hell happened to the Claremont Institute?" asks Laura K. Field, a senior fellow at the Niskanen Center and a scholar in residence at American University, in an insightful series in the *Bulwark*.[45] Daniel W. Drezner has described the institute as "the poster child for the devolution of conservative thought."[46] Over at the *National Review*, Mona Charen has written that Claremont "stands out for beclowning itself," and adds that its fellows have "thoroughly jettisoned their devotion to truth and virtue."[47] In conversation with me, Bill Kristol dismissed the current incarnation of Claremont as "off-putting and depressing and stupid." Steve Schmidt, cofounder of the Lincoln Project, was even more direct. Claremont, he told me, "is becoming like the West Point of American fascism. It has collected a creature cantina, like the *Star Wars* scene, and has nurtured and midwifed the birth of a political ideology"—he means fascism—that "leaves most commentators deeply discomfited by calling it by its name."

But is it really a story of decline? "It's not like there were no signs of ideological trouble or shortsightedness at the Claremont Institute going back nearly to the start," Field tells me. "The more I read the less surprised I am." In Kristol's view the signs were there too. "If you look at the *Claremont Review of Books* ten years ago, there were some intelligent articles." However, Kristol notes, "What I would say is that some of them have fallen into legitimizing violence and really fundamental illiberalism." A closer examination of the intellectual trajectory of the Claremont Institute, however, suggests a darker story. The ideas—the illiberalism, the legitimations of violence—were always there as subtext. The balance shifted when the bearers of those ideas smelled power.

THE INTELLECTUAL ORIGIN story of the Claremont Institute gets its start in the 1970s with a circle of graduate students gathered around a charismatic professor of political philosophy named Harry Victor Jaffa.[48] Jaffa's story begins about three decades before that, when he experienced the 1940s equivalent of a red-pill moment.

Jaffa gratefully attributed his awakening from somnolent relativism to his mentor, Leo Strauss, the German-born Jewish political philosopher who later found a home at the University of Chicago before his death in 1973. As a graduate student at Yale, by his own account, Jaffa had lived "within the historicist dogma that we are all prisoners of our own time, and that we had no access to any truth outside of it."[49] For reasons mostly to do with forgotten chapters in nineteenth-century European intellectual history, he, like Strauss, attributed the miasma of historicism to the nineteenth-century German philosopher Georg Wilhelm Friedrich Hegel. Fortunately, he said, "Strauss frees one from this prison."[50] Plato's dialogues, Aristotle's treatises on ethics, and the rest of the works that he studied with Strauss are more than just great, Jaffa realized in his moment of clarity; they are the source of absolute truth. This truth is far more durable than the compromising relativisms and historicisms of liberal dogma and reveals something that can be called "natural right."

The other teaching that Jaffa took from Strauss is that the great philosophers don't always say what they mean. According to Strauss, philosophers routinely engage in "esoteric" and "exoteric" writing. That is, they disguise their most important teachings in the face of political persecution (with which Strauss, as a German Jew who escaped to the United States, may have had some familiarity) and pass them along to followers in between the lines, as it were, or esoterically. To the general public, they offer only the outward or exoteric surface of their words. The implication is that philosophical writings are deeply political. They have an external message, aimed at influencing the public in some way; but only their intellectual fellow travelers can decode the internal meaning of the texts.

Strauss's teachings about natural right and the art of writing involve an often grim assessment of the human condition, and it seems to have been drawn from his personal experience. The failure of the Weimar Republic in 1920s Germany was a trauma for Strauss, and it is possible that he took it as a failure of the entire liberal project of modernity. The theory of esoteric writing sometimes appears to rest on the premise that human society is incapable of the kind of rational, deliberative government that liberal democracy requires. Only Strauss and his likeminded followers can handle the eternal truths vouchsafed to us by the Greeks, it seems to suggest; most ordinary people must be content to live in what Plato called "the cave"—a state of permanent delusion. A recurring theme in the writings of the men of Claremont is the depravity of the human condition—a depravity that they (and their Greek philosopher-companions) alone have the sagacity to perceive.

Strauss is hard to pin down, politically speaking. What else is to be expected of a philosopher who believes in deliberately writing in between the lines? His influence on a range of successors across the political spectrum in any case suggests that a partisan political program does not follow in any obvious or necessary way from his philosophy. Jaffa, too, was a politically complex figure, and not without appeal to progressives. Central to the vision articulated in his seminal work on the Lincoln-Douglas debates of 1858, *Crisis of the House Divided*, is the argument that equality is the founding principle of the American republic, and that Lincoln achieved incomparable greatness in wielding this principle in a revolutionary way against slavery.[51] "Reading Jaffa's early work is very illuminating—if only to see how far things have fallen over at Claremont from that higher standard," Field says. "*Crisis of the House Divided* is a rich exploration of the Lincoln-Douglas debates. It's a strange book, but anyone will learn a lot from reading it . . . Today, the people at Claremont don't seem to grant the benefit of the doubt to anyone on the other side."

Field is right; the Straussian legacy has its subtleties—but the men of Claremont don't do subtle. Much of their worldview comes down to three terms borrowed from the Straussian legacy and compressed into a single polemical point. Historicism, according to the men of Claremont, is the doctrine that we are all "prisoners of our own time," to borrow Jaffa's phrasing.[52] "Nihilism" is the supposedly consequent view that there are no absolute truths or values. And "progressivism" (which steps in for Strass's "liberalism" to some extent) is the self-destructive political program that afflicts people who are presumed to have mistakenly fallen for nihilistic historicism.

Even such a brief review of this Straussian legacy raises some difficult questions. How do we know that absolute truth landed on the texts of Plato and Aristotle, and not, say, Lao Tzu or the Vedic philosophers? If the real message was intended to be misread, how can we ever know that our self-appointed interpreters have decoded it correctly? And then there is the matter of pinpointing the moment of the crisis and the subsequent decline. The metanarrative that Claremont took over from Jaffa and Strauss is essentially a declinist one. Once there was Plato; now we are "woke" historicist-nihilist-progressives. So where did it all go wrong?

Depending on which issue of the *Claremont Review* you happen to have in hand, it turns out, the golden age is centered variously on 1776, 1787, Abraham Lincoln, the roaring twenties, the 1930s, or the 1950s; and the villains are, depending on the writer, Lincoln (who can be blamed for the administrative state, too, as it happens), Reconstruction, the New Deal, the civil rights movement, or women. As Field explains to me, "One pattern I've noticed is that when they look back . . . it's like they think there was some magical moment in history, a blip in time in 1866, 1933, or 1966, or what have you, when there was a perfect equilibrium, and all racial or civil rights problems were solved."

A still deeper problem can be glimpsed in even a cursory summary of the Straussian legacy at Claremont. It comes down to the question: Who is the nihilist now? The men of Claremont defeat nihilism, they say, by discovering absolute truth and values in the works of Plato and friends. But within the universe they describe, these supposed absolutes have no hope of surviving on their own merits. They can only be imposed on other people through deceit. If you're not brainwashing the masses with some vulgarized ideology that is derivative of Plato, the premise seems to be, then somebody else will brainwash them with something worse. It doesn't help that the men of Claremont routinely invoke the ancient doctrine of "natural right,"[53] which (at least in large parts of their tradition) can be translated as "the right to do whatever nature does not prevent you from doing." In brief, the world the men of Claremont think they inhabit—as opposed to the vision they wish to promote among the public—appears to recognize no truth beyond power and no value other than victory. Who, really, is the nihilist in this picture?

THERE IS ANOTHER figure in the Claremont Institute's intellectual genealogy, not hallowed like Jaffa or Strauss in the official pantheon, yet arguably even more central in any effort to make sense of its paradoxical worldview. Carl Schmitt was an ultraconservative German political theorist. He identified strongly with the Catholic church, though he managed to get himself excommunicated and, by his own admission, was something of a sex addict. Unlike Strauss, Schmitt is very easy to place, politically speaking. He was a Nazi and a vicious anti-Semite: not just a fair-weather Nazi but an influential legal adviser to the regime who promoted book burnings, worked to destroy the careers of Jewish scholars and scientists,[54] and refused to participate in de-Nazification after the war.

Like Strauss, Schmitt was unhappy with the Weimar Republic, which he perceived as unforgivably weak. He took his unhappiness out on the very idea of liberal democracy. Liberalism, he argued, is a failure because it refuses to acknowledge the distinction between "friend" and "enemy"—a distinction that he took to be the foundation of all politics.[55] What makes humans special and genuinely political, according to Schmitt, is that they are willing to fight one another and die for a higher cause. The other defect of liberalism, according to Schmitt, is that it fails to acknowledge that the sovereign must be he who can act in a "state of exception" or "state of emergency."[56] That is, a ruler must be able to break all the rules, ostensibly in the name of the common good, or he isn't much of a ruler at all.

At first glance, Schmitt's friend-enemy distinction might sound like a way of separating citizens from "foreigners." And indeed Schmitt, in works such as *Concept of the Political*, pointed to enemies both foreign and domestic.[57] But a main source of his appeal to conservatives has to do with the domestic enemies. To today's right wing, the more important enemies are those citizens who either fail to acknowledge that we have enemies (liberals and insufficiently reactionary conservatives, or RINOs, as they are sometimes called) who are supposedly actively plotting against the country. Trump (who may be presumed innocent of any direct knowledge of Schmitt's work) explained the point at the 2022 Road to Majority conference: "The greatest danger to America is not our enemies from the outside, as powerful as they may be," he said. "The greatest danger to America is the destruction of our nation from the people within. And you know the people I'm talking about."[58]

Even from this sketch, it is possible to glimpse how Schmitt, at least, resolves the question about nihilism that hovers over the Straussian legacy. For him, there is no good outside or above the triumph over our (internal) foes. Apparently, the way to make meaning in life is by going out and fighting liberals to the death. It's a lesson that resonates in the halls of the Claremont Institute.

Schmitt's anti-Semitism, too, is more complex (if no less despicable) than it first appears. "The Jew," in his thought, is the paradigm of the secularized, cosmopolitan, educated elite on which liberalism necessarily relies. Even some people who are not Jews can be very "Jewish," according to this variant of anti-Semitism. While the nature of Schmitt's anti-Semitism is the subject of some debate, observers note that it did not follow traditional theological patterns but was rooted in his political theory. His anti-Semitism was thus an expression of his antiliberalism, filtered through the grotesque racial prejudices of his time.

Some of his successors would learn how to draw on the same antiliberalism, while dropping the anti-Semitism in favor of hating on other groups ostensibly playing the same role. "At a time of dizzying and dynamic technical change, instantaneous communication, abolished borders, and global, de-territorialized conflict, Schmitt proves a prescient guide," Claremont contributor Aaron Zack wrote in his largely favorable review of Schmitt's 1942 book *Land and Sea:*

A World-Historical Mediation, published in the *Claremont Review of Books*, which ran in January 2017. "It is well worth reading."[59]

Strauss appears to have had some sympathy with this kind of thinking—and therein hangs another characteristically convoluted tale. Schmitt may have been an anti-Semite, but he was instrumental in getting Leo Strauss the fellowship that helped him leave Germany in 1932; Strauss had reason to be wary of Nazis, but he had few qualms about engaging directly and deeply with Schmitt's work. Indeed, one of Strauss's various and complex responses to Schmitt's work was to suggest that maybe Schmitt was just too liberal. It's all well and good to observe that humans exist in a state of nature where they will fight one another to death over their higher causes, Strauss pointed out; but if you aren't willing to name and defend a specific higher cause, you are implying that one higher cause is just as good as another, and so you are opening the door to liberalism all over again. Schmitt thought Strauss had offered an extraordinary "X-ray" of his philosophy.[60]

Strauss later wrote that Schmitt had provided him with "the most honorable and obliging corroboration of my scholarly work" he had ever been accorded.[61]

THE PARALLELS BETWEEN Carl Schmitt and Claremont hero Michael Anton's "intellectual" case for Trumpism are clear. In the essay that launched his career as one of Claremont's chief polemicists, Anton essentially claims that we are in a state of emergency. The plane is going to crash! We have friends and foes; Hillary Clinton is the enemy right in our faces. But our worst enemies are the internal ones who don't get that we have enemies. That means you, Conservatism Inc.! If you don't get that we need to rush the cockpit and save ourselves, we are all doomed.[62]

At the time, Bill Kristol perceptively characterized Anton as a minor-league Carl Schmitt. "From Carl Schmitt to Michael Anton: First time tragedy, second time farce," he noted on Twitter.[63] In later communication with me, Kristol emphasized the connection anew. "If you look at recent issues, it becomes like Carl Schmitt," he said of the *Claremont Review of Books*. "They are sending the message that extreme measures are needed to defend against the tyranny of liberal Democrats. They seem to want to blow through all the guardrails and are okay with that."

The Schmittianism radiating from the Claremont Institute is so boldface that even the conservatives at the *National Review* noticed it. Mike Watson published a piece there that extends Kristol's analysis and connects it with other representatives of the New Right today.[64] Watson's piece elicited a vituperative response from Anton, and the response is worth reading as a good example of the cheap bullying that now passes for debate among much of the New Right.[65] (Mike Watson? Never heard of him! The *National Review*? Nobody who is anybody reads it!) But a more compelling reason to read it is that Anton does get one thing right in his response: Leo Strauss did indeed like Schmitt's friend-enemy distinction. So there.

The crypto-Schmittianism in the Claremont narratives helps make sense of another, rather disturbing aspect of the conservative movement's "war on woke" and the supposed evils of liberalism. Recall that Schmitt was notable in finding new justifications for hatred of Jews. It really isn't such a big step to hate on other groups of people in the same way. Now, I don't believe for a moment that Anton is anti-Semitic. But if one substitutes "the Jew" for "the woke" in his tales of a sinister cabal driving the world to ruin, he sounds a lot like Schmitt.

"The emergency" is at the heart of everything the New Right does, and it has extended well beyond the imaginations of the men at Claremont. Kevin Roberts, president of the Heritage Foundation, frames his group's Project 2025 in the same Schmittian terms. "With enemies at home and abroad, there is no margin for error," he intones.[66] "Time is running short. If we fail, the fight for the very idea of America may be lost."[67] Faced with the totalitarian evil of the "Great Awokening," he suggests, Project 2025 may offer "the next conservative President's last opportunity to save our republic."[68]

Even the Supreme Court appears to be sipping the authoritarian Kool-Aid. In its stunning July 2024 decision, the radical majority effectively granted Donald Trump immunity from criminal prosecution in connection with his attempted coup and effectively elevated all future presidents to the status of a "king above the law," as Justice Sotomayor put it in her blistering dissent. "Never in the history of our Republic has a President had reason to believe that he would be immune from criminal prosecution if he used the trappings of his office to violate the criminal law."[69] The premise of the majority's reasoning is that a President unable to rise above the law will be unable to lead the nation. Schmitt—or the men of Claremont—could hardly have said it better.

Claremont's full intellectual legacy, not just from Schmitt, shows up most clearly where it is most damning: in the case of John Eastman. Though initially identified only as Co-Conspirator 2 in the federal charges against Donald Trump (Eastman has pled not guilty), Eastman left his philosophical signature all over the indictment.

Like the defendant and the other conspirators, according to the allegations, Co-Conspirator 2 knowingly and repeatedly lied about the election results, and he pushed schemes that he knew to be illegal. To a far greater extent than his fellow conspirators, however, Co-Conspirator 2 supplies in his own words the rope on which to hang any theory that he was some kind of "crackpot" who did not know what he was doing. While serving as legal adviser to Trump on his lawsuit against the governor of Georgia, he stated in an email that he and the defendant had "been made aware that some of the allegations (and evidence proffered by the experts) has been inaccurate"—an admission that he knew fraud claims were wrong.[70] And yet he "caused the Defendant's signed verification to be filed nonetheless." He asked the Arizona Speaker to reject his state's results.[71] And while urging the vice president to interfere with the certification of the electoral college results, he acknowledged to the vice president's counsel "that he hoped to prevent a judicial review of his proposal because he understood that it would be unanimously rejected by the Supreme Court," according to the indictment.

Nearing midnight on January 6—after Congress had reconvened and certified the vote for Biden—Co-Conspirator 2 wrote in an email to the vice president's counsel, "I implore you to consider one more relatively minor violation [of the law regarding the counting of electoral votes] and adjourn for 10 days to allow the legislatures to finish their investigations."[72] It's just one word, but the "implore" here stands out—it frames the request as a moral appeal. Even as he put forward a plan that he himself acknowledged to be illegal, Co-Conspirator 2 seemed to believe he was the good guy. How so? He tells us himself, in the evidence collected in the indictment. When White House counsel Eric Herschmann told him "You're going to cause riots in the streets," Co-Conspirator 2 responded with "words to the effect of, 'There's been violence in the history of our country in order to protect democracy, or protect the republic.'"[73]

One could hardly ask for a finer example of Claremont's idea of the Straussian man in action. His mission is to save the Republic. He must tell a few lies, yet he is nonetheless a noble liar, at least in his own mind. He acts in the political world, where natural right reigns, and not merely in the legal world where lawyers are supposed to toil. Aware of the crooked timber from which humanity is made, he is prepared to break off whatever branches are needed for the bonfire of liberty.

Eastman himself soon supplied confirmation of his mission. In a recorded interview with Thomas Klingenstein, the private equity investor and Claremont Institute funder, which was first reported by Peter Montgomery of Right Wing Watch, Eastman justified his couping this way: "We are talking about whether we as a nation are going to repudiate every one of our founding principles, which is what the modern left wing, which is in control of the Democrat [*sic*] Party, believes. This is an existential threat to the very survivability, not just of our nation, but of the example that our nation, properly understood, provides to the world. That's the stakes."[74] He then turned to the Declaration of Independence to justify his participation in the 2020 coup attempt: When a series of abuses becomes intolerable—he mentioned health care, OSHA regulations on home office chairs, mythical bans on gas stoves, and drag queens as examples[75]—"it is not only [the] right [of the people] but their duty to alter or abolish the existing government."[76]

Let freedom ring! From Eastman's perspective, it is easy to see how the effect of the Claremont brand of Straussianism can feel quite liberating. If the nation is now in a genuine state of emergency, after all, then none of the old rules apply. The times call for bold thinkers capable of imagining and building new worlds. Like a Prometheus unbound, the sage of Claremont is sure to rise to the task.

HARRY JAFFA PASSED away in 2015 at the age of ninety-six. I thought his son Philip Jaffa might have something to say about the evolution of the Institute. Indeed, he did.

On a fall afternoon, I meet up with Philip Jaffa in the locale he suggests, which is the lobby of the Four Seasons Hotel in Georgetown, not far from his home in Arlington, Virginia.

Tall and slim, in his early seventies, he shows up in the type of functional, outdoorsy clothing that suggests practicality and modest self-regard. As soon as we are seated, he launches into the beginnings of the Claremont story.

Philip's father believed in justice and equality. With staunch pro-immigrant views, he provided money to help undocumented immigrant families. A gifted teacher, he had an extraordinary ability to take complicated political philosophy and "explain it in ways that ordinary people could understand," Philip says. "He didn't make much money, but he supported the Claremont Institute because he believed above all in the American democratic experiment."

When Larry Arnn left the Claremont Institute for the more overtly reactionary Hillsdale College, Harry Jaffa wasn't sad to see him go. "My father referred to Hillsdale as a cesspool of libertarianism," Philip tells me. "He said, 'Libertarians believe you can recreate the Garden of Eden here on earth by abolishing everything except the pursuit of private property.' This becomes the goal of libertarians—to replace the idea of free people with a free market."

"My father believed you cannot be a Christian and a libertarian," Philip adds. "Libertarians believe in survival of the fittest. Christians believe in sacrifice of the fittest, the father getting into the water to save his wife and kids in the lifeboat."

Starting in 2001, Philip says, his father started getting pushed out of the institute. His mood visibly darkens. "My father considered [Charles] Kesler a philosophic adversary, not an ally . . . a political enemy, not a friend."

The Claremont Institute of today, Philip says, has betrayed its origins. "Kesler is a nihilist. He doesn't believe that morality exists at all. But you don't want to live in a society where people believe that. So you teach morality to everybody else while keeping the dark secret to yourself that it is all an illusion. Rules for thee. No rules for me.

"This is an anarchist movement," he continues. "The triumph of the libertarian wing of the conservative movement is Claremont, which is an anarchist movement. And anarchists break things. They destroy things. If you take a look at Trump's plan, it's just dismantling things. But this is what anarchists do." He pauses. "Charles Kesler is a libertarian and a nihilist. Most anarchists are.

"My father said, 'Never forget the dictatorship of the proletariat is the withering away of the state.' The Claremonters of today want to skip the dictatorship of the proletariat and go straight to the withering away."

He shrugs in disgust. "What can you say about someone who says there are 'people like us,' and then there are 'woke communists'"?

I ask what role religion plays in all this. "Eastman's and Ryan Williams's plan is to merge the neoconservatives and evangelicals through Christian nationalism," he tells me. "It's very straightforward." He makes it clear that, in his view, it has nothing to do with any actual faith.

As I exit the lobby of the Four Seasons hotel and walk a short distance to the home of my local host, I ponder how much has changed in a short time frame. Fifteen years ago, movement leaders made some effort to convey to the wider public the idea that they merely aimed for a seat at the table in the noisy forum of American democracy. We're well past that now. The reactionary right no longer feels the need to disguise their pursuit of totalitarian power.

In an email to me, Philip Jaffa condenses his outrage into a few lines: "My father's exact words to describe what was going on over there: 'They put a top hat on Jefferson Davis and call him Abraham Lincoln. They put the dust cover of *Nicomachean Ethics* on *Atlas Shrugged* and call it Aristotle.'"

CHAPTER 6

The Resentment of the Campus Misfits

When I published a lengthy essay on the Claremont Institute in September 2023, I anticipated that the organization might respond in some official way. They did not—just as their leaders and representatives had declined to respond to my emails while I was preparing the piece. As soon as my work went live online, however, the comments on social media from Claremont supporters started to roll in. The fact that I am female seemed first on the minds of many; the possibility that I might be of an undesirable ethnic identity preoccupied some of them even more. A typical comment was: "Jewish physiognomy. That's all we need to know. No point reading the piece." Others offered obscene suggestions, unprintable here. Christopher Rufo's complaint, mild by comparison, was that my prose was "hysterical." (This would be the same Rufo who has argued that America is so beholden to "the woke" that the only way to save it is to "lay siege" and "reconquer public institutions all over the United States.") Since one of the points of my essay was to report that the Claremont Institute is wallowing in misogyny and racial hate, the responses by its defenders, I thought, provided evidence in favor of the analysis. My experience was trivial in comparison with what some close colleagues in my field, particularly Black women, were receiving from the haters and troll farms on the right.

Around the same time that my small corner of social media was bubbling with male grievance, Samantha Casiano was trying to scrape together several thousand dollars for the burial of her stillborn child. Casiano was twenty weeks pregnant when she discovered that her fetus had anencephaly—a condition in which the brain and skull fail to develop—and stood no chance of surviving after birth. But Casiano lives in Texas, where abortion became effectively illegal the moment the Supreme Court issued its Dobbs decision. Casiano, who resides in a mobile home with her husband and five children, didn't have the money to take time off work, arrange childcare, and seek an abortion out of state. The state of Texas thus compelled her to carry an unwanted and doomed pregnancy for months; to endure a painful labor and high-risk childbirth, only to watch her baby "gasping for air" and dying within minutes; and then, even as she was trying to explain this confusing situation to her traumatized children, to arrange for the burial.[1]

Casiano is just one of dozens of women who have launched lawsuits against their home states for abortion bans that severely impact their health, endanger their lives, and inflict unnecessary suffering. A report on the state of maternal health care in the "pro-life" state of Louisiana shows the alarming and ludicrous impacts.[2] Women experiencing miscarriage complications have been given wholly unnecessary C-sections so that the doctors treating them could avoid accusations of having performed abortions. Others had their care delayed until they became desperately ill, even suffering permanent damage to their health, so that the doctors or hospitals could "justify" the intervention to save their lives. Many doctors in the state now decline to treat women in the first trimester, when miscarriage is most common.

In fact, growing numbers of pregnant women with cancer are prevented from accessing lifesaving treatments altogether. In Ohio, several women who were forced to travel out of state for abortions to access such treatments filed a legal action, in which they remain anonymous. Others have been denied life-saving abortion care until they develop sepsis, nearly die from severe blood loss, or suffer injuries from which they will never recover. In Idaho, which passed an extreme abortion ban, multiple women have been airlifted out of the state to save their lives; sepsis, organ failure, loss of fertility, and even death are tacitly understood by religious extremist lawyers and lawmakers as the acceptable cost of such bans. These cases underscore how abortion bans have compelled doctors to operate with extreme medical negligence, trauma-tizing and brutalizing patients and upending their lives.

The war on abortion rights is also, in effect, a war on miscarriages; in the United States, women have been jailed after seeking miscarriage care.[3] In 2023 an Ohio woman faced a felony charge after miscarrying into a toilet.[4] (After the case received widespread media coverage, the Ohio grand jury declined to indict her.) It is also a war on some of the most widely used forms of contraception—and assisted reproductive technologies to boot; in February 2024 an Alabama Supreme Court judge classified frozen embryos as "children" while citing scripture in his decision, and several hospitals promptly suspended IVF treatments.

When the Alabama judge's decision was met with wide-scale accusations of outrage and hypocrisy, some Republican politicians hastened to promise a carve-out for IVF specifically. It is worth noting what they did not offer a carve-out for. The theological doctrine that life begins at the moment of conception imperils some of the most effective forms of birth control, as long-time observers of the movement know well. At the 2018 Values Voters Summit in Washington, D.C., speaking on a panel titled "Restoring a Generation's Identity," Chelsea Patterson Sobolik, a policy director for the Ethics and Religious Liberty Commission of the Southern Baptist Convention, laid the blame for "gender confusion" squarely at the feet of family planning. "I want to dial back about one hundred years ago, to when birth control and the pill were introduced," she said. "What that did is that's the very beginning of breaking down marriage and divorcing intimacy and sex from reproduction."[5] The war on abortion rights is quite plainly a war on women's rights and dignity, and by extension on the individual freedoms at the foundation of modern democracy.

Under the influence of Trump and the MAGA movement, this war on women and democracy has become the prime focus of right-wing politics in America. The reactionary political organization Concerned Women for America invited Donald Trump to deliver the keynote address at their 2023 convention. Founded in 1979 by Beverly LaHaye to promote "Biblical values for women and families,"[6] CWA has been at the forefront of the reaction to women's rights ever since. The CEO and president of CWA, Penny Young Nance, favors stiletto heels and likes to present herself as the feisty, hyper-feminized champion of a certain kind of female empowerment. When I heard her speak at a right-wing conference in Washington, D.C., in the run-up to the 2016 presidential election, my impression was that she found Trump so disgusting that she could not bring herself to say his name. But by 2023 she was eager to put him on center stage. At the CWA convention that year, she and her group evinced no qualms about honoring a man who has been accused of rape and sexual abuse by twenty-six women, was found to be a sexual abuser in one judicial proceeding, and routinely describes women in objectifying and demeaning terms.

To be sure, CWA had much to celebrate. After all, with his appointment of three Federalist Society ideologues to the Supreme Court, Trump could take credit for the most significant rollback of women's rights in the nation's history. Republican legislatures in red states were building on that achievement by creating the policing apparatus that would track and punish women seeking reproductive care, along with any family, friends, health-care providers, and online vendors who might dare to help them. The reality of Penny Nance's uplifting "empowerment" story is that she represents a small clique of women who have traded in other women's rights for a seat at the front row of the MAGA party.

"It's important to understand how pervasive and nonnegotiable patriarchal teachings are in these religious spaces," author Kristin Kobes Du Mez tells me. "One's identity and sense of belonging as a Christian woman requires assenting to these conditions, and women who resist them can be shunned or expunged."[7] In such settings, she adds, "women's access to power is contingent on pleasing male leadership, however narcissistic and unyielding."

The confluence of the attacks on women's rights makes clear that the antidemocratic reaction in the United States is little different from that of right-wing authoritarian movements around the world and throughout history. Notwithstanding the advances made by women over the past century and the resolve, by most women, to never regress, the movement here in America is determined to subject women to a degree of state coercion from which men are exempt. Indeed, having deemed that the wombs of women like Samantha Casiano are state property, the leaders of the movement seem intent on making them the property of their male partners, too. The purpose of so-called consent laws—in which Justice Samuel Alito has expressed interest—is to require women to seek approval for their decision to have an abortion from the men who impregnated them against their wishes.

The response I received from the defenders of the men of Claremont, however, clarified my understanding of the antidemocratic, antiwoman reaction. In the story that these men are telling themselves, I realized, they cast *themselves* as the victims. It's not women who should be worrying about losing their rights and bodily autonomy; it's beleaguered young men who can't express their hateful views without receiving a bit of criticism in response. The problem with Black people, with gay people, and with women, in their view, is not that they are testy but that they are tyrants. It's past time for the victims of this persecution to rise up, stomp on their oppressors, and take back control!

As I dwell on this reversal, where grievances projected onto a scapegoat become a device for organizing oppression, I realize that it is a very familiar one. Authoritarian movements always begin with a feeling of persecution and always thrive on the demonization of seemingly all-powerful others. Terms like *white supremacy*, *patriarchy*, and *ethnonationalism* suggest confident programs arrogantly indifferent to outsiders and aimed at consolidating existing privilege. But the reality is that the movements that gather under such labels are coursing not just with entitlement but also with fear and fragility. Which made me wonder: Who, or what, do the men of Claremont really fear? And how does their fear shape the antidemocratic reaction in which they now have a significant role?

OF CLAREMONT'S NINETEEN board members, all appear to be male. As of this writing, of forty-one fellows and senior fellows, all but three are male. Even these numbers, however, understate the masculinist ethos of the place. The men of Claremont aren't just men; they are manly men by their own estimation, or at least men preoccupied with their own masculinity. To get into the mind of Claremont, it helps to browse the *American Mind*, which is aimed somewhere beneath the brow of the (putatively) high-minded *Claremont Review of Books*.

Recently, the *American Mind* featured an interesting piece from a frequent contributor who calls himself "Raw Egg Nationalist" (REN).[8] REN is the author of a cookbook. He advocates "slonking," that is, a diet he describes as part of "a physical and political ethic built around the massive consumption of raw egg."[9] The eggs are said to help with bodybuilding and other manly pursuits (remember Rocky Balboa arising before dawn and chugging down raw eggs?). But the benefits don't end there! It turns out that raw eggs can also counteract "the globalists' plan for world government."[10] In Tucker Carlson's 2022 film *The End of Men*, REN cameos with other figures in the "manosphere" to link the consumption of animal products with a back-to-the-land nationalism.[11] This is somehow meant to strengthen the traditional moral values of Western males, which may explain why Tucker often shows up in a plaid shirt.

The problem with the world today, according to REN, starts with "the agricultural revolution and its consequences" and ends with a "crisis of masculinity."[12] "We have it drilled into us, this instinctive revulsion for inequality in any form. And actually, I think we need to ask instead whether inequality has its uses," REN muses.[13] Once you get past REN's abstract world-historical patter about globalism and the agricultural revolution, it becomes clear that the real issue for him is women. "Maybe men and women shouldn't work together in the same spaces," he says.[14]

A related problem would appear to be ugly people, by which REN seems to mean the kinds of people who show up at racial justice events. In an interview with Jack Murphy, the recipient of a Lincoln Fellowship at Claremont who reportedly once wrote "feminists need rape,"[15] REN has this to say about the BLM protesters of 2020: "All of these people look the same. I mean, they are hideously ugly, malformed people."[16] The publisher of REN's antiglobalist cookbook, as it happens, is Antelope Hill, otherwise known for its Nazi and white nationalist titles, such as *Michael*, a novel written by none other than the young Joseph Goebbels ("Antelope Hill Publishing is proud to present a new English edition").[17]

REN is far from the only writer with woman problems to score a platform at the Claremont Institute. In 2021, a Boise State University political philosophy professor named Scott Yenor went viral—not in a good way—with a speech at the National Conservatism Conference in Orlando, in which he characterized women with professional aspirations as "medicated, meddlesome, and quarrelsome."[18] Yenor's views could hardly have been news to Claremont. Six months previously, the institute had invited him to deliver a keynote titled "Does Feminism Undermine the Nation?"[19] Yenor seized the opportunity to inveigh against women's pursuit of economic security and a satisfactory sex life. He maligned the "pernicious trajectory of feminism" and argued that it is "fatal to family life and fatal to the country."

Claremont hired Yenor to be the think tank's inaugural senior director of state coalitions for their new center in Tallahassee, Florida. From his speeches and writings, it would seem his actual plan looks more like an affirmative action program for reactionary males.[20] "Every effort must be made not to recruit women into engineering, but rather to recruit and demand more of men who become engineers. Ditto for med school, and the law, and every trade," he said.[21] According to Yenor, state officials should conduct civil rights investigations of academic programs ("especially colleges of nursing and education") that attract larger numbers of women than men.[22] Ron DeSantis's wife, Casey DeSantis, tweeted her support for Yenor's appointment, saying "Thrilled to welcome @scottyenor from the Claremont Institute to his new home in Tallahassee."[23]

As Bill Kristol observes, the fanaticism here is even worse under the surface. "They are not just against the legalization of same-sex marriage. They are so extreme they are for permitting gender discrimination in salaries, changing divorce law to what it was seventy years ago, for criminalizing homosexuality. They don't want to say that because of political reasons, but certainly you don't get the sense that they feel any compulsion to restrain their extremist rhetoric."

Setting aside the rabidly misogynistic agenda, the most curious thing about Yenor's work is just how unserious it is. If you want to make the case that women's struggle to realize inherent natural rights and secure equality under the law is connected to various social ills in some way, you could look for evidence to test that remarkable hypothesis. You might, for example, compare countries with different levels of gender equality with economic outcomes, life expectancy, and health measures. You would surely want to explain the inconvenient fact that some of the places that are least hospitable to women's rights happen to be those with the worst social and economic outcomes for *all* people. You might consider that around the world, the countries that seem to best satisfy Yenor's urgent desire to keep the genders in their lanes are also among the most repressive, unsafe, nepotistic, and corrupt. You would, at the very least, want to consider alternative explanations for the collapse of marriage rates among working-class Americans and the decline in male health indicators, such as the erosion of working- and middle-class wages and job security, the decline in manufacturing, and the rise of a winner-take-all economy.[24] You might also consider that among those in the higher income brackets—the upper middle classes, within which ideals of women's equality are widespread and robust—divorce rates are low, and men (as well as women) are living longer and healthier lives.

But Yenor doesn't have to do analysis because Claremont already gave him the answer. The culprit, ever and always, is relativism, historicism, nihilism, liberalism, progressivism, wokeism, and—it is all the same thing to them—feminism. So if white working-class men are suffering, that can only be because the "woke Left" has mounted a merciless assault on—here's a word Yenor uses a lot—"manliness."[25]

THE SALVATION OF men, however, is not just a matter for the lower-brow readers of the *American Mind*. The serious people of the *Claremont Review of Books* can pitch it into their work, too. Apart from his "Flight 93" masterwork of intellectual Trumpism, Michael Anton contributed at least one other piece that, in a happier world, would mark a turning point in the history of the Claremont Institute. That would be his review of a book titled *Bronze Age Mindset*, whose author goes by the name Bronze Age Pervert (BAP) and has since been identified as Costin Alamariu, who received his PhD in political philosophy from Yale.[26]

BAP writes as if he were some modern-day Zarathustra descended from a mountaintop cybercollective.[27] "I was roused from my slumber by my frog friends, and I declare to you, with great boldness, that I am here to save you from a great ugliness," he intones.[28] ("Pepe the Frog" is a meme widely associated with the far-right blogosphere.) If a right-wing Yale PhD student woke up one morning after another dateless night on 4chan and thought he was the second coming of Nietzsche, this is the book he might write.

BAP abhors women. He refers to them as "roasties" (a crude reference to female genitalia), "whores," and "property."[29] "Your friends are more important, far more important, than the girlfriends or wives you'll have," he writes in a self-helpy aside to his presumptively male readers.[30] "And actually, your girl will admire you for this—not that you should do it for that reason," he hastens to add. The "liberation of women," he whines, amounts to an "infection" from which the West "can't recover without the most terrible convulsions and the most thorough purgative measures."[31]

BAP isn't into gay people either. He thinks they represent "the most profound of social and political problem" of the modern world. Then again, as he recounts in his book, he managed to ejaculate without touching himself while gazing upon an ancient statue of a Greek boy; so perhaps he is part of the "problem"? For what it's worth, Alamariu sprinkles his Twitter feed with images of muscled beefcake.[32] Oh, and that Twitter feed is also a collection point for racial hate.[33]

BAP thinks the Bronze Age was just great. This would be the same Bronze Age in which human sacrifice was widely practiced and a great many humans were enslaved to other humans. But none of that bothers BAP, because he identifies with Achilles and the master race—those superior beings who ride herd over their inferiors without apology, without false ideas about human equality, without woke politics.[34] "The free man is a warrior," says mini-Nietzsche; "the only right government is military government."[35] In fact, he encourages his followers to join the military, where he seems to think they will be able to organize coups against womanly democracy (or as he, along with Yenor and much of the manosphere call it, "the gynocracy").[36]

What do BAP's legions of followers glean from his analysis of the modernity's woes at the hands of our female overlords? If BAP fan Justin Murphy is a guide, they want to blow stuff up, starting with the universities. At an event in September 2023 celebrating BAP's new self-published book, a revision of his 2015 dissertation at Yale titled *Selective Breeding and the Birth of Philosophy*, Murphy praised BAP as "a tremendous example of someone pushing the limits impressively and originally and powerfully and winning," gushing, "Wow, all of the energy is leaving the institutions and is already outside of the institutions and is crushing it."[37] A former professor at the University of Southampton, England, Murphy, who is American, was earlier suspended from his position over a "plethora of disgusting," "bizarre," and "hateful" tweets and videos and subsequently resigned.[38] Given his penchant for donning chaotic wigs, and for posting video confessionals of his sexual encounters along with images of himself in the nude, many college students at the University of Southampton expressed concern for his mental health. But in BAP he clearly found a kindred spirit. "I'm excited by an imminent future where simply all of education, all of philosophy, all of the production of ideas and society is essentially happening in this kind of radically decentralized and uncontrollable, ungovernable outside," Murphy enthused during the Twitter Space event. "And you're going to see education reformed by this kind of decentralized exodus."

MANLINESS. WHERE EXACTLY did that word enter the conversation? In the New Right world, manliness is a bit of a dog whistle, and Senator Josh Hawley has blown it hard with his recent book *Manhood: The Masculine Virtues America Needs* (Regnery, 2023). True to Claremont formula, Hawley traces the crisis to our departure from ancient sources. When we were schooled in the classics, we had "moral uprightness": "Machiavelli called it *virtù*" (from the Latin *vir*, meaning "man"); and the Bible has "a mission for men."[39] You might think that the man who raised his fist on January 6 and then scurried away from the manly men attacking the Capitol would see some complexity in the issue, but Hawley does not. The problem, as ever, is the "priests of wokery," as he said at the 2023 Road to Majority conference, who have apparently succeeded in infiltrating the C-suites and learned to dispense their toxic doctrines through the corporate hierarchy.[40]

Hawley, Yenor, and REN, however, are just taking a page from an earlier chapter in Claremont history. The story of manliness at Claremont might be said to begin with Harvey C. Mansfield Jr., the author of the 2006 book *Manliness*. A fixture of the Harvard University faculty of government for decades, Mansfield counts as nobility among Claremont's extended family. His father, Harvey Sr., helped Henry Jaffa land a career-making teaching job; Harry introduced Harvey Jr. to Leo Strauss; Harvey Jr. was Charles Kesler's teacher.

Manliness offers a lightly informed romp through some work in biology and the social sciences on gender and sex, from which we supposedly learn that gender stereotypes are all true. "War is hell but men like it," and women will never make good soldiers because "they fear spiders."[41] The patriarchy is just a biological fact of life. "Lacking as women are, comparatively, in aggression and assertiveness, it is no surprise that men have ruled over all societies at almost all times,"[42] Mansfield concludes. And that's that.

The book then rushes to Mansfield's home ground, the seminar room, where the ideals of the great philosophers are held up against present-day reality—which inevitably falls short of Aristotelian (or Machiavellian, it really doesn't matter) virtue. We get tips on manliness from Plato's dialogues and Homer's story about ancient Greek warrior Achilles and his captive Briseis, whom Achilles enslaves and rapes until King Agamemnon takes her for himself.

Mansfield is at least twice as subtle as REN; he knows enough to divide manliness into two basic types. The bad type is "nihilistic." In a neat exercise of philosophical jujitsu, he argues that the real problem with feminism today is that it tries too hard to be "manly"—but (gotcha!) in the bad, nihilistic way. This is especially true for Mansfield's bête noire, Simone de Beauvoir. As Diana Schaub elaborates in a retrospective on Mansfield's book in the *Claremont Review*, "Manly nihilism was embraced by the woman warrior, Simone de Beauvoir, who refashioned it into radical feminism's womanly nihilism."[43] If it sounds like Mansfield is blaming harlot Eve and her uppity sisters for ruining manliness for everyone, that's because he is, at least according to Schaub's deferential take: "Mansfield insists on women's weakness. Returning manliness to these civilized bounds, however, will be difficult, because getting manliness to walk the line, Johnny Cash–style, depends greatly on how that weaker sex behaves."[44] Lady behave!

Mansfield is far too sophisticated—or perhaps too Straussian—to openly argue for stripping American women of the rights they have fought for over the past two centuries. The "public" sphere, he insists, should remain gender-neutral. But in the "private sphere" (don't bother looking for any definition of how the spheres are distinguished), those highly accurate stereotypes should reign triumphant. Only by acknowledging that women hate spiders and men alone can be properly manly can we retain the "moral moorings" of manliness, as Schaub explains. Meanwhile, outside the seminar room, the demand that men alone should perform manliness has been pretty much standard practice for non-gender-neutral societies from South Sudan to Kazakhstan to Taliban Afghanistan.[45]

In short, *Manliness* is not the lowbrow male supremacy that bubbles up from the manosphere into the pages of the *American Mind*. It is the kindly, highbrow version of it. The raw egg fellow and Florida's new thought leader on antiwoke education don't represent a break with Claremont's misogynist past. The novelty is just that REN and Yenor are departing from the Straussian code and saying the quiet part out loud.

As for the beautiful citations of Aristotle and Homer in a tome like Mansfield's, the matter can be condensed to a basic rule of interpretation that applies to much of Claremont literature: "Plato" (or whoever) is the noise the men of

Claremont make when they want to represent indefensible prejudice as absolute truth.

YOU DON'T HAVE to spend much time with the men of the New Right to realize that they aren't sticking up for men in general. They are sticking up for conservative white men. To be sure, the more refined representatives cling to figures such as Thomas Sowell, the Black libertarian economist, and Supreme Court justice Clarence Thomas like gold dust. What better proof can there be that the virtue they celebrate rises above any color prejudice? In their garrulous way, however, other representatives of the movement can't help but reveal where it is all coming from. A helpful case study can be found in the makeover of higher education in Florida.

New College isn't the only institution in Florida that bears the fingerprints of New Right ideologues. In 2022, the Hamilton Center for Classics and Civics Education at the University of Florida was little more than an idea on a piece of paper. But it quickly picked up $3 million in state funding thanks to advocacy from the Council on Public University Reform, a mysterious group whose representative, Josh Holdenried, was previously associated with the Heritage Foundation and has a long history of working with conservative religious causes.[46] The Florida legislature then approved an additional $10 million. According to the council's draft proposal, the center would hold the power to appoint its own staff and educators in classics, history, and the humanities without consulting the existing faculties at the university. The backers of the Hamilton Center had in effect managed to create, in the space of one year, a rival academic enterprise in the humanities within the University of Florida answerable only to them.

The nonprofit behind the Hamilton operation is headed by a *Claremont Review* contributor, and the center's arrival was music to the ears of Claremont's Florida man, Scott Yenor. A hint about the center's ideas in civics education may be gleaned from its decision to hire Nathan Pinkoski, a senior fellow at the Edmund Burke Foundation, which backs NatCon, and who took up his position as a visiting faculty fellow at the center around the same time he released a review in *First Things* of Jean Raspail's *Camp of the Saints*.

Published in France in 1973, Raspail's novel imagines the horror that unfolds when one million nonwhite immigrants land on French shores. The subhuman invaders, as Raspail describes them, wallow in their own feces and delight in trampling over the misguided liberals who thought to welcome and feed them. The book has long been a favorite among white supremacists, but Hamilton's man thinks it is a work of "genius" that exposes the—you guessed it—"cancel culture" and "nihilism" that is stabbing the West in the back.[47] *The Camp of the Saints* is "the most important dystopian novel of the second half of the twentieth century," he writes. Move over, *Handmaid's Tale*!

The Hamilton Center is one of many such centers springing up around the nation.[48] It is also one piece of DeSantis's plan for higher education in Florida, along with the makeover of New College. Christopher Rufo has been as transparent about his plan for Florida and the nation's universities as he was about whipping up the fraudulent hysteria on critical race theory. In a lecture delivered in the safe space of Hillsdale College, Rufo revealed that America's universities—all of them, apparently, with the exception of Hillsdale and a handful of allies—are in the hands of the woke and discriminate rampantly against right-wingers.[49] The time has come, says Rufo, to counter this nefarious development with a new, parallel university system that would use a combination of state funds and right-wing money to hire the right people, fire the lefties, and at long last teach Aristotle, Raspail, manliness, and all that.

Affirmative action, it turns out, is just fine as long as it is deployed to advance the careers of individuals who promise to believe in what their billionaire friends know to be true. Meritocracy is a nice theory, but it must take a back seat to hiring the kind of people who will go on record about the greatness of *The Camp of the Saints*. Cancel culture is a positive good as long as you are canceling strident women, woke professors, their books, and their students.

One person who gets it, by Rufo's own estimation, is journalist and January 6 conspiracist Darren Beattie, who Trump inexplicably appointed to the commission that oversees U.S. Holocaust memorials abroad.[50] Beattie gushes about the results of the program in Florida so far, citing an unsigned piece in right-wing outlet *Revolver News* that compares the right-wing conquest of Florida's university system with Napoleon's lightning victory over the Austrians in 1805.[51]

Beattie was too far out even for the first Trump administration; he was fired from his Holocaust memorial position after it emerged that he spoke at a conference attended by well-known white supremacists (you just can't make this stuff up).[52] A listserv for Claremont alumni swiftly accumulated messages of support for Beattie that included some amount of racist and white nation-alist commentary, notably from alt-right troll and Holocaust denier Charles Johnson.[53] That prompted some participants holding more polite positions to withdraw from the listserv; eventually, Claremont shut it down. But Johnson himself had been, in fact, a Publius Fellow at Claremont and a contributor to the *Claremont Review*.[54] And he had scored a flattering foreword to his own book on Calvin Coolidge from none other than Charles Kesler.[55]

WHILE THE BRIGHT young things of the New Right were busy remaking higher education in Florida, John Poulos, the executive editor of the *American Mind*, and the writers he publishes were dipping into forms of reactionary thought with a much longer history. Back in the early twentieth century, racist anxieties helped fuel advocacy for eugenics and pronatalism in the form of calls for more white babies—and in the United States that tended to mean Protes-tant babies. The nativist physician Horatio Robinson Storer, an early antiabor-tion crusader, lamented that "abortions are infinitely more frequent among Protestant women than among Catholic," and wondered whether America's western and southern territories would be "filled with our own children or by those of aliens? This is a question that our women must answer; upon their loins depends the future destiny of the nation."[56]

Well, the natalists are back, and in November 2023 they gathered in Austin, Texas, to lament the baby bust of the twenty-first century.[57] REN showed up alongside Poulos. The promotional materials for the event claimed concern for lowering birth rates globally, and warned that "thousands of unique cultures and populations will be snuffed out."[58] The vaguely multicultural language seemed intended to express a concern for babies of all colors.

But when you dig into the work of the participants, you can see there is nothing kinder and gentler about this form of eugenics. Presenter Benjamin Braddock set out to address the baby bust, but his talk, like his online trail, reflects an obsession with "open borders" and "mass migration."[59] Another speaker, who goes by the pseudonym Peachy Keenan, a contributor to Clare-mont's *American Mind* and the author of a book titled *Domestic Extremist: A Practical Guide to Winning the Culture Wars*, refers on Twitter to immigration as "replacement" and swipes at American support for Ukraine in its war against Russian aggression, describing Ukrainian president Volodymyr Zelensky as "despicable human trash."[60] Another presenter, Indian Bronson, denigrates women facing unwanted pregnancies as "sluts" and combines his disdain for American support for Ukraine with a defense of actor Russell Brand, who has been accused of sexual abuse by four women. (Brand has denied the allegations.) The smearing of Brand, he says, is "being used as a pretext to censor him for saying bad things about the war in Ukraine."[61]

For Bronson too the problem is not really birth rates but national borders. "Given Italy's (ongoing, but recently ramped up) migrant crisis I do not think Italy survives as a nation-State in 100 years," he writes.[62] Another charming speaker, tweeting under the name Tiger Lily, cited Bronze Age Pervert in poetic faux-Zarathustra mode:

W*m*n: Canceled
Gamers: Arisen
Trump: President, first of Four Terms
Eat shit!

ROUNDING OUT THIS end of the creature cantina was shampoo magnate Charles Haywood, who has ties to the Claremont Institute and who has envisioned himself as a warlord in a post-civil-war America. Haywood, as the journalist Jason Wilson has reported in the *Guardian*, is the founder of the Society for American Civic Renewal, which condemns "those who rule today" as "corrupt[ing] the sinews of America" and promises to "counter and conquer this poison."[63] This rhetoric, Wilson explains, is "a feature of fascism that proposes revolution as a means of national rebirth."

Why is Claremont helping to normalize white supremacist, ultramisogynist, and Putinist narratives? It would be comforting to suppose that the bigotry that peeps up from the subtext at the slightest provocation is an accidental development, some kind of cross-contamination from the darker sections of the web. Yet here too, just as with manliness, a glance at the past belies any such happy conclusions.

In the metanarrative that Claremont and its fellow travelers in the New Right share, greatness comes from a distinctive civilizational tradition. This tradition allegedly got its start in Athens, then picked up something in Jerusalem, and eventually became "the West." If you want to know why "Santa just is white" and "Jesus was a white man too," in the onetime words of former Fox News presenter Megyn Kelly, there is your answer.[64] To be fair, the Claremonters generally avoid identifying this tradition explicitly with a racial group, and some are savvy enough to include a smattering of people of color in their narratives about the triumph of the West (Frederick Douglass being a favorite). But their followers likely have little trouble seeing through such feints. The whole point of reviving *Camp of the Saints* is to conflate the desire to preserve "our" glorious civilization with the fear of people of color.

The kind of people who pass around copies of Raspail's novel certainly get the point. John Eastman's views on race may be presumed to be benign, but those of the Proud Boys who stormed the Capitol on January 6 are not. And yet the Proud Boys' oath could just as well serve as a Claremont motto: "I am a proud Western chauvinist. I refuse to apologize for creating the modern world."[65]

None of which is to suggest that immigration policy should not be debated. Nation-states inevitably involve immigration controls, and some of them will be reasonable. Policies that facilitate cultural integration—the acceptance of Western norms of gender equality and freedom of speech, to give but two examples—can be encouraged or implemented. But by converting the discussion into a culture war polemic, Claremont and its NatCon allies effectively shut down exchanges of ideas. They replace rational deliberation with a loyalty test. They loudly demand that we build that wall not necessarily because it is the best policy, but because it satisfies this emotional need to take a performative stand in favor of the (presumably white) West.

A truly scholarly history would show that what we call "the West" is the work of human interactions spanning the globe. The fabled Greeks drew inspiration from as far afield as India, and many encounters with different cultures shaped history decisively. It is also clear that not every person who has mattered in the process was white or male. Jesus himself, a Jew living in Galilee and Judea in the first century, would hardly conform to the dominant images portrayed in much of Western art. But Claremont doesn't do intellectual history, properly speaking. There is a better name for what it does do, and that is identity politics.

The men of Claremont's obsession with identity politics is evident in the treatment they mete out to diversity, equity, and inclusion programs. Certainly there are valid critiques to be made of some such programs, and maybe some of these critiques make it through the apocalyptic rhetoric coming out of the New Right. What you won't hear, however, is any serious consideration that such programs came into being to address real problems in a diverse society with a long history of racial oppression and institutionalized discrimination. That's because the men of Claremont aren't here to propose practical policy solutions to the problems facing America. They come to rile up a grievance-addled base and satisfy their own resentments. They are playing identity politics even harder than most of those who they claim to be advancing it, and they understand well enough the first rule of the game, which is to dehumanize the "other," those internal enemies that fail to conform, as well as those who wash up on your shores.

IT WOULD BE comforting to write off the woman trouble at Claremont as merely the personal pathologies of a few young men. The trouble is that manliness on the New Right comes with a distinctive—and extremely dangerous—politics. It defines the imaginary enemy around which the movement is united—and it also marks out the political endpoint of its fantasies. What the New Right wants to destroy is in essence democratic government; what it wants to create is the rule of the strongman.

"Supposing that truth is a woman—what then?" Nietzsche once wrote.[66] This may help explain why the men of Claremont have so much trouble with the truth. More exactly, they have developed an aversion to the kind of rational policymaking characteristic of modern, liberal states but associated in their minds with the woke gynocracy that is allegedly making their lives so miserable. BAP helpfully fleshes out the analysis. The great threat to "beauty" in the modern world, he preaches from his virtual mountaintop, is "the left, or what I have termed the Bug-man." (Nietzsche's term, by the way, was "the last man.")[67] Anton and others at Claremont, as we know, simply call them "the woke." There are other epithets out there, little nuggets of hate, but they all refer to the same thing.

The Bugmen, to stay with BAP, are the "pretentious bureaucrats" who harbor "a titanic hatred of the well-turned out and beautiful."[68] They believe in "social justice" and "first-world regimented hygiene." (BAP doesn't like clean, well-lit streets "made safe for women" because they kill "the mood of the city.") Oh, and these bureaucrats are women, or at least unforgivably womanly. They are right now operating a "global slave project" for the benefit of the "gynocracy." To the finely tuned ears of Claremont, that sounds like a description of the Democratic Party.

BAP seems to agree. "It took 100 years of women in public life for them to almost totally destroy a civilization," he writes.[69] He tells his followers that a tactical alliance with conventional right-wingers "would get you 99% of what you want." He urges political leaders who are persuaded by his plan to bring back the Bronze Age to "use Trump as a model of success." But he is savvy enough to advise those of his followers who go into politics to disavow his work publicly, and even suggests they should attack it. Oddly, the men of Claremont have ignored this sage piece of Straussian advice.

If the BAP plan for military rule sounds fascist, that's because it is. In his case, the likely story is that he is well aware of where his politics are going— indeed, he is on record taunting that he wants "something worse" than fascism. If there is a prize anywhere for radical chic, BAP is clearly aiming to win it. "Now imagine a man of Trump's charisma, but who is not merely beholden to the generals, but one of them, and able to rule and intimidate them as well as seduce the many," he writes. "Caesars and Napoleons are sure to follow."[70]

It's worth pausing here to marvel at the breathtaking nihilism encoded in this new politics of unreason. Yes, the rationality of the modern state is limited. Anyone who has attempted to file taxes knows this. But does that mean we should blow it all up to pave the way for a return of feudal lords? A state that deliberates public policy according to facts and logic and holds itself accountable to the public good is a remarkable historical achievement. It was centuries—millennia—in the making. But what the New Right seems to want is a state that appeals only to signs from heaven and holds itself accountable to the needs of the local warlord equivalent and his favored holy men.

For many of the other young men of the New Right, the destination seems clear only after they've been going down the road for some time. An excellent illustration of the point comes from Nate Hochman's work on behalf of Ron DeSantis's campaign for president.

Hochman is a twentysomething graduate of Claremont's Publius fellowship program and a contributor to both the *Claremont Review* and the *American Mind*. He found employment with the DeSantis campaign when the governor, fresh off signing a bill into law banning abortions in Florida after six weeks from a woman's last period, effectively a total ban, thought he could use some support from the social media set. Hochman obliged with a YouTube video that flashed images of the governor at moments of maximum manly cruelty—take that, immigrants, wokesters, the gay!—to the sound of pounding techno music. It climaxes with what look like armed troops marching into the governor's face, a giant Sonnenrad in the background.[71] Hochman may well have been telling the truth when he said that he had no idea that the Sonnenrad symbol was part of Nazi iconography (though even someone who doesn't know much about Nazis might think it looks Nazi-like). But that just makes his effort even more revealing. The whole subtext of the video is that you, the viewer, are supposed to identify with troop leader DeSantis as the kind of manly man you would like to be. He isn't there to enact your preferred immigration policies or tax cuts or whatever; he is there to fluff your fantasies of power and world mastery. He appears to be the model authoritarian ruler. If the Nazis happened to have made use of the same symbols, well, that's because the Nazis were trying to make the same point.

One person who appears to grasp the authoritarian connection quite explicitly is Curtis Yarvin, a software entrepreneur sometimes described as a political theorist. Like so many others in the New Right space, unsurprisingly, Yarvin comes with a link to Claremont: he has contributed to the *American Mind* and appeared as an honored guest on Claremont podcasts.[72]

Yarvin's name for the woke baddies is "The Cathedral," though he has been known to slip into talk about "dark elves" and "hobbits," too.[73] The Cathedral is more or less where BAP's Bugmen live. It is the tyrannous complex of professional bureaucrats and liberal elites who worship at the shrine of DEI offices and pray to the woke with every cancellation. Thankfully, Yarvin spares us the sophomoric faux-Nietzschean rhetoric. Instead he delivers the message in the self-congratulatory patois of the tech bro: America needs a "reboot." Opposition will be "totally pasted." Napoleon and Lenin are to be admired because each was "a start-up guy."

Yarvin's solution, like BAP's, is simple and deserves an older name: the iron fist. He thinks America needs a king, or at least a dictator with total military power. He offers tips on how a president might become such a kingly king. The first part of the plan: pave the way with humor. "The entire project of 21st-century monarchism" should be "both utterly ironic, and completely sincere. Every part of making it happen will feel like a joke. The result, however, will be completely real—both sincere and irreversible." The other part: ignore court rulings and laws you don't like. The kicker: maybe have "taped behind your balls, a non-fungible token (NFT) which controls the nuclear deterrent. Now that's power."[74]

As political theory, this is all painfully incoherent and juvenile. The most unnerving part of the Yarvin experience, however, comes when you hear his views soberly deliberated among those who claim to worship the founders—the same founders who, if memory serves, wanted to get rid of their king and who set up a system of checks and balances to prevent any future king from arising. No matter. Intellectual integrity is not the strong suit of people who give airtime to REN and the Pizzagate man. Talk about a superempowered dictator, on the other hand, gets lots of likes from the New Right coalition and its allies. They've been bullied enough; it's time to bully back!

Casey DeSantis, the Florida governor's wife, got to the point in a September 2023 tweet: "What does it tell you when the DC Establishment, the Corporate Media and the Left are all against you . . . Honestly, it should tell you absolutely everything. Enough of the elites imposing their will against us, it's about da** time we impose our will on them!"[75] For the record, Casey DeSantis built her career at NBC and ABC.

In their pseudoclassics way, naturally, the men of Claremont frame their not-so-hidden longing for revenge as a series of ruminations about the rise of an American Caesar.[76] How glorious! Sometimes the reveries are tucked inside high-sounding language about "statesmanship." The "man of action" is Claremont's favorite character in Aristotle, mainly because, as in the case of Christopher Rufo, the former Claremont fellow behind the anti-critical-race-theory hysteria, the men of Claremont explicitly aspire to become such figures themselves.[77]

What will the manly dictator do once in power, apart from smashing the Cathedral to bits? Yarvin has little to say on that point. Who cares about the morning after? Like BAP, he practices what Nietzsche called "grand politics." It's all about magnificent gestures and look-at-me explosions. Details are for the Bugmen.

Anton's approach to the Caesar question is particularly revealing and provides an example of what Straussianism has come to mean for the New Right. In his book *The Stakes: America at the Point of No Return* (Regnery, 2020), along with his appearances on several podcasts, including a two-hour discussion with Yarvin, he frames the prospective rise of a fascist dictator as prophesy, not policy, and "laments" that such an eventuality now seems plausible, nay, likely.[78] But then he turns around and declares that we have a choice. On the inevitable slide into a postconstitutional order, we can choose to have a Blue Caesar or a Red Caesar. According to Claremont contributor Charles Haywood—he who would be warlord—the Blue man would be "a combination of Hillary and Pol Pot," and his appearance is just one or two election cycles away, after the Democrats succeed in creating a one-party state and presumedly start packing conservatives off in boxcars to reeducation camps.[79] The Red Caesar, on the other hand, would at least draw from the part of the population with high "social capital," which is fit to manage the "necessities" of life—this appears to be Anton's euphemism for Trump-supporting white working-class Americans. But such a Red Caesar is unlikely, says Anton, because—woe to us!—conservatives are still too weak and disorganized. Damned RINOs!

Anton pretends merely to offer prophesy grounded in the wisdom of the ancients. But his target audience had little trouble deciphering the hidden message for today. "Me, I like, if not love, the idea of a Red Caesar," gushes self-annointed warlord Haywood.[80] Nathan Pinkoski, the *Camp of the Saints* fan now on antiwoke duty in Florida, explains Anton's communications strategy. "In good Straussian fashion, what he teaches is not what he says, at least not outright. With great moderation, he explicitly teaches us how to act prudently within the framework of the republican constitution; with great daring, he implicitly teaches us how to act prudently when the republican constitution is gone."[81] This is what Straussianism in Claremont now means: joining a small, privileged boys' club that pushes fascist fantasies in not-so-secret code while cosplaying visionary philosophers.

So, who gets to join the secret society of latter-day Greco-Roman boy-authoritarians? Something to keep in mind is that Costin Alamariu, aka the Bronze Age Pervert, got his PhD from Yale. Curtis Yarvin did time at Johns Hopkins, Brown, and UC Berkeley. Anton is a graduate of UC Berkeley. Their hero Ron DeSantis has both Harvard and Yale on his CV. Manly man Josh Hawley is Stanford and Harvard. Vivek Ramaswamy met his wife, a doctor, when they were both graduate students at Yale. Yes, Virginia, these very men are themselves the Bugmen. When they talk about sticking it to the administrative state or fantasize about having their dictator buddy manhandle the libs, they seem to be dreaming about revenge on the people down the hall. They are going to show those professors, administrators, girls who wouldn't date them, and fellow students who were mean to them on their way up who's who.

It is with that in mind that one can make sense of the strangest aspect of the Claremont pathology: its obsession with elite higher education. Is demolishing critical race theory—hitherto confined to a tiny clutch of undersized academic departments—really going to save the working classes? Is the gut renovation of the seven-hundred-student New College really the first step on the path to restoring the glory of the Republic? A safe conclusion is that these people are unable to leave school, at least in their own minds. To put it in the Nietzschean language that perhaps some of them will understand, the accelerant of the New Right is the *ressentiment* of the reactionary campus cranks.

IN A MORE just world, the dangerous political fantasies of a few well-read misogynists might be dismissed as a fringe phenomenon, of little more consequence than a latter-day gathering of the Rosicrucian Society. But the antics of Mansfield, Yenor, Yarvin, and BAP take place in a world that suffers from no shortage of woman haters and racists and demagogues. In their bursts of hate-fueled creativity, the men of Claremont have supplied the legitimation and the permission structure for the antidemocratic reaction in America. While they rage against the gynocracy, women like Samantha Casiano face the real consequences of life under a rather more pedestrian form of patriarchy.

Large and influential religious organizations and parachurch networks continue to tell women that they should be subservient to their husbands. The term *male headship* has a lot of currency in this world, and it basically means that men should "lead" their families, and women should submit. The doctrine emphatically applies to roles in church, too. The Southern Baptist Convention, for example, ruled in 2023 that it would no longer allow women in the pulpit.[82] The fact that the SBC, like other religious organizations and denominations, has tolerated and covered up for sexual abusers in their midst often has the paradoxical effect of reinforcing this impulse toward patriarchy. Men are beasts, the logic goes; they can only be contained within a rigid order that places them on top.

In this world of religious conservatives, there is little interest in fine distinctions such as the one Harvey Mansfield floats between private-sphere manliness and public-sphere feminism. For them, the personal is the political. Trump allies like Laura Loomer, Jason Whitlock, and Nick Fuentes, for example, have advocated stripping women of the right to vote through something called "head-of-household voting." The theory is that the "head" decides which candidate the family unit will support. Head-of-household voting is practiced in some ultratraditionalist religious communities, where men are universally the decision-makers. The Twitter account @godlywomanhood, also known as the Transformed Wife, popular among "new traditionalists," posted an image of a woman wearing a T-shirt that read WOMEN SHOULDN'T VOTE and commented, "Thank you for the modest shirt, @pearlythingz! I am sure I will receive many great compliments on it!"[83] Antiabortion activist Abby Johnson puts the argument this way: "In a Godly household, the husband would get the final say."[84] Abby Johnson, by the way, was invited to speak at the Republican National Convention.

Regressive noises of this sort can also be heard on the extreme Catholic right. Michael Warren Davis, a contributing editor at the *American Conservative* and the editor of *Crisis Magazine*, has this to say about the Nineteenth Amendment: "One hundred years later, any sober and dispassionate mind must conclude that giving ladies the right to vote was the single greatest catastrophe in the history of our storied republic."[85] (Davis, for what it's worth, also seems to think that medieval serfs had a wonderful life, that the Inquisition never happened, and that Protestant religion—all of it—was a colossal mistake.)

Maybe there was a time when some people might reassure themselves that the sexism of the religious right on the whole was a form of nostalgia or an appeal to traditional values. But the antidemocratic reaction has moved on from that. The function of reactionary misogyny and racism today is not to do the impossible—even if you wish it so, you can't go back to a time that never existed the way you think it did. Nor will this agenda end with the enactment of punishing policies on all those who defy the gender order. Rather, the function is also to perform the subordination in a public way, to humiliate an "other" openly and with impunity. The aim is to mobilize racial, gender, and sex-related anxieties in support of an authoritarian political project. It is to gather up the grievances and resentments that many people have concerning race, sex, and family arrangements and then offer to crush their perceived malefactors with an iron fist. It is that promise of vengeance that draws in support. This is where the young men of the New Right come in: they are there to help you enjoy the show, and to project those good feelings of release on the heroic leader, the man in the Sonnenrad.

In the prevailing narratives about the rise of authoritarianism in the United States, the resentment that matters is thought to be the one that afflicts a sector of the working classes—the animus that arises from the uneducated, sometimes rural, often religious white people who feel left behind in an economy run by and for cosmopolitan elites. Those resentments are real, and indeed they matter. They figure centrally in the next part of this book. But resentment among the elites—the inevitable emotional damage in a society where the funnel is narrowing and relentless competition bars entry to those circles near the top, somewhere just below the all-forgiving grace of the superwealthy— this special flavor of elite-on-elite resentment matters at least as much. If and when the Red Caesar arrives, he can thank the oligarchs for funding his rise, and he can thank the rank and file of the movement for supporting him in the name of "authenticity." But he would owe at least as large a debt of gratitude to the unhappy men of Claremont, those spurned would-be members of the intellectual elite and their frog friends, for explaining just who he is, and why he should go ahead and blow the whole place up.

CHAPTER 7

Smashing the Administrative State

When Steve Bannon suggested, in the weeks after President Trump's 2017 inauguration, that the agenda of the new administration would center on the "deconstruction of the administrative state," he was greeted with many quizzical expressions.[1] Whatever is an "administrative state," and how does one "deconstruct" it? But the term had long been in currency at places like the Federalist Society and the Claremont Institute.[2]

The "administrative state" sounds a little like the "big government" specter of Reagan-era market-fundamentalist lore. Undoubtedly it resonates with Reagan's claim that "government is the problem." Yet it has evolved into something very different from the object of a boomer father-in-law's Thanksgiving lectures on the virtues of freedom and the badness of moochers. The old beef was that government bigfoots the nimble efficiency of the marketplace, dampens innovation, and coddles the takers in society at the expense of the makers. The new dispensation, on the other hand, portrays the administrative state as something far more sinister than a mere money waster or a stepping stone down the path to socialism. It is itself, in its present form, evil incarnate, a tyrant aiming to destroy the people and everything they hold dear.

By 2023 "the administrative state" had been elevated alongside "the woke" to the status of a prime evil and the object of ritual denunciation among right-wing elites. "Woke ideology is now embedded within the very DNA of the federal bureaucracy," wrote Christopher Rufo and Russ Vought, a Trump administration official who went on to set up a think tank, Center for Renewing America, with Jeffrey Clark, the deputy attorney general indicted for his role in Trump's attempted coup, as senior fellow and director of litigation.[3] (Clark has pleaded not guilty.) In the run-up to the 2024 presidential election, Republican candidates Ron DeSantis, Vivek Ramaswamy, and Donald Trump vowed to destroy, demolish, and obliterate the administrative state. In a ten-year budget proposal that he circulated on Capitol Hill, Vought demanded $2 trillion in cuts to Medicaid, hundreds of billions of dollars in cuts each to the Affordable Care Act and food stamps program, and a halving of the State Department, among other measures. "America cannot be saved unless the current grip of woke and weaponized government is broken," he explained.[4] "That is the central and immediate threat facing the country—the one that all our statesmen must rise tall to vanquish . . . The battle cannot wait."[5]

In his introduction to Project 2025, Kevin Roberts defines the administrative state as the entire apparatus of the federal government, with its hundreds of agencies and millions of employees.[6] In that case, demolishing the administrative state would presumably mean airplane pilots flying wherever they want, drug manufacturers making whatever sells, and the Coast Guard mothballing its ships. As Harry Jaffa's son, Philip Jaffa, suggested, it does indeed sound like anarchism, pure and simple. On closer inspection, though, it becomes clear that wielding administrative power is just fine with leaders of the New Right—as long as they can wield it against their enemies.

One of the many elements of the administrative state that Vought proposes to annihilate, for example, is the Gender Policy Council, which has a particular focus on tackling violence and discrimination against women and girls. But in the next breath he demands the creation of a new office tasked with "ensuring agency support for the implementation of policies related to the promotion of life and families in the United States."[7] It's really a case of "administrative state for me but not for thee."

Ideology is too gentle a word for the kind of incoherent rage that the New Right offers on the administrative state. Many of us have had bad experiences at the Department of Motor Vehicles or at the hands of our local recycling enforcers. Even the temperate Eisenhower was aware of the dangers posed by those military-industrial complexes, and sensible people can agree that, at least some of the time, government programs can get in the way of better solutions to our problems. But there is little that is temperate in the rhetoric about the administrative state on the right today. It looks more like pathology than policy.

Where did the madness come from? And if its attachment to the old market-fundamentalist synthesis has come undone, what is its real function in the antidemocratic reaction now?

IN REPORTING ON the Claremont Institute, Charles Kesler typically comes off as the éminence grise. As a gray-haired, bespectacled, sixtysomething professor with an avuncular manner, he certainly looks like the adult in the room. He writes extensively on American constitutionalism and political thought, is the editor of the *Claremont Review of Books*, hosts its *American Mind* video series, and teaches in the Claremont Institute's fellowship programs. His position at Claremont McKenna College as Dengla-Dykler Distinguished Professor of Government presumably adds some intellectual respectability to the enterprise. (On the other hand, he joined the board of Florida's New College after Governor Ron DeSantis's right-wing takeover, and he apparently played a significant role in the propagandistic 1776 Report. So there's that.) At any rate, he appears well poised to become the center of gravity in the brain trust on which a Republican president may be expected to draw.

Kesler's writing must therefore come as something of a disappointment to any who aspire to éminence-grise status. Much of his academic work wears only the thinnest intellectual patina to disguise its partisan thrust. You get a feel for his style of analysis from his interpretation of the speech that Trump delivered at the Ellipse on January 6, 2021. Where Trump says that former vice president Mike Pence and other Republican leaders in Congress would be "ashamed of themselves throughout history, throughout eternity"[8] if they failed to overturn the election, Kesler sees proof that Trump believes in "a form of right, based not merely in history but in 'eternity.'"[9] Trump the Platonist—who knew?

Kesler offers a summary of his political wisdom in his *Crisis of the Two Constitutions* (Encounter Books, 2021). The title is a self-conscious homage to Harry Jaffa's seminal book on Lincoln, *Crisis of the House Divided: An Interpretation of the Issues in the Lincoln-Douglas Debates* (University of Chicago Press, 1959), and it appears to promise subtle insights from American history. Between the covers, however, readers will find potshots at "the 1619 riots" (Kesler's label for the Black Lives Matter protests of 2020), repetitive attacks on "multicultur-alism," analysis of why liberalism "looks increasingly, well, elderly," laments about the reliance on "her truth" at the Kavanaugh hearings, representations of Donald Trump as a "truth-speaker," and, to be sure, sweeping and often partisan generalizations about American history.[10]

Although it is usually unwise to judge a book by its cover, an exception can be made in the case of Kesler's book, which presents the author's argument in all its simplicity. In a custom-drawn cartoon in shades of red and yellow, the U.S. Capitol stands in the distance, majestic and forlorn. Barring the entrance squats a monster with vaguely Mesoamerican features, labeled "the living Constitution."[11] The monster represents the great evil of the world as Kesler appears to understand it. The nature of the evil will be self-evident to anyone familiar with the version of Straussianism that has come to define the Clare-mont project: historicism, nihilism, and progressivism. More specifically, according to the historical narrative on which Kesler hangs his party hat, the evil originated with Strauss's nemesis Georg Wilhelm Friedrich Hegel, and it achieved its ultimate expression in President Woodrow Wilson, the supposed überprogressive and, according to Kesler, the creator of—wait for it—"the administrative state."[12]

Off to the right on the cartoon book cover, a small but heroic knight on horseback flies the flag of the true U.S. Constitution ("We The People," it reads), tilting his lance in the direction of the progressive beast. Call him the white knight of Claremont, ever ready to return control of the government to people who presumably think like the founders. As a matter of fact, he looks set to storm the Capitol. The book was finished before January 6, 2021, but it came out about a month afterward. The timing was impeccable.

It's a strange narrative. Did some nineteenth-century German philosopher really ruin it for all of us? Few Americans read Hegel, and even fewer still can make much sense of his incredibly opaque writings. And why pick on Woodrow Wilson? Why not another progressive figure, such as Teddy Roosevelt, Louis Brandeis, John Dewey, Alice Paul, or Robert La Follette? Come to think of it, why pick on progressives at all, given that the largest expansions of federal power in the nineteenth century undoubtedly occurred on Lincoln's watch as a consequence of the Civil War?

Claremont happens to be one of those places that engages largely in conver-sation with itself. Figuring out Kesler's cartoon history, it turns out, is just a matter of picking up another Claremont tome. Kesler appears to have cribbed most of his Hegel-to-Wilson "administrative state" narrative from John Marini, a senior fellow at the Claremont Institute whose association with the organization goes back decades. With editor and coauthor Ken Masugi, a fellow Claremonter, Marini spells out the story in his book *Unmasking the Administrative State*.[13]

To be sure, there is a sensible analysis of the administrative state that long precedes Marini and the Claremont Institute. As noted by Dwight Waldo, the subtle political theorist and onetime federal official who brought the idea to attention in a 1948 book, the administrative apparatus of the modern state has emerged as a new and powerful political function, distinct in important ways from a traditional conception of the legislature and executive.[14] The administrative state often attempts to justify its power through an ideology valorizing scientific efficiency and managerial expertise. Yet, as Waldo points out, government administrators engage in inherently political tasks; they seek negotiated solutions among constituencies, and they ultimately answer to a democratic people through their elected representatives.[15] The point of this kind of critique isn't to destroy the administrative state—certainly we'll want to hold on to the air traffic controllers and food safety inspectors—but to ensure that it remains accountable to the people in a democratic polity.

But the Claremont Institute doesn't do complicated—possibly this is one of the consequences of running affirmative action programs for committed reactionaries—and Marini is a case in point. He is a black-and-white kind of thinker, and one can get a sense of where he locates the color line from his analysis of Donald Trump's candidacy for president in 2016. Marini lauds Trump for his interest "in unifying the country" by "appealing to the common good." And: "Trump has appealed to the rule of law and has attacked bureaucratic rule as the rule of privilege and patronage."[16] Trump loves the rule of law—what a brilliantly unexpected analysis!

In Marini's narrative, the administrative state is not to be reformed or improved; it is inherently illegitimate. "The tacit promise of the rational state, and the defense of the administrative state," he claims, "rests upon the assumption that the power of government cannot be limited," which, in his reading, directly contradicts the wisdom that the founders supposedly gleaned from Aristotle.[17] Consequently, as his coauthor Ken Masugi writes, "the administrative state is the modern face of tyranny—an issue on which thinkers as diverse as Leo Strauss and Carl Schmitt apparently agree."[18] The references are apt indeed (though the suggestion that Strauss and Schmitt represent diversity speaks volumes about the scope of the Claremont intellectual universe).

Who exactly does Marini think is behind the modern face of tyranny? The "knowledge class," the "legal, technocratic, and educational elites" whose "intellectual authority derived from history, science and social science" grants them "justification for rational, or administrative rule."[19] Those fiends who ride the Washington Metro every morning, with their affinity for "science" and "reason," have apparently manipulated public opinion in a dastardly plot to advance their bureaucratic power! Trump represented "an existential threat" to their plans for administrative state, and the secret reason why many progressives still oppose Trump is that they love nothing more than the smell of bureaucracy in the morning.[20] Shorter Marini: The Bugmen did it. Does this mean that the National Parks Service people and the folks at the Federal Maritime Commission are in on the scam? Is it past time to abolish the FDA, the CIA, the FBI? Who knows. Details. Go ask the Bugmen.

Marini knows that something as big as the administrative state needs a big history. It all goes back to Hegel, he says.[21] Wait, what? Hegel again! The unintelligible German philosopher whom nobody actually reads turns up here, too? This is where the intellectual genealogy of Claremont becomes interesting—and alarming.

There are roughly two ways in which one can interpret Hegel's apparent identification of the modern state with "reason." A generous reading, favored by Hegel's many liberal admirers, says that he is emphasizing that, insofar as the individual can embrace the laws of a liberal state as an extension of her own quest for freedom, the state may be considered an artifact of reason. According to this understanding, the rationality of the liberal state is neutral, inasmuch as it serves as the place where various ideas about the good are contested and ultimately resolved through deliberation.

According to a reactionary, even paranoid reading, on the other hand, Hegel attributes to the state a kind of rationality that is not neutral and directly opposes human longings. The rationality of the state, in this reading, is of the kind that says, all in all, you're just another brick in the wall.

Carl Schmitt, as it happens, plumped for the paranoid reading. In Schmitt's view, the rational, Hegelian state represents the death knell of genuine politics. It is an attempt by professionals and bureaucrats to suppress the friend-foe-emergency world of genuine politics in favor of the suffocating rationalism of an administrative state. The Schmittian hero triumphs not with reasoned argument but by crushing the enemies of the nation in combat. On the happy day in 1933 that Adolph Hitler came to power, according to Schmitt, "one can say that 'Hegel died.'"[22] He meant that a new kind of politics was emerging, a politics that set aside the pretenses about a rational, neutral, liberal state and instead identified the state with one party, one people, and one leader. Sieg Heil!

Marini's critique of the administrative state, and even his identification of Hegel as its evil mastermind, tracks Schmitt's critique of the liberal (Jewish) order with uncanny precision.[23] In brief, the genealogy of the reaction is this: Kesler is Marini redux; Marini is Schmitt redux; and Schmitt is about as Nazi as political theorists get. Which is by no means to suggest that the men of Claremont are Nazis by association. Surely they are not. A much safer bet is that this follows the pattern of Nate Hochman's accidental Sonnenrad. They fell into the logic of fascism because they just happen to have the same tastes and prejudices as a man like Carl Schmitt.

FOUR YEARS OF the first Trump presidency afforded the world some insight into what the "deconstruction of the administrative state" looks like on the ground, and it consisted of a series of big hits for democracy. The payoff for the right, apart from epic levels of corruption and nepotism, came mainly from the Supreme Court majority Trump appointed.

A first example was the ruling that curtailed the EPA's ability to regulate greenhouse gas emissions and other sources of pollution, a reduction in states' ability to regulate firearms (so much for "states' rights"), a vast expansion in direct taxpayer funding to religious organizations, and many other causes they hold dear. The environment, public health, and religious freedom may have lost, but Marini hailed those decisions as steps in the right direction.

In June 2024, the Court delivered much more to the enemies of the administrative state. In a pair of decisions, it effectively overturned the *Chevron U.S.A., Inc. v. Natural Resources Defense Council.* The Chevron doctrine, as it was known, had long served as a platform for government agencies as they formulated the specific rules required to execute duly passed laws. Overturning the doctrine "gives unelected judges free-floating veto power over the enforcement of virtually all laws and puts a heavy thumb on the scale of deregulation," according to Dahlia Lithwick and Mark Joseph Stern in *Slate*.[24] "They want to stop government from working," Stern added, "because they believe when government functions properly . . . it's bad for industry that wants to dump pollution into our waters, or sell drugs that aren't safe, or make a ton of money and shelter it from taxation." The deconstruction of the administrative state, in short, is just the destruction of public administration and its replacement with a privately controlled, corporate-managed state.

Perhaps the best illustration of what the deconstruction looks like on the ground would be the reporting on the tenure of Michael Pack as head of the U.S. Agency for Global Media (whose flagship is Voice of America). Pack was president and CEO of the Claremont Institute from 2015 to 2017, so one may presume that he was well informed about the darkness at the heart of the administrative state. His reign at Voice of America began late in Trump's first term, lasted seven months, and ended two hours after President Biden took office. During those seven months, according to reporting on National Public Radio and in the *Washington Post* and other publications, Pack "inspired multiple formal investigations and rebukes" from various federal and D.C. judges who found that he acted "illegally and even unconstitutionally."[25]

Pack reportedly examined ways to sideline or purge staffers suspected of being not on the Trump team. (Firing a civil servant over political affiliation typically violates federal law.) After those suspected staffers were reinstated and exonerated by the inspector general's office of the U.S. State Department, according to the *Washington Post*, Pack then sought to tear down the statutory firewall that is meant to protect the independence of journalists from partisan interference, focusing on network heads, journalists, and other agency employees.[26] He also reportedly gave an open-ended, no-contract deal to a $1,470-per-hour law firm with conservative connections to investigate employees who he believed were opposed to Trump—work that, if it needed to be done at all, could have been carried out by interns with Twitter and Facebook accounts.[27] This cushy arrangement ended up costing taxpayers $1.6 million, according to reporting in the *Washington Post*.[28] A 145-page report compiled by three outside experts and endorsed by the U.S. Office of Special Counsel asserted that Mr. Pack "abused his authority" and "engaged in gross mismanagement and waste."[29] (The report appears to have been subsequently removed from the website of the U.S. Office of Special Counsel.)

"I don't think he had a plan other than to just blow the place up," said Dan Hanlon, a Trump appointee who had previously served as a top aide to Trump's chief of staff Mick Mulvaney. "We would come in at nine o'clock and stamp out at five o'clock," Hanlon added. "And we played foosball all day. And we would just sit there, commenting about how absurd this whole thing was."[30]

BROADLY SPEAKING, THE kind of antigovernment nihilism that Marini preached and Pack appeared to practice has two natural constituencies. The first consists of those people who generally do not suffer from discrimination and take things like clean water for granted and who, unaware of the role of the administrative state in creating and sustaining their own freedoms and those of others, see no place for government in securing their safety and civil rights. Thus they seek to demolish the house in which they live, and they call this freedom. The Claremont Institute and its fellow travelers on the New Right exist to gather some number of such individuals from their unhappy stations on campus, as we know from the preceding chapter.

The other constituency consists of those economic interests whose activities cause harm (such as pollution or the degradation of communities) or depend on monopoly profits, and who therefore wish avoid being regulated by any kind of state agency. The Claremont Institute, like the Heritage Foundation and much of the rest of the New Right, pays for its breakfast with money that flows from the representatives of this group.

And therein lies a paradox. Nihilism may offer some short-term benefits for oligarchs, but it isn't a winning strategy in the long term. Sensible oligarchs don't want to destroy the state; they just want to have the right kind of state. The slaveholding oligarchs of the Old South did not want to destroy the federal government; on the contrary, they wanted a federal government strong enough to compel other states to chase down their missing "property"—that is, enslaved people who managed to escape. The corporations that thrived under the "antigovernment" politics of the Reagan era did not wish for the absence of the state in the market; on the contrary, they wanted a strong state to enforce the rules that kept them in the money. In the past decades, large-scale financial institutions have seemed perfectly content to be considered too big to fail. But right-wing oligarchs of the twenty-first century appear to be funding a movement that wants to take a wrecking ball to a state that pursues the common good, equality, "wokery," or anything else they don't like.

So who is paying for this party at the end of the world? Apart from whatever small dollars it wrings from anxious recipients through its mass mailers, the Claremont Institute appears to get the largest chunk of its money from Thomas Klingenstein, the New York-based finance executive who serves as its current chairman and who, in the summer of 2023, expressed his support for Co-Conspirator 2 John Eastman for his role in the coup attempt in several YouTube interviews.[31]

Claremont has other funders, too, as I mentioned in chapter 5,[32] including the Dick and Betsy DeVos Foundation, the Sarah Scaife Foundation, the Bradley Foundation, DonorsTrust, and the Donors Capital Fund. They are among the same groups that top the list in funding climate science denial, the privatization of public education,[33] and other causes known to warm the hearts of religious right leaders. Through their contributions to the Freedom Foundation, they also support the weakening or destruction of unions and aim for the reduction of taxes (especially of inheritance taxes) for the wealthy.

The direct funding from ultrawealthy interests is only part of the story of how money has made Claremont. New Right luminaries like Ron DeSantis, Josh Hawley, and J. D. Vance are to an important extent creatures of the donor class.[34] Their careers exist in large measure because a small number of private equity and real estate investors have decided to conjure them into existence. The money that these political leaders receive from their friends turns into jobs, status, and power for the Claremont Institute and its fellow travelers on the New Right.

It would be a simple story if the money flowing to the Claremont Institute was merely there in pursuit of financial self-interest—and to some extent it is. The real estate investor who ponied up $1 million for DeSantis (not counting the gift of a golf simulator installed in the governor's mansion) would seem to have gotten cold, hard payback with a new exchange on Interstate 95 conveniently located to maximize the value of his property portfolio.[35] The reigning theory is that donors will put up with the raw eggs, the Bronze Age nuttery, the Sonnenrad, the end of democracy, and all that, as long as it delivers lower taxes and a government small enough to be unable to defend the public, but big enough to defend their own private interests.

A deeper consideration of the antics of the Claremont men, however, suggests that the moneymen may not always have a clear idea of what they are buying. Do they know anything about human history? Fascism always looks promising for big money, but it always ends badly. The end state of the vaunted "deconstruction of the administrative state" is corruption and cronyism. Caesars of every kind and throughout history have used the resources of the state to reward those who keep them in power. The study of history and political science exists for a reason, and it is in part to convey such simple and well-attested facts.

Also, have they read Project 2025? They might want to look again at the part that says that the enemy is not just "culture warriors" but "elite rule." That's you, Mr. and Mrs. DonorsTrust! Those genius funders of Claremont and friends might also want to glance at the rest of Kevin Slack's book. In the parts that the *American Mind* didn't excerpt, the good professor makes clear that a big reason to line up with the AR-15 crowd is to bring pain to the corrupt financial elites who have bought the political system.[36] That would be you, Mr. Klingenstein, and your friends at the Sarah Scaife Foundation.

So why do they keep writing the checks? Possibly some of them missed the moment in the theatrical production *Cabaret* where, after a scene in which the ordinary people of Germany, starting softly, deliver a rousing Nazi anthem, one member of the elite asks another, "Do you still think you can control them?"[37]

There is, however, another theory, and it is possibly more flattering to the men of Claremont. One thing you can say for Plato's imitators is that they can certainly tell a story. It may not be a true story, but it will pack a punch. It may not be good for you, but you might like the taste anyway. You could say that they are expert mixers of Kool-Aid. And to judge from the effect on Thomas Klingenstein, it seems to be working.

Klingenstein does not appear to believe that the Claremonters are spinning yarns to manipulate the public into supporting a government that will work for his financial interest. On the contrary, all signs indicate that he is a true believer. He really does seem to think that America is in "a Cold Civil War" between the forces of righteousness and the "Woke Comms."[38] We really are still on board Flight 93. "What the enemy wants is the destruction of the American way of life," he has said. And this enemy has many faces, "education, corporate media, entertainment, big business, especially big tech" among them. The enemy is devious indeed. "Instead of violence, there is cancelling," he writes. "Censorship is becoming a fact of life." In his YouTube absolution of John Eastman, Klingenstein all but pats his buddy on the back and encourages him to get back to work on another coup attempt.[39]

I put the question to Steve Schmidt, cofounder of the Lincoln Project, and he lit up with enthusiasm. He urged me to read a speech that Hitler gave in 1932 in Dusseldorf to an audience of business executives.[40] Hitler makes an explicit argument against democracy, he said, and "it's not an unsophisticated argument—it's what Tucker Carlson said every night on Fox and now on Twitter." The core of the argument, in its American form, is that "America needs a Caesar." Why does America need a Caesar? "To protect freedom and liberty—because democracy threatens the privilege of those who 'built the country,'" Schmidt continues. "All fascist movements require the cooperation and capitulation of conservative movements. The conservative party is the party that is devoured by fascism in any type of right-wing fascist descent."

There is a further irony to the story. In earlier times, intellectuals drifted into fascist modes of thought mostly on their own streams of rumination and resentment, and activists created their movements in sewing circles or in pubs with cheap beer. That is not what happened this time. The brilliant moneymen of DonorsTrust bought and paid for their own Kool-Aid. Over the past five decades, wealthy conservatives have conducted a grand experiment in American political discourse. They invested massively in organizations and think tanks that have sought to shift the center of public debate in a direction favorable to their interests and privileges. The Claremont Institute is representative of the many operations that blossomed with this well-financed effort. The unintended consequences of the experiment are now the story. When you pay people to be unreasonable, you attract many unreasonable people. You might even become a bit of a crank yourself. It goes back to a problem at least as old as Plato. If your power depends on lying to the people, that doesn't make you noble. It just leaves you with a choice: accept that you are a fraud or embrace the lie.

PART III

Demons

CHAPTER 8

The Rise of the Spirit Warriors

J ulie Green is a "prophet." She claims to be in direct communication with God, and she regularly offers prophesies through her YouTube channel.[1] In one video, she foresees that one day soon all those political leaders who continue to deny that the 2020 election was stolen will be executed for their crimes against the nation.[2] In the 2022 election cycle, she spoke at rallies on behalf of Doug Mastriano, the coup supporter who had converted his calls to overturn the 2020 election into the Republican nomination for governor of Pennsylvania. A leader in a charismatic religious network and movement that I will describe in this chapter, she belongs to a group of political actors who often refer to themselves as spiritual warriors—or, as I will call them, by way of slapping an admittedly simplistic phase on a complicated reality, "spirit warriors."

Green was not the only spirit warrior on the hustings in the 2022 campaign. Over in Arizona, Sean Feucht hit the stumps for gubernatorial candidate Kari Lake.[3] An antivaccine, pro-Trump, guitar-strumming preacher, Feucht stages "praise concerts" on public lands through his ministry Let Us Worship. His other ministry, Burn 24-7, features a "Spiritual Oversight" board that includes prominent neocharismatic spirit warriors like Cindy Jacobs and Lou Engle. In 2022, Feucht also lent support to Doug Lamborn, a Republican candidate from Colorado, and Lauren Boebert, the congresswoman from Colorado.[4] In one instance, he and his bandmates showed up at the Capitol Rotunda with Boebert, accompanying her as her prayers echoed through the building.[5] Feucht also rang in the New Year on December 31, 2021, with Ron and Casey DeSantis. At a concert in support of the Florida governor, he prayed over the couple, saying, "I thank you for the gift they are to America."[6]

Lance Wallnau is arguably an even more successful spirit warrior. He has campaigned for Mastriano in Pennsylvania, prayed over Marjorie Taylor Greene before a cheering crowd in Atlanta, and amassed a robust following on social media for his prophesies, which tend to involve political predictions, sales pitches, or a combination of the two. A Texas-based businessman-cum-conspiracist and evangelist, Wallnau was little known outside of charismatic telehuckstering circles until he hitched his wagon to the Trump train. In *God's Chaos Candidate: Donald J. Trump and the American Unraveling* (2016), Wallnau revealed that Trump was "anointed" by God. "I believe the 45th president is meant to be an Isaiah 45 Cyrus" who will "restore the crumbling walls that separate us from cultural collapse," he added.[7] (Cyrus was the Babylonian king who, despite not being Jewish, encouraged the return of Jewish people to the former Kingdom of Judah in the Southern Levant.) In 2020, Wallnau backed Trump again—as did God, by his reckoning. Apparently eager to turn his fiery predictions into cold hard cash, Wallnau set up a business venture selling $45 coins with the image of Trump on one side and King Cyrus on the other. He claimed the coins could be used by their holders as a "point of contact" with God in their prayers for Trump's reelection.[8]

Wallnau peddles a rotating selection of theologically inflected conspiracy theories. For example, he has alleged that environmentalists and anti-fossil-fuel activists are controlled by demons.[9] He has also identified Tucker Carlson, the racist former Fox TV host, as a "secular prophet" who is "used by God" and is "more powerful than a lot of preachers."[10] In Wallnau's world, clerical positions and religious affiliations appear to matter less in establishing an individual's religious status than having the right politics. During the 2022 elections Wallnau was a busy man, speaking at churches around the country, making frequent appearances on popular Christian nationalist podcasts, such as Truth & Liberty Coalition, on whose board he sits, and keeping his two million followers apprised of the latest prophesies. By October 2023 his conspiracism had taken an especially sinister turn; he suggested it was Soros-backed anti-Netanyahu protesters who distracted the Israeli army, allowing Hamas to breach the Gaza Strip barrier and murder civilians.[11]

Over in California, the politically connected pastor Jim Garlow offers what appears to be a similar flavor of spiritual warfare. His ministry, Well Versed, cultivates government leaders, and he has called the state's Democratic governor, Gavin Newsom, "the chief of the baby-killers." He invited "intercession prayer leader" Maryal Boumann to his show *World Prayer Network*, which is posted on YouTube, to discuss California's "diabolical" Proposition 1, the referendum that added the right to contraception and abortion to the state's constitution.[12]

Speaking at a gathering of City Elders, a national network of "spiritual, political and business leaders" that seek to "establish righteousness in governance" and "draft civil laws which reflect and uphold Biblical values and Judeo-ecclesia ethics," Wallnau attributed a "loss of trust" to "big tech, big pharma," "media, much of business," "the 'woke' church" and "the top ranks of (woke) military," among others, and vowed to transform the culture through "biblical truth."[13] He added, "This is a strategy that is executable . . . this is doable and it is so strategic in its nature that county by county . . . across America this can be done. I like to run with people that have strategy that makes sense. That is doable. And that's why I'm here."[14]

Today, the language of the spirit warriors appears to be everywhere on the right. On Eric Metaxas's right-wing radio show, repeat guest Roger Stone told him that a "demonic portal" had opened above the Biden White House.[15] Pentecostal pastor Mark Burns has riled up his fan base at political gatherings by saying, "I've come here to declare war on every demonic, demon-possessed Democrat that comes from the gates of hell."[16] Sean Feucht, the roving guitarist-preacher, has cast Democratic initiatives as "schemes of the devil in the political realm."[17] At the Family Research Council's 2023 conference, the first speaker, Jonathan Cahn, said America is presently possessed by a trio of ancient and evil spirits that are turning the country into a pagan nation because it has turned away from the Lord.[18] And Chad Connelly of Faith Wins, who appeared on the 2017 membership list of the United States Coalition of Apostolic Leaders (USCAL), appeared, in advance of the 2024 presidential election, to still be touring churches on the Lindseys' dime, bringing a message of political battle against the demonic forces of the left.

Donald Trump's defenders cast his 34 felony convictions and 57 outstanding felony charges (as of this writing) as part of a "spiritual battle." Trump encouraged these views by characterizing his 2024 presidential campaign as part of a "Final Battle," telling the National Religious Broadcasters convention that his opponents are part of a "wicked" system intent on attacking Christianity, and by praising QAnon, which promotes Christian nationalist and dominionist tropes, along with spirit warrior ideas and conspiracies.[19]

Political leaders in the Republican Party have taken note of the spirit warriors—and have rejoiced in the harvest of potential voters. GOP leaders have imitated the new crusaders, and some have even joined their ranks. Florida governor Ron DeSantis is rarely described as charismatic, yet he certainly knows when and how to parrot the language of the spirit warriors. In a speech at Hillsdale College, the nondenominational Christian institution that is a major player in the religious right's war on public education, he paraphrased a passage from Ephesians that serves as a guidepost and virtue signal for this new style of religion: "Put on the full armor of God. Stand firm against the Left's schemes," he said, substituting "the Left" where the Bible refers to "the devil."[20] He repeated the same trope at the 2021 Road to Majority conference, an influential annual gathering of conservative activists, strategists, and politicians sponsored by Ralph Reed's Faith and Freedom Coalition, and his campaign produced an ad that said he was sent by God to "take the arrows."[21]

Other politicians at the conference drew on the same variety of religious expression. "We are soldiers in God's army engaged in spiritual warfare for our country," Texas congressman Louis Gohmert declared at the 2022 Road to Majority conference in Nashville, Tennessee. "We can fight or fail."[22] In North Carolina, Lieutenant Governor Mark Robinson is also on record with his view that his political opponents (meaning Democrats) are "demonic" and full of "the spirit of the anti-Christ." He thinks LGBT people are "filth" and has said that Jewish bankers represent one of the "four horsemen of the apocalypse."[23]

The combination of nationalism, conspiracism, and demon obsession received a kind of canonical expression in the Jericho March held in Washington, D.C., on the night of January 5, 2021, in anticipation of the next day's attack on the Capitol.[24] At that rally, the pastor Robert Weaver stated that God wanted Americans to march around "the spiritual walls of this country."[25] Rev. Kevin Jessip, also speaking at the event, said, "This battle cry is a Christian call to all Christian men . . . as we prepare for a strategic gathering of men in this hour to dispel the Kingdom of Darkness."[26] Father Greg Bramlage, who pastored at Catholic parishes and incorporated "Healing/Deliverance" into his ministry before founding his organization, Missionaries of the New Evangelization, conducted an exorcism onstage. Telling the crowd, "We are in a spiritual battle, this cannot be solved by human means," he prayed that "no demonic bondage, door, entity, portal, astral projection, or disembodied spirit may enter this space."[27] Bishop Leon Benjamin, senior pastor of the New Life Harvest Church in Richmond, Virginia, said, "The demons we kill now, our children will not have to fight these devils. These are our devils, and we will kill them now."[28] On the following morning, of course, many who prayed took up arms—or at least flags, along with barricades and other objects they could use as blunt instruments. They assaulted police officers, and they ran free through the Capitol with banners proclaiming that "Jesus Saves." One group brought a large wooden cross, another a flag with a cross, and one man added a Confederate flag for good measure.

In October 2023, the spirit warriors notched another stunning victory when one of their own, in a manner of speaking, became Speaker of the U.S. House of Representatives. Congressman Mike Johnson of Louisiana indicated on his first day as Speaker that God himself had a hand in his ascension to a position second in line to the presidency. "God is the one who raises up those in authority," he told the House when, after three weeks of infighting, the Republican caucus at last settled on him as their fifth candidate for the position.[29] It's abundantly clear that Johnson fully subscribes to the Christian nation myth. The pseudohistorian and propagandist David Barton, says Johnson, had "such a profound influence on me, and my work, and my life, and everything I do."[30]

Johnson has long been associated with the Southern Baptist Convention but is fluent in the language of the spirit warriors. On a broadcast of the World Prayer Network with Jim Garlow, Johnson called America "dark and depraved." "Is God going to allow our nation to enter a time of judgment for our collective sins?" he asked. "Or is he going to give us one more chance to restore the foundations and return to Him?"[31]

Johnson ran a podcast with his wife, Kelly, for several years, and on it the pair insist that the "biblical worldview" is the only valid one, and that the separation of church and state is a myth.[32] Speaking at an antiabortion gathering, Johnson told the crowd that America can be saved only if it returns to "eighteenth-century values."[33] The biblical worldview, to judge from the support Mike Johnson has provided to the Creation Museum, appears to include the doctrine that Earth was created in its present form six thousand years ago. It also involves rejecting action to deal with the climate crisis, which, according to Johnson, "defies the created order of how this is all supposed to work." God, he explains, commanded us "to take dominion of the earth. You subdue it . . . We're supposed to eat those animals."[34] The biblical worldview also apparently supports spreading lies about election results to advance a coup. Johnson played a lead role in filing spurious court cases intended to derail Biden's victory in the 2020 presidential election and then, on the evening of January 6, 2021, after the Capitol had been ransacked, led 147 of his fellow congressional Republicans in voting against the certification of the election results.[35]

In brief, the spirit warriors have arrived—and they have almost conquered. But where did they come from?

THE STORY THAT many Americans like to tell themselves is that America's God landed around 1620 near Plymouth Rock, and He hasn't changed much since.[36] Of course, it isn't true. American religion has undergone massive transformations in its long history, from the Great Awakening to the rise of the social gospel.[37] Such changes happen in this country episodically. We are undergoing another such transformation right now—arguably the least well reported yet most politically problematic one yet.

The aspect of the change in the religious landscape that generally attracts the most media attention is the rise of the "nones," that is, individuals who do not identify with any religion.[38] But this apparent move toward secularism can be misinterpreted. The rise of the nones has occurred alongside a countervailing trend among those who do identify with religion. The nones, moreover, cannot simply be identified with secularism; an appreciable fraction of them reject religious labels not because they lack religion but because they do not see their own sense of religion reflected in those labels.

Alongside the nones and the "somes," as it were, a hotter and more reactionary style of religion is surging in America. It cuts across traditional denominational divides.[39] And it tracks some global shifts in religion, shifts in which America is a follower as well as a leader.[40]

The new religious sensibility in America is not all or even mainly about a fixed set of doctrines or denominations. While it finds its most comfortable home in Pentecostal and charismatic forms of faith, which include multiple networks and movements such as the New Apostolic Reformation, not everyone who adheres to this mode of religion is affiliated with those groups, conforms to those doctrines, or identifies with those labels. It is rather a certain style of religion: an attitude, a set of dispositions, patterns, behaviors, and a shared language. For simplicity's sake, I will refer to it generally as the religion of the spirit warriors.

Although not everyone caught up in the fervor subscribes to the same theology or comes down on the same side of the political spectrum, Pentecostals and other spirit warriors are often targeted for political exploitation, and they are exploited overwhelmingly on behalf of the extreme right. Through doctrines about global conspiracies, the supposed right of Christians to assume control over all aspects of social and political life, and the political mobilization of sexual and gender anxieties, this new religious movement thrives in times of high political and economic instability, and it has become a significant factor in the rise of the antidemocratic reaction in the United States. Perhaps not surprisingly, its origins in America go back to an earlier time of great instability. A good place to start would be that warm summer night in April 1906 when a thirty-five-year-old traveling preacher named William Seymour and seven of his friends sat down to talk with God.[41]

THEY SAT PATIENTLY, waiting for His divine presence, when suddenly they all fell to the floor "as though hit by a bolt of lightning."[42] They writhed on the ground and began speaking in tongues. Seymour, by all accounts a gentle and contemplative character whose parents had been emancipated from slavery with the end of the Civil War, found in that experience the key to a new kind of religion in America.[43] The Azusa Street Revival, named after the street in Los Angeles where the event took place, was unabashedly multiracial and gender-inclusive from the start.[44] Not surprisingly, representatives of the mainline denominations considered it wildly unorthodox, and believed the scandal was all the worse for the interracial aspect of the festivities. An article in the *Los Angeles Times* sneered at the religious presumptions of the revival and its "disgraceful intermingling of the races."[45] By 1915 the Azusa Street Revival had lost much of its momentum, yet in retrospect it looks more like the first act in the extraordinary rise of a new branch of Christianity called Pentecostalism, which in turn contributed to subsequent waves of charismatic and neocharismatic expression.[46]

"Pentecostalism represents a rare feat in American religion—a tradition that is growing," according to Ryan Burge, assistant professor of political science at Eastern Illinois University. "The Assemblies of God, which stands as the largest Pentecostal denomination, has seen a 50 percent increase in membership over the last three decades, while every other prominent Protestant denomination has seen their membership decline precipitously."

In socioeconomic terms, Pentecostalism in America appears to fare best among lower-income groups and the non-college-educated. According to a 2016 survey by Pew, only 9 percent of members of the Church of God in Christ and 10 percent of members of the Assemblies of God, both Pentecostal congregations, had family incomes above $100,000 per year. That compares with 35 percent of Episcopalians and 19 percent of Catholics. The statistics on educational attainment are similarly skewed, with college and graduate degrees more heavily concentrated among the old mainline denominations.[47]

Pentecostalism also remains an outlier in the American religious landscape when it comes to race. An old saw has it that America is never so divided by race as on Sunday mornings.[48] Starting with the Azusa Street Revival, however, that rule has not really applied to Pentecostals. To be sure, some Pentecostal communities remain segregated, but many others are notable for their racial diversity.[49] According to Burge, 44 percent of Pentecostals in America are Black and Latino. Pentecostals are also, not coincidentally, notable for their political diversity. Many Black Pentecostal traditions in America are strongly associated with the pursuit of racial and economic justice and social ethics.[50] Diversity, however, is not the same thing as general tendency; some of the largest and fastest-growing Pentecostal and neocharismatic communities lean decidedly to the right.[51]

"Religious identity is one of the biggest divides among Latinos," notes Robert P. Jones, founder and CEO of the Public Religion Research Institute, pointing to the 2020 AP/Votecast exit polls showing that Latino Catholics voted 67 percent for Biden while Latino Protestants (including Pentecostals) voted 58 percent for Trump. "Most Latino Protestants identify as evangelical, and in the American context, that shared religious identity with white evangelicals has brought along with it a Republican partisan identity and set of political attitudes and priorities."[52]

But Pentecostalism is not merely an American phenomenon. And Pentecostal celebrity evangelists now play an outsize role in the religious life of large parts of the globe. Argentina native and now California-based Alberto Mottesi, who describes himself as "an evangelist who prophesies but I'm not a prophet" and has been referred to as "the Billy Graham of Latin America" and "crusader to the world," tours extensively in Central and South America and has a robust global radio and TV presence.[53] According to *Charisma* magazine, Mottesi works to "transfer the anointing of an evangelist to young people and women in Latin America, a region that is in the midst of an unprecedented *avivamiento spiritual*—or 'spiritual revival.'"[54]

Motessi has hailed the region's shift away from Roman Catholicism. "For the past forty years I've seen the Latin American people depressed, abused, downcast from idolatry, witchcraft, and political corruption," he said. Today, "eighty percent of Christians in Latin America are Pentecostals or charismatic. This is the era of the Holy Spirit in Latin America."[55]

Many commentators on the religious right still remain focused on the "white evangelical" label. But those who report on the movement at the ground level have noted the shift. "The Pentecostal and charismatic movement is one of the biggest surges in the history of global and American Christianity," says Frederick Clarkson, senior research analyst at Political Research Associates, who has been reporting on the religious right for four decades. In the most expansive definition, Pentecostalism now claims as many as six hundred million adherents worldwide, or more than a quarter of all Christians.[56] It has a huge presence in Brazil, where it played a decisive role in the rise of the populist demagogue Jair Bolsonaro;[57] in Hungary, where it helped elevate the explicitly illiberal Viktor Orban;[58] and in Guatemala, where Pentecostal evangelicalism was exported from the United States to counter the influence of the Second Vatican Council and the rise of liberation theology, with its apparently dangerous theories about social justice and the common good.[59] It is surging among migrant workers in Gulf states, where some Pentecostal networks provide key services to the disempowered,[60] and also in Nigeria, where human trafficking organizations have infiltrated certain Pentecostal networks.[61] From the perspective of some global leaders of the movement, the United States looks like an aging and corrupt capital. It's now the kind of place to which missionaries must go, rather than the place from whence they come.

THE SAFEST GENERALIZATION about the theology of Pentecostalism is that it is "a religion of the here and now" and "not of the forever beyond," as author Elle Hardy, author of *Beyond Belief: How Pentecostal Christianity Is Taking Over the World* (Hurst, 2021), told me.[62] A key attraction is not some heavenly reward in the next life but greater material blessings in this one. Many varieties of Pentecostalism blend well with America's Prosperity Gospel, along with elements of the New Age.

The other promise that Pentecostalism and its charismatic offshoots make is that its followers will become heroes in an epic struggle between good and evil, to be played out very much in the here and now. Demons are real, "spiritual warfare" is the way to contain them, and adherents are called to serve in the battle. To engage in the battle, naturally, one must understand and speak the language of the spirits. Among many of these denominations, networks, and groupings there is a great interest in speaking in tongues.

Among some expressions of Pentecostalism, the emphasis is on overcoming adversity and gaining mastery over one's own "demons" in order to live a healthier, happier, and holier life. But in the reactionary, politicized U.S. spirit warrior circles, the conflict is also taking place on the public stage. You can read about it—or more likely catch it on TV—every day in the headlines. Hence the "apostles" and "prophets" and their allies who claim to be engaged in "spiritual warfare" on behalf of anointed political leaders and political parties (mostly Trump and the Republican Party).[63]

The paradox of a demon-haunted world, of course, is that the demons are always in charge, for the moment, even if the angels are assuredly destined for ultimate victory. The Reform Prayer Network, for example, which I describe in my previous book *The Power Worshippers* (Bloomsbury, 2020), aims to "reverse the curse over America" by "igniting a holy reformation in every sphere of society."[64] When the televangelist Paula White, a longtime friend of Donald Trump who served as an adviser to the first administration's Faith and Opportunity Initiative, famously said "We command all satanic pregnancies to miscarry right now" from "satanic wombs," she likewise meant to suggest that the demons appear to be winning—for the moment.[65]

MY ONE ATTEMPT to speak in tongues ended in embarrassment. It all started back in 2010, when I was researching my book about the religious right's war on public education. I found myself spending some time at the Life Challenge Church, a moderately sized charismatic church in Odessa, Texas. At the time, Life Challenge was busing "prayer warriors" to public school board meetings to oppose comprehensive health education classes and support the introduction of an explicitly sectarian Bible program. Churchgoers were by and large working class, the racially integrated services were warm and welcoming, and the worship music was magnificent.

Life Challenge is where I began to grasp the appeal of this style of religion. On several occasions I fell into conversation with a modestly dressed congregant who arrived with her three children. She had the disheveled appearance of a new mother just struggling to keep it together. She told me she held down a part-time job and received little help from the children's father. As services began, the children were whisked from her side and taken to the kids' area in another section of the church. The worship band launched into a contemporary gospel track, and she swayed in prayer, eyes closed; as they picked up the pace, she danced with joyful abandon.

Her eldest child, she told me, was thriving at the local public school thanks to the services for kids with learning challenges. She planned for the younger two to attend the neighborhood public school, too. But the attitude toward public education at Life Challenge was decidedly oppositional. I heard several speakers and members of the congregation refer to public schools as "government schools." Parents were encouraged to send their kids to Christian schools or homeschool if they could afford to do so. The feeling about education in general was ambivalent at best. During one sermon the lead pastor Daniel Smesler, a tall, stern white man, said, "We do support you going to college . . . but don't let it make you so analytic that it ruins your faith. Get your degree, and then get victory over your degree."[66]

Over the week that I spent at Life Challenge, I was also befriended by one of the staffers' wives, an elegant woman of Native American ancestry who favored long skirts and whose hair fell like a curtain to the back of her knees. She and her friends were determined to get me to speak in tongues. I could see that it meant a lot to them, and so I really did try to get into the right frame of mind. During portions of the service, they instructed me to repeat, over and over, "Hallelujah" and "I love you." They assured me that repeating these phrases would "loosen your tongue." Truly I gave it my all, but the Holy Spirit never overtook me, and the reporter in me couldn't go along with the idea of faking it. The ladies seemed disappointed and a bit irritated. I left wondering if maybe they did expect me to fake it, just a little, at least until I broke through.

Toward the end of my time at Life Challenge, my elegant friend recommended I attend a church in my then hometown. She wrote down the name of the church and the letters NAR beside it, underlined twice. This was my first introduction to the New Apostolic Reformation (NAR).

ANDRÉ GAGNÉ, A theology professor at Concordia University in Canada and the author of *American Evangelicals for Trump: Dominion, Spiritual Warfare, and the End Times* (Routledge, 2023),[67] has studied the NAR for some number of years. "The movement," he tells me, is "dominion in and of itself—bringing about God's Kingdom in these networks." It took off with the late C. Peter Wagner, an author and missionary who spent a decade and a half in Bolivia.[68] Wagner no doubt absorbed some of his ideas in his extended encounters with the spiritual practices of other religions. In 1971, he became a professor of church growth at Fuller Theological Seminary's School of World Missions in Pasadena, California, and authored many books, including the seminal *Dominion! How Kingdom Action Can Change the World.*[69] Wagner was instrumental in popularizing the vision of modern-day apostles and prophets, "spiritual warfare" with demons, and "territorial spirits."[70] Above all, he gave voice to the ideology of Seven Mountains Dominionism—though Wagner gave credit to Lance Wallnau for some of his ideas.

The basic proposal behind the Seven Mountains ideology is that there are seven critical peaks of modern culture—government, business, media, education, entertainment and arts, family, and religion—and that Christians of a certain reactionary variety should rightfully dominate all of them.[71] The ideology reportedly got its start in 1975, when Loren Cunningham, a missionary leader, and Bill Bright, the founder of Campus Crusade for Christ (now known as "Cru"), allegedly heard messages from God urging them to invade the "seven spheres" of society. According to Wagner, the responsibility of Christians to take over "whatever molder of culture or subdivision God has placed them in" is really a matter of "taking dominion back from Satan."[72]

At the heart of the NAR is a political theology of power, and it spreads well beyond NAR networks. Victory Channel, owned by the televangelist Kenneth Copeland, consistently pushes far-right and pro-Trump disinformation, including the lie that the 2020 election was stolen. Gene Bailey, a pastor at Eagle Mountain Church in Colorado and the host of *Flashpoint*, which airs on the Victory Channel network, often appears at megachurches alongside Andrew Wommack and Lance Wallnau, where he leads the congregations in a prayer called the Watchman Decree:

> Whereas: we have been given legal power from heaven and now exercise our authority . . .

> Whereas: because of our covenant with God, we are equipped and delegated by Him to destroy every attempted advance of the enemy . . .

The prayer shifts to a series of declarations:

> We declare that we stand against wokeness, the occult, and every evil attempt against our nation . . .

> We declare that we take back and permanently control positions of influence and leadership in each of the Seven Mountains.

It continues in this vein for some time. Judicial rulings will be biblical, the one true God will be honored, and "AMERICA SHALL BE SAVED!"[73]

Not surprisingly, given its quest for dominion, the NAR sometimes behaves more like a political party than a church—a revolutionary political party that imagines itself destined not just to win elections but to rule the earth one day in the name of God. As Frederick Clarkson puts it, "Visions of global religious and political dominion have moved to the center of their religious identity and animate their activities. Increasingly this broad movement, led by the New Apostolic Reformation, has become an integral part of authoritarian politics around the world and is deeply infused in American politics at all levels."

THE NAR IS not just in some sense a political party, but a political party that guards its own identity as a kind of political secret. Unlike more traditional religious orders, the NAR seems reluctant to admit to its own existence. It does not have a readily accessible centralized website, nor does it advertise its system of hierarchy. In fact, the NAR does have a hierarchy, which goes by the name of the Fivefold Ministry, with apostles at the top, prophets one step down, then evangelists, pastors, and teachers.[74] It also has affiliated congregations, like Life Challenge in Odessa, Texas, and its sister church in my hometown, among many others. But you won't find them listed in any convenient public-facing guidebook. What you'll get from NAR affiliates is something like the note my friend at Life Challenge gave to me—a couple of lines, underscored, to let you know that this or that person or place is the real deal.

"Quantifying the membership of networks within the NAR is difficult, as it operates as relational networks rather than a denomination," explains André Gagné. "This creates a level of opacity within the NAR. The networks within the NAR function similarly to enterprises, with members embedded in various societal spheres, such as the Seven Mountains of culture." Lance Wallnau, Jim Garlow, Julie Green, and Cindy Jacobs are all the subject of reports that connect them with this movement, and if you listen to their sermons and the podcasts in which they participate, it's not hard to discern the features and language of the NAR's theology of power.[75] But you won't hear about the connection from them.

When I reached out by email to Julie Green, I received a response from "Julie's assistant," who perhaps protested too much. "Katherine," she wrote, "I have never heard of the New Apostolic Reformation. Is it an organization with members? Or just a title that has been conferred by the media on those who are preaching & teaching about what God is doing in this nation? Since we are not sure what you are referring to, I apologize, but I can't confirm anything for you."

"While the term New Apostolic Reformation has stood the test of time for more than a quarter of a century, some don't like it, mostly because others in the movement have been harshly criticized," says Clarkson. He points, by way of example, to a 2023 conference of the U.S. Coalition of Apostolic Leaders (USCAL), the U.S. arm of the International Coalition of Apostolic Leaders (ICAL). The event was "an attempt to distance the movement from its widely accepted name," he reports. But "while much of the summit sought to define what they are (and what they are not) in the face of criticism and controversy, the Dominionist agenda of the movement remains unchanged."

TO BE CLEAR, not all spirit warriors are explicitly affiliated with New Apostolic Reformation networks. Some are associated with other groups, and some appear to have switched affiliations and allegiances enough times to count as freelancers. I think of Leigh Valentine as one of them.

I came across Valentine in person at the 2023 Road to Majority conference, an annual gathering of Christian nationalist activists and strategists. As speaker after speaker proclaimed the attack on "wokeness," I briefly noticed the impeccably groomed woman seated behind me. With blond hair styled in lush waves and what appeared to be a Chanel suit in creamy shades, she epitomized a certain type of female Trump superfan. I couldn't tell if I'd spotted her on social media before, or if she just had the look of a woman I'd imagine attending one of Trump's black-tie parties at Mar-a-Lago.

Leigh Valentine is in fact a member of Women for Trump, and she has spoken from the podium in at least one Trump rally. Her social media accounts are well stocked with photos of herself alongside major figures from Trump world—Paula White, Kari Lake, Mark Meadows, Roger Stone, and MyPillow conspiracy monger Mike Lindell. Like many other aligned spirit warrior leaders, she claims to have foreseen the Trump experience long before anyone knew it would be a thing. "God had given me a dream back in the '80s and showed me that [Trump] would run and that he would win. A literal dream from heaven," Valentine said in 2018 on the *Faith & Freedom* TV program. "If you don't like the president, well, there's a lot of other countries you can go to. Just get out. This is the time to get out because the Trump train is rolling."[76]

Valentine's story properly begins in the 1980s, around the time she says she had that dream. A former Miss Missouri USA who had been forced to give up on pageant competitions after a brutal car accident, she developed close friendships with the leaders of a North Carolina sect called the Word of Faith Fellowship, which had affiliated churches in Ghana, Brazil, and elsewhere. According to a February 1995 exposé in the TV show *Inside Edition*,[77] as well as articles in the Associated Press,[78] *People* magazine,[79] and the *Washington Post*,[80] Word of Faith Fellowship practiced something called "demon-blasting," or forming a circle around people, including children and babies, who are accused of demon possession and shouting at them for hours.

At times the shouting turned into physical beatings, with reports eventually coming out about broken ribs, punched noses, and sexual abuse. "It wasn't enough to yell and scream at the devils. You literally had to beat the devils out of people," said Rick Cooper, a U.S. Navy veteran who belonged to the church for over twenty years.[81] The group was the subject of several investigations by

North Carolina state authorities; several members were charged and sentenced for criminal activities. According to state officials, however, some allegations of child abuse were hampered by the victims' reluctance to speak out.[82] (A portion of the Word of Faith website, titled "Response to Media Lies," includes video testimony from those who are presumably current members of the church; they dismiss the allegations as "absurdities" and attest to the "example of godly living" of Word of Faith church leaders.)[83]

Valentine's next move was to divorce her first husband, the evangelist Robert Valentine. Somewhere along the line she met Rev. Robert Tilton, a wealthy older televangelist and religious entrepreneur who was close to the Word of Faith leaders, and whose own church, Word of Faith Outreach Center Church, was based in Dallas. His television show, *Success-N-Life*, was running on over two hundred stations nationwide and taking in $80 million per year from its viewers.[84] An early master of telemarketing, Tilton employed hundreds of "prayer warriors" to answer his toll-free hotlines and collect callers' data, which he then used for mass mailings that generated still more cash.[85] It all came to an end with multiple lawsuits from disgruntled donors amid allegations of racketeering and fraud.[86] (None of the plaintiffs appear to have prevailed, in part due to the religious nature of Tilton's organization and First Amendment prohibition on the court's consideration of "the truth or falsity of religious convictions and the power of prayer, matters obviously beyond the cognizance of the state."[87])

Tilton had a wife of twenty-five years, but four months after his divorce he married Valentine. That marriage lasted only twenty-one months, but it was long enough, in Valentine's eyes, that Tilton's church and telemarketing assets should count as communal property.[88] She lost that claim in court. Forced to make her own way, Valentine reinvented herself as a cosmetics entrepreneur and "international evangelist."[89] There followed a bankruptcy in which it was revealed that she had continued to support the Word of Faith Fellowship in North Carolina with regular contributions—well after the allegations of child abuse were made known.[90] She appears to remain in contact with Word of Faith founder Jane Whaley, and stood beside her at a Trump rally in 2016.[91] At the same time, she appears to have become involved in a Holocaust museum for children.[92]

At the 2023 Road to Majority conference, shortly after taking my seat, I felt a tap on my shoulder. Turning around, I saw it was the Chanel-suited blond lady seated behind me, and I took note of her name tag. Valentine looked in fine form, and it was easy to sense that the Trump train had indeed come for her like a dream come true. Her conversational opener was to ask, "Are you Jewish?"

The vibe seemed oppositional, but I smiled in response. "Yes," I replied. "Are you?"

"No," she said, as though surprised by the question, but then added, "Well, I have some Jewish blood."

Then she asked, angrily, "Are you a journalist?"

THE SPIRIT WARRIORS believe that demons appear in a variety of forms and with all sorts of agendas. As perhaps befits a group that comes predominantly (but not exclusively) from lower income groups with lower educational attainment, the warriors often seem to see in the demons the face of "the expert." Evil takes the form of the scientist who tells you that vaccines save lives, the people who base their moral code on the principles of rationalism and empathy rather than biblical truth, or the professor who advocates a devious theory. "Satan has taken over the academic mountain, he's taking over government and the FBI, he's taking over Hollywood and Netflix," said Lance Wallnau at a July 2023 event at the Faith Life Church in Ohio.[93]

But the demons that matter most, and most reliably feature in the redemption narratives of spirit warriors, are those that have to do with sexuality and perceived sexual deviance. Anxieties about the gender order, and a particular concern with "the homosexual agenda" and "transgender ideology," are the rocket fuel that sends them hurling against the (perceived) establishment. These are the demons that get people out of the pews and ready to fight the decadent, liberal, secular enemy.

When I attended the Values Voters Summit (now called Pray, Vote, Stand) in Washington, D.C., in 2016, I was surprised to discover that nearly every speaker had bathrooms on their mind. One presenter after another announced some variation of "We've got to talk about transgender bathrooms!" The focus on the bathroom issue seemed to suggest that movement leadership had discovered a new and potentially unifying theme that would resonate with their base. And, as the polling suggested, once it could be linked to concerns about the maintenance and integrity of all-female spaces, such as prisons and shelters, or the principles of fairness in competitive sports and access to college sports scholarship money, the issue had potential as a kind of political kryptonite, with appeal well outside the conservative bubble.

Setting aside the merits of such concerns, a full-throated defense of women's sports was quite a paradox for leaders of the Christian nationalist movement, who wished to evince concern for the rights of women on one hand while eviscerating them with the other. Journalist Amy Littlefield recorded the impact at the 2023 Pray Vote Stand conference in a piece filed for the *Nation*. "That devotion to gender essentialism has always animated the Christian right; what's new is the intensity with which it is now focused on trans people. And as that focus intensifies, the rhetoric itself is darkening. I lost count of the number of times speakers mentioned 'demons' or the 'demonic agenda' they believe is at work on the Left."[94]

For some conservatives, issues related to transgender identity get to the essence of their religion—but for a great many others it matters even more in the political context. In July 2023, speaking at a gathering of the Her Voice Movement, a religious organization affiliated with "apostle" Lou Engle that aims to evangelize women and mobilize them for political causes on the right, Lance Wallnau said, "When it comes down to a movement in America, not everybody's going to become a Christian to fight transgenderism. But everybody will fight transgenderism if we frame it as an attack against your children. So the battle of public persuasion is on us."[95]

IN THEORY, THE spirits could play on either side of the political aisle. In reality, its anti-intellectualism and belief in the reality of demons makes this style of religion a more natural fit with the right than the left in America today. In the United States, according to Ryan Burge, conservative Pentecostals have proven to be among the most reliable—and reliably extreme—supporters of Christian nationalism. In his Survey of Church Going Americans in March 2022, Burge developed a system for scoring individuals on a scale of Christian nationalism. The analysis rests on responses to key questions, such as whether the federal government should declare the United States to be a Christian nation and whether the federal government should enforce the separation of church and state. According to his conclusions, Pentecostals score highest on measures of Christian nationalism.[96]

Some of the best evidence for the impact of the spirit warrior religion comes from data on voters identified as Hispanic or Latino.[97] Between 2016 and 2020, Trump picked up eight points among Latino voters (the numbers vary somewhat by source); in the 2018 midterm elections, Republicans cut into the Democratic advantage by an estimated ten points.[98] The state-level results should concern Democratic strategists even more. In heavily Latino Miami-Dade County—the largest county in what was once considered the biggest swing state in the nation—President Joe Biden won only 53 percent of the vote in 2020, compared with the 63 percent share won by Democratic presidential candidate Hillary Clinton in 2016 and the 62 percent share won by former president Barack Obama in 2012.[99] In 2024, Harris won even fewer.

Although the survey data linking these major shifts to Pentecostalism is thin, the anecdotal evidence is compelling. Pastor Frank Lopez, who heads the Jesus Worship Center, a Miami-based church with two campuses that is allied with KCIA, "an alliance of apostles and prophets," has characterized former president Biden, in Spanish on Twitter, as "an ignorant leader with a destructive agenda"[100] who is "rebelling against God." He hosts prominent Latin American conservatives on his YouTube show, where he has vied with the Argentinian writer Agustin Laje Arrigoni to serve up the reddest of meat to the culture warriors in the audience. The "New Left," as he calls it, promotes abortion as a way of killing off the poor. It seeks economic chaos. Its main beneficiaries are universities, journalists, feminists, and "globalist organizations." Ronald Reagan and Donald Trump were as one, in his telling, in opposing this defining agenda of the Democratic Party.[101]

Lopez is hardly a voice in the wilderness; he serves on the board of directors of the Asociación de Ministros Hispanos del Sur de la Florida, a Miami-based association of pastors that has coordinated activities with Ralph Reed's Faith and Freedom Coalition.

Even as it makes inroads among Latino communities, the religion of the spirit warriors appears to be surging among white nationalist extremist groups. Some factions of the Oath Keepers and the Proud Boys—both associated with the January 6 coup attempt—have aligned themselves with neocharismatic forms of Christianity. Some sectors of the Constitutional Sheriffs and Peace Officers Association, a reactionary group that aims to recruit inside law enforcement agencies, also promote the movement's ideas.[102] The group's founding meeting in 2013 featured a man who was reportedly a New Apostolic

Reformation adherent and who went on to become the leader of the Republican caucus in the Washington State House.[103] Stewart Rhodes, then leader of the Oath Keepers, now convicted for seditious conspiracy, was present at the creation, too.[104]

Neocharismatic forms of Christianity are rife with "the idea that God's army of soldiers is in an active conflict with Satan's forces," Brad Onishi, author of *Preparing for War: The Extremist History of White Christian Nationalism—And What Comes Next* (Broadleaf, 2023), tells me. The movement "envisions the role of the Church as the dominating agent of God on earth," he says. "White nationalist and militia groups find in these theologies a call to battle that resonates with their worldview—one that sees the United States in conflict against domestic enemies."

As the language of spiritual warfare has taken hold across America, it has gotten consistently more bloodthirsty. Paul Doyle, a Pentecostal pastor of the Cornerstone Church in Batavia, New York, offers a case in point. In April 2022, he took aim at "leftist agenda policies," "woke churches," and "vaccines and critical race theory." He framed the midterm elections as "a new battle of good and evil," and he left no doubt that the political color of evil is blue. "Jesus bloodied himself for me," he said, "and I am ready to bloody myself for him."[105]

At the 2022 Road to Majority conference in Nashville, Florida congressman Byron Donalds, who is Black, showed how this kind of Christian nationalism could unite at least some reactionaries across color lines. Later nominated by members of the House Freedom Caucus as House speaker prior to Kevin McCarthy's confirmation, Donalds served on a panel titled "Draw the Line: The Hijacking of Our Mountains of Societal Influence and How to Reclaim Them."[106] Emceeing this panel, with its overtly dominionist title, was Madgie Nicolas, the Faith & Freedom Coalition's National Strategist of African American Engagement. She introduced Donalds and the four other participants as "four gatekeepers that [have] been helping, enforcing the Seven Mountains of influence." "We need to reclaim our dignity in this country," Nicholas declared. "We need to reclaim our sovereignty, and we need to reclaim our White House."[107]

Much of the panel discussion was centered on the supposedly false history of racial oppression in America. As Michael Harriot, author of *Black AF History: The Unwashed Story of America* (Dey Street Books, 2023), noted in the *Grio*, "To successfully rise in the ranks of the GOP, Black conservatives have to do more than deny the existence of racism; they must validate their conservative credentials by proving that they are willing to sacrifice Black lives." Referring to South Carolina senator Tim Scott and Kentucky attorney general Daniel Cameron, he added, "In their cases, erasing the lives of Black people is just part of their job descriptions."[108]

Recounting a story about what she claimed to be a Democratic voter registration operation, Adianis Morales Robles, a GOP operative, spoke at the Road to Majority conference in spirit warrior vernacular when she said, "God was showing me the injustices that these organizations, these demonic organizations, are doing to our people."[109] In fact, the spirit warrior formula has proven so politically effective that it has been adopted even by leaders who are not in any formal way part of the religious movement. Political figures like former national security adviser Michael Flynn and former president of Brazil Jair Bolsonaro identify as Catholic, and yet they outdo many Pentecostals in their commitment to spiritual warfare, their professed belief in the reality of demons, and the way they fuse national identity with a reactionary idea of religious righteousness.[110] The extraordinarily violent rhetoric coming out of right-wing political gatherings is a reflection of the movement's influence. At the 2021 Road to Majority conference, which I attended, speakers inveighed that America is "on the precipice," careening toward a "socialist revolution," "anarchy," and "chaos," and is under the thumb of the most despicable human beings imaginable—namely Democrats, who were referred to as "the enemy," "Satanic," and "agents of evil." "The backlash is coming," Senator Rick Scott of Florida warned. "Just mount up and ride to the sounds of the guns, and they are all over this country. It is time to take this country back."[111]

"'TIS THE TIME's plague, when madmen lead the blind," writes Shakespeare in *King Lear*.[112] It is a helpful image to bear in mind when considering the relationship between the spiritual leaders of the antidemocratic reaction and their congregations of rank-and-file warriors. The two ends of the new hierarchy suffer from distinct pathologies; yet both arise from the same fundamental conditions of society. The prophets and the demagogues—the Thinkers and Sergeants—have figured out how to lift themselves above the crowd in a time when competition for status is brutal; the infantry have found a way to resolve the anxieties and grievances associated with life in the lower middle of the distribution.

There is a tendency today to reduce social and political analysis to studying the antics of a handful of powerful personalities. Many people have blamed America's current political dysfunction on Donald Trump. They take for granted that the problem will go away when he, along with his fellow religious nationalist demagogues, at long last depart for wherever they are going. But the spirit warriors aren't going to disappear with them. They might very well choose leaders who are even madder. Major religious transformations don't happen for shallow reasons. Their causes run deep. In certain instances, they help clear the ground and set the stage for the rise of authoritarian leaders who tell us that they alone can fix whatever ails us.

Will the burdens of the single mother of three who dances with abandon at the Life Challenge Church really ease when the movement shutters her children's public school, when her government benefits are brought to a halt, when her birth control pills are outlawed, and when her boss is legally permitted to demote or fire her simply because she is a woman? There is no reason to think so. But the appeal of the spirit warrior religion isn't hard to fathom. It is easily discernible in the demographic data. The religion of material demons in the here and now works best with those for whom the here and now doesn't work. Religion in America is starting to look more like religion in Brazil and Guatemala because some parts of America, in some respects, are starting to resemble Brazil and Guatemala: rife with conspiracies and disinformation, increasingly unequal, bitterly divided, and unstable. If we want people to choose different gods, we might think about tackling the conditions that lead them to prefer one kind over another. In the meantime, we can expect the ranks of the spirit warriors to grow, and we can predict that, under the direction of their leaders, they will fight valiantly against any effort to solve the problems from which they emerged.

CHAPTER 9

God and Man in Las Vegas

L as Vegas, August 2023. The documentary film team from Germany meets me in the hotel lobby near the Strip. They are young, vigorously athletic, tall, mostly blond, and dressed in hipster grunge. They are vegetarian, drink moderately if at all, and are devoted to their early morning workouts at whatever hotel gym they happen to find themselves, like a perfectly Teutonic Fantastic Four. They have spent much of the past year traveling and filming in conflict zones around the world. They laugh and tell me about their Starbucks game, which they call "Starbies," where each of them orders something crazier than the last. They are here to show their viewers some of the glorious weirdness of America, and they are in a good mood. I am happy to have been invited to accompany them as a guide of sorts. With Trump facing, at this time, ninety-one felony counts across four criminal cases and his supporters growing increasingly surly, I am especially eager to get their take on what we are about to experience here in Las Vegas.

We bundle into the team van, drive about a half hour from the Strip, and spill out in a parking lot crammed with pickup trucks and midsize SUVs. We head into a public park whose grounds are dominated by enormous white tents. A large placard announces the event: REAWAKEN AMERICA. The setting is somewhat atypical for the ReAwaken America Tour, as I know from prior experience. The organization usually prefers to host their roving events at megachurches.[1]

Outside it is scorching, with temperatures in the low hundreds; thankfully, the tents are lightly air-conditioned. Inside the tent complex, the mood is collegial, with the sense of kindred solidarity that comes with shared struggles against a common enemy.

The first thing I notice is that the T-shirts are getting nastier. SIZE MATTERS blares one man's shirt over enlarged images of bullets of various calibers. IT'S RINO SEASON, reads another, with an image of Trump carrying a long gun. Another man's T-shirt features dozens of white male soldiers and the words DIVERSITY IS DESTRUCTION across the bottom. Quite a few bear slogans associated with QAnon, along with numbered fragments of text from the Bible that are associated with battle. To be sure, I see plenty of the old standbys: GOD, GUNS, AND TRUMP, a few F*CK BIDENS, and a MAKE MEN MEN AGAIN on a man who glares around the room like he wants to start a fight.

And then there is BLITZKRIEG. The Germans find this genuinely shocking, and I see them attempting to capture the wearer on video as he sits in his seat.

The first tent, closer to the entrance of the complex, is filled with rows of booths hawking "non-woke" books for children, antivax books for all ages, membership in evangelistic communities led by "prophetic" entrepreneurs, drinking water purifiers and nutritional supplements, the *Epoch Times*, a conspiracy-filled far-right media outlet affiliated with China's Fulan Gong religious movement and whose CFO was later arrested and indicted for a $67 million money-laundering scheme (he has pleaded not guilty)[2], Trumpy swag, and a whole lot of survivalist gear.[3] At one booth, women are raising donations for the January 6 insurrectionists, cast here as heroes unfairly imprisoned "in the DC Gulag." As I walk past the menacing T-shirts and through to the entrance of the second, much more capacious tent, I estimate that today's attendance is just south of two thousand. Most ReAwaken America tour stops, including one I recently attended at a California megachurch, draw crowds of this size or larger.[4]

The man behind ReAwaken America is Clay Clark, a Tulsa, Oklahoma–based entrepreneur and business coach who discovered a whole new angle on life during the COVID pandemic.[5] When his media production company began to run short on business in 2020, he knew who was to blame. He filed suit against the city of Tulsa for its mask mandates, and quickly gained prominence in the rapidly emerging antipandemic movement.[6] Like so many who came of political age in that moment, he soon discovered cures that the government was supposedly hiding. He also maintained that the COVID vaccines contained "luciferase," a dreadful compound allegedly made of Jeffrey Epstein's DNA.[7] Having lighted on a plot that went all the way to Davos and involved every bad actor imaginable—Bill Gates, Black Lives Matter, the World Economic Forum, the Serbian conceptual artist Marina Abramović, along with a nefarious climate activism movement—Clay resolved to spread the word through his movable conference series. In publicity materials for its gatherings, ReAwaken America bills America's political and spiritual challenges as a battle between "the Great ReAwakening" and "the Great Reset," the Holy Bible versus the evil masterminds behind COVID-19.[8]

Other key figures in the ReAwaken syndicate include Mike Flynn, the disgraced former national security adviser; Mike Lindell, the pillow man and election fraud funder; Eric Trump, who speaks frequently at these events; and Trump's longtime mentor Roger Stone. Sean Feucht, the guitar-strumming spirit warrior, often drops in to lead the crowd in song, and maybe raise some extra cash—at a previous ReAwaken America Tour, a woman who claimed to be a representative of his ministry, Let Us Pray, was selling stickers bearing the organization's name for $5 apiece. Robert F. Kennedy Jr. delivered presentations at several ReAwaken America events before launching his run for president (with a massive wad of cash at his back thanks to Timothy Mellon, heir to the Mellon banking fortune, who is also a Trump megadonor).[9] Speakers scheduled for appearance in Las Vegas include Alex Jones, the infamous purveyor of the most heinous conspiracy theories;[10] Sherri Tenpenny, identified by the Center for Countering Digital Hate as one of the top twelve most influential COVID deniers;[11] the podcaster and conspiracist Mel K, who pushes elaborate fairy tales involving global treachery;[12] Jackson Lahmeyer, who founded Pastors for Trump, which claims to have over seven thousand pastor members across the nation;[13] Peter Navarro, a former adviser to Trump who was convicted of contempt of Congress for failing to comply with a subpoena from the House select committee investigating the January 6 coup attempt;[14] and a squadron of demon-haunted apostles and prophets from the Christian nationalist movement.

The Las Vegas conference is the third such event I have attended in person, and it is by a significant measure the most bloodthirsty. The rhetoric coming from the podium is even more violent than the slogans on the T-shirts.

Clay Clark, speaking at a breakneck pace, cheerfully gets the conspiracy machine cranked up like an auctioneer on crystal meth:

"The World Economic Forum has the logo 666, look it up, their logo is 666, and if you're new to reading the Bible, in the Bible it tells you where Satan lives. The Bible tells you in the book of Revelation, it tells you Revelation 9-11, okay, that Satan dwelleth by the former temple of Apollo. Satan dwells where the former temple of Apollo is. Who knows that? Revelation 9-11. Okay? And it also tells you that Satan dwells where Antipas was partnered. And Geneva is the location of that, and that is the location of the World Economic Forum, and that is the location of the World Health Organization, and that is the location of the United Nations, and that is the location of SERVE, and SERVE's logo is 666, are we all on the same page here?"

Clay hands off the microphone to Mike Flynn, who describes the "global alliance against the United States America." He offers a variant of the Great Replacement conspiracy theory—the idea that devious elites are plotting to replace good (white) Americans with aliens, Jews, or other undesirables. With the help of Alex Jones, this kind of garbage has spread faster than fidget spinners through the far-right propaganda-sphere.

Stew Peters, a former bounty hunter and antivax conspiracist with a large online following, steps up to the podium next, and the gathering takes a grisly turn. "When [Anthony Fauci] is convicted after a short and fast but thorough trial, he will hang from a length of thick rope," says Peters. The audience roars their approval. "When [Hunter Biden] is convicted . . . he will get . . . Death!" More roars.[15]

"We all have one common enemy, his name is Satan, and right now his minions are trying to run the country," Peters continues. "Liberals, democrats, communists, lizard things, we got a lot of words for these creatures."

He demands the "restoration of the rightful president of America." What does he want the anointed one to do once restored? Revenge, cold and bloody. "All we need is a body of water, a length of rope, and a heavy millstone." "What we want is Nuremburg trials 2.0." "We are going to see extreme accountability. Natural accountability," he shouts, his voice getting louder. "Permanent accountability with extreme prejudice!"

One of the German team members asks me, uneasily, "Are we safe here?" I reply that this place is probably no more dangerous to us personally than the rest of Las Vegas. I believe this to be true, but it sounds hollow even as I say it. "So the danger is to the rest of the country," he says, nodding.

The racism, too, is more transparent than usual. "Big Fani. Big fat Fani. Big fat *Black* Fani Willis," Peters shouts as he launches into an attack on Fulton County DA Fani Willis and on the Georgia judge who is presiding over Trump's criminal charges in that state. While the overwhelming majority of attendees at ReAwaken America events are white, people of color are not entirely absent. They show up in similarly themed T-shirts and are featured on the podium. At a ReAwaken America tour stop I attended the previous year in San Marcos, California, I spotted in the audience several dozen individuals wearing caps or T-shirts bearing the word LEXIT, an acronym for a faith-based organization that encourages Latino voters to exit the Democratic Party and support Republican candidates instead. In Las Vegas, the presence of a smattering of people of color in the audience doesn't stop speakers like Peters from linking Blackness with everything bad in America or displaying an interest in lynching-style retribution.

Even the preachers invited to speak at the event seem exceptionally focused on making their enemies feel the pain. The Black pastor Mark Burns, a stalwart warm-up act at Trump rallies, follows Peters onstage. There is no acknowledgment of Peters's anti-Black racism, but there is plenty of additional rhetorical bloodshed. "This is a God nation, this is a Jesus nation, and you will never take my God and my gun out of this nation," he says. "I have come ready to declare war on Satan and every race-baiting democrat that tries to destroy our way of life here in the United States of America."

Jews are not entirely absent from the event, either, although their religious identity may be like that of Roseanne Barr, who was born to a Jewish family but has gone on to push Holocaust denial and anti-Semitic tropes. Introduced from the stage by Clay Clark as "sure to offend, challenge, trigger and force you to wake up to the mind control of your underlings,"[16] Barr opened her fifty-minute religious confessional with the declaration that "I am here to do some spiritual warrior stuff with you guys today." Then she begins to shout. "It's time for the heavens to open and people to receive, people to receive the truth about Jesus!"[17] She continues in ever-higher registers, "No weapon formed against us shall have dominion, it shall not proffer. On earth as it is in heaveeeeeeeeeen!!!" She screeches for some time, then moderates her tone.

"That's our task, to lift this place from the hell they've created for our children!"[18]

Who is the "they" she's talking about? It's "the people who own every cent in this world and also keep track of it," she explains. For the record, Barr recently put one of her two L.A. homes on the market for $3.5 million and then purchased an additional home before decamping to her forty-six-acre macadamia nut farm on Hawaii's Big Island.[19]

In Las Vegas, as at other ReAwaken America tour stops, Jews, or at least their supposed cosmopolitan alter egos, inevitably come in for abuse. In preparation for the tour stop in Miami, the organizers invited Charlie Ward, who had praised Hitler for "warning us," and Scott McKay, a "Patriot streetfighter" who has expressed openly pro-Hitler views on Rumble. They were meant to share the stage with Eric Trump, who had appeared on podcasts with each man on numerous occasions.[20]

"Hitler was fighting the same people we're trying to take down," McKay had said. "These people are so elusive and slippery and cunning that we ended up having World War II."[21]

When the clips were publicized on MSNBC, McKay and Ward were disinvited.[22] Even so, as my German friends can easily pick up, the dog whistles keep playing the old fascist tunes, and you don't even need a dog to hear them. Mike Flynn, Clay Clark, Peters, and conspiracy podcaster Mel K all identify the archvillains as "globalist billionaires." The masterminds are "the IMF, the World Bank, and financial elites," Ms. K intones. In case there was any doubt about what these villains look like, she and the others repeatedly name George Soros and "the Rothschilds."[23]

Flynn takes back the floor to hawk his latest book, *The Citizen's Guide to Fifth Generation Warfare (CG5GW)*. The point, he says, is "to prepare Americans and freedom loving people everywhere for our current global wartime reality."

Clay Clark pops up again to say that there is hope for persecuted real Americans after all. You just need to put your money in the right place. As ever at these events, the transition from demonizing to fleecing is seamless—at least for those who are cashing in. Clark introduces the audience to the head of a company called Beverly Hills Precious Metals. The man from L.A. offers the promise of a financial bolt-hole for the coming apocalypse. "Typically people are saying, I'm going to turn my 401K or my IRA into one of the gold or precious metals, and not have it be a taxable asset," he says. "You can do that now for minimal fees."

The fact that some number of people here have retirement accounts with enough money on hand to consider precious metals investment strategies strikes the Germans as curious. The amounts under discussion—you can start with as little as $100!—are perhaps more revealing, I reply. There appear to be few genuinely poor people in this crowd, but apart from those on the podium or their support staff, no obviously rich people, either—at least as far as the eye can tell. You can see it in the parking lot, which features neither clunkers nor Range Rovers. You can see it in those clothing choices that are not conspiracy-themed: Tommy Bahama shirts for men, department-store clamdiggers and light jewelry for the women. The attendees are older than the average American—I'm going to guess the median age is fifty—and they look on balance slightly overfed but not in a terribly unhealthy way. Many appear to spend a fair amount of time outdoors. Even the one woman who lets me know she has a vacation home in Las Vegas doesn't look like the kind of urban professional that populates the law firms and banks in America's big cities. They are in a sense what is left of the non-college-educated middle class in a country that has left that class behind in a cloud of dust.

I fall into conversation with a woman who is wearing a T-shirt with the Bible verse Ephesians 6:11, and the words "Put on the whole armor of God, that ye may be able to stand against the wiles of the devil." This passage is especially popular with today's spirit warrior charismatics, and from what I can glean from our conversation, she communes with the Holy Spirit every Sunday. She briefly tells me her life story: She runs her own hair salon but revenue has flatlined. Her marriage fell apart a decade earlier, and one of her kids no longer speaks to her. "I think they got to him," she says. "Who?" I ask. "Them," she says distractedly, gesturing toward some presumably evil plot taking place outside the tent. "The homosexual lobby."

When she speaks of her son, her expression is so sad and desperate that I feel a certain sympathy. The spirit warrior creed is undoubtedly her answer to the frustrations of her own life, a means of securing the joy and self-respect she struggles to maintain at work and is unlikely to find in her turbulent home life. But then she blames it on the "gay agenda" and would no doubt support a nihilistic strongman to smash it. It is perfectly understandable that some people develop the urge to burn it all down. But that doesn't make it a victimless crime.

MY INFORMAL IMPRESSION of the Las Vegas crowd matches with economist John Komlos's analysis of 933 individuals arrested in connection with the January 6 attack on the Capitol. (By January 2024, more than 1200 individuals had been arrested in connection with their actions on January 6, with charges ranging from disorderly conduct and assaulting police officers to seditious conspiracy. Over 700 pled guilty. Around 170 had been convicted, including 210 who pled guilty to felony offenses, while some individuals had their cases dismissed.)[24] Only 36 insurrectionists came from zip codes with average incomes below $20,000—whereas one would have expected 230 such people from a random sample of the population. Only 18 came from zip codes making $150,000 or more—compared with an expected 165 from a random sample. "This finding dovetails with the argument that the right-wing populist movement is driven primarily by the anxieties associated with transition from an industrial to a postindustrial economy," says Komlos. "That includes America's enormous income inequality, the frustrations caused by globalization for those without a college education, and the financial crisis that bailed out the upper echelons of society without paying much attention to the problems of Mainstreet America."[25]

But there are other factors at play. A 2021 survey published by the University of Chicago's Chicago Project on Security & Threats, titled "Understanding American Domestic Terrorism," reports that many of those who were arrested for the Capitol attack live in communities with increasingly diverse populations.

"The greater the decrease in non-Hispanic white, the higher the rate of sending insurrectionists," say the authors. Principal investigator Robert Pape gets to the heart of the matter: "We're finding evidence that the key driver is fear that rights of Hispanic people and Black people are outpacing the rights of white people." A complete explanation, then, does not reduce to either economic anxiety or racial anxiety on their own. We need to think in terms of the toxic combination of these factors (and others).[26]

The German crew and I decide to take a break from the speeches and walk the crowd. I chat with a man working one of the vendor booths. He is hawking nutritional supplements for people who believe they have been harmed by COVID vaccines. Literature for his product bears an endorsement from Mike Flynn. The man working the booth tells me Flynn is a partner in the business. Another man joins the conversation and turns to me for a view. I confess that I have been vaccinated and feel just fine. He edges away, laughing nervously. His fear seems genuine.

I notice boxes of free booklets at the entrance to ReAwaken America, and I see the same booklets throughout the event—placed on seats, stacked in a few tables, and in boxes scattered around the event for free distribution. As I pick up a copy, a man working at one of the booths nods and tersely adds, "You should read that." It is titled "Battlefield United States." The cover features photoshopped tanks and warplanes attacking the Statue of Liberty. The all-caps subtitle speaks in prepper code: PREPARE FOR EMP "GRID DOWN" NUCLEAR ATTACK WHEN SUMMER IS NEAR. TIME IS SHORT. STOCKPILE SUPPLIES A.S.A.P. A line at the bottom helpfully reminds readers that "Coronavirus was planned 'event 201' global pandemic exercise." The back cover adds, "All human population to be RFID chipped *All firearms to be confiscated *All resistance to be eliminated . . . TOTAL ENSLAVEMENT OF MANKIND."

Mainly Las Vegas is about fear. The overriding message is that nowhere is safe. "They" will come after you in the churches; they'll come after your kids in the schoolhouses; they're out to destroy your health; and they won't stop until they have robbed you of every penny and changed your gender against your will. The thirst for blood raging through these tents, I can't help but think, is unmistakably an index of this ever-growing, ever-morphing fear.

If there is a savior for this crowd, a man who will face down the demons and set the world right, his name is Donald Trump. Apart from the occasional grumble that Trump is sometimes not Trumpy enough, you are no more likely to hear a bad word about Jesus than about the orange-skinned savior that this crowd appears to worship. Enlarged pictures of Trump's face, superimposed on a young Arnold Schwarzeneggeresque body, with eagles and crosses and Jesus by his side, are displayed throughout the venue.[27] And even while the event is taking place, everyone knows that Trump is the front-runner—by far—in the race for the Republican nomination for the 2024 presidential election. The runners-up in the Republican contest are notable mainly for promising to pardon Trump and/or fill his mighty shoes. Which makes clear that this conference, contrary to outward appearances, is a partisan political gathering.

In another time, ReAwaken America could have been laughed off as just another festival of snake oil hucksterism in the long American tradition of separating suckers from their money through entrepreneurial grifting. But this group isn't fringe; it is representative of what one of the nation's two major parties has become. Majorities of Republican voters live in the same fear-filled, fact-free world that the Las Vegas crowd inhabits. They continue to believe in the Big Lie that the 2020 election was stolen; they think Trump was the greatest president ever; they say that Trump's indictments are just political persecution from a "weaponized" system of justice; and they have been persuaded that a global cabal is trying to strip away from them everything they hold dear.

To be sure, ReAwaken America has many devotedly Christian critics, and some of them are organized. Among the most prominent is an Episcopal priest, Rev. Nathan Empsall, leader of the group Faithful America, which runs digital campaigns to mobilize the social-justice Christian vote. "ReAwaken America's speakers and organizers have bragged that God is on their side," Empsall tells me. "It's either 'Team Jesus' or godless globalism, with no middle ground. The irony here is that in spite of the religious right's victim complex, and its constant complaints about liberals attacking Christians, it's the self-professed Christian nationalist leaders like Mike Flynn who are erasing countless other Christian voices by blotting out the Black church tradition, mainline Protestants, progressive Catholics and more." Faithful America has paid for billboard messages that counter ReAwaken America's messages of hate. But this does not seem to have put much of a dent in the ReAwaken roadshow's schedule.

THE FIRST DAY of the tour has left the Germans looking perplexed but still somewhat upbeat. I recognize in them the ability to compartmentalize, an indispensable skill for anyone who routinely works in conflict zones. Though they seem disgusted by what they have seen and heard, they, too, are reporters, and they are clearly pleased with the footage they collected. "The worse the better," I quip, sticking to the strategy of deflection for the sake of the story. We agree to meet up in the hotel lobby the next morning.

Day two of ReAwaken America proves mercifully brief. We head off into another scorching morning and arrive at the tour's patch of parkland. But the Germans are not in the mood to linger. After two hours in the hot and dusty tents, a member of the team tells me they've seen enough. They seem exhausted. On the ride back home, he turns to me with a grim expression and says, "How does this happen?"

Paranoia and conspiracism have always been a feature of American life, I suggest to my German friends. From the assassination of JFK to the attack on the World Trade Center, some number of Americans have responded to moments of crisis by embracing conspiracy theories, and others have sought to gain profit or power by exploiting this vulnerability. In the aftermath of 9/11, David Ray Griffin, a professor at the Claremont School of Theology, developed a cottage industry retailing evidence-free theories that the Twin Towers fell through an internal demolition job intended to mobilize the American public for war.[28] He persisted in pushing these conspiracy theories through a series of books and interviews with people like Alex Jones, even after they had been thoroughly and repeatedly debunked by independent experts.

I add that this kind of conspiracy theorizing has appealed to many people on the American left, too, pushing them into the political fringes and often into total distrust of the entire political system.[29]

In the annals of conspiracy theory history, however, as the ReAwaken America Tour makes clear, the COVID pandemic was an epic event that may ultimately loom much larger than JFK or 9/11. And Sergeants and Power Players of the Christian nationalist movement were at the forefront of the war on the pandemic response. On March 15, 2020, the Florida pastor Guillermo Maldonado urged the congregants at his Miami megachurch to show up for worship services in person. "Do you believe God would bring his people to his house to be contagious with the virus? Of course not," he said.[30] Rodney Howard-Browne, pastor of the River at Tampa Bay Church in Florida, mocked people concerned about the disease as "pansies" and insisted he would only shutter the doors to his packed church "when the rapture is taking place."[31] In a sermon that was live-streamed on Facebook, Tony Spell, a pastor in Louisiana, said, "We're also going to pass out anointed handkerchiefs to people who may have a fear, who may have a sickness and we believe that when those anointed handkerchiefs go, that healing virtue is going to go on them as well."[32] Jerry Falwell Jr., the disgraced president of Liberty University, joined the chorus: "You know, impeachment didn't work, and the Mueller report didn't work, and Article 25 didn't work, and so maybe now this is their next, ah, their next attempt to get Trump," he said.[33]

The paranoia far outlasted the pandemic. Groups like Moms for Liberty and ReAwaken America rose up on the anger and frustration of the pandemic period, yet they found new ways to grow even after the threat of the disease subsided. With the public health crisis mostly resolved, the Germans want to know, why is the mood still so dark?

The immediate cause, I suggest, has much to do with Donald Trump and the movement that supports him. The Big Lie about election fraud took up where the pandemic left off. And the criminal indictments and convictions of Donald Trump were proof positive of the crowd's fondest fears. For the leaders of the ReAwaken event, Trump's legal problems are not a setback; they are like Red Bull on a Saturday night. They prove, in effect, as other T-shirts pronounce, that ALEX JONES WAS RIGHT and ROGER STONE DID NOTHING WRONG. More than that, the Trump indictments and convictions have lent audiences like this a political focus and meaning that far transcends their marginal status.

The Germans don't seem reassured. The open endorsements of fascism, the grift, and especially the threats of violence against political enemies—it troubles them. "Isn't that illegal?" they say to me. They seem genuinely shaken. "What has happened to these people? In Germany this kind of thing would be against the law."

I note that much of America's political class have mostly decided that they would rather look away than acknowledge what is happening on the ground in America. It's easier for everybody, they think, if we just pretend that this is another round of politics as usual.

On the Republican side, the representatives of the supposed "establishment"—including some that the Las Vegas crowd calls RINOs, along with the ultra-wealthy donors who bankroll the operation—have, with several notable exceptions, signaled that they are fine with the ReAwaken America mindset. They have let us know that it is okay to regard a convicted felon who put himself above the Constitution (in his own vice president's words) as just another horse in the race. Sure, they may have at times put their money and hopes into other candidates who message differently—but they stop short of criticizing Trump, and they too echo his election lies and assert that his multiple felony convictions are nothing more than political persecution. They grasp that what really matters is defeating the big-government, woke-mob Democrats, who may, well . . .

I lose the thread of the argument for a moment, and we sit in silence. I realize I'm getting worked up, but I resume.

Even some of the anti-Trump Republicans seem to participate in the delusion, I point out. They tell themselves that it is all about Trump, a single bad actor, and that the old Republican Party will come back with its patrician civility, small-government conservatism, and support for traditional values. They seem oblivious to the reality that, when asked to choose an alternative, much of the Republican base has been groomed to opt for whichever candidate most resembles Trump. The candidate that promises to break the most laws, crush the most skulls, offend the most liberals, and bulldoze through all democratic institutions tends to be the one that gets their vote.

It is the self-censorship of the rest of the American political world that I find harder to explain to my German friends. A good number of those who populate the political analysis desks at the big news operations and take seats on major media panels keep telling us that America has become increasing "partisan," that it is divided into "tribes" that have their own "epistemes" or "moral language" and prefer to signal in-group loyalty than acknowledge the truth. Some say this is a matter of letting "free speech" do its magic. They assure us we can restore civility by opening ourselves to the perspectives of others. If only we would listen to and empathize with the other side, everything would return to normal.

"I guess they haven't been to Las Vegas," one of my German friends says, and I laugh.

She is right, of course. There is no "episteme" in the ReAwakened world. There is no supposed fact that can't be flipped with the next turn of the conspiracy wheel. There isn't the slightest interest in other "perspectives." There is only a concerted and well-funded effort to promote as much incivility as possible.

Above all, the idea that this event has much of anything to do with free speech is laughable. That principle is about establishing the basis for open discussion in a society that wishes to be governed by reason. The point of Las Vegas is to demolish the very possibility of reasonable discussion. Speech here is just the weapon of choice, and it is unapologetically aimed at anxious, vulnerable people for the purpose of separating them from their money and making them politically useful.

What the people on the podium are selling, and what the people in the crowd are buying, is the license to ignore reality altogether, and to deny any fact that contradicts their emotional desires, including the desire for revenge.

One of my German friends smiles at me, as if suggesting that I can relax. By the time we pull up at the Strip, I can see that she and her colleagues got the point many miles ago.

CHAPTER 10

No Exit

The red-white-and-blue world of Christian nationalism is a fascinating place, but it can also get claustrophobic. After a dozen years of reporting on the subject, I began to feel restless and perhaps at times a little unsafe. When I relocated, temporarily and for family reasons, from the United States to the UK in 2021, I therefore welcomed the distance. Though I planned to continue my reporting with regular return trips and a seemingly permanent virtual presence, I felt lighter and more carefree. London was my escape.

We found lodgings through an old friend in the Clerkenwell neighborhood, a jumble of Georgian row houses and converted warehouses that, almost two centuries ago, provided the setting for Charles Dickens's novels *Oliver Twist* and *Great Expectations* and that now serves as a hub for media, design, and technology firms. It felt as far from MAGA-land as seemed decent to imagine. In those first days after the move, I set off on late-summer morning walks past eclectic restaurants and pub staff sweeping out the remains of the previous evening. I was elated. Here was a faraway perch from which to gain some perspective on the madness back in the homeland.

ON A SUNDAY morning shortly after moving in, I step outside our new apartment for another exploratory ramble, and I hear singing. Humming along to a familiar-sounding tune, I discover a church at the other end of our very short block. The Clerkenwell Medical Mission is an elegant, square-shaped Victorian structure, and as the plaque outside explains, it was built to evangelize the disabled. A newer banner overhead announces the current incarnation of the building as the GraceLife Community Church.

The tune that I'm humming, I belatedly realize, is "Great Is Thy Faithfulness," a contemporary worship classic at America's evangelical and nondenominational churches. The songwriter, Chris Rice, was something of a celebrity until 2019, when a church in Lexington, Kentucky, launched an investigation following accusations from a former student that Rice had sexually assaulted him on multiple occasions at youth retreats. (The church's pastor issued a public statement deeming the allegations "credible because of the source of the allegations and corroborating evidence we have discovered.")[1] No matter, I think; the church on my street can't be blamed for the misdeeds of the songwriter, and likely they don't even know about it. I decide to take a look.

A friendly woman who appears to be in her mid-twenties, wearing a blue dress and box braids with a toddler at her side, waves me in at the door. "Are you new here?" she asks. She introduces herself as Dorcas and invites me to take some literature at the front table. I pick up several titles: *Your Local Church and Why It Matters*; *Answering the Hard Questions About Forgiveness*; and *The Believer's Armor: God's Provision for Your Protection*. Opening the last one to the front page, I read: "Every time God's Word leads a person to salvation, it demonstrates its power to cut a swath through Satan's dominion of darkness and bring light to a darkened soul."

The interior of the church is as olde-world as the outside. Time-worn rows of wooden pews face an elevated pulpit in the old style, and a dozen arched windows line the second story. The crowd inside is alive with smiles and hugs, and groups of congregants are engaging in boisterous conversation before the service. Perhaps the majority, like Dorcas, are Black, but I also see a mix of white, East Asian, and South Asian congregants, too. On the surface, I think as I look around the light-filled room, this gathering bears little resemblance to some of the traditional Southern Baptist services I have attended in the U.S., with their suburban settings and often racially homogenous congregations. Then the preacher ascends to his pulpit, and I take my seat for the sermon.

*   *   *

"WOULDN'T YOU BE happy for it all to be over?" the preacher intones. He is Black, and he speaks with an American accent. From the literature I gather his name is Adam Waller.

"Don't you wish that the issues of this world, the sin of this world, this fallen creation, don't you wish it was all over?" He pauses and looks around the room searchingly.

"God's people say YES," he announces, gathering up the silent stares. "We wish it was over and we didn't have to deal with this fallen world."

"Well, soon it WILL be over," Waller assures us. "The sun will darken, and the stars will fall from heaven and the heavens will be shaken," he says, appearing to read from the Bible in front of him. "There will be wars across the surface of the earth," he continues with palpable menace. "Nations against nations, kingdoms against kingdoms, famines, pestilence, earthquakes, lawlessness, the Antichrist." He inhales audibly, and I realize that this is the windup. He is just getting started with the end of the world.

"It will be massive and cause great destruction, great death. And it will be interrupted by the lights going out. No man will be able to stop this. This will be something that has never been seen before. You can't explain away that the sun is gone, the moon is dark, the stars are falling from the heavens. You can't imagine this happening, and everyone is looking up in wonder, what is happening? And the prophet tells us that 'God personally will bring his wrath upon the nations.'" It will be, Waller says, "a day of distress and anguish, a day of distress and ruin." God, he says, "will come to make war with the earth." Mountains will tremble, we are told, the earth may come off its axis, and indescribable pain will be inflicted on all the men, women, and children who do not believe with their whole hearts in Waller's preferred version of the Christian religion.

The sermon at the end of time continues for almost an hour. The only interruptions come from the pew behind me, where a young boy, who looks to be about eight years old, punctuates the gore with loud sniffles and the occasional cough. Now he clings to his mother, eyes at half mast, resting his head against her shoulder, his cheeks streaked with tears.

While the talk of global annihilation continues, I discreetly scan the literature in my hands. I find a piece titled "The Church Must Confront Homosexuality as a Sin," in which I am informed that "unrepentant homosexuality excludes one from inheriting the kingdom of God," and that "Christians are under obligation to confront the sinfulness of homosexuality . . . nor can they stay silent about the terrible consequences that await those who practice homosexuality."[2]

Then comes an essay on "Marriage Busting Myth #2," by Tom Drion, a pastor who helped to establish GraceLife Community Church. "By examining God's word, we can see that gender equality was not a foundational cornerstone God used to create paradise," he writes. "In contrast to our 21st century ideals, God did not make men and women equal." In Drion's view, it all goes back to the Garden of Eden. "Eve's role in her marriage was to be Adam's helper. She was to help him carry out his will." Lucky Adam, unlucky Eve: There isn't much nuance in the theology of gender here. "To help anyone complete a task, we must submit ourselves to sit under the authority of the one who was commissioned to do the job. We must allow ourselves to be guided by the person who is leading the task . . . Eve's God given role was to help [Adam]."[3]

While Waller continues his catalog of the horrors that the earth's people will endure on account of their failure to respect God's gender order and other alleged moral crimes, I discreetly pull out my iPhone to check up on his Twitter feed. One of his retweets (now apparently deleted) from the previous summer gives a flavor of his social media presence: "Black Lives Matter (BLM) is inspiring a generation of young people to be angry, hateful, violent, rebellious, destructive, covetous, and envious under the guise of 'justice.' But true justice (impartial equity) is not what BLM wants. It has never wanted that and never will." As a Black pastor from the States, Waller must know that he has strategic value for higher-ups in a church that is widely thought to be complicit in the racist demagoguery of right-wing American politics. In his sermon, however, he leaves no hint of self-awareness on the point.

After the service, I chat with Dorcas. She joined the church nine years ago, shortly after it was established. She lights up when I tell her I used to live in California. "We traveled to the Masters Seminary in Los Angeles, which is where this church comes from," she explains. "It's where our pastors went through training before they started this church." I smile and pretend I didn't know that already.

* * *

THE GRACELIFE COMMUNITY Church in London is what is known as a "church plant." It is one of hundreds of affiliated churches and ministries scattered around the world. It belongs to a church-planting parachurch network headquartered at Grace Community Church in Sun Valley, California. John MacArthur, who took over the pastorate of Grace Community Church in 1969, is a lion in America's Christian nationalist circles but little known outside of them. His Sun Valley church draws nearly ten thousand weekly attendants, and the Masters Seminary in Los Angeles, which he has led since 1986, has trained some of the most politically influential and connected of America's Christian nationalist preachers in the same hyperpatriarchal, homophobic, end-times religion on display at GraceLife Community Church in London.[4]

MacArthur's insistence on male domination over women leaves no room for any hopeful reinterpretation. He has instructed male seminarians not to speak at conferences with female speakers because it is "a total violation of Scripture."[5] His ministry has instructed victims of abuse to "submit" and remain with their abuser.[6] In a typical 2012 sermon titled "The Willful Submission of a Christian Wife," MacArthur instructs women to "rank yourself under" husbands. "A woman's task, a woman's work, a woman's employment, a woman's calling is to be at home," he explains. "Working outside removes her from under her husband and puts her under other men to whom she is forced to submit."[7] In other writings, MacArthur turns repeatedly to familiar passages from Ephesians ("Wives be subject to your husbands") and Colossians ("Wives, be subject to your husbands, as is fitting in the Lord"). In another representative essay, MacArthur announces, "Biblical love excludes homosexuality because of its sinfulness. Christians can best share the gospel with homosexuals by calling their lifestyle what the Bible calls it—sin."[8] In yet another typical effort, this time on "Creationism Versus Evolution," MacArthur offers a series of Bible verses that appear to condemn the theory of evolution and favor instead creationist doctrine.[9]

Nominally, MacArthur and his church subscribe to Calvinist theology that purports to base its teachings on a literal reading of the Bible.[10] But lumping his group in with "evangelicals" in general would be to overlook some subtle but important distinctions among those who fall under that label. The mainline Protestant denominations in the United States are shedding members, and the evangelical Southern Baptist Association has trended toward decline.[11] But MacArthur appears to represent that variety of hard-line, reactionary religion that is actually growing. Indeed, as far as MacArthur is concerned, the more conventional evangelicals are part of the problem. "Sadly, the broader evangelical church finds itself unprepared for the storm clouds of persecution gathering on the horizon. The net effect of weak theology, shallow preaching, syrupy sentimentalism in worship, and a consumer-driven approach to ministry has left the church vulnerable and infirm," he has preached. "The world is indeed spiraling down at breakneck speed, and to a significant degree, the church is going down with it."[12]

Setting aside the apocalyptic visions of the Book of Revelation, the Bible is of limited help in understanding the doctrines and appeal of the style of religion that MacArthur represents. Perhaps a better guide can be found on the daily talking points of conservative propaganda platforms. When MacArthur came out against COVID-19 vaccines, he cited scripture, to be sure, but his arguments came straight from the disinformation mills of right-wing social media. The "government," he claimed, had cooked up a pandemic, exaggerated the threat, and then pushed fake vaccines.

"There is no pandemic," he said.[13]

In America, Christian nationalism has thrived in the same disinformation space that has sheltered the MAGA movement and will host its inevitable successors. The religious leaders in this sector have their eyes fixed on the political leaders of the nation. One of the Masters Seminary graduates, Ralph Drollinger, the president and founder of Capitol Ministries, led prayer sessions attended by some of the most powerful members of the first administration at the Trump White House even as he built a missionary network aimed at high government officials across dozens of countries.[14]

The politico-religious ambitions of reactionary religion extend far beyond U.S. borders. Grace Community Church in America may appeal to the America First crowd, but as with Capitol Ministries, it has undertaken a massive worldwide expansion. Its website offers a helpful map function, which lights up its affiliated church plants all over the United States, Central and South America, Ireland, France, Ukraine, Germany, the Czech Republic, Italy, Azerbaijan, Kenya, Tanzania, South Africa, and of course my temporary hometown of London.

What exactly are they doing in the UK? This is a country where nonbelief appears headed for an absolute majority of the population. Less than 1 percent of the population can be found in church on any given Sunday. Only 9 percent of Britons told Gallup pollsters that God created humans in their present form ten thousand years ago, as compared with 42 percent of Americans.[15]

MacArthur and his seminarians don't mind the long odds. When they look at the UK, they see a lost country that needs to be retaken. And they plan to participate in the conquest using methods developed and tested in the United States. Alongside its English founders, GraceLife Community Church has now received reinforcements in the form of two additional ministers sent over from the United States. Adam Waller is one, and Michael Dionne of Faith Bible Church in Spokane, Washington, is the other.

"The vision of GraceLife London is not the revival of England, but the re-evangelization of England," Dionne explains on his blog. "What the country needs is a resurgence of faithful ministers and families ready to plant churches and preach the gospel, which is what GLL longs to do. The encouraging thing about this vision is that it is strictly biblical." The goal, he adds, is to plant enough churches so that every inhabitant of Greater London is within forty-five minutes of salvation—"meaning that almost 1/4 of England can be reached with sound, expository preaching, faithful shepherding and discipleship, and clear biblical evangelism."[16]

If there is a statistical grain of hope for ambitious churches seeking to re-evangelize the homeland, it is this: While the mainstream forms of Christianity in the UK, primarily the Church of England, have declined precipitously over the past two decades, the Pentecostal and charismatic varieties that are on the rise around the world are up by double digits.[17] The hotter and harder forms of evangelical religion are also gaining traction, often setting up shop by renting underutilized religious facilities, such as the Clerkenwell Medical Mission. And influential evangelical organizations in the UK are pursuing their agendas through a range of religious organizations as well as political strategies.

This, of course, is happening alongside the steady growth of Islam, which is up 44 percent in the UK over the last decade and now comprises at least 6.5 percent of the UK population.[18] If there is religion in the UK's future, it's probably not going to center on the stately, museum-quality rituals of the Anglican church.

ON MY SUNDAY morning in London, I say goodbye to Dorcas and leave the church. I feel in need of some fresh air. The sight of the Australian fusion restaurant across the street, with its stylish clientele and fanciful coffee options, somehow offers relief from the lingering visions of damnation. Not more than two hundred yards to the west of GraceLife Community Church I spot the storied St. James Church on Clerkenwell Green. Founded as a nunnery in the twelfth century, it rose to fame as a burial site for playwrights and thieves. It served as the venue for the 1632 wedding of Pocahontas's and John Rolfe's son, Thomas Rolfe, to his bride, Elizabeth. The churchyard, with its charming coffee kiosk, now functions as an unofficial community center and dog park. As I stroll over to St. James, I notice a bright, modern-looking banner over the door, INSPIRE ST. JAMES CLERKENWELL.

St. James Church turns out to be now occupied by a group that delivers "biblical teaching" in a different flavor of the evangelical tradition. A separate group from GraceLife Community Church at the Clerkenwell mission, but a parallel message nonetheless.

In a November 2023 talk on "God's Good News for Our Sexuality," Inspire St. James Clerkenwell's vicar, Mark Johnson, offers a "biblical overview" of human sexuality. Among the consequences of Eve's sin is that "He [Adam] will rule over her," as Jackson says.[19] Good news for whom? Inspire St. James Clerkenwell is a member of the Gospel Coalition (TGC), cofounded by the late Tim Keller. TGC-affiliated churches are required to conform to the organization's theological doctrines. Marriages should be "complementarian"— which is a rather nicer way of saying that men are entitled to control and women must submit. God loves everyone, even gay people! But make no mistake, being gay is a sin. Above all, every person who fails to believe as they do will endure conscious torment for all eternity.

"Why are some people born with sexual attraction to those of the same sex?" Jackson asks. "It is all a consequence of the Fall. It's Adam and Eve, turned from God's goodness to their own way."[20]

That evening I stop in at the local pub, hoping to revive my spirits with a pint and some conversation. My new friends prove to be as convivial and reassuring as I had hoped. But one tells me he heard a rumor that a blizzard that struck the United States earlier that year, leaving four million Texans without power, had been generated by the government; he seems unsure as to whether or not this is true. I overhear a man at the next table haranguing his friend about another, supposedly liberal plot: "fifteen-minute cities." On my very short walk back to our apartment, I wrestle with the reality that the transitory move to London will not offer quite the kind of escape I had anticipated.

THE LONGER I stayed in London, the more I became convinced that you cannot map the politics of one country easily onto another. But on the margins at least there are some distinct similarities. The UK Christian right is increasingly drawing on a U.S.-forged playbook. And while the UK movement draws substantially on funding and support from the U.S., they have their own Funders, too.

Take, as an example, the UK hedge fund manager Paul Marshall, who is reportedly worth £800 million, according to the *London Times*.[21] Marshall is determined to use his wealth to combat liberalism, which he believes "has lost its moorings," in religion as well as politics. He and his wife worship at Holy Trinity Brompton, a very large and extremely well funded church with a strong evangelical and charismatic slant. HTB, as it is known, is home to Alpha, an evangelistic organization with a global reach. In recent years HTB has been more forthcoming on their antipathy to liberal reforms—opposing, for instance, blessings for same-sex couples. Marshall has invested in a range of religious initiatives, including a scheme to place a Bible in every state school in the UK and support for a theological training center that inculcates in its pupils a more conservative form of theology and the culture war positions that accompany it. He has also invested in church-planting initiatives which the writer Andrew Graystone described in the *Prospect* as "a Marshall Plan for the beleaguered Church of England, [that] is widely loathed in other parts of the Church for its flatpack formula of guitar music and easy certainties."[22]

But Marshall's efforts go well beyond support for religion in the UK. His aims are clearly political. He has forged alliances with number of conservative politicians and launched an organization called the Alliance for Responsible Citizenship, which draws in right-wing activists and personalities that promote a range of conservative positions. He made an initial investment of £10 million into GB News, a conservative media outlet that frequently veers into right-wing culture war territory à la Fox News, and has subsequently invested millions more. He has also invested £18 million in Ralston College, a tiny Savannah, Georgia–based liberal arts college with a robust online platform, whose chancellor is the right-wing culture warrior Jordan Peterson. As of this writing, he is attempting to take over the conservative-leaning UK publications the *Spectator* and the *Telegraph*. In doing so, he will play a pivotal role in shaping conservative politics in the UK for years to come.[23]

For now, of course, people like Marshall are swimming against the UK tide; American-style culture wars remain unpopular in the British Isles. Most British people were stunned when the U.S. Supreme Court overturned *Roe v. Wade*. One friend, a Tory Brexiteer, asked me in genuine confusion, "Why would anyone want to ban abortion?" But the U.S. religious right has found willing UK partners and is carefully laying the groundwork for an assault on abortion rights there, too.

On an early February morning, I ride the train to Birmingham and head to St. Mary's College Oscott, a Catholic seminary. I have signed up to observe "Rethink Abortion Day," a seminar aimed at motivating and training antiabortion activists in England.[24] I enter an elegant building, adorned with stained-glass windows, elegant wooden carvings, and marble sculptures, which dates from the early nineteenth century. Passing through the somber stone hallways and serene cloisters, I make my way to the gathering spot for the day's activities.

Several dozen attendees are already assembled in the cozy, wood-paneled conference room, and I take a seat on one of the fold-out chairs. An older lady in a colorful sweater smiles as she makes room for me. To my right is a young woman with auburn hair and thick glasses. She seems a bit nervous. As we chat a bit before the program begins, I begin to grasp the source of her anxiety; she feels out of step with her peers. "It's good to be here with people who share the same views," she tells me. Recently, she says, one of her closest friends, impregnated against her will by a guy she dated only briefly, decided to have an abortion. She now regrets that she didn't interfere. "I just didn't know what to say," she tells me. She's here today in hopes of learning the tactics of persuasion.

Overhearing our conversation, the older lady leans over. "I've joined some clinic pickets, but the young girls don't pay attention to me. One of them said something rude," she adds; the memory clearly stings. "But you're young," she adds, smiling encouragingly at the auburn-haired woman. "They'll listen to you."

With fifty or sixty participants settled into our seats, the day's presentations begin. Much of the training is focused on the how-to of mounting demonstrations outside women's health centers. Long a feature of abortion politics in the United States, antiabortion protests outside UK clinics and hospitals have surged in recent years, and the presenters at the Birmingham event can claim much of the credit.[25] They include Ben Thatcher, director of March for Life UK, a spinoff of the U.S.-based March for Life, which draws tens of thousands of participants to Washington, D.C., annually.[26] Another speaker, Dave Brennan, is the director of Brephos, a project of the U.S.-based Center for Bio-Ethical Reform (CBR), which aims to help "churches respond to abortion."[27] Apart from the Catholic entities cohosting the event, the four groups principally involved in presentations at the Birmingham event are UK affiliates of U.S.-based organizations, and several of the presenters have deep ties to other major groups in America's Christian nationalist movement.[28]

Leading the discussion on demonstrations and antiabortion messaging are representatives of 40 Days for Life UK, an affiliate of the U.S.-based 40 Days for Life.[29] Founded in 2004 in Bryan, Texas—a small city that antiabortion activists have described as "the most antichoice place in the nation"—40 Days for Life specializes in training and organizing protests in front of abortion clinics and other providers.[30] The stated goal is to dissuade women from going through with an abortion, though the usual effect is simply to bully and shame them for doing so. The group also runs a "university," that is, an online program where, for $497, users can access multiple training videos on recruiting fellow protesters and performing sidewalk "counseling." Participants can also obtain antiabortion signs and materials and receive personal coaching.[31]

Forty Days for Life now claims to operate more than a thousand branches in sixty-five countries.[32] The UK branch kicked off with campaigns in Northern Ireland in 2009 and now boasts at least fifteen chapters in the island nation.[33] The organization's UK leader, Robert Colquhoun, received support for his work when he enrolled in the Leadership Institute's International School of Fundraising[34]—the same parent organization that offered training and support to Moms for Liberty and that hired Bridget Ziegler as their director of school board programs before she resigned in disgrace.[35]

HEADQUARTERED IN VIRGINIA, the Leadership Institute offers various forms of training and networking opportunities to right-wing politicians and activists in the U.S. and around the world. Its founder and president, Morton

Blackwell, is the former executive director of the Council for National Policy, one of the leading networking organizations of the Christian nationalist movement, and he signs his name to some memos from the Conservative Action Project, which is associated with the CNP and serves to unite the right in its policy positions.[36] In the fiscal year 2019, according to publicly available tax forms, the organization spent $92,494 on "educational seminars" and $25,871 on grantmaking in Europe, along with substantial sums in the Middle East, East Asia, sub-Saharan Africa, Central America, and elsewhere.[37]

In the conference room at St. Mary's Oscott, as speakers from each organization launch into their presentations, the young woman to my right takes copious notes. We receive verbal as well as written instruction on all aspects of how we ought to comport ourselves during our future adventures in clinic demonstrations, the harassment of women seeking abortions, and related activities. We are given remarkably specific recommendations on verbal messaging and body language; we are told to smile; we are even advised on our personal hygiene and fashion choices. We are offered scripts for engaging others in conversation about abortion, and techniques for "winning" those conversations by manipulating points relevant to the zeitgeist. To best support people like my young auburn-haired seatmate, we get a surprising amount of discussion about our own feelings and reactions to the imagined scenarios. There is no discussion of what it feels like to be on the other side of the picket line.

In the United States, 40 Days for Life is distinctive in that it focuses heavily on creating a certain kind of experience for its activists. The "40 Days" refers not to pregnancy terms, as one might at first suppose, but to the duration of the demonstrations. Participants commit to forty-day "vigils," the founders have explained, because forty days is a period with strong biblical associations.

At our UK conference there is a detailed discussion of "rights"—though, again, it is all about the rights of abortion opponents—from Isabel Vaughan-Spruce, the leader of the Birmingham chapter of 40 Days for Life. In December 2022, police charged Vaughan-Spruce with four counts of breaching an exclusion zone, or buffer zone, at a maternal health-care center. She promptly appeared in a YouTube video in which, wearing a pastel coat, her hair neatly pinned, she softly complains that she has been indicted for nothing more than "silently praying in my head." Her case was taken up by the UK branch of the Alliance Defending Freedom (ADF), the U.S.-headquartered right-wing legal advocacy juggernaut. In a well-coordinated PR campaign, conservative Christian media outlets joined Vaughan-Spruce in characterizing her alleged crime as "standing silently near an abortion clinic" or a "silent prayer crime." The incident received widespread media coverage in the UK, and the charges were soon dropped. None of the mainstream outlets identified Vaughan-Spruce as a leader of 40 Days for Life UK. Several months later she got herself rearrested and repeated the same talking points.[38] (The police later released her without charges.)

Today, in blue jeans, tall black boots, and a black sweater, blond hair tumbling over her shoulders, she tells us antiabortion demonstrations are all about "free speech." The praying was presumably never silent after all.

Father Sean Gough, a young Roman Catholic priest with soulful eyes and a close-cropped beard, steps to the front of the room to continue with this "free speech" theme. Gough has asserted in interviews that he is the product of sexual violence, and that "my mother chose life for me."[39] He appears to be one of the UK's most determined faces of the antiabortion movement, and his gentle demeanor belies his determination to force other women into what his mother appears to have actively chosen. Previously, Gough was charged with "protesting and engaging in an act that is intimidating to service users" of a Birmingham clinic.[40] With the help of the ADF, the charges against him, too, were dropped.[41] In a clever bit of PR jujitsu, he appeared almost immediately on Tucker Carlson's Fox News show. "You know, I was praying for free speech, which I believe is threatened in the United Kingdom," he said.[42]

To make sure participants get the point, we are offered a flyer: "Is the Law our Enemy or Our Friend? A lawyer's guide for pro-lifers." The flyer advertises a presentation by Jeremiah Igunnubole, who serves as legal counsel to the UK branch of the ADF and represented Sean Gough. Igunnubole has argued for the organization's position that the "safety barriers" erected in response to increasingly aggressive protests at clinics and maternity hospitals violate speech rights.[43]

At the antiabortion recruitment gatherings that I have attended in the United States, there is invariably the moment where speakers treat the audience to a slide show involving gory images of aborted fetuses. Birmingham does not disappoint. Taking the podium in a navy sweater and jeans and cheery attitude, Dave Brennan of the UK branch of CBR delivers the goods. The CBR is known in the U.S. for its use of graphic images, which are often enlarged and displayed as placards and billboards near playgrounds, schools, and other places where children congregate.[44] The organization also attracted notice when some of its leaders compared aborted fetuses with victims of lynching and Nazi genocide.[45]

But it's not just abortion that they're coming after; CBR has a much broader and more radical agenda. In line with its parent organization, Brennan's UK affiliate opposes the most effective forms of contraception, including birth control pills and mini pills, implants, IUDs, and vaginal rings. Any method that prevents a united sperm and egg from implanting into the vaginal wall, Brennan's group maintains, amounts to "ending a human life."

"We must acknowledge that we are in spiritual warfare for our souls . . . and HE [Satan] is determined," he tells the gathering, as we take in the stream of images. He sketches a theology according to which "saving the unborn" is the greatest moral issue of our time. Implicitly acknowledging that the activists gathered in Birmingham represent both Catholic and Protestant traditions, he calls for "co-belligerence." The idea—crafted in America over a period of fifteen years and enshrined in a key 2009 document titled "Manhattan Declaration: A Call of Christian Conscience" and signed by a broad range of reactionary activists and theologians—is that Catholics and Protestants should set aside centuries of theological differences in order to fight their common enemies who support abortion, same-sex marriage, and other liberal causes.[46]

Brennan ends his presentation with a handout on the "ABCs of Abortion," which amounts to a series of rebuttals of counterarguments one is likely to hear while harassing patients at health centers. "Take control of the conversation," Brennan says, his voice animated with a can-do lilt. "We're trying to get this person to acknowledge that it's a human life or baby." He nods and smiles. "If they raise point B or C, get back to point A. We're not trying to bring in religious values at that point. We're just being scientific."

During a break in the activities, the older lady to my left confides to me, "I read that now Satanists are getting pregnant on purpose so that they can have abortions." I ask her where she picked up this idea. "I think it was Eternal Word," she replies, referencing Eternal Word Television Network (EWTN), a worldwide media empire that some of its critics refer to as "the Fox news of Catholicism" and Pope Francis has called "the work of the devil."[47]

She furrows her brow. "We've got to do something, because things keep getting worse and worse."

The next speaker, Rachel Mackenzie, takes the stage. With her short pink hair, oversize poncho, and recurring scowl, she looks like she would fit right in at an Extinction Rebellion demonstration.[48]

Mackenzie is affiliated with Rachel's Vineyard, a faith-based U.S. organization dedicated to "healing the trauma of abortion."[49] It appears her specialty is promoting the familiar trope that frames abortion as a harm to mothers and fathers. Dr. Theresa Burke, the founder of Rachel's Vineyard, built her activist career as a pastoral associate of Priests for Life,[50] whose national director is the provocateur and defrocked priest Frank Pavone. A close associate of former president Donald Trump, Pavone drew attention to himself by actively promoting the Stop the Steal movement that spread the lie that the 2020 election was stolen.[51]

"Focus on truth and love," Mackenzie advises us, her eyes flashing with righteous fury. "If truth is communicated without love, it won't help." Then her presentation takes a bizarre and sadistic turn. Mackenzie insists that even a ten-year-old rape victim should be expected to carry a pregnancy. "You don't get unraped by an abortion," she sternly admonishes the Birmingham audience. "If a ten-year-old is raped, the most loving solution is to consider an alternative to go through an abortion. The most loving solution is Life."

Rounding out the speakers in Birmingham is Ben Thatcher of March for Life's UK spinoff. With a steady demeanor, Thatcher echoes the messages of the earlier speakers, though he seems to want to soften the edges. Participants should avoid being "aggressive" in promoting their views, he tells us. Abortion is the "greatest moral issue of our time," but we should "avoid calling it murder. We don't want to win the arguments," he concludes, "we want to win souls."[52]

HAVING HEARD FROM one side of the picket line, I reach out for voices from the other side. I find Lucy Grieve, a twenty-five-year-old from Scotland, whose life took a fresh turn on the day she accompanied her friend, Alice Murray, to a reproductive health center in Glasgow.

When she and Alice arrived outside the clinic, a group of protesters attempted to force antiabortion literature into their hands. When she and Alice declined to accept the literature, she recounts, the protesters flung the papers at them.

"They claimed to be trying to help and pray for my friend," Lucy says, but they were really attempting to "intimidate, humiliate, and shame. It felt like harassment." So much for winning souls.

The experience motivated Lucy and Alice to organize Back Off Scotland, an advocacy group that lobbies for 150-meter "exclusion zones" around reproductive health clinics.

One impression that seems to stick with Grieve is the demonstrators' preoccupation with their own feelings and concerns. When she suggested to the protesters that they might make their case in a better setting than accosting strangers on the street, she recalls, they insisted they had a right to "free speech."

"It wasn't about the women or the girls obtaining abortions," she observes with chagrin. "It was all about *their* rights." She pauses, and then adds that the demonstrators also seemed indifferent to the impact of demonstrations on the medical staff at clinics or hospitals, many of whom are not involved in elective pregnancy terminations but are instead offering prenatal care, delivering babies, assisting women with pregnancy complications, or working in neonatal units tending to newborns with severe health problems. "It affects [medical staff's] care they can provide because they are being called murderers at their own work," she says. She notes that 40 Days for Life has regularly conducted demonstrations at Scotland's largest hospital, in an area near the neonatal unit and maternity ward. The activity, she points out, is incredibly disruptive to both patients and staff.

THE UK REMAINS far behind the United States in the vigor of its culture war over women's health-care rights. Indeed, the growing antiabortion activity around reproductive health facilities has sparked a backlash that appears to be limiting the movement's policy gains for now. In early 2023, the UK's highest court recognized that harassment around health-care facilities violates the rights of those seeking reproductive and sexual health services. Even many regional courts are enforcing clinic buffer zones. The courts acknowledge that they are protecting women from harassment, rather than casting this as a "free speech issue," and the UK parliament recently moved toward legislating the establishment of buffer zones around abortion clinics.[53]

Even so, ritualized harassment and humiliation of women seeking medical care is hardly the only American contribution to the budding culture war over reproductive services in the UK. U.S. organizations are also contributing to the influx of antiabortion counseling centers. Billed as "crisis pregnancy centers," these groups attempt to dissuade women from seeking abortions, often by offering misleading or unethical advice. In the United States there are about four thousand such operations, the majority affiliated with large networks like Heartbeat International and Stanton Healthcare.[54] These organizations and others have now established multiple UK affiliates. According to an investigation by the BBC's *Panorama*, at least fifty-seven such centers have opened in the UK, and more than one-third were found to provide unsound or unethical medical advice.[55]

The U.S.-based Stanton Healthcare, which operates a clinic in Belfast, recently expanded into Scotland.[56] In 2018 a UK reporter for the *Times* of London visited the Belfast clinic and recorded a conversation in which she was told abortion would make her breasts "fill with cancer." She was warned, "You could get your womb perforated, you might be left sterile."[57]

To get a better sense of these developments, I check in with Katherine O'Brien, a spokesperson for the nonprofit British Pregnancy Advisory Service. "We've seen a real uptick in protest activity over this year," she tells me. O'Brien cautions that it would be dangerous to underestimate the potential impact of these groups. "We know that antiabortion groups are well funded, well organized, and well connected with influential parliamentarians," she says. "They are going into schools, into universities, and have a real drive to recruit the 'next generation' of antiabortion activists. They know they are playing the long game, and they believe that they will win, even if it takes decades."

The American leaders of the antiabortion movement are well aware of the long-term potential of utilizing their resources to build up the movement overseas. A joint investigation by the UK publications the *Observer* and *Citizens UK*, published in 2023, revealed that Right to Life UK increased its Facebook advertising budget more than ten times over the past three years.[58] At the UK March for Life in September 2022, Sean Carney, the U.S. CEO of 40 Days for Life, stood in front of a banner bearing the slogan LIFE FROM CONCEPTION, NO EXCEPTION and referenced the overturning of *Roe v. Wade*. "If we can do it," he told the cheering crowd assembled in London's Parliament Square, "you can do it."[59]

The train from Birmingham back to London leaves me at Euston Station in the late afternoon. As I take a meandering walk back to my apartment in

Clerkenwell, I find it difficult to imagine an American-style culture war erupting here and taking aim at democratic institutions. But then I wander in my memory back to my childhood in 1970s Boston, and it occurs to me that Americans then might have had equal difficulty imagining what has become of our national politics. At that time, abortion was thought to be of concern mainly to a subset of Catholics, and it didn't divide along partisan lines. In 1972 the popular television show *Maude*, executive-produced by the late Norman Lear, featured two segments in which the lead character faced an unintended pregnancy and chose abortion. Lear later remarked that this storyline generated no controversy.[60] By then many conservative Protestants and their institutions, including the Southern Baptist Convention, had welcomed the Supreme Court ruling that for half a century secured the right of American women to reproductive freedom. Even after the religious right succeeded in convincing conservatives that all evil came down to abortion, the issue was initially thought to be a social one, to be resolved by democratic means within the existing institutions.

Few people at the time would have imagined that antiabortion activism would become an indispensable tool for mobilizing large groups of people to join in an assault on democracy itself. The recent developments in the UK, I realize, are like a window on the American past. This is how things must have looked before the antidemocratic reaction really took hold.

CHAPTER II

Exporting the Counterrevolution

In the decades immediately following the Declaration of Independence in 1776, the new American republic became the modern world's first great exporter of democratic revolution. As America's founders watched the strategic alliances between priests and kings tumble before the advance of ideas of human equality, individual rights, and representative government in France, Haiti, Greece, the Spanish colonies, and eventually much of Europe, they were exultant. "From that bright spark which first illumed these lands / See Europe kindling, as the blaze expands," wrote Philip Freneau, the so-called poet of the American Revolution.[1] His friend Thomas Jefferson was equally pleased. "This ball of liberty, I believe most piously, is now so well in motion that it will roll round the globe, at least the enlightened part of it, for light and liberty go together," he wrote. "It is our glory that we first put it into motion."[2]

Today, however, sectors of the American right have become exporters of the antidemocratic counterrevolution. Not satisfied with their efforts to roll back individual rights in the United States and replace democratic pluralism with sectarianism and authoritarian forms of governance, America's Christian nationalists have pushed their ideas and agendas out to other countries around the world. Joining them in the effort are a host of "antiwoke" culture warriors from the New Right along with the white supremacists, men's rights activists, New Traditionalists, and others they inspire. Some groups in those other countries have proved receptive to the new ideologies. A global antidemocratic reaction has emerged that in turn contributes to the counterrevolutionary process in America.

The axis around which a sector of the global antidemocratic reaction now turns is an extraordinary alliance between a dominant wing of the Republican Party in the U.S. and the Russian dictator Vladimir Putin. Only twenty years ago, the same Republican Party was willing to go to war to overthrow a dictatorship in Iraq and (supposedly) promote democracy.[3] Yet the faction of the Republican Party that has mortgaged itself to Donald Trump balked at providing relatively small-scale aid to Ukraine as that country attempted to fend off a brutal and unprovoked Russian invasion.[4] And even while Vladimir Putin continues to crush democracy in his home country and abroad, with assassinations of journalists and political opponents, widespread imprisonment, and kleptocratic arrangements, to say nothing of the suspiciously convenient "suicides" and "accidents" of Russian business, political, and military leaders, the right wing of the Republican Party hails him as a hero and a strong leader.[5] To be sure, after months of pressure from the White House, House Speaker Mike Johnson managed to squeak out approval for aid to Ukraine in April 2024, bypassing opposition of a number of Republicans. And yet out on the far right, among the kind of people who contribute to Claremont Institute publications and who now form the "brain trust" for Donald Trump and other Republican leaders, one can hear Ukraine's resistance to Russia described as a "woke war."[6]

It is important to note that Russia and other hostile foreign powers have avidly targeted sectors of the American left in order to intensify and exploit divisions in U.S. society. This activity and its consequences are grossly underappreciated. Russia-sponsored troll farms create content that seeks to draw left-leaning Americans into irrational or polarizing positions and elevate existing content that can be used to foster mistrust in American institutions.[7] Scholars and investigative journalists have traced extremist messaging wrongly associated with the Black Lives Matter movement and a made-up organization called LGBTQ United to Russian operatives connected to the Internet Research Agency.[8] Similarly, in the run-up to the 2016 election, Russian companies with Kremlin ties promoted Facebook ads that cast Bernie Sanders as a gay superhero—along with other Facebook ads targeting the right, like the image of Jesus arm-wrestling a Hillary Clinton-supporting Satan.[9] Bots, troll farms, and purveyors of disinformation have also amplified polarizing narratives around international conflicts, including the war in Ukraine, the war between Hamas and Israel, and other conflicts in the Middle East.

In 2016, according to a report commissioned by the U.S. Senate, Moscow-led internet trolls with handles like @woke_blacks launched a social media blitz supporting Jill Stein in order to help Trump win.[10] In the 2024 election cycle, Jill Stein, for her part, exploited the crisis in the Middle East by first echoing the characterization of Joe Biden as "Genocide Joe," then doing pretty much the same for Kamala Harris, as a means of generating disappointment in the Democratic party and suppressing turnout for the Democratic candidate.[11] Sexual identity, and particularly transgender issues, provide an especially fertile ground for exploitation. Fake LGBT content, distributed through Telegram and Twitter, is often timed to coincide with specific celebrations such as Gay Pride month. A 2023 EU report analyzed over 30 cases of false content related to sexual diversity and pro-LGBT messaging and found that more than half was of Russian origin. Clarifying the strategy, Lutz Gullner, director of strategic communications and information analysis for the European External Action Service, said, "There's always an agenda behind it, amplifying certain voices."[12] The aim, of course, is to undermine faith in the values of liberalism and tolerance and foster mistrust in democratic institutions, and thus destabilize democracy worldwide.

It's not often clear whether foreign interests work directly or indirectly through individuals embedded within a subset of far-left organizations. But what is plain to see is that groups such as Code Pink and the Revolutionary Communist Party, USA, along with its affiliated organizations RiseUp, RiseUp4AbortionRights.org, and Refuse Fascism, seem to be doing their work for them. Many of these organizations appear to live-action role-play for the reactionary right by staging events that generate the chaotic imagery, such as the burning of American flags, that can be used to taint by association and discredit the entire liberal-left.[13]

To what extent are such American groups and others aware of the benefit that hostile foreign interests may derive from their work, and do they even care? It is difficult to say. In an episode of the Revcoms' talk show, host Rafael Kadaris—a proud flag-burner—said, "the U.S. is the one that is threatening to attack China. Over Taiwan. Even though Taiwan is part of China," and added, "Whatever China is doing it pales in comparison to the crimes of U.S. imperialism and its world-wide war machine."[14] In another episode, interviewee Raymond Lotta dismissed Ukraine's fight for its independence as "cannon fodder in the U.S. efforts to encircle Russia" and said "the people of the world have no interest in being part of or being drawn into as supporters and backers" of that conflict. "No U.S. NATO war with Russia," his interviewer said with a satisfied look. "No World War Three."[15]

And then there is the "left-to-right acceleration" of a subset of "journalist-provocateurs and the readers who have followed them rightward," as the authors Kathryn Joyce and Jeff Sharlet wrote in a vital piece for *In These Times*. While the phenomenon long predates the current political era, it began in earnest "with the onset of the Trump years," Joyce and Sharlet note, pointing to Glenn Greenwald's *Rumble*, Max Blumenthal's *Grayzone*, and the writer Naomi Wolf, whose career has devolved from feminist author of "big ideas" books to frequent guest on Steve Bannon's *War Room*.[16] In June 2024, the *Washington Post* reported that an editor at *Grayzone*, who had worked extensively for Russia's *Sputnik*, had taken money from Iranian government-owned media.

To be clear, many of the left-to-right accelerationists are doing it all on their own steam. And of course there are those leftist activists who find themselves strange bedfellows with some of the world's most repressive, kleptocratic, and gender-unequal foreign interests. But it is important to note that no reasonable equivalence can be drawn on foreign manipulation between left and right. That is because the individuals and groups described here, along with others like them, are not anywhere near the Democratic establishment; in fact, their representatives often promote third-party spoilers or foster voter apathy. Indeed, the general thrust of Russian intervention has been to support Trump, right-wing populism, and everything that destabilizes American democracy, and along with it the NATO alliance. Some Chinese, Iranian, and other social media accounts have often mirrored Russian tactics.[17] Meanwhile, the Republican establishment has embraced and elevated Putin's would-be defenders in their midst.

Among Americans with a sense of history and respect for democracy, the emergence of the Russian-American axis of reaction has mostly come as a shock. But those who have followed the rise of Christian nationalism in the U.S. over the past several decades cannot be surprised. Even while the Cold War was still hot, American reactionaries and their Russian counterparts started building bonds over their shared hatred of secularism, nontraditional gender and family relations, immigration, and modernity. In fact, the process that led to this rapprochement began decades earlier, when America's culture warriors set off on their first crusades and began preparing the world for the coming reaction.

PAUL BENNO MARX was born on a dairy farm in Minnesota in 1920, the fifteenth child of a devout Catholic family.[18] At twenty-two he took vows as a Benedictine monk. At thirty-seven he obtained a PhD in sociology. By fifty-three, when he toured Ireland, he had risen to be one of the world's first truly global antiabortion crusaders. Over the last three decades of his life, as founder and leader of the Human Life Center in 1972 and Human Life International in 1981, he travelled the world preaching the horrors of reproductive health care.[19] "Contraception is an enormous evil and the gateway to abortion and all manner of sexual abuse," he said. "If parents contracept, their teenagers will fornicate."[20] He gave dozens of lectures around Ireland, some of them at girls' schools, and they mostly followed the same script: he showed slides of aborted fetuses and played a soundtrack said to be of a fetal heartbeat at three months. The pièce de résistance was the exhibition of a fourteen-week-old fetus in a jar, which attracted great publicity but also controversy, especially at the girls' schools, as he placed it in front of pupils without the administrators' foreknowledge or approval.[21]

From the start, Marx's antiabortion activism was entwined with a deep-seated terror of women's equality. "I shudder with revulsion over the modern secular feminism that has weakened or destroyed so many fine institutions, including many women's religious orders, our Catholic school system, and now our Catholic hospitals," he wrote in his 1997 autobiography. In the summer of 1959 his travels with thirty-four female Catholic college graduates and nurses through ten countries "confirmed what I had always known and taught" when, one evening, the women enjoyed a few glasses of champagne: "There is a vast, inherent, God-planned, emotional, and psychological difference between male and female. This truth, of course, is sadly and vehemently resented and denied by die-hard feminists, who hate Freud's dictum, 'Anatomy is destiny,'" he wrote in his condemnation of the women's merriment. No doubt he would have preferred them more like his mother, of whom he wrote, "Did not do much reading, because she had no time. But she was an excellent housekeeper."[22]

MARX WAS FAR from the only global antiabortion crusader to emerge from America. Joining him was Joseph Scheidler, the founder of the U.S.-based Prolife Action League. Born in Indiana in 1927, Scheidler was an advertising executive who believed in direct action. He was a pioneer in demonstrating at maternal health-care centers and organizing angry gatherings outside doctors' homes. "Some pro-life directors have spoken about winning brownie points by condemning violence," he once explained. "I am not interested in brownie points."[23] One of his followers, Randall Terry, went on to found Operation Rescue and boasts, on his own website, that he has been arrested forty-nine times and spent time in various federal, state, and local prisons in connection with illegal forms of activism.[24]

A tall man with a big voice and a taste for dapper business suits, Scheidler took pleasure in his crusade. He described himself as a "tireless, aggressive, imaginative, daring, cocksure, and optimistic individual." When the mother of an eleven-year-old girl arranged an abortion for her child in 1985 in Chicago, Scheidler hired a private detective, located her apartment, parked outside, and harangued her and her family from the street and neighboring balconies with a megaphone, then demonstrated in front of the hospital where the mother and her young daughter were expected to appear. The mother "was almost hysterical. We couldn't reason with her," he told the papers.[25]

From his mentor Paul Marx, Scheidler picked up the tactic of displaying images of aborted fetuses at his protest actions and in speeches. In 1983, he took his slides and his message to Ireland, where he would have a dramatic impact in energizing the antiabortion movement. One of his stops was the family home of Úna Bean Mhic Mhathúna. As secretary of the Irish House-wives' Union, Úna advocated for the needs of Irish women inside and outside the home from a traditionalist perspective—that is, in opposition to feminist goals.[26] It was on Úna's teenaged daughter Niamh, however, that Scheidler's visit left an enduring mark. We'll get to her in a moment.

It was Marx's work in Eastern Europe, in any event, that would ultimately have the greatest impact.[27] As Irish activists responded to his call, Marx turned his attention to other countries, including those in Europe and Latin America.

In the late 1980s he notched a particular success in Poland. Under communism, Poland had no restrictions on abortion. As that country was extricating itself from Soviet domination, Marx brought "financial, material, and spiritual aid" to its emerging antiabortion movement.[28] The right-wing governments that followed communism imposed increasingly severe restrictions on abortion, culminating in what was an essentially a total ban in 2021. The Polish triumph, in retrospect, would be the first of several major victories for the illiberal reaction in the former Soviet sphere.

Today, a number of powerful and well-funded organizations are carrying on the work of Marx and his brethren, whose culture wars helped young governments and political movements forge new identities. The Political Network for Values (PNfV), an umbrella organization drawing in politicians and organizations from dozens of countries, describes itself as "a global platform of worldwide political representatives and leaders who actively promote and defend the values of family, life and freedom."[29] One of its key supporters is the government of Viktor Orban, a flagbearer for European illiberalism and the populist right.[30]

In 2023, the PNfV held its annual gathering in New York City, hosted at the United Nations. U.S. politicians and policy group leaders joined together with representatives from Sudan, Uganda, Finland, Argentina, Mexico, and Spain. Partner organizations included the ADF, the Heritage Foundation, Family Watch International, C-Fam, and the International Organization for the Family. The gathering produced a declaration, called the New York Commitment, "to rescue the original meaning of the Universal Declaration of Human Rights"—a slap back at the allegedly "woke" idea, enshrined in that very document, that all human beings are equal in dignity and rights, "without distinction of any kind, such as race, colour, sex," and that "all are deserving of equal protection against discrimination."[31]

It isn't hard to discern the anxiety around sex and sexuality that underlies PNfV's determination to eliminate gender equality as a human right worthy of defense. Topping the PNfV's list of priorities, printed on their website and other materials, is that "life is the first of all human rights" and that "the defense of life should begin from its moment of conception." Others include the idea that "marriage is between a man and a woman" and the "state cannot and should not replace parents in this task" of educating children, an item written in the idiom of those who wish to abolish public education. The PNfV is also committed to "the defense of the right to conscientious objection in every sphere," which may be seen as a demand by religious conservatives to exempt themselves from the laws that apply to everyone else in society.[32] In short, it is a list that closely follows the agenda of America's Christian nationalist movement.

But organizations like the PNfV did not come together by accident. The global counterrevolution had some early pioneers, and their stories are worth considering for what they reveal about the aims of the movement today.

ALLAN C. CARLSON WAS born in Iowa in 1949 and is now professor emeritus at Hillsdale College, the private Christian nationalist enterprise in Michigan. Early in his academic career, Carlson concluded that the collapse of "the natural family" was the source of every major social problem in the United States.[33] By "natural family," he meant a family consisting of a male head of household winning bread and embodying the dominant masculine virtues in overseeing his brood; a subordinated female domestic worker embodying the feminine virtues; and their (preferably numerous) children.[34] Abortion was a threat to the natural family, but much bigger threats, to judge from Carlson's preoccupations, were feminism and, perhaps worst of all, "the homosexual agenda."[35]

In 2023 Carlson mourned the passing of Cardinal George Pell of Australia, a "tall and muscular" man whom he praised for his "unperturbable masculinity." It was the end of "masculine Christianity," he lamented.[36] He waved away the fact that Pell presided over an epidemic of horrific child abuse perpetrated by priests with whom he served and shared houses. He had no interest in noting that Pell was himself convicted in 2020 of child abuse (the conviction was subsequently overturned when a church investigation did not find sufficient evidence to corroborate the accusation), or that a report from the commonwealth of Australia's Royal Commission into Institutional Responses to Child Sexual Abuse found that Pell not only knew about the child abuse committed by others but failed to take the proper steps to respond to complaints about predator priests.[37] Carlson was certain that "the gay community" of Sydney was behind the accusations against Pell.[38]

Carlson announced his hatred of all things homosexual very early in his career, and he was rewarded in 1988 when the Reagan administration appointed him to head a National Commission on Children, a position he held until 1993.[39] It was in the context of that work that Carlson took a fateful trip to Russia in 1995. In Moscow, Carlson met with a pair of sociology professors, Anatoly Antonov and Victor Medkov, who shared his concerns about the rise of women's equality and gay rights. By their own account, the Russians learned a great deal from Carlson, and they translated his work with reverence. Mainly, they learned how to frame their passionate homophobia and revulsion to equality as a project on behalf of "the natural family," and how to package the resulting demographic paranoia for the benefit of a nationalist political movement. The outcome of the meeting was the establishment in 1997 of the World Congress of Families (WCF), a group intended to unite America's Christian right with like-minded activists in Russia and Europe.[40]

The WCF soon picked up support from its two main constituencies. In America, Brian S. Brown and his fellow leaders of the National Organization for Marriage formed common cause with other reactionary groups such as the ADF and Focus on the Family, along with international allies such as the Spain-based advocacy group CitizenGO, representatives from the Vatican, the far-right Fidesz Party in Hungary, and the far-right Law and Justice (PiS) party in Poland, among others.[41] In Russia, the contributors and participants came from the echelons of the new ruling elite and priestly class. Over the subsequent three decades, Carlson's American-born-and-bred politics would rise to power alongside the new Russian oligarchy—and then it would turn around to hit back hard at America.[42]

SOME OF THE reforms that the Irish activist Úna Bean Mhic Mhathúna promoted as a leader of the Housewives Union might count as progressive. She advocated for school meals for children, free travel for pensioners, and the right of women to serve on juries. Other aspects of the program were distinctly regressive. She achieved fame with a letter to the prime minister of Ireland in which she denounced "career women" and demanded that mothers be laid off from the Irish public sector. She was also vehemently opposed to any form of sex education or premenstrual advice for girls.[43]

Like her American counterpart Phyllis Schlafly, Úna appeared to have been convinced that greater employment opportunities and equal rights for women would undermine any security and dignity women might claw back from a deeply and irredeemably unequal society. Women's rights activists, she said, were nothing but "fornicators," "dirty sluts," "tarts," and "filthy bastards who should never get married." At the 1995 referendum count of the Divorce Referendum, which resulted in the liberalization of divorce law, she shouted at the victorious campaigners, "G'way ye wife-swapping sodomites!"[44]

Úna's young daughter, Niamh, was just fourteen years old at the time of Joseph Scheidler's visit, and she was struck by the graphic images he brought with him of aborted fetuses. Niamh was transfixed. She resolved on the spot to dedicate herself to the global antiabortion movement.[45]

It is plausible that Niamh had also absorbed her mother's view that dignity for women hinged on restriction, rather than loosening, of freedoms. "They embraced the pretense that abortion is healthcare, and they voted for a lie that tells women they have a choice, when really what they're telling them is that when you have a crisis pregnancy you are on your own," she said at the 2019 All Ireland Rally for Life, commenting on the 2018 vote that repealed the country's abortion ban. "So much for caring about women."[46]

It isn't hard to detect the undercurrents of social class and nationalist identity that seem to have informed Niamh's antiabortion politics from the beginning. In her speeches, she references Thomas MacDonagh, one of the seven leaders of the Easter Rising of 1916, which played a role in Ireland's struggle for independence.[47] She and her movement have portrayed their enemies on the prochoice side of the debate as foreign interlopers who introduced the toxins of global liberalism into the Emerald Isle. With an affinity for bold lipstick and leather and denim jackets, she is a well-cultivated representative of the retro-feminist side of today's prolife movement. "Women deserve better than abortion's empty promises," she says, castigating Ireland's recently liberalized abortion laws for "treating women and their preborn babies with contempt."[48]

Even as her rhetoric suggested conflict with a purportedly global elite, Niamh herself was soon enmeshed in a global fellowship of antiabortion crusaders. Her brassy, militant tactics won admirers from the same network of Paul Marx acolytes that had brought forth her own activism. Soon she was collaborating with antiabortion organizers in the UK and Europe.[49] As the cofounder of Youth Defense, one of Ireland's most influential antiabortion organizations, she occupies a prominent position at international prolife conferences, and her work is routinely featured on leading Catholic Church–sponsored news platforms as well as secular platforms.[50]

The impact of these international influences is easily discernible in Niamh's own political practice—and especially how that practice continues the work of her mother but in a very different register. Abortion has long been a major issue in Ireland; Niamh has absorbed how to make it *the* issue. She appears to use "life" as the doctrine that not only defines religion but also divides the political world between the pure and the tainted, between an authentic local "nation" versus a global, cosmopolitan "other."

Paradoxically, Niamh herself, along with her fellow antiabortion activists, is a kind of globalist, even arguably an imperialist. The implicit political vision of a righteous oligarchy founded on a certain gender hierarchy is a convenient means of vastly expanding the power that Niamh and her cadre of like-minded zealots hold. Antidemocratic nationalism makes heavy use of antiglobalist rhetoric, yet its success depends critically on the creation of a likeminded global power structure and uniform imposition of global religions' norms. The supposedly local regimes it promotes depend for their survival on an illiberal oligarchy that operates without borders.

On the other side of the struggle is Grainne Griffin, the contemplative, thirtyish codirector of Together for Yes, an umbrella group of over seventy organizations representing a cross section of Irish civil society. With her law diploma, hipster-lite wardrobe, and passion for Irish literary fiction, Griffin is a relatable, if somewhat reluctant, spokesperson for a generation of young Irish women and men who are pushing back against the influence of the conservative wing of the church in politics and society.

In 2018, Together for Yes scored a historic victory when the Irish public voted overwhelmingly to support abortion law liberalization. Yet access remains scarce. Following the examples set by their American counterparts, antiabortion campaigners like Niamh have adopted new tactics: creating sham websites and fake pregnancy centers, introducing legislation to enforce restrictive time limits, establishing twenty-four-hour demonstrations outside maternity hospitals, using messaging and influence techniques crafted by U.S. activists, and working behind the scenes with political and clerical allies to roll back recent gains.[51]

"There is more intimidation happening, and it's more aggressive," says Griffin. "It isn't just deterring women from getting the care they need, it is also driving women toward unsafe abortions and making their lives grueling and dangerous. It is also deterring doctors to come on to the lists in terms of them being able to provide services to those in need. So for us this is a really critical issue."

Meanwhile, for Niamh Ui Bhriain, the U.S. Supreme Court's decision in the case of *Dobbs v. Jackson Women's Health Organization* to overturn *Roe v. Wade* came like a shot in the arm. At a 2022 antiabortion rally organized by March for Life UK, she enthused, "We have renewed hope and energy and a sense of excitement, but more than that we know the importance of defiance— of refusing to bow down to the establishment, of being unafraid [to] be counter-cultural when that's what it takes to end abortion."[52]

IN THE YEARS immediately following Allan Carlson's trip to Moscow, the cultural "technology transfer" moved in the same direction as the electronics technology transfer—mainly from West to East—that is, from America's Christian nationalists to Russia's emerging oligarchic-nationalist class. The Americans, led by figures such New Right activist Paul Weyrich, effectively taught the emerging Russian elite how religious nationalism could be deployed in service of illiberal and antidemocratic ends.[53] In particular, the Americans shared with their Russians counterparts a determination to frame the fear and loathing of gay people and hostility to women's equality as part of a nationalist, "pro-family" vision that could be used to secure authoritarian forms of governance and protect the privilege and property of an elite. Vladimir Putin seized the opportunity and swiftly adopted these and other religious-nationalist strategies to consolidate his power, as well as raiding the state to enrich his cronies and create a protective oligarchy.[54] He was quick to see the geostrategic value of an alliance with the "pro-family" forces in the West, and he was just as quick to sacrifice the rights of people inside Russia to curry favor with Russia's reactionary sectors as well as extremists on the outside.

A central figure in bringing America's reactionary right into alignment with the Russian kleptocracy was Brian S. Brown, a founder and longtime leader of the National Organization for Marriage.[55] Raised in Whittier, California, Brown grew up in Cold War America, and he eyed Russia accordingly—as part of the axis of evil. While studying at Oxford University in England in the 1990s, however, he converted to Catholicism—not just any Catholicism, but the reactionary variety associated with so-called natural law theorist and

Oxford don John Finnis.[56] A key mentor for figures such as Supreme Court justice Neil Gorsuch and the Princeton University–based professor and ultraconservative legal activist Robert P. George, Finnis has argued that, in virtue of natural law, same-sex intimacy is the moral equivalent of bestiality.[57] For his part, Brown has said that he believes gay people should not exist.[58]

In 2007, Brown joined with George in creating the National Organization for Marriage and became its president.[59] His leadership squad included Chuck Stetson, chair of the Bible Literacy Project and its arm Essentials in Education, which seeks to promote sectarian religious coursework in public schools. Also on the leadership team was John Eastman, aka Co-Conspirator 2 in the Trump federal indictment, who took over as chairman of the board in 2011. Brown went on to establish the International Organization of the Family (IOF), which aims to promote a broad reactionary agenda worldwide. His trajectory was destined to lead him to Russia; in 2013, he traveled to Moscow and spoke before a committee of Russia's parliament, the Duma.

Brown came to see Russia as a critical ally in the struggle to impose "the natural family" by force of law.[60] He has played a key role in the IOF-affiliated WCF, and through his contacts became a key figure in related organizations in several countries. He sits on the board of CitizenGO and appears to be an important intermediary in the movement of funds across the "natural family" world. He is on the board of directors of the PNfV and has scored private meetings with Supreme Court justices Brett Kavanaugh and Samuel Alito.[61]

The global "natural family" has clearly learned much from its American originators—though it sometimes has a rather different public face or advocates for different policy preferences. As always, there are nuances specific to different countries. On the other hand, it might also be said that the Americans are starting to learn from their counterparts, inasmuch as American activists in recent years have been even less guarded than previously, especially with regards to their homophobia.

Journalist M. Gessen, who is married to a woman and has children, interviewed Brown at a 2016 gathering of the WCF in Tbilisi. Gessen asked him whether he could imagine a world in which Gessen's family and his might coexist. His answer: "No."[62] None of this makes Brown unwelcome in the highest Republican political circles in the United States.

The closely aligned organization Agenda Europe similarly seeks a "restoration of the natural order," and Agenda Europe's man in Poland is Aleksander Stepkowski.[63] Born in 1974, Stepkowski is a professor of sociology and law. In 2014 he participated in a WCF conference and drafted and endorsed a "World Family Declaration."[64] "Never before has there been a universal banner uniting all people to rally in protection of the natural family," the declaration reads.[65] Stepkowski returned to Poland and cofounded the Ordo Iuris Center for Legal Culture, an extremely well-funded think tank.[66] From his new perch, Stepkowski went on to help draft legislation tightening Poland's existing abortion bans, which were already among the most restrictive in the world. The legislation prohibited abortion even for gross fetal abnormalities and has resulted in the deaths of women experiencing pregnancy complications.[67]

The draconian restrictions ignited the largest Polish protest movement since the 1980s—the so-called coat-hanger rebellion.[68] Stepkowski and his fellow travelers paid a steep price at the ballot box in the 2023 parliamentary election, when enough voters supported opposition parties that right-wing populists were denied a majority.[69]

But the American connection, no less than the Russian connection, remains alive and well at Ordo Iuris. One of its partners on a variety of projects is the right-wing legal advocacy juggernaut Alliance Defending Freedom (ADF), which is U.S.-based but has established multiple offices in Europe, the UK, and Asia. Another partner is the European Center for Law and Justice, founded by former president Trump's lawyer Jay Sekulow, which has funneled over $3.3 million to religious lobbyists, many of them with ties to the Kremlin. Thanks to the efforts of Stepkowski and his colleagues and allies, Poland became a textbook case of rising religious authoritarianism in Europe, with a state-controlled media that trumpeted their talking points at every turn. President Andrzej Duda declared that support for gay rights is "an ideology" and "even more destructive to the human being" than communism,[70] and a third of municipalities declared themselves "LBGT-free zones"—all in order to defend "Christian values," as one leader of the ruling party put it.[71]

The ADF certainly recognizes the benefits of exporting the counterrevolution. Greg Scott, vice president of communications for the ADF, confirmed for me that the organization's budget exceeded $102 million in the fiscal year

2021–22. That's an increase from $60 million in 2018. Between 2015 and 2020, according to the ADF's publicly available tax data for 2020, overseas expenditures rose from $3 million to almost $10 million.[72] When I asked Scott if overseas expenditures had increased in subsequent years, he and other ADF representatives declined to offer a direct response.

"We are dedicated to the promotion of fundamental freedoms for all, and ADF International's efforts are focused on areas where human rights are under threat," ADF International's legal communications director, Elyssa Koren, told me instead. Protecting human rights, according to the ADF mindset, involves promoting antisodomy laws around the world, including a law in Belize that, before it was overturned, made gay sex punishable by ten years' imprisonment.[73] According to the platform 76crimes.com, 65 nations have laws against homosexuality, and seven countries, six of them Muslim majority, impose or permit the death penalty for consensual gay sex. One can be fairly sure that the ADF will not intervene in the human rights and religious liberty violations upon which these laws are based.

IN 2018, LEONARDO Garnier, the former minister of education from Costa Rica, was sitting at his kitchen table with two of his three teenage daughters at their home in a leafy San José neighborhood when he began to hear a cacophony of chants, shouts, and other strange sounds from just outside. In hushed tones, he told his daughters to retreat to the back of the house, and then the bearded university professor gingerly made his way into the living room and peered through the window. Outside his front door was a writhing sea of people—men in clerical robes, young men with clenched fists held aloft, middle-aged women bearing signs and bullhorns. Buses, which had apparently been used to transport the motley crew, lined the opposite side of the street. Leading the unexpected spectacle was a brigade of angry-looking nuns in long black habits. As Garnier peered through the window, one of them caught his eye and spat in his direction.

Garnier's sin was to have introduced sex education into Costa Rica's public schools. As he saw it, sex education was the key to protecting teenagers— starting with his own daughters—and empowering them to control their fertility and their lives. The data backed up his claim. Prior to Garnier's work as minister of education, in 2011, the teenage birth rate in Costa Rica had stood at nearly 20 percent. By the time the protestors showed up at his doorstep, it had fallen to 12 percent. Garner was proud that he had been able to succeed where so many others had failed. "Every time a previous minister had tried to introduce sex education it was derailed by the Catholic Church," he said. "But with our efforts we were able to have it included in every public high school."

During his tenure in the ministry of education, Garnier had become accustomed to being on the receiving end of angry messages on social media. Many posts included threats along the lines of "You should die" or "Your mother should have aborted you." Sometimes angry handwritten letters appeared in the mail. While most appeared to be from people who simply wanted to let off steam, in recent months, Garnier had noticed, the attacks had become more sustained, and the threats more specific. Still, the demonstration in front of his home came as a shock. There was nothing haphazard about it; the event had clearly been planned and funded well in advance.

From the beginning, Garnier's program had met with opposition from representatives of the Catholic Church. By 2018, however, Catholic leaders had joined with those from the growing and powerful evangelical movement. The difference was striking. "The opposition became more violent in the rhetoric and the social networks," Garnier says. The tone had become "apocalyptic," he notes; the protestors seemed to think that sex education for teenagers was just one step short of global catastrophe. "Some of these people take this very personally," Garnier remarks, "and they can be quite aggressive." The politics were different, too. "Politicians who had previously seemed favorable to the program now began to speak out against it." For the first time, Garnier began to wonder whether his short-lived yet successful reform program would be scuttled.

Today, as special adviser to the UN's secretary general for transforming education and a lecturer at the University of Costa Rica, Garnier watches as the movement unfolds in his country in real time. "A big chunk of our electorate is now responding to this big religious pressure," Garnier tells me, "even within my party, which is liberal. If politicians don't want to lose votes, they have to say nice things about these religious interests. Our own candidate from our party, which is the more liberal party, has even started saying things against our sex ed program, which has been so successful in reducing rates of unwanted pregnancy among our teenagers, because he now needs support from right-wing Catholics and evangelicals. It is affecting our whole society." Garnier pauses for a minute, then shakes his head. "That is very dangerous."

Reflecting on the hostile demonstration that landed on his doorstep, Garnier admits, "It was a bit scary. But the funny thing," he continues, "was that if you dig deeper, it is really about the money and power, and not just sex."

To understand the roots of the opposition, Garnier began to look for the source of the ideas that seemed to animate evangelical and Catholic opponents of the curriculum. Abortion was not the issue, as he knew; abortion is already illegal in Costa Rica, with very few exceptions. As he searched through the material on the opposition, he was surprised to come across a certain phrase, repeated over and over: "gender ideology." This, he concluded, was a signifier that appeared to unite evangelical and Catholic religious leaders—two groups that Garnier had previously assumed were somewhat at odds.

The idea of "gender ideology," as Garnier saw it, encompassed opposition to female equality and intolerance of gay people, as well as transgender identity. It also seemed to be accompanied everywhere with an embrace of right-wing economic theory and a rejection of rights and protections for the workforce. "Gender ideology," in short, did not simply refer to transgender people. It had become the signifier in which all social change that threatened the existing gender and economic order could be inscribed. Conservative religious forces of all denominations had united in the fight for far-right market fundamentalist economics. The phrase was being used in the way that "critical race theory" was being used in America—a catchall for a range of issues that could trigger anxieties about identity in order to push forth a broad reactionary agenda.

The other surprising fact that Garnier discovered is that the anti-gender-ideology project that had shaken his country's political balance did not originate anywhere near Costa Rica. The impetus, as he saw it, came from Spain, from a group associated with an extremist Spanish activist and lawyer named Ignacio Arsuaga. But Arsuaga's group appeared to be interlinked with a collection of activist organizations whose principal leaders and funders are to be found in the United States and Russia, among the Christian nationalists and the oligarchs.

BACK IN THE 1990s, Alexey Komov was a nightclub impresario with a keen interest in yoga and a deep attachment to one particular guru. When his yogi came down with terminal cancer, however, Komov was devastated. His guru concluded that yoga is "satanic" and, before his death, was baptized in the Orthodox church and became a monk. The day Komov attended his funeral, he began to study theology. Pretty soon he switched vocations and become the helpmeet of the rising oligarchs of Russia.[74] From a business standpoint, it was surely a good move.

Komov was soon working with Konstantin Malofeev, an oligarch who funded Russian separatists in Ukraine and who has been accused of multiple financial crimes and sanctioned by various Western governments.[75] In 2014, Malofeev hosted a secret "antigay" meeting with like-minded European conservatives in Vienna.[76] Another Russian oligarch close to the WCF is Vladimir Yakunin, who trails a cloud of accusations of wrongdoing. Malofeev and Yakunin have long records of stoking both far-right and far-left movements around the world in ways that redound to the benefit of Russia's moneyed elite, and Komov cast himself as the man to lead the effort with the growing Christian nationalist movement in the West. "Russia should become the prime defenders of faith of conservatives of the world," he told an interviewer.[77]

Komov has become a fixture at the WCF and at IOF events. He has cultivated a special interest in America's religious-right homeschooling movement, hosting some of its most prominent advocates at Russian conferences. He has also made himself indispensable to the massive conservative Christian film industry, an important component of the religious right's messaging strategy. Komov is also closely connected with a Russian oligarch in the media industry whose platform has promoted Russia's own brand of religious nationalism. The fruit of his efforts is apparent in the dense, international network of leaders and funders of religious authoritarianism. "We have hundreds of American conservative leaders coming in the Kremlin like dear guests," he boasts.[78]

Among Komov's various entanglements is one based in Spain. Together with his fellow crusader Brian S. Brown, Komov sits on the board of CitizenGO, the "pressure group" founded by Spanish lawyer and activist Ignacio Arsuaga.

IGNACIO ARSUAGA WAS born in 1973 to an affluent family well stocked with finance ministers, business leaders, and prominent figures in conservative

Spanish society. From an early age he seemed deeply motivated by his anxieties about the existence of gays and lesbians. He also displayed profound hostility to the notion of women's equality. After attending university in Madrid and law school at Fordham University in New York, he committed himself to fighting the culture wars.

His activism began with the promotion of boycotts against the tony Spanish department store El Corte Inglés, as well as a popular restaurant chain, for showing same-sex couples in their advertisements. In 2001, he founded an activist organization, HazteOir ("Make Yourself Heard"), which supports the criminalization of same-sex relationships and opposes birth control as well as abortion. In 2010, he published his ideas in the form of a book, *The Zapatero Project: Chronicle of an Attack on Society*, co-written with M. Vidal Santos.

In his book, Arsuaga lays out the case against "gender ideology." The new laws and cultural norms that grant legitimacy to same-sex relationships, he argues, will lead inevitably to the eradication of gender itself. "These new rights replace the man and woman, the couple who make up the nucleus of the family unit, with any kind of cooperative agreement between two parties," he claims, and thus place "common law partners on the same footing as married couples." Asserting a conspiracy of "secularists, relativists, radical feminists, abortionists, representatives of the homosexual lobby and totalitarians of all stripes and colours" that has infiltrated "almost all institutions concerned with international cooperation," he inveighs with horror against the "shining universe of absolute equality." He is opposed to laws intended to limit domestic violence or to allow women access to family planning services. These and other efforts on behalf of women's rights and dignity represent a "vulgarization" and amount to a direct attack on the family unit. According to Arsuaga, in brief, "gender ideology" is a "tyrannical project designed to subvert our society" and "a totalitarian project designed to suppress *us*."[79]

In 2013, Arsuaga founded CitizenGO. Drawing money and support from American and Russian sources, including Malofeev, CitizenGO perhaps inevitably includes Komov and Brown.[80] In a speech at WCF 2022, Arsuaga was emphatic in aligning himself with the authoritarian project of global illiberalism in both its Christian nationalist and New Right variants. "We are in a religious war," he declared, and the other side consists of "secular progressives" who want to impose "their dictatorship of the politically correct," "a totalitarian ideology" also called "woke ideology."[81]

In the Spanish political context, Arsuaga is explicitly aligned with Vox, the ultraconservative nationalist party.[82] Not surprisingly, his reactionary agenda makes him likewise a supporter of today's Republican Party in the United States; Poland's Ordo Iuris; Hungary's avowedly "illiberal" strongman Viktor Orban; former president Bolsonaro's version of Brazil; and Putin's Russia. CitizenGO's street-level activism, however, extends much farther afield. The organization was recently found to be behind vicious attacks on reproductive rights in Kenya and Ghana, for example.[83]

In Latin America, Arsuaga's movement received a boost when a pair of Argentinian authors, Agustín Laje and Nicolás Márquez, seized upon his ideas. The work they produced, *The Black Book of the New Left*, has enjoyed explosive popularity among Latin American conservatives, who have been known to flash it at conferences and public appearances to demonstrate their intellectual bona fides.[84] Their work too now has a global reach; in 2024, Laje was an honored speaker at Ralph Reed's Road to Majority conference, where he informed his audience about funding sources for the "LGBT agenda." Like Arsuaga, Laje and his coauthor of *The Black Book of the New Left* promote the idea that "gender ideology" is a front for a global conspiracy of secular progressives bent on destroying capitalism and all that is holy.[85]

"The funny thing is that the book starts out as an academic work and seems well written, even if you don't agree with what they are saying," says Costa Rica's erstwhile education minister Garnier. "But then they're expressing an incredible amount of hatred toward women, feminism, and gay people. They are right-wing in terms of economic policy, but mainly they have this conservative obsession with gender order."

Garnier pauses to stroke his beard thoughtfully. "They came to Costa Rica in 2017," he says, "and that's when our problems really began."

The rapid worldwide rise in the reactionary assault on democracy and human rights has not gone unnoticed. "In recent years, different groups and individuals from different religious communities have emerged. Mostly Catholics, but there are also Protestants and Orthodox, who see human rights progress, especially in sexuality, education, and equality, as a threat to their religious freedoms and practices," says Neil Datta, director of the European Parliamentary Forum for Population and Development and a longtime observer of the global conservative movement. "In recent years, ultraconservative groups in Europe have grown stronger, and the attack on fundamental human rights has intensified. We see it most obviously here in Europe, but the effects of their work are felt all over the world."

The important thing to understand, however, is that the growth in the anti-democratic reaction in countries around the world is no accident. It is not merely the result of parallel social changes or convergent cultural evolution. It is to a significant degree the result of intentional and coordinated action on the part of powerful political forces. Above all, the movement is the result of strategic investment on the part of well-connected groups, some of them directly linked to states and national political parties.

Financial surveys that involve investigative teams scraping and analyzing data on thousands of U.S. funders speak to the power of money in the rise of the global far right. According to a 2020 report in OpenDemocracy, Christian-right groups in the United States spent at least $280 million on campaigns against the rights of women and LGBT people across five continents.[86] A subsequent report, released in 2023, showed that anonymous donors funneled $272 million through donor-advised funds in just four tax years from 2017 to 2020; the initial analysis found that more than 40 percent of the donor-advised funds, totaling $113 million, went to four groups: the Alliance Defending Freedom, the Family Research Council, Family Watch International, and Liberty Counsel.[87]

The European Parliamentary Forum has conducted its own studies. From 2009 to 2018, their analysis of the data turned up funding totaling $707.2 million. Of that amount, according to their study, $81.3 million originated from the United States; $188.2 million originated from the Russian Federation; and $437.7 million came from EU sources. The list of contributors— including foundations established by European oligarchs and Russian kleptocrats, along with U.S. organizations such as the Alliance Defending Freedom, the Billy Graham Evangelistic Association, and the Federalist Society—shows the deep and interconnected nature of the movement.[88]

This cross-border activism, moreover, is mutually reinforcing. The movement's achievements in places as widely separated as Costa Rica, Ireland, and Poland would not have been possible without those early exchanges of ideas and staff. A group like the ADF does not establish a global network of offices merely for branding purposes; its network advances goals in the home country by advancing them elsewhere. Perhaps the biggest payoff from the cultivation of the Russia-America axis came with the election of Donald Trump in 2016 and its consequences, which arguably would not have been possible without support from Putin in Russia.

The victims of the global reaction will by no means be limited to women seeking reproductive care or gay people who wish to join together in marriage with those they love. Religious nationalist countries are often "theocratic" in a certain fake sense—that is, they are regimes that endorse a particular religion and attempt to impose that religion and its patriarchal values on society. But they are more accurately described as cronyistic kleptocracies with strong militaristic features and absolute suppression of free speech and political opposition.

It is no mystery why the so-called natural family finds its natural home in authoritarian regimes; it is equally plain why the principal financial backers of the movement come from the Russian oligarchy and the American plutocracy. The activists descended from Paul Benno Marx are free to imagine that they are just "saving babies" or "protecting families." In truth they are the grave-diggers of democracy.

The Way Forward?

Any survey of the antidemocratic reaction in the United States is bound to provoke alarm and perhaps even a feeling of hopelessness. There is no getting around the grim facts about the threat facing the nation. And yet, if we take the long view, I continue to think other facts can give us some grounds for optimism.

I draw some of that hope from a consideration of the American past. This isn't the nation's first visit to the pro-authoritarian rodeo. In the struggle against the slaveholding oligarchy, in the taming of what, in 1907, President Theodore Roosevelt called the "malefactors of great wealth," and in the advancement of the civil rights movement, justice ultimately prevailed, however imperfectly. In the long run, it can be hoped, the MAGA movement and its defenders won't look that different from Patrick Buchanan and the America Firsters. They, like Tucker Carlson, Stew Peters, and Laura Ingraham, will recede into the grubby footnotes of history, where they may join the likes of Father Coughlin, Bob Jones Sr., Gerald L. K Smith, and other purveyors of grievance and race hate. But the descent into fascism—if it hasn't already happened by the time these pages reach you—remains the most likely path through which the American experiment ends, if it is to end.

Meeting the present challenge won't be easy, and there is no guarantee of success. Still, those who hope for progress can take comfort in the knowledge that the facts are on our side. In this brief afterword, I want to draw attention to six principal findings reported in this book, and which should be of interest to a pro-democracy movement:

- We are (still) in the majority.
- They are divided.
- The separation of church and state is a good idea—and we should try it.
- Extreme levels of material inequality are eroding democracy.
- Knowledge is power.
- Organization matters.

WE ARE STILL IN THE MAJORITY

Those who wish to protect democracy in the United States should hold at the front of their minds a simple fact: We—that is, those of us who reject the politics of conquest and division—are in the majority. Though they claim to speak for "real Americans," the antidemocratic reactionaries are nothing more than a disproportionately mobilized minority. It follows that those of us who believe in democracy must build a tent big enough to keep the pro-democracy majority together, and mobilize accordingly.

This is what Lincoln accomplished in prosecuting the Civil War, and it was what the Germans failed to accomplish in the interwar period, when various factions to the left of the Nazi party failed to put the commitment to democracy ahead of their many differences. In the last several years I have heard multiple keynote speakers at right-wing and Christian nationalist gatherings repeat a quote famously attributed to Ronald Reagan: "The person who agrees with you 80 percent of the time is a friend and an ally—not a 20 percent traitor."[1] We would do well to follow that advice.

Of course, being in the majority is no guarantee of success in the American system. We have to face up to the fact that the U.S. Constitution can be and has been exploited for countermajoritarian purposes. The guardrails of our democracy were meant to protect the rights of minorities, not to facilitate the rise of a militant minority that wishes to dominate. If we are to guard against the new American fascism, we will have to consider some political reforms.

- Some components might include examination of the Electoral College, which is a debilitating legacy from the founding period that

THE WAY FORWARD? 237

favors minority rule and distorts presidential campaigns by funneling
them into a nonsensical collection of "battleground states."
- The Supreme Court and the federal judiciary, too, must be rescued
  from corruption and partisan capture. Enforceable (rather than
  "self-monitored") ethics guidelines, among other measures, should be
  deliberated and are within the power of Congress to achieve. Term
  limits and other reforms must be considered in the efforts to create a
  legitimate court from the ruins of the present one.
- Voting rights must be protected, too. Here again the path to
  reforming race-based gerrymandering and targeted
  disenfranchisement runs through the legislative and judicial processes
  that we already have.

MORE FUNDAMENTAL REFORMS to America's governmental institutions are
also worth considering, if only to remind us of how hard the work of democracy
is. In another legacy from the past, the Senate, for example, gives the six
hundred thousand residents of Wyoming as much say as forty million Cali-
fornians. The system of territorial representation, according to which congressional representatives are elected within geographically defined districts, may
offer trade and land protections and other advantages. But a more proportional
system of representation could place a check on the antidemocratic reaction's
ability to leverage a radicalized minority.

Structural reforms aside, building a majority for democracy means
convincing Americans that democracy matters—and that it matters more than
the many policies that are rightly the subject of debate within any democracy.
Moderates, liberals, and progressives can learn something here from the right.
Their tent includes lots of people who really should not be getting along with
one another. Which brings up the next lesson gleaned from the reporting:

THEY ARE DIVIDED

Human beings have an unfortunate tendency to construe adversaries as
diabolically unified in their monomaniacal pursuit of evil. The antidemocratic
reaction epitomizes this tendency when proponents like Flight 93 guru
Michael Anton identify the pro-democracy enemy as "the globalist borg"—a

characterization that anyone who has been inside the tent at a gathering of disputatious liberals and progressives knows to be laughably optimistic.

But the same caution applies to understanding the antidemocratic reaction. It isn't under the thumb of Satan or any of his deputies. It may be organized, but there are cracks in the coalition. It is a gathering of sometimes un-like-minded people wrapped in a bundle of incompatible beliefs and agendas. That is its great weakness, and it should be exploited.

The source of the contradictions in the antidemocratic reaction is that it rests on an alliance between oppressors and many of their principal victims. It relies on the money of the few whose primary interest is to protect their power and privilege at the expense of the rest of society, and it relies on the votes of the many who will by and large suffer under the same extractive arrangements. To add to the mix, it trades in the ideas of an intellectual class that is parasitic on both sides—sucking money out of the oligarchs while offering right-wing identity politics and false hope to the resentful.

The reliance on grievance and fear as a main political binding agent may offer the satisfaction of group identity, in the short term at least, but its contradictions are easily exposed. This is why reactionaries like J. D. Vance and Josh Hawley point in so many directions at once. On the one hand, these graduates of elite universities expect us to believe that they are the genuine representatives of the common man, the forgotten hillbillies, and all that. With reactionary intellectuals at their side, they pretend to stand up for workers against oppressive corporations. On the other hand, there is zero realistic chance that they will deviate in any significant way from the preferred policies of the private equity managers that have funded their careers. The only thing we can be sure of is they will retire to places like the Claremont Institute, where they may join a new priestly elite that promises to justify the ways of money to man.

This is why the ideology of the antidemocratic reaction is such a mess. Does it want "small government"—or does it want a government big enough to share your bedroom and your body? Does it want "free speech"—or does it want to ban books, limit the information doctors are allowed to share with their patients, and compel religious speech in public schools? Does it want "deregulation"—or does it want to bring "the woke corporations" of the world to heel? Does it want religious freedom, or does it want theocracy? Is it standing up for "hardworking Americans"—or is destroying workplace protections and setting up the rule of a new, righteously conservative elite and helping the funders grow their fortunes?

One job of the pro-democracy movement must be simply to heighten and expose these contradictions—not just for the benefit of the general public but for the enlightenment of supporters of the antidemocratic reaction themselves.

EXTREME LEVELS OF INEQUALITY ARE ERODING DEMOCRACY

Those who would defend democracy should also keep in mind that the grotesque levels of inequality in our time are contributing to the present crisis. It's not just colossal differences in wealth that matter, but immense gaps in status, health, and life opportunities. To be clear, this doesn't mean that the have-nothings are leading the revolution. On the contrary, the bulk of the danger comes from a sector of the have-everythings: the Funders of the antidemocratic reaction, along with their Thinker, Sergeant, and Power Player enablers.

The facts reported in this book may count as proof that Louis Brandeis was right when he reportedly said: "We can have democracy in this country, or we can have great wealth concentrated in a few hands, but we can't have both."[2] The Supreme Court in its current, antidemocratic incarnation would not exist were it not for Leonard Leo and his billionaire friends. The gerrymandered state legislatures would not be suppressing voter rights, plundering public education budgets on behalf of right-wing cronies and religious groups, and passing regressive antilabor legislation if it weren't for the State Policy Network and the various other groups representing the paranoid wing of the plutocracy. To be clear, not every wealthy person throws their money at antisocial causes; a good number are funding existing democracy-building initiatives as well as starting new ones. But as I have detailed in this book, right-wing money has tended to be more strategic, and in this struggle it may well be more plentiful.

Among the solutions to consider: Let's try having a progressive system of taxation. The present system of taxation is flat at best, and even regressive at the top.[3] Anybody who parrots the market fundamentalist nonsense that taxing the superwealthy hinders prosperity should be given a ticket back to the 1950s, when the United States combined progressive taxation with widely shared economic growth.

It's also time to dispense with the religion of economism, which asks us to take as an article of faith the idea that the rich deserve every penny they get because they and they alone are the creators of wealth. The massive fortunes we see today are largely the work of extractive monopolies, major market inefficiencies, and the soft (and sometimes hard) corruption that goes with them. Such concentrations of titanic wealth arise from antidemocratic means; it is little surprise, then, that they are deployed, as I have shown in this book, for antidemocratic ends.

Also, how about we shine a light on all that dark money? The idea that money is speech and that speech isn't free unless rich people can hide behind shell companies and anonymous donations is one of many crimes against democracy that can be laid at the feet of the present Supreme Court. It can be fixed with legislation, and it should be.

At the other end of the inequality spectrum, where most of the population lives, the outlines of the solution are also clear, if rather more difficult and complex to implement. The key may be to give the non-college-educated supporters of right-wing populism everything they say they don't want. They've signed up for antilabor "right-to-work" politics, when what they need is stronger unions and the right to negotiate better wages and conditions. They've bought into the antigovernment meme, when what they need is representative government, healthy and well-funded public education at all levels, better information systems, and some sort of public or at least affordable health service. Some have been persuaded that abortion is the great evil of our time, but they should be able to decide with whom to form their families, if and when to have children, and how many they wish to raise. Many have come to believe that "others" are the source of their troubles, when in fact "others" may be their natural allies.

To be clear, giving voters what they say they don't want at a time when workplace safety regulations are equated with socialism and contraception is equated with baby murder isn't a great way to win their votes in the moment. It is necessarily a long-term strategy. It aims to change the fundamental conditions that provoke the anxieties and misunderstandings that in turn drive people to vest their hopes in strongman fantasies and racist demagoguery. While navigating from here to there, democracy's defenders need to be alert to messaging and identity politics on the right, which generally succeed by misrepresenting efforts to help *all* the people as narrow efforts to only help *those* people.

For now, the identitarian messages and disinformation to which these voters are subjected may well drown out these material improvements. In fact, a great number have been persuaded that God has a partisan identity—which brings me to the next point:

THE SEPARATION OF CHURCH AND STATE IS A GOOD IDEA—AND WE SHOULD TRY IT

Those who would defend democracy in America must recognize that certain kinds of religion have been exploited and weaponized. The network of reactionary faith leaders, houses of worship, and national organizations described in this book—the pastors who whipped up the crowd that later stormed the Capitol on January 6; the "prophets" who take to the hustings on behalf of election deniers; the various institutes and centers that train up prospective school board members and activists to prosecute culture wars across the country—this network may claim to be religiously inspired, and parts of it may even look like a religion on Sundays. On most days of the week, however, it is a component of a political party. More exactly, it is an anti-American, antidemocratic, authoritarian party that exploits its spiritual claims over its congregants to advance its own power and its own political and economic agenda. Moreover, it is a party that operates with public subsidies and special privileges not granted to other parties. The separation of church and state is a noble ideal; but it is not the reality on the ground in America today.

The alliance of church and state in its present form is not merely a matter of symbols and monuments, or pastors expressing their political convictions. It's about money. Currently, political parties and their candidates are exploiting the loophole that allows them to run unregulated, tax-exempt political campaigns out of churches and other houses of worship. We ought to at least recognize political campaigns run out of churches and faith-based organizations as what they are, instead of pretending that they are exercises in the freedom of religion, and we should consider ways to address this loophole in campaign finance regulation.

Making the matter worse are features of our system of taxation. In the late eighteenth century, when Virginia attempted to impose a tax on the public in support of the established Anglican church, the Baptists objected, and Thomas Jefferson and James Madison joined them in opposition. Compelling Peter to pay for the religion of Paul through taxation, they said, was a gross injustice and a violation of religious freedom. With the creation of tax deductions and ongoing development of unique exemptions for religious organizations and philanthropies, however, we have brought about exactly what they opposed. American taxpayers of every religion and no religion are now compelled to subsidize every church, temple, and mosque. The arrangement might have been seen as desirable or at least acceptable as the price of life in a complex economy, had some of the churches, temples, and mosques not turned themselves into political cells. Today, it makes no sense. Why should Peter be compelled to subsidize groups that seek to deprive him of his right to marry or vote?

Making things still worse are the many schemes intended to siphon public money, much of it from public education budgets, into religious organizations. Such arrangements are devastating for public education systems, but the comingling of church and state they represent is possibly even more damaging. Under the inaccurate name of "religious liberty," we are moving step by step toward a system in which the government funnels money to religious groups, and those religious groups in turn deploy their spiritual hold over congregations to keep their favorite political party in power. This is exactly what America's founders meant when they barred "an establishment of religion," and they prohibited it in the best piece of real estate in our Constitution—the Establishment Clause, which is the first clause of our First Amendment.

Some of the harms here are due to misguided jurisprudence on religious liberty coming from the Supreme Court. The First Amendment right to the free exercise of religion, in the current court's thinking, can be roughly translated as the right of conservative Christians to discriminate against those who offend their religious sensibilities. The First Amendment prohibition against an establishment of religion, in the current jurisprudence, has been tossed aside in favor of the preposterous position that denying conservative Christian groups access to public money, no questions asked, represents a violation of their "religious liberty."

While better laws and better justices could take us a long way toward a genuine religious freedom, including freedom from having to fund any religion if you don't want to, the freedom from having your most impactful healthcare decisions guided by the religion of others, and the freedom from religious coercion in public schools, these legal reforms can only go so far in strengthening democracy against the theocratic wing of the antidemocratic reaction.

A key reform can come from within churches and religions. A great many Christians believe the religion of Jesus has more to do with loving thy neighbor than chasing fugitive pregnant women across state borders, the destruction of child labor protections, and protecting the right to own AR-15s. I regret to say that I have not had room in this book to adequately present their side of the story. If they can win the hearts and minds of the faithful, democracy is sure to benefit.

KNOWLEDGE IS POWER

The antidemocratic reaction combines counterrevolutionary elements aiming to preserve their power with revolutionary elements seeking to destroy the existing order. This alliance thrives in confusion and covert arrangements. Expose it to the light, and enough people to the truth, and it will wither away. As a matter of principle, anything that advances rational public discourse advances democracy. As a practical matter: the pro-democracy movement must be committed to the defense of strong public education and to the creation of a media system accountable to the public and the truth.

The assault on public education from the antidemocratic reaction isn't just about prosecuting the culture wars on the playgrounds, and it isn't just about privatization cronies cashing in, either—although it is in part both of those things. It is also about raising a population compliant with authoritarian rule. Nothing scares a right-wing oligarch more than a populace capable of questioning the idea that market forces will solve all their problems. Nothing scares would-be theocrats more than a student body educated to think for themselves. The antidemocratic reaction is well aware of the wisdom of Thomas Jefferson—in essence that a people that wants to be ignorant and free wants what is impossible—and it has decided that ignorance is preferable to a free people.

The crisis in media is too big to cover in detail here, but a couple of aspects are worth highlighting. A first step is to recognize that the system is broken not because "both sides" apply their partisan biases in equal measure. It is failing because the assault tilts definitively to one side. Studies such as *Partisanship, Propaganda, and Disinformation: Online Media and the 2016 Presidential Election* by authors associated with Harvard University's Berkman Klein Center for Internet & Society, to give but one example, have made clear that the system is not symmetrical.[4] While there is certainly disinformation on the left, too, the right-wing ecosystem is far better at pushing manufactured untruths into mainstream discourse. The chief flaw of the moderately well-functioning media in the center is that, in its defensive and misguided efforts to appear nonpartisan, it breathes air into the bellows of antidemocratic propaganda. Furthermore, the system of private ownership and exploitation of the data we all generate in our online activities is a giant machine for dysfunction.

ORGANIZATION MATTERS

The most important lesson I draw from observing the antidemocratic reaction to date is that its success has largely been an organizational one. Victory (such as it is) did not come from better ideas; it has been the result of a massive, decades-long, farsighted investment in the people and infrastructure of an antidemocratic shadow party, and this investment has deposited its toxic fruit in courthouses and state capitols across the country. A pro-democracy movement can learn a few things from this success, even if it does not wish to emulate the reaction. The imperatives are:

- *Think long term.* The people who built the conservative think tank world and legal ecosystem were not merely planning to win the next election. They were aiming to win a culture war spanning decades. The success of the Federalist Society and related organizations in packing the judiciary was forty years in the making. The campaign to make a holy scripture out of market fundamentalism started even earlier.
- *Invest in organizations and people.* With some exceptions, liberal and progressive money tends to go to siloed causes. Conservative money goes to people, institutions, and organizational networks. One approach aims at policy and electoral victories, the other aims at fielding an army. At this point, it is pretty clear which tactic is more effective. Just about every antidemocratic operative of note has passed through the Leadership Institute, taken up a fellowship at a right-wing think tank, accepted a position within a right-wing policy group or ultraconservative religious network, or dined, proverbially speaking, with the Council for National Policy. The strength of the

antidemocratic reaction lies in its dense organizational infrastructure and the network of individuals who know they can count on building careers and shoring up their own economic security within it.

- *Build coalitions.* While the left often divides itself into purity cliques or operates out of relatively siloed causes, the right has shown a willingness to make plenty of bedfellows.
- *Go local.* The chief supports of the antidemocratic reaction are the networks of faith-based organizations that mobilize the Infantry. This is where you create poll watchers, door knockers, school board candidates, and town council members.

ULTIMATELY THE QUESTION I would like to address is the one I am asked repeatedly when I discuss the antidemocratic movement in public settings: What can I do? What can one person do in the face of such a powerful and well-funded threat?

To which I can only say: Put this book down and get to work now! Support your school community. Get involved in local governance. If you belong to a church or house of worship, work to bring your fellows to the side of justice and democracy. Find others who are committed to protecting the vote or involved in voter engagement and education campaigns. Reach out to those who feel politically disenfranchised. Tell them democracy matters. Tell them the republic is theirs—if they can keep it.

ACKNOWLEDGMENTS

My work in this field began more than fifteen years ago with an article published in the *Santa Barbara Independent* on the appearance of a Good News Club in my daughter's public elementary school. I owe an enduring debt of gratitude to *Independent* cofounder and editor Marianne Partridge.

I'd like to thank the wonderful people at Bloomsbury Publishing, including my editors Anton Mueller, Morgan Jones, and Ryan Kearney, for championing and improving the work. Cheers to my brilliant agent, Andrew Stuart, for his insight, humor, patience, and unflagging support.

This project would not have been possible without the many individuals who invested their time and tested their patience in sharing their experiences with me. I regret that I could not include them all. Some are acknowledged in the text, but others prefer to remain anonymous, so I thank them anonymously.

My research is informed by the work of other writers, researchers, academics, and others in the field. Some of their names appear directly in the text. A good number of others are acknowledged in the footnotes. I offer the names of the rest, in no particular order—with a few caveats: (a) this list is incomplete, and (b) the opinions in this book should be blamed on me, not on those who have been generous enough to assist me:

Melissa Deckman, Aaron J. Koller, Peter Montgomery, Anthea Butler, Sarah Posner, Rev. Kelly Brown Douglas, Amanda Tyler, Bradley Onishi, Jonathan Wilson-Hartgrove, Laura Field, Matthew Taylor, Maura Conway, Philip Gorski, Kathryn Joyce, Ana Brakus, Cynthia Idriss, Ruth Braunstein, Michelle Boorstein, Robert O'Harrow, Lauren Sandler, Michelle Goldberg, Andrew Whitehead, Jay Michaelson, Dahlia Lithwick, Jamie Manson, Sam Perry, Jemar Tisby, Julie Ingersoll, Tom Carter, Kristin Kobes Du Mez, Bill Kristol, Robert P. Jones, Michelangelo Signorile, Obery Hendricks, Rachel Tabachnik, Frederick Clarkson, Marci Hamilton, David Nasaw, Steven K. Green, Lauren Francis Turek, Jane Mayer, Steve Schmidt, Jared Holt, Doug Pagitt, Ryan Stoller, Amanda Marcotte, Jeff Sharlet, Damon Linker, Rachel Laser, Rob Boston, Eboo Patel, Teddy Wilson,

Andrew Seidel, Kyle Spencer, Nick Fish, Michael Podhorzer, Jessica Valenti, Mary Ziegler, Nancy MacLean, Heidi Schlumpf, Jack Jenkins, Daniel K. Williams, Claire Conner, Lisa Graves, Dave Neiwert, Anne Nelson, Steven Livingston, and André Gagné.

Several sections of text draw on findings that I have laid out in earlier pieces for the *New York Times*, NBC, the *New Republic*, the *New York Review of Books*, the *Guardian*, *Religion Dispatches*, and elsewhere. I'd like to thank editors who have supported that work, including Aaron Retica, Michael Tomasky, Jason Linkins, Meredith Bennett-Smith, Jarvis DeBerry, Noa Yachot, Matt Seaton, Paul O'Donnell, and Evan Derkacz.

I'd like to thank Thea Smith and Kira Smith for some editorial assistance and the *God & Country* team for amplifying the message.

To those who hosted me on my travels: thank you for your warmth, generosity, and the morning coffee. A special thanks to the Levinson clan, Skin & Lady, Green Heart, David Lonsdale, and Michelle Gittelman.

Above all I wish to thank my husband, Matthew Stewart.

NOTES

INTRODUCTION

1. Justin Stabley, "What You Need to Know About John Eastman's 2020 Election Charges," PBS, September 21, 2023, https://www.pbs.org/newshour/politics/what-you-need-to-know-about-john-eastmans-2020-election-charges.

2. Jacques Billeaud, "Attorney John Eastman Pleads Not Guilty to Felony Charges in Arizona's Fake Elector Case," AP News, May 17, 2024, https://apnews.com/article/arizona-fake-electors-charges-john-eastman-2020-1d6df9ac00b810a0d54d6fc4ae97ec57.

3. Emmanuel Saez and Gabriel Zucman, "The Rise of Income and Wealth Inequality in America: Evidence from Distributional Macroeconomic Accounts," *Journal of Economic Perspectives* 34, no. 4 (Fall 2020): 3–26, https://pubs.aeaweb.org/doi/pdfplus/10.1257/jep.34.4.3.

4. Maggie Astor, "Heritage Foundation Head Refers to 'Second American Revolution,'" *New York Times*, July 3, 2024, https://www.nytimes.com/2024/07/03/us/politics/heritage-foundation-2025-policy-america.html.

CHAPTER 1: CALIFORNIA DREAMING

1. Leah Bitsky, "Step Inside Meghan Markle and Prince Harry's Ultra-Private $14M Montecito Mansion," *Page Six*, November 16, 2023, https://pagesix.com/2023/11/16/royal-family/step-inside-meghan-markle-and-prince-harrys-14m-montecito-mansion/; Samantha Michaels, "The Escape from the Billionaire Meme Mogul," *Mother Jones*, June 21, 2021, https://www.motherjones.com/criminal-justice/2021/06/russian-sergey-grishin-421-media-billionaire-instagram-content-farm-trump-threats/.

2. Richard Mineards, "McGinity's Travels," *Montecito Journal*, July 11, 2023, https://www.montecitojournal.net/2023/07/11/mcginitys-travels.

3. "Pepsi-Cola Bottling Company of Bakersfield," OpenCorporates, https://opencorporates.com/companies/us_ca/C0258840.

4. Neal Leitereg, "Montecito Trophy Compound with Historical Cottages and Ocean Views Asks $72.5 Million," *Forbes*, April 14, 2021, https://www.forbes.com/sites/forbes-global-properties/2021/04/14/montecito-trophy-compound-with-historical-cottages-and-ocean-views-asks-725-million/.

5. "2535 Sycamore Canyon Rd, Santa Barbara, CA 93108," Zillow, https://www.zillow.com/homedetails/2535-Sycamore-Canyon-Rd-Santa-Barbara-CA-93108/15880729_zpid/.

6. "The James and Joan Lindsey Family Foundation," OpenCorporates, https://opencorporates.com/companies/us_ca/C1874817.

7. "James and Joan Lindsey Family Foundation," ProPublica Nonprofit Explorer, https://projects.propublica.org/nonprofits/organizations/770390011.

8. Katherine Stewart, "The Shock Troops of the Next Big Lie," *New Republic*, January 10, 2022, https://newrepublic.com/article/164842/christian-nationalists-trump-shock-troops.

9. Joan Lindsey, "Comm #7: History Now, or History Never," The Church Finds Its Voice, June 1, 2021, www.churchfindsitsvoice.com/post/all-previous-comms-pdf.

10. "James and Joan Lindsey Family Foundation," Tax Filings by Year, ProPublica Nonprofit Explorer, https://projects.propublica.org/nonprofits/organizations/770390011; "About," Faith Wins, https://faithwins.org/about/.

11. Ken Blackwell, "Election Integrity Reform Is Key to Preventing a Socialist Takeover of America," *Townhall*, August 15, 2021, https://townhall.com/columnists/kenblackwell/2021/08/15/election-integrity-reform-is-key-to-preventing-a-socialist-takeover-of-america-n2594161.

12. Matt Trotter, "Lahmeyer and His Supporters Target Fellow Republicans and Push 2020 Election Lies at Rally," Public Radio Tulsa, October 1, 2021, www.publicradiotulsa.org/local-regional/2021-10-01/lahmeyer-and-his-supporters-target-fellow-republicans-and-push-2020-election-lies-at-rally; "About Us," Pastors for Trump, https://www.pastors4trump.com.

13. "USCAL National Council Membership 2017," United States Coalition of Apostolic Leaders, https://static1.squarespace.com/static/54359608e4b07147d79770e1/t/58e65cccbebafbe3ac92d95e/1491492045212/USCAL+Nat+Council.pdf.

14. "September 2020 Membership Directory," Council for National Policy, https://irp.cdn-website.com/681250a9/files/uploaded/CNP-Membership -Directory-September-2020.pdf.

15. Jane Mayer, "Betsy DeVos, Trump's Big-Donor Education Secretary," *New Yorker*, November 23, 2016, https://www.newyorker.com/news/news-desk/betsy -devos-trumps-big-donor-education-secretary.

16. Public Religion Research Institute Staff, "A Christian Nation? Understanding the Threat of Christian Nationalism to American Democracy and Culture," Public Religion Research Institute, February 8, 2023, www.prri.org/research/a -christian-nation-understanding-the-threat-of-christian-nationalism-to-ame rican-democracy-and-culture.

17. Robert P. Jones et al., "How Immigration and Concerns About Cultural Changes Are Shaping the 2016 Election," Public Religion Research Institute and the Brookings Institute, June 23, 2016, www.prri.org/wp-content/uploads /2016/06/PRRI-Brookings-2016-Immigration-survey-report.pdf.

18. "New PRRI/Atlantic Survey Analysis Finds Cultural Displacement—Not Economic Hardship—More Predictive of White Working-Class Support for Trump," Public Religion Research Institute, May 9, 2017, www.prri.org/press -release/white-working-class-attitudes-economy-trade-immigration-election -donald-trump.

19. Niraj Chokshi, "Trump Voters Driven by Fear of Losing Status, Not Economic Anxiety, Study Finds," *New York Times*, April 24, 2018, https://www.nytimes .com/2018/04/24/us/politics/trump-economic-anxiety.html.

20. Diana C. Mutz, "Status Threat, Not Economic Hardship, Explains the 2016 Presidential Vote," *Proceedings of the National Academy of Sciences of the United States of America* 115, no. 19 (April 2018): E4338, https://doi.org/10.1073/pnas .1718155115.

21. Chad Connelly, "Lockdown Lessons," Faith Wins, March 30, 2021, https:// faithwins.org/lockdown-lessons/.

22. Chad Connelly, "Why Is America So Special for Christians?" September 14, 2020, in *Faith Wins Podcast*, 1:15–2:10, https://faithwins.libsyn.com/why-is -america-so-special-for-christians.

23. Connelly, 2:35, 4:08–4:27.

24. "Register to Vote," Faith Wins, https://faithwins.org/register-to-vote/.

25. "Welcome to the Virginia Project," Virginia Project, https://virginiaproject.com/home; "If They Tell You You've Already Voted," Virginia Project, https://myemail.constantcontact.com/If-they-tell-you-you-ve-already-voted.html?soid=1135298864072&aid=bQh1Fubp6JE.

26. "About WallBuilders," WallBuilders, https://wallbuilders.com/about-us/. Accessed April 2, 2023.

27. Katherine Stewart, "How a Data-Backed Christian Nationalist Machine Helped Trump to Power," *Guardian*, March 3, 2020, www.theguardian.com/us-news/2020/mar/03/bill-dallas-christian-nationalist-right-donald-trump.

28. George Barna, *The Day Christians Changed America: How Christian Conservatives Put Trump in the White House and Redirected America's Future* (Ventura, CA: Metaformation, 2017): 147–48.

29. Joan Lindsey, "Comm #2: Bet You Never Knew You Had So Many Voices!" The Church Finds Its Voice, June 1, 2021, www.churchfindsitsvoice.com/post/all-previous-comms-pdf.

30. "Welcome to the Black Robe Regiment," Black Robe Regiment, http://www.blackrobereg.org/.

31. Home page, Stand Courageous, https://standcourageous.com.

32. "What Is Stand Courageous?" Stand Courageous, https://standcourageous.com/about.

33. Christian Nightmares (@ChristnNitemare), "This is from the opening day of the 2023 Emerge Men's Conference from Awaken Church," X, March 12, 2023, 6:07 P.M., https://twitter.com/ChristnNitemare/status/1635039885089443840.

34. David Gilbert and Tess Owen, "Meet the 'Black Robe Regiment' of Extremist Pastors Spreading Christian Nationalism," *Vice News*, November 8, 2022, www.vice.com/en/article/pkgqk7/who-are-the-black-robe-regiment.

35. Jack Healy, Michael Wines, and Nick Corasaniti, "Republican Review of Arizona Vote Fails to Show Stolen Election," *New York Times*, September 24, 2021, https://www.nytimes.com/2021/09/24/us/arizona-election-review-trump-biden.html.

36. Laura Vozzella, "Youngkin Distances Himself from Controversial Rally Featuring Trump and Bannon," *Washington Post*, October 18, 2021, https://www .washingtonpost.com/local/virginia-politics/trump-bannon-youngkin-repub lican-virginia/2021/10/13/1113ad10-2bb4-11ec-985d-3150f7e106b2_story.html.

37. Benjamin Wallace-Wells, "Biden and Trump's First Debate Did Not End Well," *New Yorker*, September 30, 2020, https://www.newyorker.com/news/our -columnists/biden-and-trumps-first-debate-did-not-end-well.

38. Vozzella, "Youngkin Distances Himself."

39. Robert Jeffress, "Pastor Robert Jeffress: Biden Is President-Elect—How Should Christians Respond?" Fox News, November 7, 2020, https://www.foxnews.com /opinion/biden-elected-christians-response-robert-jeffress.

40. Mat Staver, "This Is Far from Over" . . . ," Liberty Counsel, November 9, 2020, https://lc.org/newsroom/details/20201109this-is-far-from-over.

41. Right Wing Watch (@RightWingWatch), "Former congresswoman Michele Bachmann calls on God to 'smash the delusion, Father, that Joe Biden is our president. He is not,'" X, November 9, 2020, 9:42 A.M., https://twitter.com /RightWingWatch/status/1325811083492401152.

42. Richard Antall, "A New Resistance Is Rising," *Crisis Magazine*, November 10, 2020, https://crisismagazine.com/opinion/a-new-resistance-is-rising.

43. Vassia Barba, "Preacher Absolutely Loses It After Being Challenged over His 'Private Jet Lifestyle,'" *Daily Mirror*, March 1, 2023, https://www.mirror.co.uk /news/us-news/preacher-absolutely-loses-after-being-29343654; and Kenneth Copeland, "Pro-Trump Evangelical Kenneth Copeland Laughs Manically over Media Calling Biden's Win," *Independent*, November 9, 2020, YouTube video, 2:00, www.youtube.com/watch?v=VBkegy4aDvk.

44. Rob Kuznia and Majlie de Puy Kamp, "The Pastors," CNN, January 3, 2021, https://www.cnn.com/interactive/2021/06/us/capitol-riot-paths-to-insurrection /pastors.html.

45. "My Faith Votes Launches 'Election Integrity Now' Protecting Security of U.S. Elections," My Faith Votes, May 13, 2021, https://www.myfaithvotes.org/press -release/my-faith-votes-launches-election-integrity-now-protecting-security -of-u-s-elections.

46. Katherine Stewart, "What's Missing from Popular Discussions of Today's Christian Nationalism," *Washington Spectator*, September 13, 2021, https://washingtonspectator.org/whats-missing-from-popular-discussions-of-todays-christian-nationalism/.

47. "Conservative Political Action Conference with Allen West, Representative Louis Gohmert and Others," *C-SPAN*, July 11, 2021, 9:00, https://www.c-span.org/video/?513297-101/conservative-political-action-conference-allen-west-representative-louis-gohmert.

48. Olivia Little, "Unmasking Moms for Liberty," *Media Matters for America*, November 12, 2021, https://www.mediamatters.org/critical-race-theory/unmasking-moms-liberty; home page, Moms for America, https://momsforamerica.us; and home page, Parents Defending Education, https://defendinged.org.

49. Katherine Stewart, "Christian Nationalism Is One of Trump's Most Powerful Weapons," *New York Times*, January 6, 2022, https://www.nytimes.com/2022/01/06/opinion/jan-6-christian-nationalism.html.

50. Joan Lindsey, "Comm #8: That Thing We Lost," The Church Finds Its Voice, June 1, 2021, https://www.churchfindsitsvoice.com/post/all-previous-comms-pdf.

51. Ann Pieramici, "Inaugural 'No One Bought or Sold' Event Targets Human Trafficking in Santa Barbara County," *Noozhawk*, March 4, 2024, https://www.noozhawk.com/inaugural-no-one-bought-or-sold-event-targets-human-trafficking-in-santa-barbara-county/; and home page, Strategic Alliance to Fight Exploitation, https://www.safesbc.org.

52. Home page, *Politically Basic*, podcast, https://www.politicallybasic.com/.

53. Kyle Campbell, "Kyle Campbell Corrects Media Narrative on Religious 'Nones' and Discusses Christian Outreach," Tony Perkins, January 29, 2024, YouTube video, 4:54, https://www.youtube.com/watch?v=aX1u-MerKP4.

54. Joan Lindsey and Kielle Horton, "Comm #6: Freedom Now or Freedom Never," The Church Finds Its Voice, June 1, 2021, https://www.churchfindsitsvoice.com/post/all-previous-comms-pdf.

55. Patrick Lindsey (@plindsey73), "Daaaaaaannng!!! This place was so awesome. De Blasio & Cuomo can sukkit long and hard. #reopenNOW," X, December 11, 2020, 6:32 P.M., https://twitter.com/plindsey73/status/1337540770832633856.

CHAPTER 2: A TALE OF TWO BUSCHES

1. Johnny Zokovitch, "This Week, Let Us Demonstrate What We Stand For," Pax Cristi USA, January 17, 2021, https://paxchristiusa.org/2021/01/17/this-week-let -us-demonstrate-what-we-stand-for/.

2. Home page, Thomas Merton Center, https://thomasmerton.org; and home page, St. Thomas Aquinas Parish, https://paloaltocatholic.net.

3. Dan Morris-Young, "Tim Busch, Conservative Activist-Philanthropist, Rejects Anti-Francis Label," *National Catholic Reporter*, June 12, 2019, https://www .ncronline.org/news/tim-busch-conservative-activist-philanthropist-rejects-anti -francis-label.

4. "Business School $3 Million Grant," Catholic University of America, January 22, 2015, https://communications.catholic.edu/news/2015/01/business-grant.html.

5. Tom Roberts, "Conservative Donors Aim to Shape Catholic Narrative for the Wider Culture," *National Catholic Reporter*, December 21, 2017, https://www .ncronline.org/news/conservative-donors-aim-shape-catholic-narrative-wider -culture.

6. Corwin E. Smidt and James M. Penning, "Michigan: Veering to the Left?" in *God at the Grass Roots, 1996: The Christian Right in the American Elections*, ed. Mark J. Rozell and Clyde Wilcox (Lanham, MD: Rowman & Littlefield, 1997), 128.

7. Frank Newport, "Religious Group Voting and the 2020 Election," *Gallup*, November 13, 2020, https://news.gallup.com/opinion/polling-matters/324410 /religious-group-voting-2020-election.aspx.

8. Nicholas Rowan, "'Fake Catholic': Trump Ambassador to Catholics Blasts Biden for Positions on Abortion and Gay Marriage," *Washington Examiner*, September 18, 2020, https://www.washingtonexaminer.com/news/477115/fake -catholic-trump-ambassador-to-catholics-blasts-biden-for-positions-on-abor tion-and-gay-marriage/.

9. José H. Gómez, "USCCB President's Statement on the Inauguration of Joseph R. Biden, Jr., as 46th President of the United States of America," United State Conference of Catholic Bishops, January 20, 2021, https://www.usccb.org /news/2021/usccb-presidents-statement-inauguration-joseph-r-biden-jr-46th -president-united-states.

10. Philip Pullella, "Pope Francis Laments 'Reactionary,' Politicised, US Catholic Church," Reuters, August 28, 2023, https://www.reuters.com/world /us/pope-francis-laments-reactionary-politicised-us-catholic-church-2023 -08-28/.

11. Matt Durr, "Namesake, Co-Founder of Busch's Grocery Store Chain Dies at Age 89," *Michigan Live*, November 18, 2015, https://www.mlive.com/business /ann-arbor/2015/11/namesake_co-founder_of_buschs.html; "Our People," Busch Firm, https://thebuschfirm.com/people/; and "Our Leadership," Pacific Hospitality Group, https://www.pacifichospitality.com/our-leadership.

12. NCR Editorial Staff, "Editorial: Money Shapes the US Catholic Narrative," *National Catholic Reporter*, October 25, 2019, https://www.ncronline.org/news /editorial/editorial-money-shapes-us-catholic-narrative.

13. Tom Roberts, "Koch, Turkson Speak at Catholic University's 'Good Profit' Conference," *National Catholic Reporter*, October 11, 2017, https://www.ncronline .org/news/koch-turkson-speak-catholic-universitys-good-profit-conference.

14. Roberts.

15. "14th Annual Summer Conference," Napa Institute, https://napa-institute.org /event/14th-annual-summer-conference-2/; NCR Editorial Staff, "Editorial: Money Shapes the US Catholic Narrative," Catholic Network US, October 29, 2019, https://catholicnetwork.us/2019/10/29/editorial-money-shapes-the-us -catholic-narrative/; "Religion, State of the Church Among Topics at Annual Napa Conference," Napa Institute, August 14, 2019, https://napa-institute.org /religion-state-of-the-church-among-topics-at-annual-napa-conference/; "About Legatus," Legatus, https://legatus.org/legatus; and "Mr. Tim Busch," Sacred Story Institute, https://sacredstory.net/about/board/tim-busch/.

16. "Economic Justice for All: Pastoral Letter on Catholic Social Teaching and the U.S. Economy," United States Conference of Catholic Bishops, 1986, https://www.usccb.org/upload/economic_justice_for_all.pdf.

17. Ari L. Goldman, "Catholic Bishops Criticized on Poor," *New York Times*, November 5, 1986, https://www.nytimes.com/1986/11/05/us/catholic-bishops -criticized-on-poor.html.

18. William E. Simon and Michael Novak, "Special Report: Liberty and Justice for All," *Crisis Magazine*, December 1, 1986, https://crisismagazine.com/vault /special-report-liberty-and-justice-for-all.

19. Matthew 25:29 (NIV), https://www.biblegateway.com/passage/?search=Matt hew%2025%3A29&version=NIV.

20. "Thomas S. Monaghan," Giving Pledge, https://givingpledge.org/pledger ?pledgerId=248; "Frank Hanna," Hanna Capital LLC, https://www.hanna capitalllc.com/frank-hanna/; and Jim Rendon, "Powerful Donor Quietly Supports Groups Opposing Abortion and LGBT Rights," *Chronicle of Philanthropy*, March 7, 2023, https://www.philanthropy.com/article/powerful-donor-quietly -supports-groups-opposing-abortion-and-lgbt-rights.

21. Tom Roberts, "Knights of Columbus' Financial Forms Show Wealth, Influence," *National Catholic Reporter*, May 15, 2017, https://www.ncronline.org /knights-columbus-financial-forms-show-wealth-influence.

22. "Opus: The Cult of Dark Money, Human Trafficking, and Right-Wing Conspiracy inside the Catholic Church," Simon & Schuster, https://www .simonandschuster.com/books/Opus/Gareth-Gore/9781668016145

23. Courtney Mares, "Pope Makes Changes to Opus Dei," *Inside the Vatican*, https://insidethevatican.com/magazine/pope-makes-changes-to-opus-dei.

24. CNA Daily News, "What Is Opus Dei? A CNA Explainer," *Catholic World Report*, January 8, 2019, https://www.catholicworldreport.com/2019/01/08/what -is-opus-dei-a-cna-explainer/.

25. Tom Gjelten, "For Trump, Conservative Catholics Are the New Evangelicals," NPR, October 26, 2020, https://www.capradio.org/news/npr/story?storyid= 926659149.

26. Gjelten, "For Trump, Conservative Catholics."

27. Gjelten.

28. Heidi Schlumpf, "Money Trail Tells the Tale of EWTN's Direction," *National Catholic Reporter*, July 18, 2019, https://www.ncronline.org/culture/money-trail -tells-tale-ewtns-direction; Roberts, "Conservative Donors"; and Roberts, "Knights of Columbus' Financial Forms."

29. "Father Robert Sirico on Shooting at Arapahoe High School," Fox News, February 4, 2017, https://www.foxnews.com/video/2932570621001#sp=show -clips; Victor Garcia, "Father Robert Sirico on Christmas Civility: 'We Need a Little More Corniness. I Think We've Become Far Too Cynical,'" *Fox News*, December 25, 2019, https://www.foxnews.com/media/christmas-father-robert

-sirico-corny-cynical; and Charles Creitz, "Rev. Robert Sirico Says Latest COVID-19 Recommendations for Houses of Worship Already in Place," Fox News, May 22, 2020, https://www.foxnews.com/media/catholic-priest-churches -have-been-prepared-active-fighting-covid-risks.

30. Gregory A. Smith, "White Christians Continue to Favor Trump over Biden, But Support Has Slipped," Pew Research Center, October 13, 2020, https://www .pewresearch.org/short-reads/2020/10/13/white-christians-continue-to-favor -trump-over-biden-but-support-has-slipped/.

31. Heidi Schlumpf, "The Rise of EWTN: From Piety to Partisanship," *National Catholic Reporter*, July 16, 2019, https://www.ncronline.org/culture/rise-ewtn -piety-partisanship.

32. Michael Warsaw, "Voting for a Vision, Not a Person," *National Catholic Register*, October 17, 2020, https://www.ncregister.com/commentaries/voting-for-a-vision -not-a-person.

33. Michael Warsaw, "Two Views of Freedom," *National Catholic Register*, August 15, 2024, https://www.ncregister.com/commentaries/two-views-of-freedom-kamala -harris.

34. Warsaw, "Voting for a Vision."

35. "The World Over with Raymond Arroyo," *ETWN*, https://www.ewtn.com/tv /shows/world-over.

36. David Gibson, "More Protests over Koch Gift to Catholic University of America," *Religion News Service*, February 11, 2014, https://religionnews.com /2014/02/11/protests-koch-gift-catholic-university-america/.

37. Jordon Fabian, "Trump-Allied Groups Pour $30 Million into Barrett Confirma- tion," *Bloomberg*, October 22, 2020, https://www.bloomberg.com/news/articles /2020-10-22/trump-allied-groups-pour-30-million-into-barrett-confirmation.

38. Michael O'Malley, "Alien Menace," Roy Rosenzweig Center for History and New Media, https://chnm.gmu.edu/exploring/19thcentury/alienmenace/pop _catholics.html.

39. "Chaos in the Streets: The Philadelphia Riots of 1844," Falvey Library, https:// exhibits.library.villanova.edu/chaos-in-the-streets-the-philadelphia-riots-of -1844; and "The Kensington Riots of 1844," PhilaPlace, http://m.philaplace.org /story/316/.

40. Katherine Stewart, "What the 'Government Schools' Critics Really Mean," *New York Times*, July 31, 2017, https://www.nytimes.com/2017/07/31/opinion/donald-trump-school-choice-criticism.html; Emily DeRuy, "A Tale of Two Betsy DeVoses," *Atlantic*, March 8, 2017, https://www.theatlantic.com/education/archive/2017/03/a-tale-of-two-betsy-devoses/518952/; and "Acton Institute," InfluenceWatch, https://www.influencewatch.org/non-profit/acton-institute/.

41. John Finnis, *Natural Law and Natural Rights* (New York: Oxford University Press, 1980), 37.

42. Oliver Laughland, Molly Redden, Robert Booth, and Owen Boycott, "Oxford Scholar Who Was Mentor to Neil Gorsuch Compared Gay Sex to Bestiality," *Guardian*, February 3, 2017, https://www.theguardian.com/law/2017/feb/03/neil-gorsuch-mentor-john-finnis-compared-gay-sex-to-bestiality.

43. John Finnis, "Law, Morality, and 'Sexual Orientation,'" in *Same Sex: Debating the Ethics, Science, and Culture of Homosexuality*, ed. John Corvino (Lanham, MD: Rowman & Littlefield, 1997), 31–43, www.princeton.edu/~anscombe/articles/finnisorientation.pdf.

44. John Finnis, "The Good of Marriage and the Morality of Sexual Relations: Some Philosophical and Historical Observations," *American Journal of Jurisprudence* 42, no. 1 (1998): 97–134, www.princeton.edu/~anscombe/articles/finnismarriage.pdf.

45. John Finnis, *Human Rights and Common Good: Collected Essays* (Oxford: Oxford University Press, 2011), 3:351.

46. Neil Gorsuch, *The Future of Assisted Suicide and Euthanasia* (Princeton, NJ: Princeton University Press, 2006), 157.

47. Gorsuch, acknowledgments.

48. United Press International, "Southern Baptists Approve Abortion in Certain Cases," *New York Times*, June 3, 1971, https://www.nytimes.com/1971/06/03/archives/southern-baptists-approve-abortion-in-certain-cases.html.

49. "Evangelicals and Catholics Together: The Christian Mission in the Third Millennium," *First Things* 43 (May 1994): 15–22, https://www.leaderu.com/ftissues/ft9405/articles/mission.html.

50. *Time* staff, "Bushism Made Catholic," *Time*, February 7, 2005, https://content.time.com/time/specials/packages/article/0,28804,1993235_1993243_1993306,00.html.

51. "Manhattan Declaration: A Call of Christian Conscience," Manhattan Declaration, October 20, 2009, https://www.manhattandeclaration.org; and "Staff," James Madison Program in American Ideals and Institutions, https://jmp.princeton.edu/about/people/staff.

52. Serena Sigillito and Robert P. George, "Can We Still Reason Together? A Conversation with Robert P. George," *Public Discourse*, March 20, 2021, https://www.thepublicdiscourse.com/2021/03/74871/; and Jane Mayer, "How Right-Wing Billionaires Infiltrated Higher Education," *Chronicle Review*, February 12, 2016, https://facultygov.unc.edu/wp-content/uploads/sites/261/2019/10/Mayer-article-on-Right-Wing-Billionaires.pdf.

53. "Advisors," James Madison Program in American Ideals and Institutions, https://jmp.princeton.edu/about/people/advisors; Laura Sanicola, "Who Is Republican Donor and Justice Clarence Thomas' Friend Harlan Crow?" *Reuters*, April 7, 2023, https://www.reuters.com/world/us/who-is-republican-donor-justice-clarence-thomas-friend-harlan-crow-2023-04-07/; and Justin Elliot, Joshua Kaplan, and Alex Mierjeski, "Justice Samuel Alito Took Luxury Fishing Vacation with GOP Billionaire Who Later Had Cases Before the Court," ProPublica, June 20, 2023, https://www.propublica.org/article/samuel-alito-luxury-fishing-trip-paul-singer-scotus-supreme-court.

54. David Rohde, "William Barr, Trump's Sword and Shield," *New Yorker*, January 13, 2020, https://www.newyorker.com/magazine/2020/01/20/william-barr-trumps-sword-and-shield.

55. Jonathan Hafetz and Brett Max Kaufman, "William Barr's Unsolicited Memo to Trump about Obstruction of Justice," ACLU, January 11, 2019, https://www.aclu.org/news/civil-liberties/william-barrs-unsolicited-memo-trump-about-obstruction-justice.

56. Marty Lederman, "A First Take on Bill Barr's Memo on Presidential Authority and the Mueller Investigation," *Just Security*, December 20, 2018, https://www.justsecurity.org/61975/legal-arguments-bill-barrs-memo-mueller-investigation/.

57. Maegan Vazquez and Kaitlan Collins, "Trump Nominates William Barr to Be His Next Attorney General," CNN, December 7, 2018, https://edition.cnn.com/2018/12/07/politics/william-barr-attorney-general-nomination/index.html.

58. William Barr, "Address on Religious Liberty to the Law School and the de Nicola Center for Ethics and Culture at the University of Notre Dame," American Rhetoric Online Speech Bank, October 11, 2019, https://www.american rhetoric.com/speeches/williambarrnotredame.htm.

59. William Barr, "Attorney General Barr at Federalist Society Convention," *C-SPAN*, November 15, 2019, 21:28–38:04, https://www.c-span.org/video/ ?466450-1/attorney-general-barr-federalist-society-convention#.

60. Jonathan D. Karl, "Inside William Barr's Breakup with Trump," *Atlantic*, June 27, 2021, https://www.theatlantic.com/politics/archive/2021/06/william -barrs-trump-administration-attorney-general/619298/.

61. John Gehring, "William Barr, Nation's Top Lawyer, Is a Culture Warrior Catholic," *National Catholic Reporter*, July 23, 2020, https://www.ncronline.org /news/william-barr-nations-top-lawyer-culture-warrior-catholic.

62. Patrick J. Deneen, *Why Liberalism Failed* (New Haven, CT: Yale University Press, 2018).

63. Kristin Kobes Du Mez, "Where Do Women Belong? A Critique of Patrick Deneen's *Why Liberalism Failed*," *Kristin Kobes Du Mez* (blog), December 12, 2018, https://kristindumez.com/resources/where-do-women-belong-a-critique -of-patrick-deneens-why-liberalism-failed/.

64. Rod Dreher, "French-Ahmari: A Report from the Scene," *American Conservative*, September 6, 2019, https://www.theamericanconservative.com/french -ahmari-a-report-from-the-scene/; Peter Suderman, "Sohrab Ahmari Is a Joke," *Reason*, September 6, 2019, https://reason.com/2019/09/06/sohrab-ahmari -is-a-joke/; Jake Lahut, "Republican Senate Candidate J. D. Vance Says 'Our Country Is Kind of a Joke' in Justifying His Off-Color Tweets," *Business Insider*, January 24, 2022, https://www.businessinsider.com/gop-senate-candidate-jd -vance-says-our-country-is-kind-of-a-joke-2022-1?r=US&IR=T; Henry J. Gomez, "Tim Ryan and J. D. Vance Attack Each Other over 'Great Replacement' Theory in Final Ohio Senate Debate," NBC News, October 17, 2022, https://www .nbcnews.com/politics/2022-election/tim-ryan-jd-vance-attack-great-replace ment-theory-final-ohio-senate-de-rcna52621; and Rod Dreher, *The Benedict Option: A Strategy for Christians in a Post-Christian Nation* (New York: Sentinel, 2017).

65. Adrian Vermeule, *Common Good Constitutionalism* (Hoboken, NJ: John Wiley & Sons, 2022).

66. Michael Sobolik, "Instead of Transcending Tyranny, the 'New Right' Wants to Learn from It," American Foreign Policy Council, February 24, 2022, https://www.afpc.org/publications/articles/instead-of-transcending-tyranny -the-new-right-wants-to-learn-from-it.

67. Brooke Masters, "Adrian Vermeule's Legal Theories Illuminate a Growing Rift among US Conservatives," *Financial Times*, October 13, 2022, https://www.ft .com/content/5c615d7d-3b1a-47a2-86ab-34c7db363fe4.

68. Adrian Vermeule, "Beyond Originalism," *Atlantic*, March 31, 2020, https://www .theatlantic.com/ideas/archive/2020/03/common-good-constitutionalism/609037/.

69. "A Lesson of Virtue," *Beijing Review*, July 15, 2022, http://www.bjreview.com /Opinion/Governance/202207/t20220715_800300955.html.

70. Michael Anton, "Why It's Clearly Not in America's Interest to Go to War over Taiwan," *Federalist*, December 20, 2021, https://thefederalist.com/2021/12/20 /why-its-clearly-not-in-americas-interest-to-go-to-war-over-taiwan/.

71. Sean T. Byrnes, "Patrick Deneen's Escape from Liberalism," *New Republic*, November 21, 2023, https://newrepublic.com/article/175549/patrick-deneens -escape-liberalism-jackson-lears-review.

72. Jim Graves, "The Man Behind Catholic U's Largest Donation Ever," *Catholic World Report*, May 19, 2016, https://www.catholicworldreport.com/2016/05/19 /the-man-behind-catholic-us-largest-donation-ever/.

73. Tommy Beer, "Top 1% of U.S. Households Hold 15 Times More Wealth than Bottom 50% Combined," *Forbes*, April 14, 2022, https://www.forbes.com/sites /tommybeer/2020/10/08/top-1-of-us-households-hold-15-times-more-wealth -than-bottom-50-combined/?sh=2444d62c5179; and Alexandre Tanzi and Michael Sasso, "Richest 1% of Americans Close to Surpassing Wealth of Middle Class," *Bloomberg*, November 9, 2019, https://www.bloomberg.com/news/articles /2019-11-09/one-percenters-close-to-surpassing-wealth-of-u-s-middle-class.

CHAPTER 3: SCHOOL'S OUT FOREVER

1. Bob Norman, "A Report Details How the Zieglers Prowled Pubs for Three-some Partners," NPR, May 16, 2024, https://www.wusf.org/courts-law/2024-05 -16/christian-bridget-ziegler-pubs-threesome-partners-sarasota-police-report.

2. Curt Anderson, "Florida School Board Recommends Ouster of Moms for Liberty Co-founder over Republican Sex Scandal," AP News, December 12,

2023, https://apnews.com/article/bridget-christian-ziegler-florida-republicans -rape-accusation-90df76d7f1f2f2b827d29e3d07db9741.

3. Gary Fineout, "Ousted Florida GOP Leader Christian Ziegler Won't Be Charged with Rape," *Politico*, January 19, 2024, https://www.politico.com/news /2024/01/19/christian-ziegler-wont-be-charged-with-rape-00136686.

4. https://www.mysuncoast.com/2024/03/06/state-declines-pursue-video-voyeur ism-charges-against-christian-ziegler/

5. Ali Swenson, "Moms for Liberty Reports over $2 Million in Revenue, with Bulk of Contributions from Two Donors," AP News, November 17, 2023, https:// apnews.com/article/moms-for-liberty-donors-revenue-gop-schools-70d733e02 4d81f7ad054b0f321e67647.

6. Jo Napolitano, "Exclusive: Moms for Liberty Pays $21,000 to Company Owned by Founding Member's Husband," *The 74*, October 20, 2022, https://www .the74million.org/article/exclusive-moms-for-liberty-pays-21k-to-co-owned -by-founding-members-husband/.

7. Michelle Nickerson, *Mothers of Conservatism: Women and the Postwar Right* (Princeton, NJ: Princeton University Press, 2012), xiv.

8. Nickerson, xiii.

9. Michael Feola, "Moms for Liberty Is Part of a Long History of Rightwing Mothers' Activism in the US," *Guardian*, July 6, 2020, https://www.theguardian.com /commentisfree/2023/jul/06/moms-for-liberty-long-history-rightwing-activism.

10. Kiera Butler, "'Betsy DeVos Was a Disaster. I Think Erika Donalds Could Be Worse,'" *Mother Jones*, August 10, 2023, https://www.motherjones.com/politics /2023/08/erika-donalds-byron-charter-hillsdale-optimaed-betsy-devos-edu cation-secretary-trump/.

11. Butler.

12. Butler.

13. *Gender Transformation: The Untold Realities; A Documentary Every Parent Needs to Watch*, EpochTV, June 19, 2023, https://www.theepochtimes.com/epochtv /gender-transformation-5280005.

14. "City on the Hill Youth Leadership & Worldview Conference, July 21-27, 2024," PA Family, https://pafamily.org/coth/.

15. "Legal Resources," Moms for Liberty—Williamson County, TN, https:// momsforlibertywc.org/resources/legal-resources/.

16. "Who We Are," Protect Our Kids Now, https://protectourkidsnow.org/who -we-are/.

17. "Capitol Resource Institute," Cause IQ, https://www.causeiq.com/organizations /capitol-resource-institute,680129342/; and home page, Kitchen Table Activist, https://www.thekitchentableactivist.com.

18. Anna Harris, "Dorchester District Two Book Complainant Comes Forward, Others Share Concerns," Live 5 News, February 5, 2024, https://www.live5news .com/2024/02/05/dorchester-district-two-book-complainant-comes-forward -others-share-concerns/.

19. John Fea, "In a Sermon on 'Defending Truth,' Tim Barton Makes Multiple False Claims," *Current*, September 30, 2022, https://currentpub.com/2022/09/30 /in-a-sermon-on-defending-truth-tim-barton-makes-multiple-false-claims/.

20. Chris Rufo, "Laying Siege to the Institutions," Hillsdale College, streamed live on April 5, 2022, YouTube video, 27:40, 34:48, https://www.youtube.com/watch ?v=W8HhoGqoJcE.

21. "Frequently Asked Questions," Public School Exit, https://www.publicschoolexit .com/faqs.

22. Annika Brockschmidt, "At Moms for Liberty Summit, 'Mama Bears' Declare Spiritual War on the 'Radical Left,'" *Religion Dispatches*, July 6, 2023, https:// religiondispatches.org/at-moms-for-liberty-summit-mama-bears-declare-spiri tual-war-on-the-radical-left/.

23. Teddy Wilson, "Moms for Liberty County Chapters Growing Connections to Far Right Groups," *Radical Reports*, July 22, 2023, https://www.radicalreports .org/p/moms-for-liberty-county-chapters.

24. Martha Stoddard and Joe Dejka, "Nebraska Home-School Families Denounce 'Tyranny' of New Rule," *Omaha World-Herald*, October 15, 2013, https://omaha .com/news/nebraska-home-school-families-denounce-tyranny-of-new-rule /article_83ed798a-0ba1-55d3-9a50-d5d6cf675ef5.html.

25. Robin Respaut and Chad Terhune, "Putting Numbers on the Rise in Children Seeking Gender Care," Reuters, October 6, 2022, https://www.reuters.com /investigates/special-report/usa-transyouth-data/; Kate Yandell, "Young Children Do Not Receive Medical Gender Transition Treatment," FactCheck .org, May 22, 2023, https://www.factcheck.org/2023/05/scicheck-young-children -do-not-receive-medical-gender-transition-treatment/.

26. "National Statistics on Child Abuse," National Children's Alliance, https://
www.nationalchildrensalliance.org/media-room/national-statistics-on-child
-abuse/; and Darreonna Davis, "Firearms Now No. 1 Cause of Death for U.S.
Children—While Drug Poisoning Enters Top 5," *Forbes*, October 5, 2023, https://
www.forbes.com/sites/darreonnadavis/2023/10/05/firearms-now-no-1-cause-of
-death-for-us-children—while-drug-poisoning-enters-top-5/?sh=6a2d9f3c
609e.

27. 60 Minutes (@60Minutes), "'What do you mean by that?' Scott Pelley asks
Moms for Liberty founders about claims, posted on the group's social media,
that students are being 'groomed,'" X, March 3, 2024, 7:33 P.M., https://twitter
.com/60Minutes/status/1764449124663861416?lang=en.

28. Peter Montgomery, "The Right-Wing Political Machine Is Out to Take Over
School Boards by Fanning Fears of Critical Race Theory," *Right Wing Watch*,
August 6, 2021, https://www.rightwingwatch.org/post/the-right-wing-political
-machine-is-out-to-take-over-school-boards-by-fanning-fears-of-critical-race
-theory/.

29. Kyle Spencer, *Raising Them Right: The Untold Story of America's Ultraconservative Youth Movement and Its Plot for Power* (New York: HarperCollins, 2022),
xi–xii.

30. Yascha Mounk, "What an Audacious Hoax Reveals About Academia," *Atlantic*,
October 5, 2018, https://www.theatlantic.com/ideas/archive/2018/10/new-sokal
-hoax/572212/.

31. Greg Matsen, "Wokeness Is Literally a Religion—feat. James Lindsay," Cwic
Media, February 5, 2024, YouTube video, https://www.youtube.com/watch?v
=sd6nYjRSqG4.

32. Tim Smith-Laing, "Postmodernism Gone Mad: Is Academia to Blame for
Cancel Culture?" *Telegraph*, September 19, 2020, https://www.telegraph.co.uk
/books/what-to-read/postmodernism-gone-mad-academia-blame-cancel
-culture/.

33. https://www.wlrn.org/2023-12-13/school-board-votes-for-scandal-hit-moms
-for-liberty-co-founder-to-resign-she-refuses

34. David Gilbert, "A Far-Right Moms Group Is Terrorizing Schools in the Name
of Protecting Kids," *Vice News*, April 26, 2023, https://www.vice.com/en/article
/dy3gnq/what-is-moms-for-liberty.

35. Ari Odzer, "Lone South Florida School Board Member on Gov. DeSantis' 'Target List' Speaks Out," NBC Miami, February 22, 2023, https://www.nbcmiami.com/news/local/lone-south-florida-school-board-member-on-gov-desantis-target-list-speaks-out/2979611/#.

36. Steven Walker, "Edwards Walks Out of Sarasota School Board Meeting as Anti-Gay Public Comments Continue," *Sarasota Herald-Tribune*, March 22, 2023, https://eu.heraldtribune.com/story/news/education/2023/03/22/sarasota-school-board-member-tom-edwards-walks-out-of-meeting/70033278007/.

37. Walker.

38. Tom Edwards, "Colleague: Controversial School Board Member's Policies Have 'Deliberately Harmed Children,'" interview by Michael Smerconish, CNN, December 16, 2023, 5:34, https://edition.cnn.com/videos/politics/2023/12/16/smr-florida-school-board-member-on-gop-sex-scandal.cnn.

39. Jacob Ogles, "Gay Florida School Board Member Targeted with Homophobic Slurs," *Advocate*, March 25, 2023, https://www.advocate.com/politics/florida-school-board-homophobia.

40. CBC Radio, "Drag Queen Keeps Reading to Kids after Group of Men Disrupt Pride Event Yelling Slurs," CBC, June 14, 2022, https://www.cbc.ca/radio/asithappens/as-it-happens-monday-edition-1.6486762/drag-queen-keeps-reading-to-kids-after-group-of-men-disrupt-pride-event-yelling-slurs-1.6488356.

41. Alex Paterson, "'Doom & Groom': Fox News Has Aired 170 Segments Discussing Trans People in the Past Three Weeks," Media Matters for America, April 8, 2022, https://www.mediamatters.org/fox-news/doom-groom-fox-news-has-aired-170-segments-discussing-trans-people-past-three-weeks.

42. Moriah Balingit, "Okla. Board Moves Forward with Nation's First Religious Charter School," *Washington Post*, October 9, 2023, https://www.washingtonpost.com/education/2023/10/09/oklahoma-religious-charter-school-contract-approved/.

43. Sean Murphy, "Oklahoma School Board Approves What Would Be the 1st Taxpayer-Funded Religious School in US," AP News, June 5, 2023, https://apnews.com/article/religious-charter-school-oklahoma-be6e51ffcdaeb393c4be34a6f27feba4.

44. Murphy.

45. Anna Bradley, "Notre Dame Law School Religious Liberty Clinic Supports Catholic Dioceses' Efforts to Operate the First Faith-Based Charter School in the U.S.," Notre Dame Law School, February 14, 2023, https://law.nd.edu /news-events/news/notre-dame-law-school-religious-liberty-clinic-supports -catholic-dioceses-efforts-to-operate-the-first-faith-based-charter-school-in -the-u-s/.

46. Pete Williams, "Supreme Court OKs Use of Public Money for Religious Education," NBC News, June 21, 2022, https://www.nbcnews.com/politics /supreme-court/supreme-court-oks-use-public-money-religious-education -rcna21627; Nicole Stelle Garnett, "Correcting Maine's Error," *City Journal*, December 7, 2021, https://www.city-journal.org/article/correcting-maines -error; and Denise Wagner, "ND Law's Religious Liberty Initiative Files Amicus Brief in Support of Maine Families in School Choice Case," Notre Dame Law School, March 12, 2021, https://law.nd.edu/news-events/news/notre -dame-religious-liberty-initiative-files-amicus-brief-in-support-of-maine -families-in-school-choice-case/.

47. Corey Stephenson, "4th Circuit: Skirt Requirement Violated Rights," *North Carolina Lawyer's Weekly*, July 8, 2022, https://nclawyersweekly.com/2022/07/08 /4th-circuit-skirt-requirement-violated-rights/.

48. Marian Wang, "Charter School Power Broker Turns Public Education into Private Profits," ProPublica, October 15, 2014, https://www.propublica.org/article /charter-school-power-broker-turns-public-education-into-private-profits.

49. Grace Panetta, "The Supreme Court Could Consider a Charter School's Code Requiring Skirts or Dresses for Girls," *The 19th*, January 10, 2023, https:// 19thnews.org/2023/01/supreme-court-could-consider-charter-school-dress -code/; and Galen Leigh Sherwin, "A Federal Appeals Court Strikes a Blow Against Sexist School Dress Codes," *Slate*, June 16, 2022, https://slate.com/news -and-politics/2022/06/school-dress-codes-skirts-sexist-unconstitutional.html ?via=rss.

50. CJ Staff, "Brunswick Charter School Asks U.S. Supreme Court to Take Up Dress Code Dispute," *Carolina Journal*, September 12, 2022, https://www .carolinajournal.com/brunswick-charter-school-asks-u-s-supreme-court-to -take-up-dress-code-dispute/.

51. "Our Pledge," Roger Bacon Academy, http://rogerbaconacademy.com/our -pledge-2/.

52. "Peltier v. Charter Day School," ACLU of North Carolina, Case No. 7:16-cv-30, February 29, 2016, https://www.acluofnorthcarolina.org/sites/default/files/field_documents/2016-02-29_charter_day_school_complaint_0.pdf.

53. "No. 22-238," Supreme Court of the United States, https://www.supremecourt.gov/search.aspx?filename=/docket/docketfiles/html/public/22-238.html; "Peltier v. Charter Day School (4th Cir.)," Notre Dame Law School Religious Liberty Initiative, https://religiousliberty.nd.edu/clinic/cases/peltier-v-charter-day-school-4th-cir/.

54. Meg Kilgannon, "School Board Boot Camp Was Held, and All 50 States Reported for Duty!" Family Research Council, June 30, 2021, https://www.frc.org/updatearticle/20210630/school-camp.

55. Frederick Clarkson, "Baby We Were Born for War: To Dominionist Christian Groups, No Election Is Too Small—and Colorado Is Just the Beginning," *Religion Dispatches*, November 28, 2021, https://religiondispatches.org/baby-we-were-born-for-war-to-dominionist-christian-group-no-election-is-too-small-and-colorado-is-just-the-beginning/.

CHAPTER 4: THE ROOM WHERE IT HAPPENS

1. Andy Kroll, Justin Elliott, and Andrew Perez, "How a Billionaire's 'Attack Philanthropy' Secretly Funded Climate Denialism and Right-Wing Causes," ProPublica, September 6, 2022, https://www.propublica.org/article/barre-seid-heartland-institute-hillsdale-college-gmu.

2. Kroll, Elliott, and Perez.

3. Kroll, Elliott, and Perez.

4. Andrew Perez, Andy Kroll, and Justin Elliott, "How a Secretive Billionaire Handed His Fortune to the Architect of the Right-Wing Takeover of the Courts," ProPublica, August 22, 2022, https://www.propublica.org/article/dark-money-leonard-leo-barre-seid.

5. Ed Pilkington, "How a Trump Adviser Manipulates Free Speech to Advance His Causes and 'Hurt His Adversaries,'" *Guardian*, August 9, 2023, https://www.theguardian.com/law/2023/aug/09/leonard-leo-federalist-society-manipulates-free-speech.

6. Perez, Kroll, and Elliott, "How a Secretive Billionaire."

7. Stephen Engelberg and Richard Tofel, "Why We Are Publishing the Tax Secrets of the .001%," ProPublica, June 8, 2021, https://www.propublica.org/article/why-we-are-publishing-the-tax-secrets-of-the-001.

8. James Morton Turner and Andrew C. Isenberg, *The Republican Reversal: Conservatives and the Environment from Nixon to Trump* (Cambridge, MA: Harvard University Press, 2018), 84.

9. Adam Gabbatt, "The Kingmaking Trump Ally Behind a Cadre of Rightwing Judges," *Guardian*, August 11, 2023, https://www.theguardian.com/us-news/2023/aug/11/leonard-leo-aileen-cannon-trump-conservative-judges.

10. Elbert Hubbard, *Jesus Was an Anarchist* (New Delhi: Isha Books, 2013).

11. Kroll, Elliott, and Perez, "Billionaire's 'Attack Philanthropy.'"

12. Robert Lewis Dabney, "The Negro and the Common School," in *Discussions of Robert Lewis Dabney*, vol. 4, *Secular*, ed. C. R. Vaughan (Harrisonburg, VA: Sprinkle, 1994), 177.

13. Archibald Alexander Hodge, *Popular Lectures on Theological Themes* (Philadelphia: Presbyterian Board of Publication, 1887), 283–84.

14. Hodge.

15. Rousas John Rushdoony, *The Messianic Character of American Education: Studies in the History of the Philosophy of Education* (Vallecito: Ross House Books, 1995), 337–39.

16. Jerry Falwell, *America Can Be Saved! Jerry Falwell Preaches on Revival* (Murfreesboro, TN: Sword of the Lord, 1979), 52.

17. D. James Kennedy, "Kennedy Classics—A Godly Education," Coral Ridge Ministries, September 4, 2015, YouTube video, 13:14, https://www.youtube.com/watch?v=VW5ziJUjc98.

18. Morris H. Chapman, "A Case for Christian Elementary and Secondary Schools," *Baptist Press*, April 24, 2009, https://www.baptistpress.com/resource-library/news/a-case-for-christian-elementary-and-secondary-schools/.

19. Joseph P. Overton, "An Inside Look at the Government-School Mentality," Mackinac Center for Public Policy, September 23, 2002, https://www.mackinac.org/4674.

20. William B. Allen, "Public Education: An Autopsy," *Religion and Liberty* 4, no. 4 (July 2010), https://www.acton.org/pub/religion-liberty/volume-4-number-4 /public-education-autopsy.

21. Rob Schwarzwalder, "To Save Children, Cut Education," *Washington Times*, January 21, 2010, https://www.washingtontimes.com/news/2010/jan/21/to-save -children-cut-education/.

22. Diane Ravitch, "Texas: Unmasking the Campaign to Privatize Public Schools," *Diane Ravitch's Blog*, February 14, 2023, https://dianeravitch.net/2023/02/14 /texas-unmasking-the-campaign-to-privatize-public-schools/.

23. Stephanie Saul and Danny Hakim, "The Most Powerful Conservative Couple You've Never Heard Of," *New York Times*, June 7, 2018, https://www.nytimes .com/2018/06/07/us/politics/liz-dick-uihlein-republican-donors.html.

24. Ben Schreckinger, "Rebekah Mercer," *Politico*, 2017, https://www.politico.com /interactives/2017/politico50/rebekah-mercer/.

25. Vicky Ward, "The Blow-It-All-Up Billionaires," *Huffington Post*, March 17, 2017, https://highline.huffingtonpost.com/articles/en/mercers/.

26. "2022 Impact Report: Whatever Is Praiseworthy," National Christian Foundation, https://www.ncfgiving.com/wp-content/uploads/2023/01/NCF-2022 -Impact-Report.pdf.

27. Heidi Przybyla, "'Plain Historical Falsehoods': How Amicus Briefs Bolstered Supreme Court Conservatives," *Politico*, December 3, 2023, https://www.politico .com/news/2023/12/03/supreme-court-amicus-briefs-leonard-leo-00127497; "A Major Milestone: Celebrating $4 Billion Sent," The Signatry, December 13, 2022, https://thesignatry.com/blog/celebrating-4-billion-sent/.

28. Jeremy Beaman, "Barr Slams 'Secular Progressive Orthodoxy' in Public Schools," *Washington Examiner*, May 21, 2021, https://www.washingtonexaminer.com/news /2880104/barr-slams-secular-progressive-orthodoxy-in-public-schools/.

29. Katherine Stewart, "How Christian Fundamentalists Plan to Teach Genocide to Schoolchildren," *Guardian*, May 30, 2010, https://www.theguardian.com /commentisfree/2012/may/30/christian-fundamentalists-plan-teach-genocide.

30. "What Is Ziklag," Ziklag Group, accessed March 1, 2024, https://web.archive.org /web/20230515030106/https://www.unitedinpurpose.org/uip/What_is_Ziklag.asp.

31. "Inside the Secret Right-Wing Plan to 'Take Down the Education System as We Know It,'" *Documented*, October 17, 2023, https://documented.net/investigations/inside-the-secret-right-wing-plan-to-take-down-the-education-system-as-we-know-it.

CHAPTER 5: THE PERMANENT EMERGENCY

1. Emma Brown and Rosalind S. Helderman, "For John Eastman and Clarence Thomas, An Intellectual Kinship Stretching Back Decades," *Washington Post*, December 23, 2022, https://www.washingtonpost.com/investigations/2022/12/23/john-eastman-clarence-thomas-clerk/.

2. Emma Brown, Jacqueline Alemany, and Josh Dawsey, "John Eastman Says Ginni Thomas Invited Him to Speak on 'Election Litigation,'" *Washington Post*, June 16, 2022, https://www.washingtonpost.com/investigations/2022/06/16/john-eastman-ginny-thomas-frontliners-substack/.

3. John C. Eastman, "We Are a Religious People," *Claremont Review of Books*, March 27, 2014, https://claremontreviewofbooks.com/digital/we-are-a-religious-people.

4. Justin Stabley, "What You Need to Know About John Eastman's 2020 Election Charges," PBS, September 21, 2023, https://www.pbs.org/newshour/politics/what-you-need-to-know-about-john-eastmans-2020-election-charges.

5. Kyle Cheney, "Judge Rejects Eastman Bid to Retain Law Practice While Fighting Disbarment," *Politico*, May 1, 2024, https://www.politico.com/news/2024/05/01/judge-rejects-eastman-bid-practice-00155641.

6. Kathryn Joyce, "The New Right's Grim, Increasingly Popular Fantasies of an International Nationalism," *New Republic*, January 6, 2022, https://newrepublic.com/article/164441/conservative-inspiration-orban-hungary-poland.

7. David Brooks, "The Terrifying Future of the American Right," *Atlantic*, November 18, 2021, https://www.theatlantic.com/ideas/archive/2021/11/scary-future-american-right-national-conservatism-conference/620746/.

8. Thomas D. Klingenstein, "The War Against Woke Communism," *American Mind*, October 6, 2021, https://americanmind.org/features/the-war-against-woke-communism/.

9. Katherine Stewart, "The Claremont Institute: The Anti-Democracy Think Tank," *New Republic*, August 10, 2023, https://newrepublic.com/article/174656/claremont-institute-think-tank-trump.

10. "Gov. Ron DeSantis Speaks at Faith and Freedom Coalition Conference," C-SPAN, June 23, 2023, 20:58, https://www.c-span.org/video/?528908-10/gov-ron-desantis-speaks-faith-freedom-coalition-conference.

11. "Vivek Ramaswamy Speaks at Faith and Freedom Coalition Conference," C-SPAN, June 23, 2023, 10:45, https://www.c-span.org/video/?528908-5/vivek-ramaswamy-speaks-faith-freedom-coalition-conference.

12. "Faith and Freedom Coalition Conference," C-SPAN, June 23, 2023, 01:09:32, https://www.c-span.org/video/?528908-1/faith-freedom-coalition-conference.

13. "Donald Trump Speaks at Faith and Freedom Coalition Conference," C-SPAN, June 24, 2023, 08:25, https://www.c-span.org/video/?528898-1/donald-trump-speaks-faith-freedom-coalition-conference.

14. Michael Anton, "The Flight 93 Election," *Claremont Review of Books*, September 5, 2016, https://claremontreviewofbooks.com/digital/the-flight-93-election/; and Damon Linker, "The Intellectual Right Contemplates an 'American Caesar,'" *The Week*, July 28, 2021, https://theweek.com/politics/1003035/the-far-right-contemplates-an-american-caesar.

15. Anton, "Flight 93 Election."

16. "Michael Anton: Britain's Grand Strategy for the 21st Century; NatCon UK," National Conservatism, May 19, 2023, YouTube video, 8:09, https://www.youtube.com/watch?v=OYdKXT1eJsg.

17. "Michael Anton," 7:07–7:30.

18. Christopher F. Rufo (@realchrisrufo), "The goal is to have the public read something crazy in the newspaper and immediately think 'Critical Race Theory. We have decodified the term," X, March 15, 2021, 3:17 P.M., https://twitter.com/realchrisrufo/status/1371541044592996352.

19. Christopher F. Rufo, *America's Cultural Revolution: How the Radical Left Conquered Everything* (New York: Broadside, 2023).

20. Kenya Evelyn, "Historians Rail Against Trump Administration's 1776 Commission," *Guardian*, January 22, 2021, https://www.theguardian.com/us-news/2021/jan/22/1776-commission-report-trump-administration-historians.

21. Jim Dela, "New College Students, Faculty Are Leaving After DeSantis Takeover. Here's How Many," *Bradenton Herald*, August 18, 2023, https://www.bradenton.com/news/local/education/article278368274.html.

22. Steven Walker, "New College of Florida Nets Record Number of New Students, but at Academic Cost," *Sarasota Herald-Tribune*, July 27, 2023, https://www.heraldtribune.com/story/news/education/2023/07/27/new-college-of-florida-pursues-student-athletes-at-academic-cost-richard-corcoran/70445567007/.

23. Moira Donegan, "Florida's Attacks on Academic Freedom Just Got Even Worse," *Guardian*, August 16, 2023, https://www.theguardian.com/commentisfree/2023/aug/16/florida-ron-desantis-academic-freedom.

24. Home page, Project 2025, https://www.project2025.org.

25. Jonathan Berry, "Department of Labor and Related Agencies," in *Mandate for Leadership: The Conservative Promise*, ed. Paul Dans and Steven Groves (Washington, D.C.: Heritage Foundation, 2023), 581, https://static.project2025.org/2025_MandateForLeadership_FULL.pdf.

26. William Perry Pendley, "Department of the Interior," in Dans and Groves, *Mandate for Leadership: The Conservative Promise*, 520.

27. Roger Severino, "Department of Health and Human Services," in Dans and Groves, *Mandate for Leadership*, 450.

28. Heritage Foundation (@Heritage), "'It seems to me that a good place to start would be a feminist movement against the pill, & for . . . returning the consequentiality to sex,'" X, May 27, 2023, 3:00 P.M., https://twitter.com/Heritage/status/1662534135762624520.

29. "The Patriarchal End Game: Control," *Tattooed Theologian*, December 7, 2023, https://tattooed-theologian.com/2023/12/07/the-patriarchal-end-game-control/.

30. Alexander Ward and Heidi Przybyla, "Trump Allies Prepare to Infuse 'Christian Nationalism' in Second Administration," *Politico*, February 20, 2024, https://www.politico.com/news/2024/02/20/donald-trump-allies-christian-nationalism-00142086.

31. Kevin D. Roberts, "A Promise to America," foreword to Dans and Groves, *Mandate for Leadership*, 1.

32. Jeff Stein, Josh Dawsey, and Isaac Arnsdorf, "The Former Trump Aide Crafting the House GOP's Debt Ceiling Playbook," *Washington Post*, February 19, 2023, https://www.washingtonpost.com/us-policy/2023/02/19/russ-vought-republi can-debt-ceiling-strategy/.

33. Roberts, "Promise to America," 5.

34. Charles R. Kesler, *Crisis of the Two Constitutions: The Rise, Decline, and Recovery of American Greatness* (New York: Encounter Books, 2021), 98, 401.

35. Eva Brann, "Plato's Impossible Polity," *Claremont Review of Books* 6, no. 3 (Summer 2006), https://claremontreviewofbooks.com/platos-impossible-polity /; and Glenn Ellmers, "Soul, Man," *Claremont Review of Books* 19, no. 1 (Winter 2019), https://claremontreviewofbooks.com/soul-man/.

36. Elisabeth Zerofsky, "How the Claremont Institute Became a Nerve Center of the American Right," *New York Times Magazine*, August 3, 2022, https://www .nytimes.com/2022/08/03/magazine/claremont-institute-conservative.html.

37. Christopher Flannery, "John Eastman Is an American Hero," *American Greatness*, August 4, 2022, https://amgreatness.com/2022/08/04/john-eastman-is-an -american-hero/.

38. "Claremont Institute's 2021 Annual Gala Honoring Florida Governor Ron DeSantis," Claremont Institute, November 9, 2021, YouTube video, www .youtube.com/watch?v=Li1e372UyN8.

39. Jennifer C. Berkshire, "The West Coast Think Tank Helping to Orchestrate DeSantis's War on the Woke," *Nation*, March 30, 2023, https://www.thenation .com/article/politics/the-west-coast-think-tank-helping-to-orchestrate-de santis-war-on-the-woke/.

40. https://www.youtube.com/watch?v=hK8il7p_BoI

41. Kevin Slack, "The Constitution, Citizenship, and the New Right," *American Mind*, June 15, 2023, https://americanmind.org/features/the-constitution-citizen ship-and-the-new-right/.

42. Republicans Against Trump (@RpsAgainstTrump), "MAGA influencer Jack Posobiec at CPAC: 'Welcome to the end of democracy. We're here to overthrow it completely,'" X, February 22, 2024, 4:36 P.M., https://twitter.com/Rps AgainstTrump/status/1760780642671845629.

43. "4. America: 'The Best Regime?'" *American Mind*, August 29, 2013, YouTube video, https://www.youtube.com/watch?v=pL4BkCC5fcM.

44. Jason Wilson, "US Businessman Is Wannabe 'Warlord' of Secretive Far-Right Men's Network," *Guardian*, August 22, 2023, https://www.theguardian.com /world/2023/aug/22/charles-haywood-claremont-institute-sacr-far-right.

45. Laura K. Field, "What the Hell Happened to the Claremont Institute?" *Bulwark*, July 13, 2021, https://www.thebulwark.com/p/what-the-hell-happened -to-the-claremont-institute; and Laura K. Field, "Charles Kesler Sees the Light," *Bulwark*, August 25, 2022, https://www.thebulwark.com/p/charles-kesler -claremont-institute-sees-the-light.

46. Daniel W. Drezner, "On the Matter of Political Science and the Claremont Institute," *Washington Post*, September 29, 2021, https://www.washingtonpost .com/outlook/2021/09/29/matter-political-science-claremont-institute/.

47. Mona Charen, "Claremont's New Class of Fellows Would Make Its Founders Weep," *National Review*, July 12, 2019, https://www.nationalreview.com/2019 /07/claremont-would-make-its-founders-weep/.

48. Thomas Merrill, "The Claremont Institute, Harry Jaffa, and the Temptation of Theory," *Bulwark*, November 15, 2021, https://www.thebulwark.com/p/the -claremont-institute-harry-jaffa-and-the-temptation-of-theory.

49. Harry V. Jaffa, "Straussian Geography: A Memoir and Commentary," in *Crisis of the Strauss Divided: Essays on Leo Strauss and Straussianism, East and West* (Lanham, MD: Rowman & Littlefield, 2012), 8.

50. Jaffa, 8.

51. Harry V. Jaffa, *Crisis of the House Divided: An Interpretation of the Issues in the Lincoln–Douglas Debates* (Chicago: University of Chicago Press, 2009).

52. "Harry V. Jaffa," Contemporary Thinkers, https://contemporarythinkers.org /harry-jaffa/biography/; and Peter Wood, "America Isn't Make-Believe," *American Mind*, January 26, 2021, https://americanmind.org/memo/america-isnt -make-believe/.

53. Kevin Slack, "The Natural Right," *American Mind*, July 27, 2023, https:// americanmind.org/features/the-constitution-citizenship-and-the-new-right /the-natural-right/.

54. Claudia Koonz, *The Nazi Conscience* (Cambridge: Harvard University Press, 2003), 58-59.

55. Charles Haywood, "*The Concept of the Political* (Carl Schmitt)," *Worthy House*, October 14, 2022, http://theworthyhouse.com/2022/10/14/the-concept-of-the-political-carl-schmitt/.

56. Friedrich Balke, "Beyond the Line: Carl Schmitt und der Ausnahmezustand," *Philosophische Rundschau* 55, no. 4 (December 2008): 273–306, http://www.jstor.org/stable/42572848.

57. Carl Schmitt, *The Concept of the Political: Expanded Edition* (Chicago: University of Chicago Press, 2007).

58. "Former President Trump Speaks in Nashville 6/17/22 Transcript," *Rev*, June 19, 2022, https://www.rev.com/blog/transcripts/former-president-trump-speaks-in-nashville-6-17-22-transcript.

59. Aaron Zack, "Anchors Away," *Claremont Review of Books*, January 4, 2017, https://claremontreviewofbooks.com/digital/anchors-away.

60. Heinrich Meier, *Carl Schmitt and Leo Strauss: The Hidden Dialogue*, trans. J. Harvey Lomax (Chicago: University of Chicago Press, 1995).

61. Meier, 123.

62. Anton, "Flight 93 Election."

63. Bill Kristol (@BillKristol), "From Carl Schmitt to Mike Anton: First time tragedy, second time farce," X, February 3, 2017, 11:53 A.M., https://twitter.com/BillKristol/status/827560738109718528.

64. Mike Watson, "Carl Schmitt's Disappointing American Disciples," *National Review*, May 26, 2022, https://www.nationalreview.com/magazine/2022/06/13/carl-schmitts-disappointing-american-disciples/.

65. Michael Anton, "Reductio Ad Hitlerum," *American Mind*, June 28, 2022, https://americanmind.org/salvo/reductio-ad-hitlerlum/.

66. Roberts, "Promise to America," 15.

67. Roberts, 1.

68. Roberts, 17.

69. "No. 23-939," Supreme Court of the United States, https://www.supremecourt .gov/opinions/23pdf/23-939_e2pg.pdf.

70. Zachary Cohen and Tierney Sneed, "Trump Knew Voter Fraud Claims Were Wrong, Federal Judge Says as He Orders John Eastman Emails Turned Over," CNN, October 19, 2022, https://edition.cnn.com/2022/10/19/politics/eastman -house-trump-documents/index.html.

71. "Arizona Speaker Says John Eastman Asked Him to Decertify Election Results," C-SPAN, June 21, 2022, https://www.c-span.org/video/?c5020669 /arizona-speaker-john-eastman-asked-decertify-election-results.

72. Jake Lahut, "John Eastman Asked for '1 More Relatively Minor Violation' of Election Law in Wake of Jan. 6 Attack: VP Aide," *Business Insider*, June 16, 2022, https://www.businessinsider.com/john-eastman-email-night-of-january-6 -minor-violation-law-2022-6?r=US&IR=T.

73. Clare Foran and Jeremy Herb, "Key Revelations About Attorney John East-man's Role in Effort to Overturn Election from Thursday's January 6 Hearing," CNN, June 16, 2022, https://www.cnn.com/2022/06/16/politics/john-eastman -january-6-committee-hearing/index.html.

74. "The John Eastman Interview: Part III," Tom Klingenstein, August 2, 2023, YouTube video, 22:18, https://www.youtube.com/watch?v=hK8il7p_BoI.

75. Ibid., 26:00–28:00.

76. Ibid., 23:54.

CHAPTER 6: THE RESENTMENT OF THE CAMPUS MISFITS

1. Selena Simmons-Duffin, "A Good Friday Funeral in Texas. Baby Halo's Parents Had Few Choices in Post-Roe Texas," NPR, April 6, 2023, https://www.npr .org/sections/health-shots/2023/04/06/1168399423/a-good-friday-funeral-in -texas-baby-halos-parents-had-few-choices-in-post-roe-te.

2. "Standard Pregnancy Care Is Now Dangerously Disrupted in Louisiana, Report Reveals," NPR, March 19, 2024, https://www.npr.org/transcripts/1239376395.

3. Robin Levinson-King, "US Women Are Being Jailed for Having Miscar-riages," *BBC*, November 11, 2021, https://www.bbc.com/news/world-us-canada -59214544.

4. Julie Carr Smyth, "A Black Woman Was Criminally Charged After a Miscarriage. It Shows the Perils of Pregnancy Post-Roe," AP News, December 16, 2023, https://apnews.com/article/ohio-miscarriage-prosecution-brittany-watts -b8090abfb5994b8a23457b80cf3f27ce.

5. Chelsea Patterson Sobolik, "Restoring a Generation's Identity," 2018 Values Voters Summit, Washington, D.C., September 21, 2018, 8:48 (author's recording).

6. "Beverly LaHaye—CWA Founder," Concerned Women for America Legislative Action Committee, https://concernedwomen.org/cwa-founder-beverly -lahaye/.

7. Kristin Kobes Du Mez, *Jesus and John Wayne: How White Evangelicals Corrupted a Faith and Fractured a Nation* (New York: Liveright, 2020).

8. Raw Egg Nationalist, "Do You Even Read, Bro?" *American Mind*, February 17, 2023, https://americanmind.org/salvo/do-you-even-read-bro/.

9. Joshua Molloy and Eviane Leidig, "The Emerging Raw Food Movement and the 'Great Reset,'" Global Network on Extremism and Technology, October 10, 2022, https://gnet-research.org/2022/10/10/the-emerging-raw-food-movement -and-the-great-reset/#.

10. Molloy and Leidig.

11. Tucker Carlson, dir., *The End of Men*, Tucker Carlson Originals, October 5, 2022, https://www.imdb.com/title/tt22440752/?ref_=tt_mv_close.

12. Lauren Southern, "'The End of Men'—How Modern Food Is Causing De-Evolution," October 4, 2022, YouTube video, 3:29, https://www.youtube.com /watch?v=1vVtGRSXPYw.

13. Patrick Butler, "Mars Mindset #3—Raw Egg Nationalist: Fighting Against Big Food and Destroying Our Feminized Culture," May 31, 2022, YouTube video, 43:35, https://www.youtube.com/watch?v=6qsqcDYAH2Y.

14. Butler.

15. David Corn, "J.D. Vance Appeared with Podcaster Who Once Said "Feminists Need Rape," *Mother Jones*, August 25, 2022, https://www.motherjones. com/politics/2022/08/jd-vance-appeared-with-podcaster-jack-murphy-who -said-feminists-need-rape/.

16. Laura K. Field, "The Decay at the Claremont Institute Continues," *Bulwark*, April 21, 2022, https://www.thebulwark.com/p/the-decay-at-the-claremont-institute-continues.

17. Jonny Diamond, "Here Are the People Publishing Fascist, Nazi, White Nationalist Garbage with Amazon's Help," *Literary Hub*, June 14, 2022, https://lithub.com/here-are-the-people-publishing-fascist-nazi-white-nationalist-garbage-with-amazons-help/; and Joseph Goebbels, *Michael: A German Destiny in Diary Form* (East Greenville, PA: Antelope Hill, 2023), https://antelopehillpublishing.com/product/michael-by-dr-joseph-goebbels/.

18. Kevin Richert, "'Medicated, Meddlesome and Quarrelsome': Boise State Professor's Comments on Women Draw Fire," *Idaho Education News*, November 29, 2021, https://www.idahoednews.org/news/medicated-meddlesome-and-quarrelsome-boise-state-professors-comments-on-women-draw-fire/.

19. Scott Yenor, "Does Feminism Undermine the Nation?," Claremont Institute Center for the American Way of Life, March 26, 2021, https://dc.claremont.org/watch-does-feminism-undermine-the-nation/.

20. Becca Savransky, "Boise State Professor: Don't Recruit Women into Engineering, Medical School, Law," *Spokesman-Review*, November 30, 2021, https://www.spokesman.com/stories/2021/nov/30/boise-state-professor-dont-recruit-women-into-engi/.

21. Savransky.

22. Scott Yenor, "Florida Universities: From Woke to Professionalism," Claremont Institute Center for the American Way of Life, March 11, 2023, https://dc.claremont.org/florida-universities-from-woke-to-professionalism/.

23. Casey DeSantis (@CaseyDeSantis), "Thrilled to welcome @scottyenor from the Claremont Institute to his new home in Tallahassee," X, February 8, 2022, 4:30 P.M., https://twitter.com/CaseyDeSantis/status/1623434042518515712.

24. Doug Hall, "Low-Wage Workers Have Experienced Wage Erosion in Nearly Every State," Economic Policy Institute, February 18, 2014, https://www.epi.org/publication/wage-workers-experienced-wage-erosion-state/; "The Erosion of Collective Bargaining Has Cost Middle-wage Workers Thousands of Dollars Each Year," Economic Policy Institute, April 8, 2021, https://www.epi.org/press/the-erosion-of-collective-bargaining-has-cost-middle-wage-workers-thousands-of-dollars-each-year-new-report-shows-that-deunionization-has

-fueled-the-growth-of-wage-inequality/; and Richard Hernandez, "The Fall of Employment in the Manufacturing Sector," U.S. Bureau of Labor Statistics Monthly Labor Review, August 2018, https://www.bls.gov/opub/mlr/2018 /beyond-bls-the-fall-of-employment-in-the-manufacturing-sector.htm.

25. Scott Yenor and Nick Stevens, *The Recovery of Family Life: Exposing the Limits of Modern Ideologies* (Waco, TX: Everand, 2020); and Scott Yenor, "Anatomy of a Cancellation," *First Things*, January 2023, https://www.firstthings.com /article/2023/01/anatomy-of-a-cancellation.

26. Michael Anton, "Are the Kids Al(t)Right?" *Claremont Review of Books* (Summer 2019), https://claremontreviewofbooks.com/are-the-kids-altright; Jack Butler, "Why Conservatives Must Reject the 'Bronze Age Mindset'—And Offer Something Better," *National Review*, February 14, 2023, https://www.nationalreview .com/corner/why-conservatives-must-reject-the-bronze-age-mindset-and-offer -something-better/.

27. "Bronze Age Mindset—Bronze Age Pervert (2018)," Internet Archive, https:// archive.org/details/bronze-age-pervert-bronze-age-mindset-2018/mode/2up.

28. Elijah del Medigo, "Wat Iz Bronze Age Mindset?" *American Mind*, November 5, 2019, https://americanmind.org/salvo/wat-iz-bronze-age-mindset/.

29. Bronze Age Mantis (@bronzeagemantis), "One of the most absurd aspects of contemporary so-called civilization is that you're not allowed to openly challenge another man for his property. The right to individual duel improves the stock," X, April 18, 2023, 12:33 P.M., https://twitter.com/bronzeagemantis/status /1648364179840188417.

30. "Bronze Age Mindset."

31. "Bronze Age Mindset."

32. Bronze Age Pervert (@bronzeagemantis), "Cannibalism abhorrent only when sourcing in subhuman. But imagine ritual sacrifice and partaking flesh of a young Dolph," X, January 9, 2023, 9:51 P.M., https://twitter.com/bronzeagemantis/status /1612643369301204993; Bronze Age Pervert (@bronzeagemantis), "My message to the international left, the pro-immigration unmanned right, and their peons; on occasion to celebrate soon having 100K on this heavensite," X, March 27, 2023, 2:42 P.M., https://twitter.com/bronzeagemantis/status/1640424029793439749; and Bronze Age Pervert (@bronzeagemantis), "Image found on Anna Khachiyan's phone, reports indicate she is regularly paying for visits from Polish male model as

well as vials of his sweat mixed in olive oil," X, May 11, 2023, 1:00 P.M., https://twitter.com/bronzeagemantis/status/1656705898440687616.

33. m. anje (@augureust), "'Be yourself; everyone else is already taken'—Oscar Wilde," X, May 1, 2023, 9:43 A.M., https://twitter.com/augureust/status/165303228 6936506368; ElBuni (@therealbuni), "No le digan No le digan a la colombiana en que clase de barco llegaron sus antepasados a latinoamerica," X, May 3, 2023, 11:14 A.M., https://twitter.com/therealbuni/status/1653780088343650304; Frens Wui Md. (@FrensWeMade), "War is Peace Freedom is Slavery Zendaya is Attractive," X, May 4, 2023, 2:53 P.M., https://twitter.com/FrensWeMade/status/1654197601179435008.

34. Bronze Age Pervert (@bronzeagemantis), ">Achilles stood out the Trojan War because the Trojans didn't respect conventional entitlements that only the Greeks gave to his tribe and he felt bad when he lost a minor battle," X, July 27, 2021, 2:50 P.M., https://twitter.com/bronzeagemantis/status/1420094253544484869.

35. "Bronze Age Mindset."

36. Yenor, "Anatomy of a Cancellation."

37. "Group discussing BAP's book," September 22, 2023, 4:20, 22:18 (author's recording).

38. Rory Tingle, "Politics Lecturer, 32, at Southampton University Is Suspended for Likening Abortion to NECROPHILIA on Social Media Then Responding 'It's a Great Tweet' During Student Backlash," *Daily Mail*, October 12, 2018, https://www.dailymail.co.uk/news/article-6269163/University-lecturer-32-suspended-likening-abortion-NECROPHILIA.html.

39. Josh Hawley, *Manhood: The Masculine Virtues America Needs* (New York: Regnery, 2023).

40. Peter Montgomery, "Josh Hawley Delivers Christian Nationalist Rallying Cry Against 'Woke' at Road to Majority," *Right Wing Watch*, June 23, 2023, https://www.rightwingwatch.org/post/josh-hawley-delivers-christian-nationalist-rallying-cry-against-woke-at-road-to-majority/.

41. Harvey C. Mansfield, *Manliness* (New Haven, CT: Yale University Press, 2006), 76.

42. Mansfield, 64.

43. Diana Schaub, "Man's Field," *Claremont Review of Books* 52, no. 2 (Spring 2006), https://claremontreviewofbooks.com/mans-field.

44. Schaub.

45. "South Sudan: 'Hellish Existence' for Women and Girls, New UN Report Reveals," *UN News*, March 21, 2022, https://news.un.org/en/story/2022/03/1114312.

46. Emma Pettit, "How a Center for Civic Education Became a Political Provocation," *Chronicle of Higher Education,* February 22, 2023, https://www.chronicle.com/article/how-a-center-for-civic-education-became-a-political-provocation; Ana Ceballos, "A Mystery Group Pushed for $3M in State Funding for New UF Academic Center," *Tampa Bay Times*, July 13, 2022, https://www.tampabay.com/news/florida-politics/2022/07/13/a-mystery-group-pushed-for-3m-in-state-funding-for-new-uf-academic-center/.

47. Nathan Pinkoski, "Spiritual Death of the West," *First Things*, May 2023, https://www.firstthings.com/article/2023/05/spiritual-death-of-the-west.

48. Jane Mayer, "How Right-Wing Billionaires Infiltrated Higher Education," *Chronicle of Higher Education*, February 12, 2016, https://www.chronicle.com/article/how-right-wing-billionaires-infiltrated-higher-education/.

49. Chris Rufo, "Laying Siege to the Institutions," Hillsdale College, streamed live on April 5, 2022, YouTube video, https://www.youtube.com/watch?v=W8HhoGqoJcE.

50. Kathryn Joyce, "'The Florida of Today Is the America of Tomorrow': Ron DeSantis's New College Takeover Is Just the Beginning of the Right's Higher Ed Crusade," *Vanity Fair*, February 10, 2023, https://www.vanityfair.com/news/2023/02/ron-desantis-new-college-florida.

51. Darren Beattie, "DeSantis' Educational Coup in Florida," *Wentworth Report*, February 6, 2023, https://wentworthreport.com/2023/02/06/desantis-educational-coup-in-florida/; and "Total Victory: DeSantis' 'New Florida College' Triumph Is the Blueprint for Recapturing 'Woke' Institutions Across the Country," *Revolver*, February 4, 2023, https://revolver.news/2023/02/desantis-new-florida-college-is-the-blueprint-for-recapturing-woke-institutions-nationwide/.

52. Jeet Heer, "Trump-Loving Think Tank Wracked with White Nationalist Controversy," *New Republic*, August 23, 2018, https://newrepublic.com/article

/150859/trump-think-tank-wracked-white-nationalist-controversy; and Robert Costa, "Trump Speechwriter Fired amid Scrutiny of Appearance with White Nationalists," *Washington Post*, August 19, 2018, https://www.washingtonpost.com/politics/trump-speechwriter-fired-amid-scrutiny-of-appearance-with-white-nationalists/2018/08/19/f5051b52-a3eb-11e8-a656-943eefab5daf_story.html.

53. Ben Shapiro, "Shapiro at 'National Review': Conservatives Oust Radicals, the Left Welcomes Them," *Daily Wire*, August 28, 2018, https://www.dailywire.com/news/shapiro-national-review-conservatives-oust-ben-shapiro.

54. "Charles C. Johnson," *Claremont Review of Books*, https://claremontreviewofbooks.com/author/charles-c-johnson.

55. Ken Masugi, "Why Coolidge Matters," *Law and Liberty*, August 1, 2013, https://lawliberty.org/why-coolidge-matters/; Charles C. Johnson, *Why Coolidge Matters: Leadership Lessons from America's Most Underrated President* (New York: Encounter Books, 2013).

56. Horatio Robinson Storer, "Why Not? A Book for Every Woman," Internet Archive, 1866, https://archive.org/details/whynotbookforeveoostor/page/n5/mode/2up.

57. Jason Wilson, "Revealed: US Pro-Birth Conference's Links to Far-Right Eugenicists," *Guardian*, September 4, 2023, https://www.theguardian.com/us-news/2023/sep/04/natal-conference-austin-texas-eugenics.

58. Home page, Natal Conference, https://www.natalism.org.

59. Dr. Ben Braddock (@GraduatedBen), "It's pretty weird that we've had two years of open borders mass migration yet it seems like none of the service jobs are being filled and everywhere still feels short-staffed," X, September 20, 2023, 8:57 P.M., https://twitter.com/GraduatedBen/status/1704661190268289103.

60. Peachy Keenan (@KeenanPeachy), "Anti-immigration screed in the LA Times! Reminder: you are only allowed to mourn your replacement by new arrivals if you are yourself a member of the 'oppressed' classes," X, November 26, 3023, accessed April 15, 2024; Peachy Keenan (@KeenanPeachy), "Despicable trash human Zelenskyy forced to fire his blonde mistress, aw, very sad! Nothing a few 100 billion yankee dollars can't help," X, September 20, 2023, 10:37 P.M., accessed April 15, 2024.

61. Undated screenshot of Indian Bronson Twitter, now deleted.

62. ib (@Indian_Bronson), "Re-upping, given Italy's (ongoing, but recently ramped up) migrant crisis I do not think Italy survives as a nation-State in 100 years," X, September 20, 2023, 12:38 P.M., https://twitter.com/Indian_Bronson/status /1704535547241169089.

63. Jason Wilson, "US Businessman Is Wannabe 'Warlord' of Secretive Far-Right Men's Network," *Guardian*, August 22, 2023, https://www.theguardian.com /world/2023/aug/22/charles-haywood-claremont-institute-sacr-far-right.

64. Hadas Gold, "Megyn Kelly: Jesus and Santa Were White," Politico, December 12, 2013, https://www.politico.com/blogs/media/2013/12/megyn -kelly-jesus-and-santa-were-white-179491.

65. Andrea Cipriano, "White Supremacists Win New Bragging Rights After Trump 'Stand By' Comment," *Crime Report*, September 30, 2020, accessed April 15, 2024, https://thecrimereport.org/2020/09/30/white-supremacists-win -new-bragging-rights-after-trump-stand-by-comment.

66. Friedrich Nietzsche, *Beyond Good and Evil*, trans. Helen Zimmern (Project Gutenberg, 2009), https://www.gutenberg.org/files/4363/4363-h/4363-h.htm.

67. Friedrich Nietzsche, *Thus Spoke Zarathustra: A Book for All and None*, trans. Thomas Common (Project Gutenberg, 1999), https://www.gutenberg.org/files /1998/1998-h/1998-h.htm.

68. "Bronze Age Mindset—Bronze Age Pervert (2018)," Internet Archive.

69. "Bronze Age Mindset."

70. "Bronze Age Mindset."

71. "Former DeSantis Staffer Allegedly Created Anti LGBTQ+ Video That Included Nazi Imagery," *Queer News Tonight*, July 28, 2023, YouTube video, https://www.youtube.com/watch?v=83dG7v66tuo.

72. "Curtis Yarvin," *American Mind*, https://americanmind.org/tag/curtis-yarvin/; and "The Stakes: The American Monarchy?" *American Mind* (podcast), 2020, Apple Podcasts, https://podcasts.apple.com/fr/podcast/the-stakes-the-american -monarchy/id1439372633?i=1000523635124.

73. Joshua Tait, "The Problem with Right-Wing 'Regime' Talk," *Bulwark*, August 23, 2022, https://www.thebulwark.com/p/the-problem-with-right-wing

-regime-talk; and Curtis Yarvin, "You Can Only Lose the Culture War," *Gray Mirror*, July 11, 2022, https://graymirror.substack.com/p/you-can-only-lose-the -culture-war.

74. Curtis Yarvin, "Monarchism and Fascism Today," *Gray Mirror*, December 15, 2021, https://graymirror.substack.com/p/monarchism-and-fascism-today.

75. Casey DeSantis, "What does it tell you when the DC Establishment, the Corporate Media and the Left are all against you . . . ," *Facebook*, September 17, 2023, https://www.facebook.com/CaseyDeSantis/posts/what-does-it-tell-you-when -the-dc-establishment-the-corporate-media-and-the-left/320724613839707/.

76. Michael Anton and Curtis Yarvin, "The Stakes: The American Monarchy?" *American Mind*, May 31, 2021, https://americanmind.org/audio/the-stakes-the -american-monarchy/.

77. Thomas D. Klingenstein, "Trump's Virtues," *American Mind*, March 2, 2022, https://americanmind.org/salvo/trumps-virtues/.

78. Michael Anton, *The Stakes: America at the Point of No Return* (Washington, DC: Regnery, 2020).

79. Charles Haywood, "The Stakes: America at the Point of No Return (Michael Anton)," *Worthy House*, September 8, 2020, http://theworthyhouse.com/2020 /09/08/the-stakes-america-at-the-point-of-no-return-michael-anton/.

80. Haywood.

81. Nathan Pinkoski, "Postconstitutional America," *First Things*, November 2020, https://www.firstthings.com/article/2020/11/postconstitutional-america.

82. Geoff Bennett and Shoshana Dubnow, "Southern Baptist Convention Bans Female Pastors, Ejecting Several Churches in the Process," PBS, June 15, 2023, https://www.pbs.org/newshour/show/southern-baptist-convention-bans -female-pastors-ejecting-several-churches-in-the-process.

83. The Transformed Wife (@godlywomanhood), "Thank you for the modest shirt, @pearlythingz!" X, November 11, 2023, 12:41 P.M., https://twitter.com /godlywomanhood/status/1723395585578041810.

84. Dr. Abby Johnson (@AbbyJohnson), "Then they would have to decide on one vote. In a Godly household, the husband would get the final say," X, May 2, 2020, 11:37 A.M., https://twitter.com/AbbyJohnson/status/1256608666196815873.

85. Michael Warren Davis, "Against Women's Suffrage," *Crisis Magazine*, August 18, 2020, https://crisismagazine.com/opinion/against-womens-suffrage.

CHAPTER 7: SMASHING THE ADMINISTRATIVE STATE

1. Philip Rucker and Robert Costa, "Bannon Vows a Daily Fight for 'Deconstruction of the Administrative State,'" *Washington Post*, February 23, 2017, https://www.washingtonpost.com/politics/top-wh-strategist-vows-a-daily-fight-for-deconstruction-of-the-administrative-state/2017/02/23/03f6b8da-f9ea-11e6-bf01-d47f8cf9b643_story.html.

2. Michael Uhlmann, "The Administrative State and Its Discontents," Federalist Society, January 17, 2018, https://fedsoc.org/commentary/videos/the-administrative-state-and-its-discontents.

3. Russell Vought and Christopher F. Rufo, "Republicans vs. Government Wokeness: Here's What It Will Take to Root Out This Dangerous Ideology," Fox News, March 20, 2023, https://www.foxnews.com/opinion/republicans-vs-government-wokeness-heres-what-take-root-out-dangerous-ideology.

4. Russ Vought, "Introduction to the Center for Renewing America FY2023 Budget," Center for Renewing America, December 7, 2022, http://americarenewing.com/wp-content/uploads/2024/02/CRA-Budget-Intro-1.pdf.

5. Vought.

6. Kevin D. Roberts, "A Promise to America," forward to *Mandate for Leadership: The Conservative Promise*, ed. Paul Dans and Steven Groves (Washington, DC: Heritage Foundation, 2023), 1–17, https://static.project2025.org/2025_MandateForLeadership_FULL.pdf.

7. Russ Vought, "Executive Office of the President of the United States," in Dans and Groves, *Mandate for Leadership*, 62.

8. Brian Naylor, "Read Trump's Jan. 6 Speech, a Key Part of Impeachment Trial," NPR, February 10, 2021, https://www.npr.org/2021/02/10/966396848/read-trumps-jan-6-speech-a-key-part-of-impeachment-trial.

9. Charles R. Kesler, "After January 6th," *Claremont Review of Books* 21, no. 1 (Winter 2020/21), https://claremontreviewofbooks.com/after-january-6th.

10. Kesler, 7, 163, 222.

11. Kesler, 1.

12. Kesler, 121.

13. John Marini, *Unmasking the Administrative State: The Crisis of American Politics in the Twenty-First Century*, ed. Ken Masugi (New York: Encounter Books, 2019).

14. Susan E. Dudley, "Milestones in the Evolution of the Administrative State," *Daedalus* 150, no. 3 (Summer 2021): 33–48, https://doi.org/10.1162/daed_a_01858.

15. Dwight Waldo, *The Administrative State: A Study of the Political Theory of American Public Administration* (New York: Routledge, 2017).

16. John Marini, "Donald Trump and the American Crisis," *Claremont Review of Books*, July 22, 2016, https://claremontreviewofbooks.com/digital/donald-trump-and-the-american-crisis.

17. Marini, *Unmasking the Administrative State*, 75.

18. Marini, 147.

19. John Marini, "After Trump: The Political and Moral Legitimacy of American Government," *American Mind*, October 23, 2018, https://americanmind.org/salvo/the-political-and-moral-conditions-of-legitimacy-after-trump/.

20. Marini, *Unmasking the Administrative State*, 75.

21. Marini, "After Trump."

22. Carl Schmitt, *Staat, Bewegung, Volk: Die Dreigliederung der politischen Einheit* (Hamburg, Germany: Hanseatische Verlagsanstalt, 1933), 32, https://archive.org/details/CarlSchmittStaatBewegungVolk/page/n35/mode/2up?view=theater.

23. John Marini, "Bureaucracy, Regulation, and the Unmanly Contempt for the Constitution," interview by Richard Reinsch, *Law and Liberty*, January 16, 2019, https://lawliberty.org/podcast/bureaucracy-regulation-and-the-unmanly-contempt-for-politics/.

24. Dahlia Lithwick and Mark Joseph Stern, "The Presidential Debate Was a Big Distraction from the Latest Supreme Court Havoc," *Slate*, June 28, 2024, https://slate.com/news-and-politics/2024/06/presidential-debate-fail-supreme-court-john-roberts.html.

25. David Folkenflik, "Trumpism at Voice of America: Firings, Foosball and a Conspiracy Theory," NPR, January 27, 2021, https://www.npr.org/2021/01/27/959661875/firings-foosball-and-a-conspiracy-theory-trumpism-at-voice-of-america.

26. Washington Post Editorial Board, "How a Trump Appointee Tried to Destroy Voice of America," *Washington Post*, June 7, 2023, https://www.washingtonpost.com/opinions/2023/06/07/voa-agm-whistleblowers-michael-pack/.

27. Washington Post Editorial Board.

28. Washington Post Editorial Board.

29. Washington Post Editorial Board.

30. Folkenflik, "Trumpism at Voice of America."

31. Jason Wilson, "The Far-Right Financier Giving Millions to the Republican Party to Fight 'Woke Communists,'" *Guardian*, August 4, 2023, https://www.theguardian.com/us-news/2023/aug/04/far-right-republican-donor-woke-thomas-klingenstein; and John Eastman, interview by Tom Klingenstein, YouTube video, in three parts: part 1, June 21, 2023, https://www.youtube.com/watch?v=8rARmn9Dafs, part 2, July 21, 2023, https://www.youtube.com/watch?v=UFi2HGkmZHc, and part 3, August 2, 2023, https://www.youtube.com/watch?v=hK8il7p_BoI.

32. "Conservative Megadonors, Including Betsy DeVos, Funneled $1.38 Million to the Claremont Institute in 2020, a Group Closely Tied to Undermining the 2020 Election," Accountable.us, January 12, 2022, http://accountable.us/conservative-megadonors-including-betsy-devos-funneled-1-38-million-to-the-claremont-institute-in-2020-a-group-closely-tied-to-undermining-the-2020-election/; and Andy Kroll, "Revealed: The Billionaires Funding the Coup's Brain Trust," *Rolling Stone*, January 12, 2022, https://www.rollingstone.com/politics/politics-news/devos-bradley-claremont-trump-election-fraud-insurrection-1274253/.

33. Jim DeFede, "Facing South Florida for Oct. 22: Freedom Foundation/Teachers Union Targeted," CBS News, October 22, 2023, https://www.cbsnews.com/amp/miami/news/facing-south-florida-for-oct-22-freedom-foundationteachers-union-targeted/.

34. Stephanie Kirchgaessner, "Billionaire Backer Feels 'Deceived' by Josh Hawley over Election Objections," *Guardian*, January 18, 2021, https://www.theguardian.com/us-news/2021/jan/18/josh-hawley-billionaire-deceived-election-objections-capitol-attack; and Alex Isenstadt, "A Mole Hunt, a Secret Website and Peter Thiel's Big Risk: How J. D. Vance Won His Primary," *Politico*, May 3, 2022,

https://www.politico.com/news/2022/05/03/jd-vance-win-ohio-primary
-00029881.

35. Michael Scherer, Isaac Arnsdorf, and Josh Dawsey, "DeSantis Agency Sent $92
Million in Covid Relief Funds to Donor-Backed Project," *Washington Post*,
June 28, 2023, https://www.washingtonpost.com/politics/2023/06/28/desantis
-hosseini-interstate-covid-money/.

36. Kevin Slack, *War on the American Republic: How Liberalism Became Despotism*
(New York: Encounter Books, 2023).

37. Sam Moore, "Cabaret: How the X-Rated Musical Became a Hit," BBC,
February 10, 2022, https://www.bbc.com/culture/article/20220210-how-the-x
-rated-musical-cabaret-became-a-hit.

38. Thomas D. Klingenstein, "Trump's Virtues," *American Mind*, March 2, 2022,
https://americanmind.org/salvo/trumps-virtues/.

39. Tom Klingenstein, "Winning the Cold Civil War," National Association of
Scholars, September 9, 2021, https://www.nas.org/blogs/article/winning-the
-cold-civil-war.

40. Adolf Hitler, "Hitler's Speech to the Industry Club in Düsseldorf (January 27,
1932)," German History in Documents and Images, accessed April 16, 2024,
https://ghdi.ghi-dc.org/sub_document.cfm?document_id=3918.

CHAPTER 8: THE RISE OF THE SPIRIT WARRIORS

1. "Julie Green Ministries Official," YouTube, https://www.youtube.com/@julie
greenofficial/videos.

2. Eric Hananoki, "Doug Mastriano Campaign 'Prophet': Political Executions
Are Coming, Biden 'Is No Longer Alive,' Pelosi Drinks 'Children's Blood,'"
Media Matters for America, August 17, 2022, https://www.mediamatters.org
/qanon-conspiracy-theory/doug-mastriano-campaign-prophet-julie-green
-political-executions-are-coming.

3. Brian Kaylor and Beau Underwood, "Will Christians Sing Praises for Democracy's Demise?" *A Public Witness*, November 1, 2022, https://publicwitness
.wordandway.org/p/will-christians-sing-praises-for.

4. Heidi Beedle, "Lamborn and Boebert 'Hold the Line' at CO Springs Event,"
Colorado Times Recorder, May 24, 2022, https://coloradotimesrecorder.com/2022
/05/lamborn-and-boebert-hold-the-line-at-co-springs-event/45961/.

5. Sean Feucht, "Lauren Boebert's Powerful Prayer in the Capitol Rotunda," March 16, 2023, YouTube video, https://www.youtube.com/watch?v=tvo BeEOoQiU.

6. Kyle Morris, "DeSantis Touts 'Freest State' of Florida During Appearance at New Years Eve Christian Concert in Miami," FOX 13 Tampa Bay, January 1, 2022, https://www.fox13news.com/news/desantis-touts-freest-state-of-florida -during-appearance-at-new-years-eve-christian-concert-in-miami.

7. Lance Wallnau, *God's Chaos Candidate: Donald J. Trump and the American Unraveling* (Keller, TX: Killer Sheep Media, 2016), 19.

8. John Fea, "Why a $45 Trump Prayer Coin Is No Joke," *Religion News Service*, May 17, 2019, https://religionnews.com/2019/05/17/why-a-45-trump-prayer-coin -is-no-joke-lance-wallnau-jim-bakker/.

9. Gustaf Kilander, "MAGA Pastor Says Climate Activists Are Being Controlled by 'Demons,'" *Independent*, July 14, 2022, https://www.the-independent.com /news/world/americas/us-politics/lance-wallnau-maga-pastor-climate-b212 3364.html.

10. David French, "Tucker Carlson's Dark and Malign Influence over the Christian Right," *New York Times*, May 7, 2023, https://www.nytimes.com/2023/05 /07/opinion/tucker-carlson-christian-right.html.

11. Lance Wallnau, "Episode #632: The Real Story Behind What Soros Is Up To," May 31, 2022, https://lancewallnau.com/episode-632-the-real-story-behind -what-soros-is-up-to/.

12. "World Prayer Network," YouTube, https://www.youtube.com/playlist?list =PLveqmiOZzJ_eY4-5aOocPMrmDEoA_G3DT.

13. City Elders, "Dr. Jim Garlow—Who Has Occupied Our Country?" September 7, 2023, YouTube video, 19:33, https://www.youtube.com/watch?v =LDDiPFc7J3w.

14. City Elders, 23:55.

15. James Lasher, "Roger Stone Tells Eric Metaxas: 'A Demonic Portal Opened Above the White House,'" *Charisma News*, December 14, 2022, accessed March 4, 2024, https://www.charismanews.com/culture/90958-roger-stone-tells -eric-metaxas-a-demonic-portal-opened-above-the-white-house.

16. Katherine Stewart, "The Rise of Spirit Warriors," *New Republic*, January 23, 2023, https://newrepublic.com/article/170027/rise-spirit-warriors-christian-right-politics.

17. Sean Feucht, "Are the Left's Policies Satanic?" *Charisma News*, August 29, 2022, accessed March 4, 2024, https://www.charismanews.com/opinion/90009-sean-feucht-are-the-left-s-policies-satanic.

18. Right Wing Watch (@RightWingWatch), "The first speaker at the Family Research Council's activist conference is author Jonathan Cahn, who says America is possessed by 'the dark trinity,'" X, September 15, 2023, 9:21 A.M., https://twitter.com/RightWingWatch/status/1702673953964093472.

19. Jill Colvin and Michelle L. Price, "Trump, Facing Potential Indictment, Holds Defiant Waco Rally," AP News, March 25, 2023, https://apnews.com/article/trump-waco-rally-texas-9a5676b734bb087a977ffe0216d0a6a8; Nathan Layne and Tim Reid, "Trump Portrays 2024 Race as a Christian Battle, Akin to D-Day," Reuters, February 23, 2024, https://www.reuters.com/world/us/trump-portrays-2024-race-christian-battle-akin-d-day-2024-02-23/; Michael Gold, "Trump Frames Election as Battle Against 'Wicked' System Bent on Attacking Christians," *New York Times*, February 23, 2024, https://www.nytimes.com/2024/02/22/us/politics/trump-national-christian-broadcasters.html.

20. John Fea, "Florida Governor Ron DeSantis at Hillsdale College: 'Put on the Full Armor of God. Stand Firm Against the Left's Schemes,'" *Current*, September 13, 2022, https://currentpub.com/2022/09/13/florida-governor-ron-desantis-at-hillsdale-college-put-on-the-full-armor-of-god-stand-firm-against-the-lefts-schemes/.

21. Ron DeSantis, "Faith and Freedom Coalition: Road to Majority Conference—2021," *Fox Nation*, accessed April 16, 2024, https://nation.foxnews.com/watch/7457d0501d9b29cd4164795d19d3e258/; and Amy Eskind, "Ron DeSantis' Campaign Ad Says He Was Sent by God to 'Take the Arrows,'" *People*, November 7, 2022, https://people.com/politics/ron-desantis-god-made-fighter-ad/.

22. Stewart, "Rise of Spirit Warriors."

23. Adam Gabbatt, "Fears Grow in North Carolina as Ultra-Extreme Republican Eyes Governor's Mansion," *Guardian*, May 5, 2023, https://www.theguardian.com/us-news/2023/may/05/mark-robinson-republican-north-carolina-governor-race.

24. Emma Green, "A Christian Insurrection," *Atlantic*, January 8, 2021, https://www
.theatlantic.com/politics/archive/2021/01/evangelicals-catholics-jericho-march
-capitol/617591/.

25. NTD Newsroom, "Jericho March Co-Founder: 'God Told Me to Let the
Church Roar,'" *NTD*, December 13, 2020, https://www.ntd.com/jericho-march
-co-founder-god-told-me-to-let-the-church-roar_539706.html.

26. "Christian Nationalism and the January 6, 2021, Insurrection," Christians Against
Christian Nationalism, February 9, 2022, https://static1.squarespace.com/static
/5cfea0017239e10001cd9639/t/6203f007e07275503964ab4d/1644425230442/Chris
tian_Nationalism_and_the_Jan6_Insurrection-2-9-22.pdf, 17.

27. "Christian Nationalism," 18.

28. "Christian Nationalism," 19.

29. Jack Jenkins, "Mike Johnson Suggests His Election as House Speaker Ordained
by God," *Washington Post*, October 27, 2023, https://www.washingtonpost.com
/religion/2023/10/27/house-speaker-mike-johnson-evangelical/.

30. Robert Downen, "Texas Activist David Barton Wants to End Separation of
Church and State. He Has the Ear of the New U.S. House Speaker," *Texas
Tribune*, November 3, 2023, https://www.texastribune.org/2023/11/03/david
-barton-mike-johnson-texas-church-state-christianity/.

31. Tim Dickinson, "Mike Johnson: 'Depraved' America Deserves God's Wrath,"
Rolling Stone, November 15, 2023, https://www.rollingstone.com/politics/politics
-features/mike-johnson-america-god-wrath-jim-garlow-1234879233/.

32. David Corn, "Mike Johnson Conducted Seminars Promoting the US as
a 'Christian Nation,'" *Mother Jones*, October 28, 2023, https://www.motherjones
.com/politics/2023/10/mike-johnson-seminars-christian-nation-speaker-far
-right/.

33. Martin Pengelly, "New House Speaker Mike Johnson Praised '18th-Century
Values' in Speech," *Guardian*, October 27, 2023, https://www.theguardian.com
/us-news/2023/oct/27/mike-johnson-value-moral-conservative-republican.

34. Corn, "Mike Johnson Conducted Seminars."

35. April Rubin, "How Mike Johnson's Denial of Trump's 2020 Loss Helped Pave
His Path to Power," *Axios*, October 26, 2023, https://www.axios.com/2023/10
/26/mike-johnson-house-speaker-2020-election-denialism.

36. David Barton, "Plymouth Colony with David Barton," Eagle Mountain Church, September 16, 2020, Vimeo video, https://vimeo.com/458748600.

37. "Religion and the Founding of the American Republic: Religion in Eighteenth-Century America," Library of Congress, accessed March 4, 2024, https://www.loc.gov/exhibits/religion/rel02.html; and *Encyclopedia Britannica*, s.v., "Social Gospel," February 7, 2022, https://www.britannica.com/event/Social-Gospel.

38. Jana Riess, "The 'Nones' Are Growing—and Growing More Diverse," *Religion News Service*, March 24, 2021, https://religionnews.com/2021/03/24/the-nones -are-growing-and-growing-more-diverse/.

39. Aaron Earls, "Study: Conservative Churches Most Likely to Grow," Lifeway Research, January 27, 2017, https://research.lifeway.com/2017/01/27/study-con servative-churches-most-likely-to-grow/.

40. John Micklethwait and Adrian Wooldridge, *God Is Back: How the Global Rise of Faith Is Changing the World* (London: Penguin Books, 2010).

41. Vinson Synan, "Pentecostalism: William Seymour," *Christianity Today*, 2000, https://www.christianitytoday.com/history/issues/issue-65/pentecostalism -william-seymour.html.

42. "General Bylaws 2020," Pentecostal Church of God, https://uploads-ssl.webflow .com/5da396c9848a167a29dc6619/5e7267812dfa3d7475710ea7_2020Bylaws_com pressed.pdf.

43. Synan, "Pentecostalism."

44. Cecelia Rasmussen, "Vision of a Colorblind Faith Gave Birth to Pentecostalism," *Los Angeles Times*, June 14, 1998, https://www.latimes.com/archives/la -xpm-1998-jun-14-me-59833-story.html.

45. Rasmussen.

46. Gary Dauphin, "#Blackhistory: On April 9, 1906, the Azusa Street Revival Begins in Los Angeles," California African American Museum, April 9, 2018, https://caamuseum.org/learn/600state/black-history/blackhistory-on-april-9 -1906-the-azusa-street-revival-begins-in-los-angeles.

47. David Masci, "How Income Varies Among U.S. Religious Groups," Pew Research Center, October 11, 2016, https://www.pewresearch.org/short-reads /2016/10/11/how-income-varies-among-u-s-religious-groups/.

48. Jeff Brumley, "Sunday Morning Becoming the Most Politically 'Segregated' Hour in America," *Baptist News Global*, August 24, 2018, https://baptistnews .com/article/sunday-morning-becoming-the-most-politically-segregated-hour -in-america/.

49. "Racial and Ethnic Composition Among Pentecostals in the Evangelical Tradition," Religious Landscape Study, Pew Research Center, 2015, https://www.pew research.org/religious-landscape-study/database/religious-family/pentecostal -family-evangelical-trad/racial-and-ethnic-composition/.

50. Kenneth L. Waters, Sr., "Afro-Pentecostalism: Black Pentecostal and Charismatic Christianity in History and Culture," *Christian Scholar's Review*, April 15, 2013, https://christianscholars.com/afro-pentecostalism-black-pentecostal-and -charismatic-christianity-in-history-and-culture/.

51. Elle Hardy, "The Rise of Pentecostal Christianity," interview by Nathan J Robinson, *Current Affairs*, April 8, 2022, https://www.currentaffairs.org/2022/04 /how-pentecostal-christianity-is-taking-over-the-world.

52. Katherine Stewart, "The Democratic Party Is Shedding Latino Voters. Here's Why," *New Republic*, May 11, 2022, https://newrepublic.com/article/166406 /democrats-losing-latino-voters-2022.

53. Eric Tiansay, "He Asked God for Nations," *Charisma*, August 31, 2003, https:// mycharisma.com/spiritled-living/he-asked-god-for-nations/.

54. Tiansay.

55. Tiansay.

56. Rebecca Randall, "Pentecostals Lead the World in Conversions, but Not in US Missions," *Christianity Today*, February 11, 2021, https://www.christianitytoday .com/ct/2021/february-web-only/pentecostal-global-growth-missions-agencies -study-bok.html.

57. Amy Erica Smith and Ryan Lloyd, "Top Pentecostal Leaders Supported the Far-Right in Brazil's Presidential Campaign," *Vox*, October 8, 2018, https://www.vox .com/mischiefs-of-faction/2018/10/8/17950304/pentecostals-bolsonaro-brazil.

58. Shaun Walker, "Orbán Deploys Christianity with a Twist to Tighten Grip in Hungary," *Guardian*, July 14, 2019, https://www.theguardian.com/world/2019 /jul/14/viktor-orban-budapest-hungary-christianity-with-a-twist.

59. Jakob Egeris Thorsen, "The CCR in Latin America and Guatemala," in *Charismatic Practice and Catholic Parish Life* (Leiden: Brill, 2015), 20–47, https://doi .org/10.1163/9789004291669_003; and Jeff Abbott, "The Other Americans: Guatemala Is Constructing a Religious Narco-State," *Progressive*, September 14, 2022, https://progressive.org/latest/other-americans-guatemala-religious-narco -state-abbott-091422/.

60. Elle Hardy, "Spiritual Union: Why Gulf Migrants Are Turning to Evangelical Christianity," *Guardian*, July 31, 2022, https://www.theguardian.com/world/2022 /jul/31/spiritual-union-why-gulf-migrants-turning-evangelical-christianity.

61. Alice Facchini, "Il silenzio delle chiese pentecostali sulla tratta delle donne nigeriane," *IRPI Media*, August 1, 2022, https://irpimedia.irpi.eu/silenzio-chiese -pentecostali-sulla-tratta-donne-nigeriane/.

62. Elle Hardy, *Beyond Belief: How Pentecostal Christianity Is Taking Over the World* (London: Hurst, 2021).

63. Sarah Posner, "The Army of Prayer Warriors Fighting Trump's Impeachment," *Type Investigations*, December 19, 2019, https://www.typeinvestigations.org /investigation/2019/12/19/the-army-of-prayer-warriors-fighting-trumps-im peachment/.

64. Katherine Stewart, *The Power Worshippers: Inside the Dangerous Rise of Religious Nationalism* (London: Bloomsbury, 2020); Stewart, "Rise of Spirit Warriors."

65. Tara Law, "Trump Spiritual Advisor Calls for Miscarriage of 'Satanic Pregnancies,'" *Time*, January 26, 2020, https://time.com/5771920/trump-paula-white -miscarriage-satanic-pregnancies/.

66. Katherine Stewart, *The Good News Club: The Christian Right's Stealth Assault on America's Children* (New York: PublicAffairs, 2012), 186–87.

67. André Gagné, *American Evangelicals for Trump: Dominion, Spiritual Warfare, and the End Times* (Routledge, 2023).

68. "C. Peter Wagner," Ywam Publishing, https://www.ywampublishing.com /p-2004-c-peter-wagner.aspx.

69. C. Peter Wagner, *Dominion!: How Kingdom Action Can Change the World* (Ada, MI: Revell, 2008).

70. Rachel Tabachnick, "The Evangelicals Engaged in Spiritual Warfare," interview by Terry Gross, NPR, August 19, 2011, https://www.npr.org/2011/08/24/139781021/the-evangelicals-engaged-in-spiritual-warfare.

71. "The Seven Mountains of Societal Influence," Generals International, https://www.generals.org/the-seven-mountains.

72. Wagner, *Dominion!*, 148.

73. "Watchman Decree," *Victory Channel*, https://flashpoint.govictory.com/wp-content/uploads/sites/7/2022/06/WatchmanDecree.pdf.

74. Frederick Clarkson, "'Unfriending' America: The Christian Right Is Coming for the Enemies of God—Like You and Me," *Salon*, June 17, 2023, https://www.salon.com/2023/06/17/unfriending-america-the-christian-right-is-coming-for-the-enemies-of-god—like-you-and-me/.

75. Home page, NAR Connections, https://narconnections.com.

76. Kyle Mantyla, "Leigh Valentine: If You Don't Like That God Is Using Trump to Save America Then 'Just Get Out,'" Right Wing Watch, June 19, 2018, https://www.rightwingwatch.org/post/leigh-valentine-if-you-dont-like-that-god-is-using-trump-to-save-america-then-just-get-out/.

77. "Word of Faith Fellowship/Inside Edition," Trinity Foundation, October 22, 2012, YouTube video, https://www.youtube.com/watch?v=YwE5fBT9RYE.

78. Mitch Weiss and Holbrook Mohr, "'Nobody Saved Us': Man Describes Childhood in Abusive 'Cult,'" AP News, December 13, 2017, https://apnews.com/article/nc-state-wire-word-of-faith-fellowship-north-america-us-news-ap-top-news-2582341fd6bb4de58dcd4249d4171463.

79. Jen Juneau, "'One of America's Most Dangerous Cults' Insists It Wants to Spread God's Love: What Ex Members Say Really Goes on Inside," *People*, March 1, 2020, https://people.com/crime/word-of-faith-fellowship-cult-new-book/.

80. Samantha Schmidt, "Gay Man Says Church Members Beat, Choked Him for Hours to Expel 'Homosexual Demons,'" *Washington Post*, June 2, 2017, https://www.washingtonpost.com/news/morning-mix/wp/2017/06/02/gay-man-says-church-members-beat-choked-him-for-hours-to-expel-homosexual-demons/.

81. Mitch Weiss, "AP Exclusive: Ex-Congregants Reveal Years of Ungodly Abuse," AP News, February 27, 2017, https://apnews.com/article/nc-state-wire-broken-faith-north-carolina-us-news-religion-e9404784f9c6428a8d4382f5ada8f463.

82. Weiss, "AP Exclusive."

83. "Statement from 'Miss Norris,'" *Word of Faith Fellowship* (blog), March 12, 2017, https://wordoffaithfellowship.org/blog/statement-from-miss-norris/.

84. Sean Rowe, "Second Coming," *Dallas Observer*, November 6, 1997, https://www.dallasobserver.com/news/second-coming-6402423.

85. Rowe, "Second Coming."

86. "Bankruptcy Filing Reveals Ties to Word of Faith Fellowship," *Religion News Blog*, July 14, 2006, https://www.religionnewsblog.com/15355/bankruptcy-filing-reveals-ties-to-word-of-faith-fellowship.

87. https://www.libertymagazine.org/article/the-prophet-of-profit1.

88. "Celestial Pleadings," *D Magazine*, March 1, 1997, https://www.dmagazine.com/publications/d-magazine/1997/march/celestial-pleadings/.

89. "Leigh Valentine," *7Figure$*, March 2021, https://issuu.com/bfgibson/docs/7figure__march/s/11815224.

90. "Bankruptcy Filing Reveals Ties."

91. Alexander Burns and Maggie Haberman, "Electoral Map Gives Donald Trump Few Places to Go," *New York Times*, July 30, 2016, https://www.nytimes.com/2016/07/31/us/politics/donald-trump-presidential-race.html?_r=0. Whaley (front row left) and Valentine (beside her, front row center) can be seen in the second photograph.

92. "About Leigh Valentine," Leigh Valentine Beauty, https://www.valentinespa.com/About-Leigh-Valentine_ep_7.html.

93. "Faith Life Church LIVE 6/10/2023: Special Guest Lance Wallnau," Faith Life Church Online, June 10, 2023, YouTube video, 1:25:00, https://www.youtube.com/watch?v=GApuQwAlVno.

94. Amy Littlefield, "At the Vote Pray Stand Summit, Christian Parents and Their 'Rights' Take Center Stage," *Nation*, September 22, 2023, https://www.thenation.com/article/politics/vote-pray-stand-summit/.

95. Kira Resistance (@KiraResistance), "When it comes to movement in America, not everybody's going to become Christian to fight transgenderism But everybody will fight transgenderism, if we FRAME it as attack against your children," X, July 14, 2023, 6:04 P.M., https://twitter.com/KiraResistance/status/1679975246869467136.

96. Ryan Burge (@ryanburge), "Was looking through some recently collected data that included Christian Nationalism questions," X, July 8, 2022, 7:45 P.M., https://twitter.com/ryanburge/status/1545554824179159040.

97. Eric Levitz, "David Shor on Why Trump Was Good for the GOP and How Dems Can Win in 2022," *Intelligencer*, March 3, 2021, https://nymag.com/intelligencer/2021/03/david-shor-2020-democrats-autopsy-hispanic-vote-midterms-trump-gop.html.

98. Zachary B. Wolf and Curt Merrill, "Anatomy of a Close Election: How Americans Voted in 2022 vs. 2018," CNN, November 9, 2022, https://edition.cnn.com/interactive/2022/politics/exit-polls-2022-midterm-2018-shift/; and Marissa Martinez, "Voters of Color Did Move to the Right—Just Not at the Rates Predicted," *Politico*, November 13, 2022, https://www.politico.com/news/2022/11/13/latino-voters-midterm-elections-republicans-00066618.

99. Levitz, "David Shor."

100. Frank Lopez (@FrankLopezJWC), "El presidente Biden dijo ayer que se añadiría la identificación sexual 'X' al pasaporte americano. Esto es una manera perversa de rebelión a Dios. Un líder ignorante con una agenda destructora," X, April 1, 2022, 8:55 A.M., https://twitter.com/FrankLopezJWC/status/1509877113050046480.

101. Frank López, "¿En Qué Consiste La Nueva Izquierda? / Agustín Laje," March 28, 2022, YouTube video, https://www.youtube.com/watch?v=jnJDT9eZ8AA.

102. Frederick Clarkson and Cloee Cooper, "Convergence of Far-Right, Antidemocratic Factions in the Northwest Could Provide a Model for the Rest of the Nation," *Religion Dispatches*, May 25, 2021, https://religiondispatches.org/convergence-of-far-right-antidemocratic-factions-in-the-northwest-could-provide-a-model-for-the-rest-of-the-nation/.

103. Clarkson and Cooper.

104. Andrea Cavallier, "Oath Keepers Leader Stewart Rhodes Is Found Guilty of Seditious Conspiracy over January 6 Riot and Now Faces up to 20 Years in Prison," *Daily Mail*, November 30, 2022, https://www.dailymail.co.uk/news/article-11483491/Oath-Keepers-leader-Stewart-Rhodes-guilty-seditious-conspiracy-January-6-riot.html.

105. Brian Kaylor and Beau Underwood, "Taking Off the Armor of God," *A Public Witness*, August 16, 2022, https://publicwitness.wordandway.org/p/taking-off-the-armor-of-god.

106. "Road to Majority 2022 Conference Agenda," Faith & Freedom Coalition, June 2022, http://www.ffcoalition.com/wp-content/uploads/2022/06/2022-FFC -Policy-Conference-Agenda-1.pdf.

107. Stewart, "Rise of Spirit Warriors."

108. Michael Harriot, "Tim Scott, Daniel Cameron and the Business of Selling Souls," *Grio*, November 16, 2023, https://thegrio.com/2023/11/16/tim-scott-daniel -cameron-and-the-business-of-selling-souls/.

109. Katherine Stewart, "What's Missing from Popular Discussions of Today's Christian Nationalism," *Washington Spectator*, September 13, 2021, https:// washingtonspectator.org/whats-missing-from-popular-discussions-of-todays -christian-nationalism/.

110. Tom Deignan, "Michael Flynn Is Embracing His Irish Catholic Heritage," *IrishCentral*, November 8, 2022, https://www.irishcentral.com/opinion/others /michael-flynn-irish-catholic; and Niklas Franzen, "How Bolsonaro Is Breaking the Divide Between the State and Church," *International Politics and Society*, September 2, 2022, https://www.ips-journal.eu/topics/democracy-and-society /how-bolsonaro-is-breaking-the-divide-between-state-and-church-6168.

111. Katherine Stewart, "Christian Nationalists Are Excited About What Comes Next," *New York Times*, July 5, 2022, https://www.nytimes.com/2022/07/05 /opinion/dobbs-christian-nationalism.html.

112. William Shakespeare, "The Tragedy of King Lear, Act IV, Scene 1: The Heath," Open Source Shakespeare, accessed March 26, 2024, https://www.opensource shakespeare.org/views/plays/play_view.php?WorkID=kinglear&Act=4&Scene =1&Scope=scene.

CHAPTER 9: GOD AND MAN IN LAS VEGAS

1. Jessica Hill, "God, Country, Trump: Thousands Gather at Far-Right Convention in NLV," *Las Vegas Review-Journal*, August 26, 2023, https://www .reviewjournal.com/news/politics-and-government/nevada/god-country -trump-thousands-gather-at-far-right-convention-in-nlv-2894465/.

2. "Epoch Times CFO Is Arrested and Accused of Role in $67M Multinational Money Laundering Scheme," AP News, June 3, 2024, https://apnews.com /article/epoch-times-cfo-indictment-money-laundering-caad358778bb6b73e32 e9f989f3b9665.

3. Brandy Zadrozny, "How the Conspiracy-Fueled *Epoch Times* Went Mainstream and Made Millions," NBC News, October 13, 2023, https://www.nbcnews.com /news/us-news/epoch-times-falun-gong-growth-rcna111373.

4. Richard Lardner and Michelle R. Smith, "Michael Flynn's ReAwaken Road-show Recruits 'Army of God,'" PBS *Frontline*, October 7, 2022, https://www .pbs.org/wgbh/frontline/article/michael-flynn-reawaken-america-tour/.

5. Carter Walker, "COVID-19, Rigged Elections and a Prophecy from God: Clay Clark's ReAwaken America Tour Comes to Lancaster," *LancasterOnline*, October 21, 2022, https://lancasteronline.com/news/local/covid-19-rigged-elec tions-and-a-prophecy-from-god-clay-clarks-reawaken-america-tour-comes /article_07937fc2-51ab-11ed-8c3b-dbdc793e4dea.html.

6. Jonathan Kelly, "Doctor Zoellner & Clark Filing Lawsuit to Lift Mayor Bynum's Mask Mandate," EIN Presswire, August 18, 2020, https://www .einnews.com/pr_news/524259724/doctor-zoellner-clark-filing-lawsuit-to-lift -mayor-bynum-s-mask-mandate.

7. Noah Phillips, "ReAwaken America Tour Fuses Trumpism and Christian Nationalism," *Moment Magazine*, May 12, 2023, https://momentmag.com/deep -dive-clay-clark-reawaken-america/.

8. "Experience Clay Clark's The Great ReAwakening vs. The Great Reset," https://www.thrivetimeshow.com/wp-content/uploads/Tulare-CA-Episode -22-Version-2-ThrivetimeShow-1.jpg.

9. Alex Seitz-Wald, "RFK Jr. Not Participating in Far-Right Event After Being Listed as a Speaker, Aide Says," NBC News, May 12, 2023, https://www .nbcnews.com/meet-the-press/meetthepressblog/rfk-jr-not-participating-far -right-event-listed-speaker-aide-says-rcna84156.

10. Eric Neugeboren, "Alex Jones, Other Far-Right Speakers to Appear at North Las Vegas-Owned Property," *Nevada Independent*, July 6, 2023, https:// thenevadaindependent.com/article/alex-jones-other-far-right-conspiracy -theorists-to-speak-at-north-las-vegas-event; and Tim Dickinson, "'Alex Jones Did Nothing Wrong': Meet the Christian Nationalist Behind 'Pastors for Trump,'" *Rolling Stone*, December 27, 2022, https://www.rollingstone.com /politics/politics-features/jackson-lahmeyer-christian-nationalist-conspiracy -theorist-pastors-for-trump-1234649049/.

11. "The Disinformation Dozen: Why Platforms Must Act on Twelve Leading Online Anti-Vaxxers," Center for Countering Digital Hate, March 24, 2021, https://counterhate.com/wp-content/uploads/2022/05/210324-The-Disinfor mation-Dozen.pdf.

12. "Mel K Worldwide Conspiracy," *Media Matters for America*, March 1, 2021, https://www.mediamatters.org/media/4004097.

13. Dickinson, "'Alex Jones Did Nothing Wrong.'"

14. "Former White House Advisor Convicted of Contempt of Congress," U.S. Attorney's Office for the District of Columbia, September 7, 2023, https://www .justice.gov/usao-dc/pr/former-white-house-advisor-convicted-contempt -congress.

15. Katherine Stewart, "The Right-Wing Conspiracy-Fest Is More Openly Blood-thirsty than Before," *New Republic*, September 13, 2023, https://newrepublic.com /article/175514/reawaken-america-political-violence-conference.

16. Roseanne Barr, ReAwaken America Tour, Las Vegas, Nevada, August 2023, 00:04–00:10 (author's recording).

17. "Roseanne Barr: Roseanne's Surprising Take on Faith and Comedy—ReAwaken America Las Vegas," FlyoverConservatives, September 16, 2023, BitChute video, 14:45, https://www.bitchute.com/video/HRZNCZIqf5h1/.

18. Roseanne Barr, ReAwaken America Tour, 30:17–31.00 (author's recording).

19. Vince DiMiceli, "Roseanne Barr Sells One LA-Area Home—After Buying Another," *Real Deal*, March 19, 2022, https://therealdeal.com/la/2022/03/19 /roseanne-barr-sells-one-la-area-home-after-buying-another/.

20. Phillips, "ReAwaken America Tour."

21. Phillips.

22. Jennifer Bowers Bahney, "Nicolle Wallace Credits Rachel Maddow for Getting Anti-Semites Booted from Mar-a-Lago Event with Eric Trump," *Mediaite*, May 12, 2023, https://www.mediaite.com/politics/nicolle-wallace-credits-rachel -maddow-for-getting-anti-semites-booted-from-mar-a-lago-event-with-eric -trump/.

23. "Mel K Worldwide Conspiracy."

24. https://www.nytimes.com/interactive/2024/01/04/us/january-6-capitol-trump
-investigation.html.

25. John Komlos, "A Revealing New Look into the January 6 Insurrectionists,"
DCReport, December 19, 2022, https://www.dcreport.org/2022/12/19/a-revealing
-new-look-into-the-january-6-insurrectionists/.

26. Robert A. Pape, "Understanding American Domestic Terrorism: Mobilization
Potential and Risk Factors of a New Threat Trajectory," Chicago Project on
Security and Threats, April 6, 2021, https://cpost.uchicago.edu/publications
/understanding_american_domestic_terrorism_mobilization_potential_and
_risk_factors_of_a_new_threat_trajectory/.

27. Sarah D. Wire, "At Far-Right Roadshow, Trump is God's 'Anointed One,'
QAnon is King, and 'Everything You Believe Is Right,'" *Los Angeles Times*,
October 12, 2023, https://www.latimes.com/politics/story/2023-10-12/reawaken
-america-trump-maga-qanon-christian-nationalism.

28. David Aaronovitch, "UN Expert? No, a Conspiracy Crank," *Times* (London),
April 15, 2008, https://www.thetimes.co.uk/article/un-expert-no-a-conspiracy
-crank-zndmplz35dp.

29. Richard Hofstadter, "The Paranoid Style in American Politics," *Harper's Magazine*, November 1964, https://harpers.org/archive/1964/11/the-paranoid-style
-in-american-politics/.

30. Bianca Padró Ocasio, "'Demonic Spirit': Miami Pastor Rejects Coronavirus
Warning," *Miami Herald*, March 15, 2020, https://www.miamiherald.com/news
/local/community/miami-dade/article241209151.html.

31. Alex Bollinger, "Pastor Who Laid Hands on Trump Says Avoiding Coronavirus Is for 'Pansies,'" *LGBTQ Nation*, March 18, 2020, https://www.lgbtqnation
.com/2020/03/pastor-laid-hands-trump-says-avoiding-coronavirus-pansies/.

32. Aila Slisco, "Pastor Holds Service with over 1,000 Parishioners in Defiance of
Large-Gathering Ban," *Newsweek*, March 18, 2020, https://www.newsweek
.com/pastor-holds-service-over-1000-parishoners-defiance-large-gathering
-ban-1493113.

33. Katherine Stewart, "The Religious Right's Hostility to Science Is Crippling Our
Coronavirus Response," *New York Times*, March 27, 2020, https://www.nytimes
.com/2020/03/27/opinion/coronavirus-trump-evangelicals.html.

CHAPTER 10: NO EXIT

1. Robert Cunningham, "Investigation into Allegations Against Chris Rice," Tates Creek Presbyterian Church, October 15, 2020, https://tcpca.org/rice -investigation.

2. Alex Montoya, "When Truth Meets Love," in *Right Thinking in a Church Gone Astray: Finding Our Way Back to Biblical Truth*, ed. Nathan Busenitz (Eugene, OR: Harvest House, 2017), 54–57.

3. Tom Drion, "Sermon: Marriage Myth Busting #2," GraceLife London, May 2, 2021, https://www.gracelifelondon.org/articles/sermon-marriage-myth -busting-2.

4. "History," Grace Community Church, https://www.gracechurch.org/about /history.

5. Julie Roys, "John MacArthur Tells Seminarians Not to Speak at Conferences with Women, Even Though He Has," *Roys Report*, May 8, 2023, https://julieroys .com/john-macarthur-tells-seminarians-not-to-speak-at-conferences-with -women-even-though-he-has/.

6. Sarah Einselen, "Head of Counseling at John MacArthur's School: Wife Should Endure Abuse Like Missionary Endures Persecution," *Roys Report*, April 5, 2022, https://julieroys.com/head-counseling-john-macarthur-school-wife-endure -abuse/.

7. John MacArthur, "The Willful Submission of a Christian Wife," Grace to You, February 19, 2012, https://www.gty.org/library/sermons-library/80-382/the -willful-submission-of-a-christian-wife.

8. John MacArthur, "God's Word on Homosexuality: The Truth About Sin and the Reality of Forgiveness," *Master's Seminary Journal* 19, no. 2 (Fall 2008): 153, https://tms.edu/wp-content/uploads/2021/09/tmsj19f.pdf.

9. "The Theology of Creation by Pastor John MacArthur," Fathers of Faith, December 2, 2023, YouTube video, https://www.youtube.com/watch?v=t_3JG PfBIZg.

10. Ryan Martin, "How I Became a 'Calvinist' (and It Wasn't Because of Piper or MacArthur)," *Immoderate* (blog), June 1, 2009, https://immoderate.wordpress .com/2009/06/01/how-i-became-a-calvinist-and-it-wasnt-because-of-piper-or -macarthur/.

11. David Roach, "Southern Baptists Lost Nearly Half a Million Members Last Year," *Christianity Today*, May 12, 2023, https://www.christianitytoday.com /news/2023/may/southern-baptist-membership-drop-baptism-rebound-sbc .html.

12. John MacArthur, foreword to Busenitz, *Right Thinking in a Church Gone Astray*, 6–7.

13. Jaclyn Cosgrove, "L.A. Megachurch Pastor Mocks Pandemic Health Orders, Even as Church Members Fall Ill," *Los Angeles Times*, November 8, 2020, https://www.latimes.com/california/story/2020-11-08/la-pastor-mocks-covid -19-rules-church-members-ill.

14. Mattathias Schwartz, "How The Trump Cabinet's Bible Teacher Became a Shadow Diplomat," *New York Times*, October 29, 2019, https://www.nytimes .com/2019/10/29/magazine/ralph-drollinger-white-house-evangelical.html.

15. Sarah Lane Ritchie, "4 Things Americans Can Learn About Faith and Evolution from Great Britain and Canada," *BioLogos*, September 27, 2017, https:// biologos.org/articles/4-things-americans-can-learn-about-faith-and-evolution -from-great-britain-and-canada.

16. Michael Dionne, "The Dionne Family's Future Plans," Faith Bible Church, November 8, 2020, https://fbchurch.org/resource/the-dionne-familys-future -plans.

17. "Pentecostal Churches Thriving in London as Traditional Denominations Decline," National Secular Society, https://www.secularism.org.uk/news/2013 /07/pentecostal-churches-thriving-in-london-as-traditional-denominations -decline.

18. Ruth Peacock, "The Future of Religion in Britain: A Rise in Islam as Christianity Declines. And Then There's Magic . . . ," Religion Media Centre, September 22, 2022, https://religionmediacentre.org.uk/news/the-future-of -religion-in-britain; and "Religion, England and Wales: Census 2021," Office for National Statistics, November 29, 2022, https://www.ons.gov.uk/people populationandcommunity/culturalidentity/religion/bulletins/religionengland andwales/census2021.

19. Mark Jackson, "God's Good News for Our Sexuality (2 of 3)," Inspire Saint James Clerkenwell, November 12, 2023, 11:55, https://inspirelondon.org/sermons /gods-good-news-for-our-sexuality-2-of-3.

20. Jackson, 13:08.

21. "The Sunday Times Rich List 2023," *Times* (London), https://www.thetimes.co .uk/sunday-times-rich-list.

22. Andrew Graystone, "The Marshall Plan," *Prospect*, March 27, 2024, https://www .prospectmagazine.co.uk/ideas/media/65415/the-marshall-plan-paul-marshall -gb-news.

23. Graystone.

24. "ReThink Abortion Day," *Facebook*, https://www.facebook.com/events/1252875 085259607.

25. Frances Ryan, "It's Not Just the US, Britain Needs No-Protest Buffer Zones around Its Abortion Clinics Too," *Guardian*, May 11, 2022, https://www.the guardian.com/commentisfree/2022/may/11/britain-protest-buffer-zone-abortion -clinics-women.

26. "Ben Thatcher; March for Life UK 2022," March for Life UK, September 12, 2022, http://www.marchforlife.co.uk/aiovg_videos/ben-thatcher-march-for-life -uk-2022/.

27. "What Is Brephos?" Brephos, https://www.brephos.org/about.

28. "Isabel Vaughan-Spruce: Challenging 'Thought-crimes'—Charity Volunteer Arrested for Silent Prayer," ADF UK, https://adfinternational.org/en-gb/cases /isabel.

29. Abbi Garton-Crosbie, "Who Are 40 Days for Life and What Does Pro-life Mean?" *The National*, April 20, 2023, https://www.thenational.scot/news/234 67694.40-days-life-pro-life-mean/.

30. Bonnie Pritchett, "Closure of Planned Parenthood Clinic Seen as Prayer Model," *Baptist Press*, September 18, 2013, https://www.baptistpress.com/resource -library/news/closure-of-planned-parenthood-clinic-seen-as-prayer-model/.

31. "University," 40 Days for Life, https://www.40daysforlife.com/en/university.

32. "University."

33. "40 Days for Life Spring 2009 Campaign Report," Archdiocese of Baltimore, July 16, 2009, YouTube video, https://www.youtube.com/watch?v=Oan1 TorDCGo.

34. Lauren Day, "The United Kingdom's 40 Days for Life," Leadership Institute, April 30, 2013, https://www.leadershipinstitute.org/news/?NR=9582.

35. Steven Walker, "Bridget Ziegler Resigns Director Position at Conservative Nonprofit Leadership Institute," *Sarasota Herald-Tribune*, December 6, 2023, https://www.heraldtribune.com/story/news/politics/2023/12/06/bridget-ziegler -resigns-position-at-conservative-leadership-institute/71829708007/.

36. Heidi Beirich and Mark Potok, "The Council for National Policy: Behind the Curtain," Southern Poverty Law Center, May 17, 2016, https://www.splcenter.org /hatewatch/2016/05/17/council-national-policy-behind-curtain; "Conservatives Oppose Funding the Far-Left's Agenda in the Lame Duck," Conservative Action Project, September 28, 2022, https://conservativeactionproject.com/conservatives -oppose-funding-the-far-lefts-agenda-in-the-lame-duck/; and "Memos," Conser vative Action Project, https://conservativeactionproject.com/memos/.

37. Andrea Suozzo et al., "Leadership Institute," ProPublica Nonprofit Explorer, April 24, 2024, https://projects.propublica.org/nonprofits/organizations/510235174.

38. "Isabel Vaughan-Spruce: Challenging 'Thought-crimes.'"

39. K. V. Turley, "Father Gough: 'I Was Conceived in the Context of Violence, and My Mother Chose Life for Me,'" *National Catholic Register*, February 26, 2023, https://www.ncregister.com/news/father-gough-i-was-conceived-in-the -context-of-violence-and-my-mother-chose-life-for-me.

40. Elaine Blackburne, "Priest and Woman Arrested as They 'Silently Prayed' Cleared of 'Thoughtcrime,'" *WalesOnline*, February 16, 2023, https://www .walesonline.co.uk/news/uk-news/priest-woman-arrested-silently-prayed-262 55478; and PA News Agency, "Priest Accuses Government of Censoring 'Silent Prayers' near Abortion Clinic," *Ealing Times*, February 16, 2023, http://www.ealingtimes.co.uk/news/national/23326365.priest-accuses-govern ment-censoring-silent-prayers-near-abortion-clinic.

41. Irene Garcia, "UK Court Acquits Woman, Priestess, of 'Thought Crime' for Silent Prayer near Abortion Clinic," *Local Today*, February 16, 2023, accessed March 5, 2024, https://localtoday.news/mn/uk-court-acquits-woman-priestess- of-thought-crime-for-silent-prayer-near-abortion-clinic-152033.html; and "Fr. Sean Gough, Isabel Vaughan-Spruce Receive 'Not Guilty!' Verdict for Silent Prayer Thoughtcrime," *Catholic Network*, February 16, 2023, https://www .thecatholicnetwork.co.uk/6413.

42. "Priest Charged after Praying Outside of Abortion Clinic Says Free Speech Is 'Threatened,'" Fox News, February 15, 2023, https://www.foxnews.com/video /6320516153112.

43. Jeremiah Igunnubole, "Don't Buffer the Truth about Censorship Zones," *Critic*, July 22, 2022, https://thecritic.co.uk/dont-buffer-the-truth-about-censorship -zones/.

44. Brian Palmer, "Mommy, Where Do Pictures of Aborted Babies Come From?" *Slate*, October 26, 2010, https://slate.com/news-and-politics/2010/10/where-do -anti-abortion-protesters-get-those-grisly-photos.html.

45. "Bishop Assailed on Exhibit's Abortion-Holocaust Linkage," *Los Angeles Times*, March 28, 2002, https://www.latimes.com/archives/la-xpm-2002-mar-28-mn -35157-story.html.

46. "Manhattan Declaration: A Call of Christian Conscience," Manhattan Declaration, November 20, 2009, https://www.manhattandeclaration.org.

47. Thomas Reese, "EWTN, Once 'The Work of the Devil,' Now Gets Blessing from Pope," *National Catholic Reporter*, May 17, 2023, https://www.ncronline.org /opinion/guest-voices/ewtn-once-work-devil-now-gets-blessing-pope.

48. Rachel Mackenzie, "Hope, Healing and Forgiveness: Facing the Canon with Rachel Mackenzie," interview by J. John, Facebook, May 29, 2022, 0:24, https://www.facebook.com/jjohnglobal/videos/705999730698942/.

49. "Pro Life Movement Supporter Rachel Mackenzie: 12-Week Limit on Unrestricted Abortions Misleading," GBC News, February 14, 2020, YouTube video, https://www.youtube.com/watch?v=fgubGCa-P4M.

50. "Theresa Karminski Burke—Founder of Rachel's Vineyard," Rachel's Vineyard, https://www.rachelsvineyard.org/aboutus/theresa.aspx.

51. "Pro-Life Leader Frank A. Pavone," Priests for Life, https://www.priestsforlife .org/staff/frank-pavone-biography.aspx; and Christopher White, "Pro-Life Activist and Trump Apologist Frank Pavone Dismissed from Catholic Priesthood," *National Catholic Reporter*, December 18, 2022, https://www.ncronline .org/vatican/vatican-news/pro-life-activist-and-trump-apologist-frank-pavone -dismissed-catholic.

52. "Ben Thatcher; March for Life UK 2022."

53. Libby Brooks, "SNP Leadership Candidates Urged to Commit to Abortion Clinic Buffer Zones," *Guardian*, March 13, 2023, https://www.theguardian.com /world/2023/mar/13/snp-leadership-candidates-urged-to-commit-to-abortion -clinic-buffer-zones.

54. "Crisis Pregnancy Centers," Planned Parenthood, https://www.planned parenthood.org/uploads/filer_public/81/a3/81a30c3d-c40f-4bd9-aa28-be52e218 ob1b/ppnc-cpc-fact-sheet.pdf.

55. Eleanor Layhe and Divya Talwar, "Abortion UK: Women 'Manipulated' in Crisis Pregnancy Advice Centres," *BBC News*, February 27, 2023, https://www .bbc.com/news/uk-64751800.

56. Home page, Stanton Healthcare Belfast, https://www.stantonbelfast.org; Joe Duggan, "Controversial Anti-Abortion Group Accused of Misleading Women Set to Expand into Scotland," inews.co.uk, June 29, 2022, https://inews.co.uk /news/anti-abortion-group-misleading-women-scotland-1710460; and home page, SHE Pregnancy Support, https://shepregnancysupport.org.

57. Isabel van Brugen, "Anti-Abortion Centre Stanton Healthcare Peddling False Cancer Claims to Women," *Times* (London), June 2, 2018, https://www.thetimes .co.uk/article/belfast-anti-abortion-centre-stanton-healthcare-peddling-false -cancer-claims-to-women-669bnk725.

58. Sian Norris and Manasa Narayanan, "UK Anti-Abortion Charity with Links to MPs Ran Misleading Facebook Ads," *Guardian*, December 16, 2023, https://www.theguardian.com/world/2023/dec/16/anti-abortion-charity-mis leading-facebook-ads-mps-right-to-life-uk.

59. Katherine Stewart, "'If We Can Do It, You Can Do It': US Anti-Abortion Groups Ramp up Activities in UK," *Guardian*, April 2, 2023, https://www .theguardian.com/world/2023/apr/02/us-anti-abortion-groups-uk-far-right.

60. "Norman Lear on the Controversial Abortion Episode of Maude—TelevisionAcademy.com/Interviews," FoundationINTERVIEWS, August 26, 2009, YouTube video, https://www.youtube.com/watch?v=bfIi96SIUrM.

CHAPTER II: EXPORTING THE COUNTERREVOLUTION

1. *Encyclopedia Britannica*, s.v. "Philip Freneau," March 4, 2024, https://www .britannica.com/biography/Philip-Freneau; and Philip Freneau, "On the Prospect of a Revolution in France," in *The Poems of Philip Freneau*, ed. Fred Lewis

Pattee (Project Gutenberg, 2012), 2:385, https://www.gutenberg.org/files/39909
/39909-h/files/38529/38529-h/38529-h.htm.

2. Thomas Jefferson, "Thomas Jefferson to Tench Coxe," Library of Congress,
June 1, 1795, https://www.loc.gov/exhibits/jefferson/181.html.

3. Carroll Doherty and Jocelyn Kiley, "A Look Back at How Fear and False Beliefs
Bolstered U.S. Public Support for War in Iraq," Pew Research Center, March 14,
2023, https://www.pewresearch.org/politics/2023/03/14/a-look-back-at-how-fear
-and-false-beliefs-bolstered-u-s-public-support-for-war-in-iraq/; and "The Iraq
War," George W. Bush Presidential Library, https://www.georgewbushlibrary
.gov/research/topic-guides/the-iraq-war.

4. Joan E. Greve, "Hard-Right House Republicans Are Against Ukraine Aid—
and They Seem to Be in Charge," *Guardian*, October 14, 2023, https://www
.theguardian.com/us-news/2023/oct/14/republican-house-ukraine
-support-gaetz#.

5. Pjotr Sauer, "Twenty Years of Ruthlessness: How Russia Has Silenced Putin's
Opponents," *Guardian*, August 27, 2023, https://www.theguardian.com/world
/2023/aug/27/history-killing-how-russia-has-silenced-putins-opponents; and
David Leonhardt, "The G.O.P.'s 'Putin Wing,'" *New York Times*, April 7,
2022, https://www.nytimes.com/2022/04/07/briefing/republican-party-putin
-wing.html.

6. "Woke War 3," *American Conservative*, October 21, 2022, https://www.the
americanconservative.com/woke-war-3/; David Sacks, "The Neocons and the
Woke Left Are Joining Hands and Leading Us to Woke War III: Opinion,"
Newsweek, October 17, 2022, https://www.newsweek.com/neocons-woke-left
-are-joining-hands-leading-us-woke-war-iii-opinion-1748947.

7. Ilya Yablokov, "Russian Disinformation Finds Fertile Ground in the West,"
Nature Human Behaviour 6 (June 10, 2022): 766–67, https://www.nature.com
/articles/s41562-022-01399-3.

8. Samantha Bradshaw, Renée DiResta, and Carly Miller, "Playing Both Sides:
Russian State-Backed Media Coverage of the #BlackLivesMatter Movement,"
International Journal of Press/Politics 28, no. 4 (February 2022): 791–817, https://doi
.org/10.1177/19401612221082052; Rachel Kraus, "Russia Stole These Activists'
Causes—But They're Not Backing Down," *Mashable*, May 15, 2018, https://
mashable.com/article/activists-respond-russia-facebook-ads.

9. Scott Shane, "These Are the Ads Russia Bought on Facebook in 2016," *New York Times*, November 1, 2017, https://www.nytimes.com/2017/11/01/us/politics /russia-2016-election-facebook.html; Cecilia Kang, Nicholas Fandos, and Mike Isaac, "Russia-Financed Ad Linked Clinton and Satan," *New York Times*, November 1, 2017, https://www.nytimes.com/2017/11/01/us/politics/facebook -google-twitter-russian-interference-hearings.html.

10. Robert Windrem, "Russians Launched Pro-Jill Stein Social Media Blitz to Help Trump Win Election, Reports Say," NBC News, December 22, 2018, https: //www.nbcnews.com/politics/national-security/russians-launched-pro-jill-stein -social-media-blitz-help-trump-n951166.

11. "Jill Stein: 'It's Not Enough to Abandon Genocide Joe. Vote for an Alterna-tive,'" interview by Katie Halper, February 18, 2024, YouTube video, https://www .youtube.com/watch?v=oU-NIAlnvqI.

12. Javier Caballero, "'Gayrope': This Is How Russia Uses Disinformation Against the LGBTQ+ Community to Attack Democracies," *El País*, December 3, 2023, https://english.elpais.com/international/2023-12-03/gayrope-this-is-how -russia-uses-disinformation-against-the-lgbtq-community-to-attack-demo cracies.html.

13. Alex Oliveira, "Communists Who Burned US Flags Outside Jason Aldean Concert Branded as 'Cult,' 'Pyramid Scheme' by Left-Wing Activists," *New York Post*, September 11, 2023, https://nypost.com/2023/09/11/us-flag-burning -communists-labeled-cult-by-other-activists/.

14. "Interview with a Brainwashed American Chauvinist on the Chinese Balloon Affair (An RNL Skit)," The Revcoms, February 22, 2023, YouTube video, https://www.youtube.com/watch?v=wlqBWeUeXfY.

15. "Andy Zee in Conversation with Raymond Lotta on No US/NATO War with Russia! No World War 3!" interview by Andy Zee, Facebook, May 2, 2022, https://www.facebook.com/therevcoms/videos/939843206683147/.

16. Kathryn Joyce and Jeff Sharlet, "Losing the Plot: The 'Leftists' Who Turn Right," *In These Times*, December 12, 2023, https://inthesetimes.com/article /former-left-right-fascism-capitalism-horseshoe-theory.

17. Madison Hall, "Chinese Social Media Accounts Are Stoking Political Chaos Ahead of the 2024 Presidential Election: Report," *Business Insider*, April 1, 2024,

https://www.businessinsider.com/chinese-social-media-accounts-stoking -political-chaos-in-the-us-2024-4.

18. Paul Marx, *Faithful for Life: Telling It Like It Is or at Least As I Saw It* (Human Life International, 1997), 1.

19. "Father Paul Benno Marx, OSB," Saint John's Abbey, https://saintjohnsabbey .org/father-paul-benno-marx-osb.

20. Paul Marx, "The Wanderer Interviews Fr. Paul Marx," interview by Arthur J. Brew, *EWTN Global Catholic Television Network*, https://www.ewtn.com /catholicism/library/wanderer-interviews-fr-paul-marx-12127.

21. Sylwia Kuźma-Markowska and Laura Kelly, "Anti-Abortion Activism in Poland and the Republic of Ireland c.1970s–1990s," *Journal of Religious History* 46, no. 3 (July 2022): 526–51, https://doi.org/10.1111/1467-9809.12870.

22. Marx, *Faithful for Life*, 25, 34–39, 12.

23. Clay Risen, "Joseph M. Scheidler, 'Godfather' of the Anti-Abortion Movement, Dies at 93," *New York Times*, January 20, 2021, https://www.nytimes.com/2021 /01/20/us/joseph-m-scheidler-dead.html.

24. "About Randall Terry," RandallTerry.com, https://www.randallterry.com/about.

25. "Man With a Mission," *Chicago Tribune*, August 11, 1985, https://www .chicagotribune.com/1985/08/11/man-with-a-mission-6.

26. Sam McGrath, "Úna Bean Mhic Mhathúna: Over 40 Years of Reactionary Politics," Come Here to Me!, July 29, 2012, https://comeheretome.com/2012/07 /29/una-bean-mhic-mhathuna-40-years-of-reactionary-politics/.

27. Marx, *Faithful for Life*, 179–209.

28. Kuźma-Markowska and Kelly, "Anti-abortion Activism."

29. Home page, Political Network for Values, https://politicalnetworkforvalues.org.

30. "The Building of Hungarian Political Influence: The Orbán Regime's Efforts to Export Illiberalism," Heinrich Böll Foundation, December 2022, https://cz .boell.org/sites/default/files/2023-01/pc_boell_the-building-of-hungarian -political-influence_en_1.pdf.

31. Redacción, "The New York Commitment Will Restore the Original Meaning of the Universal Declaration of Human Rights," Political Network for Values,

December 19, 2023, https://politicalnetworkforvalues.org/en/2023/12/the-new
-york-commitment-will-restore-the-original-meaning-of-the-universal
-declaration-of-human-rights/.

32. "Our Values," Political Network for Values, https://politicalnetworkforvalues
.org/nuestros-valores/.

33. Allan C. Carlson and Paul T. Mero, *The Natural Family: A Manifesto* (Dallas,
TX: Spence, 2007).

34. Allan C. Carlson, "The Domestic Workplace," *Touchstone: A Journal of Mere
Christianity*, May 2000, http://www.touchstonemag.com/archives/article.php?id
=13-04-017-f.

35. Allan C. Carlson, "The End of Marriage," *Touchstone: A Journal of Mere Christianity*, September 2006, http://www.touchstonemag.com/archives/article.php
?id=19-07-038-f&readcode.

36. Allan C. Carlson, "Unshaved Masses," *Touchstone: A Journal of Mere Christianity*,
May/June 2023, http://www.touchstonemag.com/archives/article.php?id=36-03
-003-e.

37. Christopher Knaus, "George Pell: What the Five-Year Royal Commission into
Child Sexual Abuse Found," *Guardian*, January 11, 2023, https://www
.theguardian.com/australia-news/2023/jan/12/george-pell-what-the-five-year
-royal-commission-into-child-sexual-abuse-found.

38. Carlson, "Unshaved Masses."

39. "Carlson, Allan C. 1949–," *Encyclopedia.com*, https://www.encyclopedia.com
/arts/educational-magazines/carlson-allan-c-1949.

40. "Exposed: The World Congress of Families," Human Rights Campaign Foundation, June 2015, http://assets2.hrc.org/files/assets/resources/WorldCongress
OfFamilies.pdf.

41. "IOF Leadership," International Organization for the Family, https://www
.profam.org/leadership/; "World Congress of Families Partners 2017," International Organization for the Family, https://www.profam.org/world-congress
-of-families-partners-2017/.

42. Tom Kington, "World Congress of Families: Russia Plays Happy Christian
Families with Europe's Populists," *Times* (London), March 30, 2019, https://www

.thetimes.co.uk/article/world-congress-of-families-russia-plays-happy-chris
tian-families-with-europe-s-populists-qmdkzwhd9.

43. McGrath, "Úna Bean Mhic Mhathúna."

44. Kathy Sheridan, "How Wife-Swappin' Sodomites Won the Right to Remarry,"
Irish Times, January 19, 2015, https://www.irishtimes.com/life-and-style/how
-wife-swappin-sodomites-won-the-right-to-remarry-1.2070412.

45. J. P. O'Malley, "Pro Lifers' Argument Consigned to History," *Times* (London),
January 11, 2015, https://www.thetimes.co.uk/article/pro-lifers-argument-con
signed-to-history-6l6rwlvqz95.

46. "Niamh Uí Bhrian Speaking at the All Ireland Rally for Life / Pro-Life Against
Abortion," All-Ireland Rally for Life, July 27, 2019, YouTube video, 2:05,
https://www.youtube.com/watch?v=XjLXzsMlCko.

47. "Niamh Uí Bhriain Speaking."

48. "Niamh Uí Bhriain : 'How Dare Westminister Trample on the People of the
North of Ireland,'" All-Ireland Rally for Life, September 12, 2019, YouTube
video, 1:10, https://www.youtube.com/watch?v=8enGw8ooxSc.

49. Youth Defence, "March for Life in UK Gets Record Numbers," Facebook,
September 7, 2022, https://www.facebook.com/YouthDefence/posts; "Youth
Defence: National and International Conferences," Life Institute, https://
thelifeinstitute.net/youth-defence/projects/national-and-international-confer
ences.

50. "Niamh Uí Bhriain," Life Institute, https://thelifeinstitute.net/author/Niamh
.uibhriain.

51. Caelainn Hogan, "Why Ireland's Battle over Abortion Is Far from Over,"
Guardian, October 3, 2019, https://www.theguardian.com/lifeandstyle/2019/oct
/03/why-irelands-battle-over-abortion-is-far-from-over-anti-abortionists.

52. "Roe v. Wade is Overturned: Come On Ireland, It's Your Turn," Life Institute,
July 2, 2022, https://thelifeinstitute.net/news/2022/roe-v-wade-is-overturned
-come-on-ireland-its-your-turn.

53. David S. Broder, "Opinion: A Republican in Moscow," *Washington Post*,
December 2, 1989, https://www.washingtonpost.com/archive/opinions/1989/12
/03/a-republican-in-moscow/71e687b9-597e-481b-8245-10a3de44fd94/.

54. "Putin Signs Law Expanding Russia's Rules Against 'LGBT Propaganda,'" Reuters, December 5, 2022, https://www.reuters.com/world/europe/putin-signs -law-expanding-russias-rules-against-lgbt-propaganda-2022-12-05/; and "The Facts on LGBT Rights in Russia," Council for Global Equality, http://www .globalequality.org/component/content/article/1-in-the-news/186-the-facts-on -lgbt-rights-in-russia.

55. Charles Joughin, "NOM's Brown Traveled to Russia to Support Bill That Would Deny Adoption to 'Abnormal' Gay Parents," Human Rights Campaign, October 3, 2013, https://www.hrc.org/press-releases/noms-brown-traveled-to -russia-to-support-bill-that-would-deny-adoption-to-a.

56. "Head of National Organization for Marriage Is Oxford Convert to Catholicism," *Catholic Culture*, August 31, 2009, https://www.catholicculture.org/news /headlines/index.cfm?storyid=3901.

57. Oliver Laughland et al., "Oxford Scholar Who Was Mentor to Neil Gorsuch Compared Gay Sex to Bestiality," *Guardian*, February 3, 2017, https://www .theguardian.com/law/2017/feb/03/neil-gorsuch-mentor-john-finnis-compared -gay-sex-to-bestiality.

58. M. Gessen, "The Homophobic Activist Who Won an Audience with Two Supreme Court Justices," *New Yorker*, November 8, 2019, https://www.newyorker .com/news/our-columnists/the-homophobic-activist-who-won-an-audience -with-two-supreme-court-justices.

59. Hatewatch Staff, "Brian Brown Named President of Anti-LGBT World Congress of Families," Southern Poverty Law Center, June 2, 2016, https://www .splcenter.org/hatewatch/2016/06/02/brian-brown-named-president-anti-lgbt -world-congress-families.

60. Rosalind S. Helderman and Tom Hamburger, "Guns and Religion: How American Conservatives Grew Closer to Putin's Russia," *Washington Post*, April 30, 2017, https://www.washingtonpost.com/politics/how-the-republican-right-found -allies-in-russia/2017/04/30/e2d83ff6-29d3-11e7-a616-d7c8a68c1a66_story.html.

61. Gessen, "The Homophobic Activist Who Won an Audience with Two Supreme Court Justices."

62. M. Gessen, "Family Values: Mapping the Spread of Antigay Ideology," *Harper's Magazine*, March 2017, https://harpersmag.wpengine.com/archive/2017/03 /family-values-3/.

63. Angela Giuffrida and Flora Garamvolgyi, "The Network of Organisations Seeking to Influence Abortion Policy Across Europe," *Guardian*, May 26, 2022, https://www.theguardian.com/world/2022/may/26/the-network-of-organi sations-seeking-to-influence-abortion-policy-across-europe.

64. Klementyna Suchanow, "Ordo Iuris and the Kremlin: Evidence Presented by Klementyna Suchanow," *Resetobywatelski*, January 24, 2022, https://resetoby watelski.pl/ordo-iuris-and-the-kremlin-evidence-presented-by-klementyna -suchanow/.

65. "World Family Declaration," International Organization for the Family, https:// profam.org/article-16/world-family-declaration.

66. Claudia Ciobanu, "Ordo Iuris: The Ultra-Conservative Organisation Trans- forming Poland," *Balkan Insight*, June 22, 2021, https://balkaninsight.com/2021 /06/22/ordo-iuris-the-ultra-conservative-organisation-transforming-poland/.

67. "Poland: Abortion Witch Hunt Targets Women, Doctors," Human Rights Watch, September 14, 2023, https://www.hrw.org/news/2023/09/14/poland -abortion-witch-hunt-targets-women-doctors.

68. Cassandra Vinograd and Ewa Gallica, "Abortion in Europe: 'Coat Hanger Rebellion' Grips Poland," NBC News, April 26, 2016, https://www.nbcnews .com/storyline/europes-abortion-fight/abortion-europe-coat-hanger-rebellion -grips-poland-n559621.

69. Jan Cienski, "Poland Election Results: Opposition Secures Win, Final Count Shows," *Politico*, October 17, 2023, https://www.politico.eu/article/poland -election-results-opposition-donald-tusk-wins-final-count-civic-platform-pis/.

70. Associated Press, "Polish President Calls LGBT 'Ideology' Worse than Communism," *Los Angeles Times*, June 15, 2020, https://www.latimes.com/world -nation/story/2020-06-15/polish-president-calls-lgbt-ideology-worse-than -communism.

71. Claudia Ciobanu, "A Third of Poland Declared 'LGBT-Free Zone,'" *Balkan Insight*, February 25, 2020, https://balkaninsight.com/2020/02/25/a-third-of -poland-declared-lgbt-free-zone/.

72. Andrea Suozzo et al., "Alliance Defending Freedom," ProPublica Nonprofit Explorer, April 24, 2024, https://projects.propublica.org/nonprofits/organiza tions/541660459.

73. Equality Matters, "This Right-Wing Legal Powerhouse Wants to Make Gay Sex Illegal," *HuffPost*, December 6, 2017, https://www.huffpost.com/entry/this-right-wing-legal-pow_b_6185878.

74. Hannah Levintova, "How US Evangelicals Helped Create Russia's Anti-Gay Movement," *Mother Jones*, February 21, 2014, https://www.motherjones.com/politics/2014/02/world-congress-families-russia-gay-rights/.

75. Hélène Barthélemy, "How the World Congress of Families Serves Russian Orthodox Political Interests," Southern Poverty Law Center, May 16, 2018, https://www.splcenter.org/hatewatch/2018/05/16/how-world-congress-families-serves-russian-orthodox-political-interests.

76. Robert Zubrin, "The Wrong Right," *National Review*, June 24, 2014, https://www.nationalreview.com/2014/06/wrong-right-robert-zubrin/.

77. Jasper Jackson et al., "Unholy Alliance: The Far-Right Religious Network Attacking Reproductive and LGBTQ+ Rights," *Bureau of Investigative Journalism*, September 25, 2022, http://www.thebureauinvestigates.com/stories/2022-09-25/unholy-alliance-the-far-right-religious-network-attacking-reproductive-and-lgbtq-rights/.

78. Jackson.

79. Ignacio Arsuaga and M. Vidal Santos, *The Zapatero Project: Chronicle of an Attack on Society* (Madrid: HazteOir, 2011).

80. Steven Forti, "Y el mejor amigo español de Putin es . . . ," *Contexto y acción*, March 3, 2022, https://ctxt.es/es/20220301/Firmas/38961/malofeev-rusia-ucrania-guerra-abascal-hazteoir-arsuaga-villar-mir-oligarcas-antigenero-ultraderecha.htm.

81. "Ignacio Arsuaga's Speech at the XIV World Congress of Families—Mexico 2022," CitizenGO, October 3, 2022, YouTube video, 1:19, https://www.youtube.com/watch?v=1xW71EUAZeI.

82. Wojciech Cieśla, "Make Spain Great Again," *VSquare*, April 26, 2019, https://vsquare.org/make-spain-great-again/.

83. Jackson et al., "Unholy Alliance."

84. Nicolás Márquez and Agustín Laje, *El libro negro de la nueva izquierda: Ideología de género o subversión cultural* (Buenos Aires: Grupo Unión, 2016).

85. Newsroom Infobae, "The Argentine Who Is Causing Controversy Among the Authors Invited to the Bogotá Book Fair 2022," *Infobae*, March 30, 2022, https://www.infobae.com/en/2022/03/30/the-argentine-who-is-causing-controversy-among-the-authors-invited-to-the-bogota-book-fair-2022/.

86. Nandini Naira Archer and Claire Provost, "Revealed: $280m 'Dark Money' Spent by US Christian Right Groups Globally," *openDemocracy*, October 27, 2020, https://www.opendemocracy.net/en/5050/trump-us-christian-spending-global-revealed/.

87. Lydia Namubiru, "Charity Loophole Lets US Donors Give Far-Right Groups $272m in Secret," *openDemocracy*, July 5, 2023, https://www.opendemocracy.net/en/5050/donor-advised-funds-daf-us-charity-law-loophole-bankroll-hate/?.

88. Neil Datta, "Tip of the Iceberg: Religious Extremist Funders Against Human Rights for Sexuality and Reproductive Health in Europe 2009–2018," European Parliamentary Forum for Sexual & Reproductive Rights, June 15, 2021, https://www.epfweb.org/node/837.

CONCLUSION

1. Ramesh Ponnuru, "Re: The WSJ Gets It Wrong," *National Review*, January 26, 2010, https://www.nationalreview.com/bench-memos/re-wsj-gets-it-wrong-ramesh-ponnuru/.

2. Irving Dilliard, *Mr. Justice Brandeis, Great American: Press Opinion and Public Appraisal* (St. Louis: Modern View Press, 1941); and Bryan W. White, "Louis D. Brandeis, Wealth and Democracy: Checking a Common Quotation (Updated)," Zebra Fact Check, March 12, 2013, https://archive.ph/2023.07.05-011135/https://www.zebrafactcheck.com/louis-d-brandeis-wealth-and-democracy-checking-a-common-quotation/.

3. Emmanuel Saez and Gabriel Zucman, *The Triumph of Injustice: How the Rich Dodge Taxes and How to Make Them Pay* (New York: W. W. Norton, 2019).

4. Robert Faris et al., *Partisanship, Propaganda, and Disinformation: Online Media and the 2016 U.S. Presidential Election*, Berkman Klein Center, August 16, 2017, https://cyber.harvard.edu/publications/2017/08/mediacloud.

INDEX

abortion, 23, 38–39
  antiabortion activism, 204–12, 217–19,
    222–24
  bans on, 121–22, 226
  and California's Proposition I, 161
  and Catholics, 38–39, 44, 51–53, 57
  and consent laws, 123
  Florida's ban on, 137–38
  Gorsuch on, 49
  impacts on medical treatments, 121–22
  impacts on women with cancer, 121
  in Ireland, 222–24
  Lopez's rhetoric on, 177
  and miscarriages, 121–22
  and needs of right-wing supporters, 240
  in Poland, 226
  and racist/anti-immigration
    sentiments, 133–34
  and religious conservatives, 51–53,
    212, 231
  and sex education, 229
  Supreme Court rulings on, 47, 49, 51,
    204, 211, 212, 224
  in Texas, 121
  training of antiabortion activists, 206
  in the United Kingdom, 204–5, 206–12
  See also reproductive health/rights
Acton Institute, 45, 48, 86
Adam and Eve (biblical), 198, 202
"administrative state," 144–52, 154
Advancing American Freedom, 18
affirmative action, 132
Affordable Care Act, 145
Agenda Europe, 226
Ahmari, Sohrab, 55
Alabama Supreme Court, 122
Alamariu, Costin (BAP), 127–28, 140

Alito, Samuel, 123, 225
Allen, William B., 86–87
Alliance Defending Freedom (ADF), 62,
  90, 91–92, 100, 206–7, 221, 226–27, 233
Alliance for Responsible Citizenship, 203
All Ireland Rally for Life, 222
Alpha (evangelical organization), 203
Amalekites (biblical), 92
American Center for Law and Justice, 90
American Mind magazine, 108, 124, 127,
  130, 133, 154
American Restoration Tour, 21
American Values, 18
Amish, 55
anarchism, 118, 145
Anderson, Carl, 42
anger and resentment, 5, 7
Antall, Richard, 33
Antelope Hill Publishing, 125
antidemocratic movement, 224
  contradictory claims of, 238–39
  division in, 237–39
  as global reaction, 213–14, 233
  ideology of, 238–39
  and inequality, 239–41
  main features of, 6
  and men of Claremont Institute, 141
  organization/planning of, 244
  scare tactics of, 21
  and Supreme Court, 239
  theocratic wing of, 6
  as threat to democracy, 4–5
  variety of personalities involved in, 3, 8
    (*see also* Funders; Infantry; Power
    Players; Sergeants; Thinkers)
  and wealth, 239, 240
anti-intellectualism, 10, 176

anti-Semitism, 50, 113, 115

Anton, Michael, 56, 101–2, 106, 114–15, 127, 136, 139–40, 237–38

Antonin Scalia Law School at George Mason University, 84

Antonov, Anatoly, 221

anxieties, sources of, 23–24

apocalyptic visions, 32, 197

Aristotle, 139

Arizona, results of 2020 election in, 30

Arnn, Larry, 106, 118

Aronson, Alex, 83

Arroyo, Raymond, 45

Arsuaga, Ignacio, 97, 229, 230–32

Asociación de Ministros Hispanos del Sur de la Florida, 32

Assemblies of God, 166

assisted suicide, 49

authoritarianism, 3, 6, 13, 54, 55, 106, 124, 138, 142–43, 224, 226, 227, 230–33, 234, 243

Azusa Street Revival, 165, 166

Bachmann, Michele, 33

Baer, Steven, 82, 84–85

Baez-Geller, Lucia, 76

Bailey, Gene, 170–71

Baines, Steven, 20–21, 26, 35

Bannon, Steve, 32, 89, 144

Barclay, Stephanie, 78

Barna, George, 28

Barr, Roseanne, 185–86

Barr, William, 54, 56, 91

Barrett, Amy Coney, 47

Barton, David, 27, 28, 65, 67, 80, 163

Barton, Tim, 27–29, 65

Bast, Joseph, 83

"Battlefield United States" (booklet), 189

Beattie, Darren, 132–33

Beauvoir, Simone de, 130

Becket Fund for Religious Liberty, 44

Belize, 227

Benjamin, Leon, 163

Beyond Belief (Hardy), 167–68

Bible and Constitution of the U.S., 25

"biblical law," 7

Biden, Hunter, 184

Biden, Joe, 32, 39–40, 45, 151, 177, 215

Biden administration, 68

Big Lie (stolen-election claims), 19–20, 27, 29, 31, 33–35, 170, 190, 192
  base primed for claims of voter fraud, 35
  claims of persecution, 159
  and pastors/leaders of religious right, 33
  Pavone's involvement in, 209
  Trump's rejection of election results, 32–33
  voter fraud claims, 19

Billy Graham Evangelistic Association, 233

birth rates, declining, 133

Black Americans, 69–70, 76
  Black Lives Matter (BLM) movement, 147, 198, 214
  as conservatives, 178–79
  factors driving support for New Right, 188
  as Pentecostals, 166
  REN's racist comments on, 125
  white men's claims of victimization by, 124

The Black Book of the New Left (Laje and Márquez), 232

Black Robe Regiment, 11, 28–29

Blackwell, Ken, 19

Blackwell, Morton, 69, 205–6

Blumenthal, Max, 216

Boebert, Lauren, 159

Bohlinger, Peter, 92, 93

Bolsonaro, Jair, 167, 179

books and book bans, 62–64, 76, 238

borders and border policy, 135

Boumann, Maryal, 161

Bow Group, 100

Boykin, Jerry, 80

Boykin, William, 29

Braddock, Benjamin, 133
Bradley Foundation, 48, 52, 72, 81, 88, 106, 153
Bramlage, Greg, 162–63
Brand, Russell, 134
Brandeis, Louis, 239
Breitbart News, 32
Brennan, Dave, 205
Brexit, 101
Bright, Bill, 170
British Pregnancy Advisory Service, 211
Brockschmidt, Annika, 60, 61
Bronson, Indian, 134
Bronze Age Mindset (Alamariu), 127
Bronze Age Pervert (BAP), 127–28, 134, 136, 137, 140, 141
Brooking Institution, 23
Brown, Brian S., 97, 98, 221, 224–25, 230, 231
Brown v. Board of Education, 85
Buchanan, Patrick, 235
Bugmen, 136–37, 140, 149
bureaucrats, resentment toward, 136–37
Burge, Ryan, 165–66, 176
Burke, Theresa, 209
Burns, Mark, 161, 185
Busch, Robert, 38–39, 41, 45–46
Busch, Timothy, 39–42, 45–48, 56–58
Butler, Keira, 62

Cahn, Jonathan, 161
California's Proposition I, 161
Callahan, David, 90–91
Call to Action, 46
Cameron, Daniel, 179
campaign finance regulation, 241
Campbell, Kyle. *See* Horton, Kielle
Camp of the Saints (Raspail), 131–32, 135
cancel culture, 100, 132, 155
cancer treatments, 121
capitalism, 39, 41–42
Capitol Resource Institute, 63
Carlson, Allan C., 220–21, 224
Carlson, Tucker, 125, 155, 160, 207, 235

Carney, Sean, 211
Carr, John, 44
Casiano, Samantha, 121, 123, 141
catastrophism, 13, 23
Catholic Information Center, 43
Catholic League, 43
Catholics and Catholicism, 52, 224–25
    and abortion, 38–39, 44, 51–53, 57, 208
    abuse of children, 43, 220
    and Biden, 39–40
    and Christian nationalism, 53
    contradictory claims of, 56–57
    and economic justice, 41
    and evangelicals, 229
    and immigrant populations, 47–48
    Latin Americans' shift from, 167
    and libertarianism, 44
    and Opus Dei, 42
    and presidential election of 2020, 39
    progressives, 46–47
    and Protestants, 47–48, 50
    and religious charter schools, 78–80
    rise of hyper-conservative, 43
    and same-sex marriage, 44
    and sex education, 228, 229
    and social justice, 46, 58
    and threats posed by progress, 232
    and Trump, 44, 45
    in the UK, 208
    on U.S. Supreme Court, 47
    waning power of, 43
    and women's equality, 50
Catholic Scholars for Worker Justice, 46
Catholics for Choice, 46
CatholicVote, 43
censorship, 155
Center for Bio-Ethical Reform (CBR), 205, 207–8
Center for Election Integrity, 30
Center for Renewing America (CRA), 105
Chantilly, Virginia, 20
Chapman, Morris H., 86
Charen, Mona, 108–9
charismatic movements, 167

Charter Day School v. Peltier, 79–80
charter schools, religious, 78–80
Chevron U.S.A. Inc. v. Natural Resources Defense Council, 150–51
Child Evangelism Fellowship, 36, 92
"childless cat ladies," 55
children, crises related to welfare of, 68
China, 56, 215–16
Christian conservatives, 8
    and "biblical law," 7
    claims of discrimination against, 24
    claims of persecution, 24
    and "in-group" membership, 6
    and religious persecution, 23
    values imposed on others, 24
    and women's access to power, 123
Christian nationalism
    about, 12–13
    and Arsuaga, 231
    audiences' responses to, 30
    author's reporting on, 195
    basic dispositions of adherents, 13
    and Catholics, 53
    cohesion and organization of, 28
    and Constitution of the U.S., 26, 27
    demonization of Democrats, 26
    domestic enemies of, 178
    and Eastman's strategies, 119
    economic doctrines of, 25, 41–42
    on "election integrity," 27
    and evangelicals, 12, 199–200
    four traits of followers, 31–33
    goals of, 19
    and "in-group" membership, 6
    and ideology of Power Players, 12
    and January 6, 2021, insurrection, 31
    mindset common to, 22–26
    and National Summit of Moms for Liberty, 65
    and the New Right, 104, 106
    pastors/leadership of, 33–34
    Pentecostals' support of, 176
    persecution narratives of, 32
    and political leaders, 200
    and political opposition, 26
    and reproductive rights of women, 47, 51
    in the UK, 195–98, 200–201
    urgency of elections for, 23
    violent/militant imagery of, 28–29, 67
    See also specific individuals, including MacArthur, John
churches
    "church planting," 199, 203
    declines in membership, 199
    and power of wealthy Americans, 41
    and separation of church and state, 241–42
    and voter recruitment/mobilization, 26
The Church Finds Its Voice, 19, 28, 36
Church Militant, 43
Church of God in Christ, 166
CitizenGO, 221, 230, 231, 232
Citizens for Educational Freedom, 87
civility, loss of, 4, 193
civil rights movement, 111
civil servants in Trump administration, 151
Claremont Institute, 10, 106–18, 120, 133
    all-male board of, 124
    ambitions of, 136
    and antidemocratic movement, 141
    and anti-regulation constituency, 152
    citation of philosophers/philosophies, 130–31, 139, 147, 149–50
    and "deconstruction of the administrative state," 144
    funding sources, 152, 153, 155
    and higher education, 141
    and identity politics, 135–36
    and Kesler, 147–48
    and "manliness," 129
    and Marini, 148
    and 9/11 conspiracies, 191
    origin story of, 109–10
    power of, 153
    and Western civilization, 134, 135
    and Yarvin, 138
    and Yenor, 125–27

Clark, Clay, 182, 184, 185, 186–87
Clark, Jeffery, 145
Clarkson, Frederick, 80, 167, 171, 172
Classical Schools Network Inc., 62
Clerkenwell Medical Mission, 196, 201
climate science, 83–84, 88, 104–5, 153, 163
Clinton, Hillary, 32, 101, 114, 140, 177, 214
Club for Growth, 88, 89
coalition building, 245
Coalition of African American Pastors, 32
Colquhoun, Robert, 205
Colson, Charles, 52
Concerned Citizens for Education, 64
Concerned Women for America (CWA), 122–23
Connelly, Chad, 21–26, 28, 29–30, 161
conscience rights, 105
consent laws, 123
Conservative Action Project, 89
Conservative Political Action Conference (CPAC), 34–35, 108
conspiracies, 5, 108, 191
constituencies of antigovernment interests, 152
Constitutional Sheriffs and Peace Officers Association, 177–78
contraceptives, 57, 105, 122, 161, 208, 217, 231, 240
contradictory aims of antidemocratic movement, 8–9
Cooper, Rick, 173
Copeland, Kenneth, 34, 170
Coral Ridge Ministries, 12
Corkery, Ann and Neil, 89
Costa Rica, 227–29, 232, 233
Coughlin, Charles, 46, 235
Council for National Policy (CNP), 12, 18, 63, 89, 206, 244
Courage International, 45
COVID-19 pandemic, 24, 37, 77, 182–83, 189, 191–92, 200
Creation Museum, 163
Crisis Magazine, 43

critical race theory (CRT), 30–31, 63, 66, 69, 70, 75, 77–78, 80, 103, 104, 141, 178
Crow, Harlan, 52–53, 56
Crow, Katherine, 53
"Cultural Marxism," 71
"cultural revolution" in the West, 71
Cunningham, Loren, 170
"Cyber Ninjas" audit, 30

Dabney, Robert Lewis, 85
Daily Signal, 32
Danube Institute, 100
Datta, Neil, 232–33
Davis, Michael Warren, 142
Declaration of Independence, 2, 117
"deconstruction of the administrative state," 144–46, 150–52, 154
democracy
    central role of organization in, 244–45
    and division in antidemocratic movement, 237–39
    early spread of, 213
    Hitler's argument against, 155
    and inequality, 239–41
    key findings for advocates of, 236–45
    proponents of, in majority, 236–37
    and public education, 243
    and separation of church and state, 241–43
    threats to, 4–5, 14, 136, 239–41
    See also antidemocratic movement
Democrats
    and critical race theory, 31
    demonization of, 26, 161, 162, 184
    denigration of, 27
    January 6, 2021, insurrection blamed on, 34–35
    and Latino voters, 185
    Lopez's rhetoric on, 177
demons, 160–62, 163, 168, 170, 173–74, 175, 176, 179
Deneen, Patrick, 54–55
depravity, 109–10
deregulation, 8, 151, 238

DeSantis, Casey, 126, 139, 159–60
DeSantis, Ron, 61–62, 69, 74, 76, 104,
    132, 145
    authoritarianism of, 138
    campaign for president, 137–38
    and donors, 153
    and Feucht, 159–60
    honored by Claremont Institute, 107
    and New College, 146
    and public education, 84
    and Republican primary, 72
    and spirit warriors, 162
    on "wokeness," 101
Descovich, Tina, 69, 74
DeVos, Betsy, 9, 86, 89
DeVos, Rich, 22
DeVos family, 48, 88
The Diary of Anne Frank (Frank), 63
Dick and Betsy DeVos Family
    Foundation, 106, 153
DignityUSA, 46
Dionne, Michael, 201
disinformation, 5, 214–15, 243–44
diversity, 135, 166, 188
Diversity, Equity, and Inclusion (DEI)
    training, 71, 104
divorces, 105, 126, 222
Dobbs v. Jackson Women's Health, 47, 49, 224
Documented (journalism project), 91, 92
Domestic Extremist (Keenan), 133
domestic violence, 231
dominionism, 162, 164, 170–71, 172, 178
Donalds, Byron, 61–62, 178
Donalds, Erika, 61–62
Donors Capital Fund, 48, 106, 153
DonorsTrust, 48, 90, 106, 153, 154, 155
Douglass, Frederick, 135
Doyle, Paul, 178
Drag Queen Story Hours, 76–77
Dreher, Rod, 55
dress codes, 79–80
Drezner, Daniel W., 108
Drion, Tom, 198
Drollinger, Ralph, 200

Drummond, Gentner, 78
D'Souza, Dinesh, 34
Duda, Andrzej, 226
Duggan, Mae, 87
Du Mez, Kristin Kobes, 55, 123
Dunn, Tim, 9, 88

Eastern Europe, antiabortion activism in,
    218–19
Eastman, John, 2, 97–99, 107, 135, 225
    and Claremont Institute, 106
    indictments against, 116
    and January 6, 2021, insurrection, 2,
        107, 108, 116–17, 153
    and Klingenstein, 153, 155
    mission of, 116–17
    and religion, 119
economy
    and economic conflicts, 5
    economic doctrines of Christian
        nationalism, 25, 41–42
    and economic inequality, 5, 43, 188
    and factors driving support for Trump,
        23–24
    instability in, 165
    and progressive taxation, 239
Edmund Burke Foundation, 100
education, 128–29, 141. *See also* schools and
    public education
Edwards, Tom, 74–75, 81
eighteenth-century values, 163
Election Integrity Now Initiative, 34
"Election Integrity Reform Is Key to
    Preventing a Socialist Takeover of
    America," 19
Electoral College, 34, 236–37
elites, Thinkers' self-identification as, 13
Emerge Men's Conference at Awaken
    Church, 29
emergency, America's supposed state of,
    114, 115
Empsall, Nathan, 190
The End of Men (film), 125
England, Karen, 63–64

Engle, Lou, 159, 176
Enlightenment ideals, 2, 25
environmentalists, 160
Environmental Protection Agency (EPA), 150
Epoch Times, 182
Epoch TV, 62
equality, 2, 135, 198, 219, 221, 224, 231, 239–41
Escriva, Josemaria, 42
Eternal Word Television Network (EWTN), 41, 208
ethnonationalism, 124
eugenics, 133
European Center for Law and Justice, 226
European Parliamentary Forum, 233
euthanasia, 49
evangelicals
    and Catholics, 229
    and Christian nationalism, 12, 199–200
    MacArthur's criticisms of, 200
    and New Right, 119
    and reproductive rights of women, 51, 52
    and sex education, 229
    style of leadership in, 53
    and surge of Pentecostal/charismatic movements, 167
    in the UK, 195–98, 200–205
evolution, 199
EWTN Global Media, 45–46
EWTN News, 43
Exodus Mandate, 66
experts, demons' influence on, 175
extremism, 67–68, 93, 177

Faith and Freedom Coalition, 12, 162
Faithful America, 190
Faith Wins, 11, 19, 20, 26, 28, 29, 35
Falun Gong religious movement, 62
Falwell, Jerry, Jr., 12, 86, 191
Family Research Council (FRC), 12, 18, 19, 69, 72, 80, 87, 90, 233
family values, 37

Family Watch International, 233
Fancelli, Julie, 60
Farris, Michael P., 68
fascism, 106, 137, 140, 154
    conservative parties' relationship to, 155
    endorsement of, 192
    and New Right—Christian nationalism, 104
    and public education, 81
Fauci, Anthony, 24, 184
fears driving New Right participants, 189
federal government and "deconstruction of the administrative state," 144–46
Federalist Society, 10
    and Catholics, 44–45
    and "deconstruction of the administrative state," 144
    as funding source, 233
    and Notre Dame Religious Liberty Clinic, 78
    and Supreme Court, 45, 47, 82–83, 123, 244
federal judiciary, 237
Fellowship Foundation, 90
feminism, 50, 97, 127, 130, 217, 220, 231
Feucht, Sean, 159–60, 161, 183
Fidesz Party, 221
Field, Laura K., 108, 109, 111
Fieler, Sean, 41–42
Finnis, John, 48–49, 225
firearms, 150, 189
First Amendment, Establishment Clause of, 98–99, 242
First Things (journal), 45
Fivefold Ministry, 172
Flannery, Christopher, 107
"The Flight 93 Election," 101
Florida, 61–62, 131–32, 137–38
Flynn, Mike, 89, 179, 183, 184, 186, 189, 190
FOCUS, 45
Focus on the Family, 18, 221
food stamps program, 145
40 Days for Life UK, 205, 206, 207, 210, 211
fossil fuels, 104–5, 160

Founding Fathers, 25–26, 27, 107, 139
Fox News, 32, 77
Foxx, Byron, 35
Francis, Pope, 40, 42, 46, 208
Freedom Foundation, 88, 153
free speech, 193, 207, 234, 238
Freneau, Philip, 213
Friedman, Milton, 86, 88
friend–enemy distinction of Schmitt,
    112–13, 115
Fuentes, Nick, 142
Funders
    about, 9–10, 13
    ambitions (and tolerances) of, 153
    analysis of donations from, 233
    behind Claremont Institute, 152, 153
    and Big Lie (stolen-election claims),
        20, 33
    and Christian nationalist mindset, 13
    dark money of, 88–91
    and "deconstruction of the
        administrative state," 154
    and inequality, 239
    oligarchic/plutocratic backgrounds of,
        234
    and Project 2025, 154
    and religious belief, 13
    role of Infantry for, 11
    in the UK, 203–4
The Future of Assisted Suicide and
    Euthanasia (Gorsuch), 49

Gagné, André, 170
Garlow, Jim, 160–61, 163, 172
Garnett, Nicole Stelle, 78
Garnier, Leonardo, 227–29, 232
gender, 70
    gender identity, 64, 80, 165 (see also
        transgender people)
    gender ideology, 72, 87, 105, 229,
        231–32
    gender roles, 6
    gender stereotypes, 129
Gender Policy Council, 145

Gender Transformation: The Untold Realities
    (documentary), 62
Gen Z, 37
George, Robert P., 45, 52, 225
George Jenkins Foundation, 60
George Mason University, 84
gerrymandering, 239
Gessen, M., 225
Gidley, Hogan, 30–31
Gillum, Andrew, 70
Gjelten, Tom, 43, 44
globalization, 188, 223
global warming, 83–84
God's Chaos Candidate (Wallnau), 160
Gohmert, Louis, 35, 162
Gómez, José H., 40
Good News Club, 17–18, 36
The Good News Club (Stewart), 17, 66
Good Samaritan parable, 58
Gore, Gareth, 42
Gorsuch, Neil, 47, 48, 49, 78, 84, 225
Gospel Coalition (TGC), 202
Gough, Sean, 207
Grace Community Church in Sun Valley,
    California, 199–201
GraceLife Community Church, 196–98,
    200–201
Graham, Lindsey, 40
Graystone, Andrew, 203
Grayzone (Blumenthal), 216
Great Awokening, 105
Great Reset, 71
Green, Julie, 159, 172
Greene, Marjorie Taylor, 160
Greenwald, Glenn, 216
Grieve, Lucy, 209–10
Griffin, David Ray, 191
Griffin, Grainne, 223
Griscom, Shannon, 39
Gullner, Lutz, 215
guns, 150, 189

Haley, Nikki, 72
Hall, J. C., 69

Hall, KrisAnne, 69

Hamas, Israel's war with, 215

Hamilton Center for Classics and Civics
    Education at University of Florida,
    131, 132

Hanlon, Dan, 152

Hanna, Frank, 41

Hardy, Elle, 167–68

Harriot, Michael, 178–79

Harris, Kamala, 32, 45, 215

Hawley, Josh, 101, 129, 140, 153, 238

Haywood, Charles, 108, 134, 140

health care, affordable, 240

Heartbeat International, 211

Heartland Institute, 83–84

Heaven, 57

Hegel, Georg Wilhelm Friedrich, 109–10,
    147–48, 149–50

Heritage Action, 35

Heritage Action for America, 81

Heritage Foundation, 10, 72, 115
    and antiregulation constituency, 152
    funding for, 90
    at NatCon conference in London, 100
    on Project 2025, 104–5
    on sex and contraceptives, 105

Herschmann, Eric, 116

Her Voice Movement, 176

higher education, 128, 132, 141

Hilarides, Robert, 89

Hillsdale College, 61–62, 84, 103, 106, 118

historicism doctrine, 111, 127, 147

Hitler, Adolf, 155, 186

Hobby Lobby, 104

Hochman, Nate, 137–38, 150

Hodge, A. A., 85

Holdenried, Josh, 131

Hollywood Prayer Network, 18

Holy Trinity Brompton (HTB), 203

homeschooling movement, 68, 230

Home School Legal Defense Association,
    68

homosexuality. See LGBTQ+

Horton, Kielle (Kyle Campbell), 36–37

"housewife populism," 61

Housewives Union, 221

Howard-Browne, Rodney, 191

Howell, Elbert, 9

Hubbard, Elbert, 84

Huizenga, J. C., 89

human condition, depravity of, 109–10

human rights, 219, 227, 232–33

human trafficking, 167

Idaho, abortion ban in, 121

identitarianism, 13

identity politics, 135–36, 238, 240

Igunnubole, Jeremiah, 207

immigrant populations, 47–48, 131–32,
    133–34, 135

inclusion programs, 135

income inequality, 188

Infantry, 9, 11, 12–13, 179–80, 245

Ingraham, Laura, 235

"in-group" membership, 6

inheritance taxes, 153

Insurrection Act as priority of CRA, 105

International Coalition of Apostolic
    Leaders (ICAL), 172

International Organization of the Family
    (IOF), 225

Ireland, 217, 218, 221–24, 233

Isenberg, Andrew, 83–84

Islam, 50, 201

Israel–Hamas War, 215

Italy, 134

IVF treatments, 122

Jackson, Mark, 202

Jacobs, Cindy, 159, 172

Jaffa, Harry Victor, 109–12, 117, 118

Jaffa, Henry, 129

Jaffa, Philip, 117–19, 145

Jamati, Edna, 39

James and Joan Lindsey Family
    Foundation, 18, 19

James Madison Center, 10

January 6, 2021, insurrection

arrests made in connection with, 188
blamed on Democrats, 34–35
and Busch, 38
demographic analysis of insurgents, 188
and Eastman, 2, 107, 108, 116–17
fundraising for patriots of, 1, 182
insurgents cast as victims of, 34
and men of Claremont Institute, 10
and pastors/leaders of religious right,
    33–34
pastors' participation in, 29, 241
and Republican Party, 4
Sergeants' participation in, 11
and spirit warriors, 162–64
and Trump's attempt to overturn
    election, 31
and Trump's presidential immunity, 115
violent, spiritual rhetoric preceding,
    162–63
Jefferson, Thomas, 213, 241, 243
Jeffress, Robert, 33
Jenkins, Jennifer, 73–74, 76
Jericho March in Washington, D.C., 162
Jessip, Kevin, 162
Jewish people, 115, 120, 162, 185, 186
John M. Olin Foundation, 52
Johnson, Abby, 142
Johnson, Kelly, 163
Johnson, Mike, 163–64, 214
Jones, Alex, 183, 184, 191, 192
Jones, Bob, Sr., 235
Jones, Robert P., 23, 166
Joyce, Kathryn, 99, 216
"Judeo-Christian" (term), 50
Judicial Crisis Network, 89
Justice, Tiffany, 69

K, Mel (podcaster), 183, 186
Kadaris, Rafael, 215
Kavanaugh, Brett, 84, 147, 225
Kaveny, Cathleen, 43
Keenan, Peachy, 133–34
Keller, Tim, 202
Kelly, Megyn, 135

Kennedy, D. James, 12, 86
Kennedy, Robert F., Jr., 183
Kesler, Charles, 103, 106, 118, 133, 146–48,
    150
Kingdom Causes Inc., 36
Kirk, Charlie, 70
kleptocracies/kleptocrats, 216, 224, 233, 234
Klingenstein, Thomas D., 100, 106, 117, 153,
    154–55
Knights of Columbus, 42
Koch, Charles, 40
Koch brothers, 9, 46, 48, 89
Komlos, John, 188
Komodo Health Inc., 68
Komov, Alexey, 97, 229–30, 231
Koren, Elyssa, 227
Kristol, Bill, 109, 114, 126

labor rights, 39
labor unions, 153, 240
LaHaye, Beverly, 122–23
LaHaye, Tim, 22
Lahmeyer, Jackson, 19, 183
Laje, Agustin, 232
Lake, Kari, 159
Lamborn, Doug, 159
Land and Sea (Schmitt), 113–14
Lang, Chuck, 84
Laser, Rachel, 78
Las Vegas, ring-wing activists gathered in,
    1–2, 181–94
Latin America and Latin Americans, 166,
    167, 177, 185, 188, 232
Law and Justice (PiS), 221
Leadership Conference on Civil and
    Human Rights, 90
Leadership Institute, 69, 72, 81, 205, 244
leadership of antidemocratic movement, 8.
    See also Funders; Power Players;
    Sergeants; Thinkers
Lear, Norman, 212
legitimacy, political, 32
Leo, Leonard, 42, 43, 56, 82–83, 84, 239
Leo, Margaret, 43

LGBTQ+, 1, 11
  BAP's abhorrence of, 128
  and blessings for same-sex couples, 203
  and book bans, 11, 63–64
  calls for war on, 97
  condemned as "sinful," 197–98, 199,
    202
  criminalized, 126, 227, 231
  demonized, 6
  disinformation about, 215
  and Drag Queen Story Hours, 76–77
  and "gay agenda," 187–88, 220–21, 232
  gay school board member, 75
  and gender identity, 64
  and gender ideology, 229, 231
  money spent on campaigns against, 233
  and natural law/family, 48–49, 225
  and Project 2025, 105–6
  and public education challenges, 77
  and religious authoritarianism, 53, 224,
    226, 227, 230, 231–32
  Robinson's condemnation of, 162
  and Russia's oligarchy, 224, 230
  same-sex marriage, 44, 126, 208, 219
  and school-age children, 76
  transgender people, 68–69, 77, 105–6,
    175–76, 215, 229
  white men's claims of victimization by,
    124
LGBTQ United, 214
libertarianism, 44, 45, 85, 86–87, 91, 118
Liberty Counsel, 33, 233
Lieberman, Myron, 86
Life Challenge Church, 168–69, 172, 180
life expectancies, declining, 5
Lincoln, Abraham, 2, 110–11, 155, 236
Lincoln Project, 109
Lindell, Mike, 183
Lindsay, James (author), 70–72, 81
Lindsey, James B. (donor), 18, 93
Lindsey, Joan Holt, 18–19, 20, 21–22, 36,
    37, 93
Lindsey, Patrick, 37
Lindsey Foundation, 18, 19

Lithwick, Dahlia, 151
Littlefield, Amy, 176
lobbyists, 12
local networks, mobilization of, 245
Locke, Greg, 34
London, England, 195–98, 200–203
Loomer, Laura, 142
Lopez, Frank, 177
Lotta, Raymond, 216
Louisiana, 121

MacArthur, John, 199–201
MacDonagh, Thomas, 222
Mackenzie, Rachel, 209
Madison, James, 241
Maldonado, Guillermo, 191
Malofeev, Konstantin, 230, 231
"Manhattan Declaration: A Call of
    Christian Conscience," 52–53, 208
Manhattan Institute, 81
*Manhood: The Masculine Virtues America
    Needs* (Hawley), 129
Manliness (Mansfield), 129–30
Mansfield, Harvey C., Jr., 129–30, 141–42
Mansfield, Harvey C., Sr., 129, 141
Mao Zedong, 71, 81
Marini, John, 148, 149, 150, 152
Márquez, Nicolás, 232
marriages, 202, 219
Marshall, Paul, 203–4
Marx, Paul Benno, 217–19, 222, 234
Marxism, progressives accused of, 101
Mastermedia International, 18
Mastriano, Doug, 159, 160
Masugi, Ken, 148–49
Matthew, gospel of, 41
Maude (television show), 212
McAuliffe, Terry, 20
McCarthy, Kevin, 178
McKay, Scott, 186
media, 31–32, 34, 243–44
Media Matters, 77
Medicaid cuts, 145
Medkov, Victor, 221

Mellon, Timothy, 183
Meloni, Giorgia, 97
men and masculinity
    claims of discrimination, 24
    claims of victimization, 124
    cultivated as Sergeants, 35
    defense of conservative white men, 131
    domination over women, 199, 202
    and male headship, 141–42
    and "manliness," 127, 129–30, 136
    masculine Christianity, 220
    masculine military virtue, 29
    REN on masculinity, 125
    submission/subordination expected of
        women, 6, 141–42, 198, 199, 202
    Yenor's defense of "manliness," 127
Mercer, Rebekah, 89
Mercer, Robert, 89
meritocracy, 132
Metaxas, Eric, 34, 161
Mhathúna, Niamh, 218, 222–24
Mhathúna, Úna Bean Mhic, 218, 221–22
Miami-Dade County, Florida, 177
Microtargeted Media, 60–61
middle-class Americans, 187
Middle East conflicts, 215
militaristic rhetoric, 29, 35
military rule, plans for, 137
Millennials, 37
miscarriages, 121–22. See also abortion
misogyny, 6, 108, 125–26, 134, 142
Mitchell, Baker, Jr., 79–80
Moms for America, 35
Moms for Liberty, 67–68, 74, 75
    and anti-public-school activism, 66
    Conference, 27, 35
    and COVID-19 pandemic, 192
    National Summit, 59–60, 62–66, 72
    origin myth of, 60
    and Republican presidential
        candidates, 72
Monaghan, Thomas, 40–41
monarchism, 138–39
Montgomery, Peter, 117

Moore, E. Roy, 66–67
Moral Majority, 12, 86
Mothers of Conservatism (Nickerson), 61
Mottesi, Alberto, 166–67
Mueller, Robert, 54
multiculturalism, Kesler's attacks on, 147
Mulvaney, Mick, 152
Murphy, Jack, 125
Murphy, Justin, 128–29
Murray, Alice, 209
Mutz, Diana C., 24
My Faith Votes, 34

Nancy, Penny Young, 122–23
Napa Institute, 40
National Academy of Sciences, 23–24
National Association of Intercollegiate
    Athletics, 103
National Catholic Prayer Breakfast, 43
National Center for Public Policy
    Research, 18
National Christian Foundation (NCF), 36,
    89–90
National City Christian Church, 20
National Commission on Children, 221
National Conservatism Conference in
    London, 99–102, 135
National Education Association, 77
National Organization for Marriage, 221,
    224, 225
National Prayer Breakfast, 12
National Review, 115
Natural Law and Natural Rights
    (Finnis), 48
natural law/family, 48–49, 224–26, 234
Navarro, Peter, 183
Network for Public Education, 61–62
NETWORK Lobby for Catholic Social
    Justice, 46
Neuhaus, Richard John, 45, 52
New Apostolic Reformation (NAR), 164,
    170–72
New College, 102–4, 106, 131, 141, 146
New Deal, 111

New Right, 6, 10, 115, 139
    about, 99
    ambitions of, 136
    and anti-regulation constituency, 152
    and Arsuaga, 231
    and Christian nationalism, 104, 106
    and "deconstruction of the
        administrative state," 145
    defense of white men, 131
    and evangelicals, 119
    and "manliness," 129
    values and goals of, 137
    and Western civilization, 134
Newsmax, 32
Newsom, Gavin, 161
New York Commitment, 219
Nickerson, Michelle, 61
Nicolas, Madgie, 178
Nietzsche, Friedrich, 136, 139
Nigeria, 167
nihilism, 11, 111, 113, 127, 130, 132, 137, 147,
    152
9/11 conspiracies, 191
Nineteenth Amendment, 142
Nista, Sally, 75
Nixon, Richard, 31
"nones" in religious landscape, 164
Notre Dame Religious Liberty Clinic, 78
Novak, Michael, 41, 52

Oath Keepers, 177
Obama, Barack, 177
O'Brien, Katherine, 211
O'Donovan, Leo, 39
Ohio, 122
Oklahoma, 78–79
oligarchy/oligarchs, 5, 143, 152–53, 223, 224,
    230, 233, 234, 235, 238, 243
Onishi, Brad, 178
OpenDemocracy, 233
Operation Rescue, 218
OptimaEd, 61–62
Optima Foundation, 62
Opus Dei, 42–43, 54

Opus: The Cult of Dark Money, Human
    Trafficking, and Right-Wing Conspiracy
    Inside the Catholic Church (Gore), 42
Orban, Viktor, 167, 219
organization and planning, 244–45
Owens, Candace, 70

Pack, Michael, 151, 152
Pape, Robert, 188
parent activist groups, 35
Parents Defending Education, 35, 62
parents' rights groups, 67–68. See also
    Moms for Liberty
partisanship, 4, 193
pastors, Christian, 11, 29, 32, 241
Pastors for Trump, 11, 19, 32
patriarchy, 6, 29, 123, 124
Patriot Mobile Action, 35, 69
Pavone, Frank, 209
Pell, George, 220
Pence, Mike, 116
Pennsylvania Family Institute, 62
Pentecostals and Pentecostalism, 166–67,
    176–78, 201
Perkins, Tony, 12, 29, 37
persecution complex, 13, 23, 124
Peters, Ken, 34
Peters, Stew, 184–85, 235
Peterson, Jordan, 204
philosophers and philosophy, 109–10,
    130–31, 139
Pinkoski, Nathan, 131, 140
Pizzagate, 108
Planned Parenthood, 64
pluralism, 26
plutocracy of America, 234, 239
Poland, 219, 226, 233
political action committees (PACs), 35
political instability, 165
Politically Basic podcast, 37
Political Network for Values (PNfV),
    219–20
Pope, Art, 79–80
populism, 25

Posobiec, Jack, 108
postindustrial economy in America, 188
Poulos, John, 133
Power Players, 9, 11, 12, 191
The Power Worshippers (Stewart), 168
Pray Vote Stand conference, 175–76
pregnancies, unwanted, 228–29. *See also* reproductive health/rights
presidential election of 2016, 32, 54, 101, 214–15
presidential election of 2020
    and audit of Arizona's ballots, 30
    and drivers of support for Trump, 24
    Lindsey's predictions regarding, 18–19
    and spirit warriors, 164
    stolen-election claims (*see* Big Lie)
    Trump's attempt to overturn, 31
    Trump's attempt to subvert certification of election results, 34, 116
    and Trump's indictment, 2
    See also January 6, 2021, insurrection
presidential election of 2024, 4, 32, 35, 72, 189
presidential immunity, 49, 115
Priests for Life, 209
Prince family, 48
privatization, 61–62
progressives and liberals, 127
    accused of Marxism, 101
    calls for war on, 97
    and deadly blizzard in Texas, 202
    defending against "tyranny" of, 114
    as defined by conservatives, 111
    demonization of, 160, 161, 162, 184
    Deneen on "failures" of, 54–55
    Kesler on evil of, 147
    liberal donors, 90–91
    Lopez's rhetoric on, 177
    Right wing's beliefs about, 97
    Schmitt on failures of, 112–13
    "victimization" claims, 70
    Yenor's take on, 127
    See also "wokeness"

progressive taxation, 239
Project 2025, 104–6
    as America's "last opportunity," 115
    and "deconstruction of the administrative state," 145
    on "enemies" of America, 115
    and funders/donors, 154
    and gender ideology, 105
    and Opus Dei, 42
prolife stance, 12, 104, 105
Prosperity Gospel, 168
Protect Our Kids, 63
Protestants
    and abortion, 208, 212
    and Catholics, 47–48, 50
    Davis on, 142
    and reproductive rights of women, 51–53
    and threats posed by progress, 232
    and women's equality, 50
Proud Boys, 67, 75, 76–77, 135, 177
public confidence undermined by Trump, 32
Public Education (Lieberman), 86–87
Public Religion Research Institute (PRRI), 23
Public School Exit, 66
Putin, Vladimir, 214, 224, 234

QAnon, 68, 162, 182

race and racism, 77
    and abortion, 133–34
    aims of racism, 142
    and Black conservatives, 178–79
    denial of existance of racism, 178–79
    Eastman's views on, 135
    and identity politics, 135–36
    and motives driving war on public education, 85–86
    at ReAwaken America Tour, 185
    and "replacement" theories, 108
Rachel's Vineyard, 209
Raising Them Right (Spencer), 70

Ralston College, 203–4
Ramaswamy, Vivek, 72, 101, 140, 145
Raspail, Jean, 131–32
"Raw Egg Nationalist" (REN), 124–25, 129, 130, 133
reactionary nihilism, 7–8
Reagan, Ronald, 41, 177, 236
Reagan administration, 152, 220
reason rejected by antidemocratic movement, 7
ReAwaken America Tour, 11, 181–94
Reed, Ralph, 12, 34, 100, 162, 177, 232
Reese, Dran, 67
Reform Prayer Network, 168
reforms to governmental institutions, 237
regulation, government, 152
relativism, 127, 231
religious freedom, 21, 238, 242
religious organizations, taxpayer funding for, 150, 241–42
renewable energy, 105
Reno, R. R. "Rusty," 45, 53–54
representative government, 240
reproductive health/rights, 6–7, 53
    and antidemocratic ideology, 238
    and California's Proposition I, 161
    Christian nationalists' work to expunge, 47
    contraceptives, 57, 105, 122, 208, 217, 231, 240
    Heritage Foundation on, 105
    and IVF treatments, 122
    and needs of right-wing supporters, 240
    as prime focus of right-wing politics, 122
    and religious conservatives, 51–53, 57, 231, 232
    and sex education, 227–28
    war on, 122
    women punished for seeking, 123
    See also abortion
Republican Party, 4
    and antidemocratic movement, 5
    anti-Trump members of, 193
    and Arsuaga, 232
    and Brown, 225
    changing culture of, 193
    and discrimination against Christians, 23
    and January 6, 2021, insurrection, 4, 34
    and spirit warriors, 162
    and Ukraine, 214
    and "voting biblical values, 22
The Republican Reversal (Turner and Isenberg), 83–84
Return of the Strong Gods (Reno), 53–54
Revolutionary War, 29
Rhodes, Stewart, 178
Rice, Chris, 196
Right to Life UK, 211
Right Wing Watch, 69
Rinderle, Katherine, 76
RINOs, 1, 192
Road to Majority (2021), 162
Road to Majority conference, 34, 100, 178, 179
Roberts, Kevin, 105–6, 145
Roberts, Tom, 42, 44
Robinson, Mark, 162
Robles, Adianis Morales, 179
Roe v. Wade, 51, 204, 211, 212, 224
Roger Bacon Academy, 79–80
Rohde, David, 54
Roosevelt, Theodore, 235
Rothschilds, 186
Rufo, Christopher, 66, 103, 104, 120, 132, 139, 145
Rumble (Greenwald), 216
Rushdoony, Rousas J., 86
Russia, 54, 214–15, 216–17, 221, 224, 230, 233, 234
Rydin, Mike, 89

Salvini, Matteo, 97
same-sex marriage, 44, 126, 208, 219. See also LGBTQ+
Sanders, Bernie, 214

Santos, M. Vidal, 231
Sarah Scaife Foundation, 48, 106, 153, 154
Satan, 178, 184, 208
Scaife Foundation, 88
Schaeffer, Francis, 51
Schaub, Diana, 130
Scheidler, Joseph, 218, 222
Schlafly, Phyllis, 50
Schlumpf, Heidi, 44, 45, 47
Schmidt, Steve, 109, 155
Schmitt, Carl, 112–15, 116, 149–50
Schneck, Stephen, 43
schools and public education, 59–81, 82–93
    and antidemocratic ideology, 238,
       239, 243
    and anti-public-school activism, 66
    and book bans, 62–64, 76
    conservatives' hostility to, 65–67
    and critical race theory, 30–31, 63, 66,
       69, 70, 75, 77–78, 80, 141
    and DeSantis, 84
    desegregation of, 66, 85–86
    and donors' dark money, 88–91
    efforts to place Bibles in, 203
    efforts to undermine, 18, 77, 80–81,
       91–93
    and gender identity, 64
    and homeschooling movement, 68, 230
    hostility toward, 4
    motives driving war on, 85–87
    nationalists' rhetoric on, 27
    and needs of right-wing supporters, 240
    opponents of, 168–69
    and pandemic, 77
    prayer/religious teachings in, 91–92, 238
    privatization of, 76, 81, 153, 243
    and pro-democracy movement, 243
    reforms/decentralization of, 128–29
    religious charter schools, 78–80
    as scapegoat, 66
    school board wars, 29–30, 69, 73–78
    and "school choice" advocates, 89
    school vouchers, 81, 87
    and secularism, 87

    and separation of church and state,
       78, 242
    sex education in, 227–28, 229
    "wokeness" treated as threat in, 72, 75,
       76, 84, 87
Schwarzwalder, Rob, 87
scientists, demons' influence on, 175
Scotland, 209–10, 211
Scott, Greg, 226–27
Scott, Rick, 179
Scott, Tim, 179
secularism, 54, 87, 231
Seid, Barre, 82, 83–85, 88, 91, 93
Seidel, Andrew, 25
Sekulow, Jay, 226
separation of church and state, 18, 25–26,
    78, 98–99, 163, 176, 241–43
September 11, 2001, conspiracy theories, 191
Sergeants, 11, 13, 35, 179, 191
Servant Foundation, 89–90
Sessions, Jeff, 54
Seven Mountains ideology, 170, 171, 172, 178
1776 Commission, 103, 146
sex education, 227–28, 229
sexual identity/orientation, 104, 215.
    See also LGBTQ+
sexuality, 48–49, 122, 165, 175–76, 202, 238.
    See also reproductive health/rights
Seymour, William, 165
Sharlet, Jeff, 216
Shuai, Peng, 56
Signatry, 90
Singer, Paul, 53, 56
Sirico, Robert A., 45
Slack, Kevin, 108, 154
slavery, suppression of history, 11
small government, demands for, 238
Smesler, Daniel, 169
Smirnov, Dmitri, 97
Smith, Gerald L. K., 235
Smith-Laing, Tim, 70
Sobolik, Chelsea Patterson, 122
social gospel, 25, 41
social justice, 46, 58, 136

Society for American Civic Renewal, 134

Soros, George, 186

Sotomayor, Sonya, 47, 115

Southeastern Legal Foundation, 62

Southern Baptist Convention, 51, 86, 122,
    141, 163, 199, 212

Southern Poverty Law Center, 70

Sowell, Thomas, 131

Spain, 230–32

speaking in tongues, 165, 168–70

Spell, Tony, 191

Spencer, Kyle, 69–70

spiritual warfare, 12, 162–63, 168, 170, 178

spirit warriors, 159–80
    appeal of religion to, 180
    and Latinos, 177
    and New Apostolic Reformation,
        170–72
    origins of, 165–67
    and political theology of power, 170–71
    and Seven Mountains ideology, 170,
        171, 172, 178
    and speaking in tongues, 165, 168–70
    and Valentine, 173–75
    violent rhetoric of, 162–63, 168, 178, 179
    and white nationalist extremists,
        177–78

*The Stakes: America at the Point of No
    Return* (Anton), 139–40

Stand Courageous, 29, 35

Stanton Healthcare, 211

State Policy Network, 27, 83, 239

status anxiety, 5, 23–24

Staver, Mat, 33, 67

Stein, Jill, 215

Stepkowski, Aleksander, 226

Stern, Mark Joseph, 151

Stetson, Chuck, 225

St. James Church on Clerkenwell Green,
    202

Stone, Roger, 161, 183, 192

Storer, Horatio Robinson, 133

Strategic Alliance to Fight Human
    Trafficking (SAFE-SBC), 36

Strauss, Leo, 109–10, 111, 113, 114, 115, 149

Straussianism, 117, 139, 140, 147

strongman saviors, 13

Sullivan, Vicky, 39

Sunday treated as "day of rest," 104

Taiwan, 56, 215

taxes, 153, 239, 241–42

Tenpenny, Sherri, 183

Terry, Randall, 218

Texas, 121, 202

Texas Public Policy Foundation, 88

Thatcher, Ben, 205, 209

theocracies/theocrats, 6, 7, 36, 89, 105, 234,
    238, 242, 243

Thiel, Peter, 56

Thinkers, 10–11, 13, 179

Thomas, Clarence, 53, 78, 84, 98, 131

Thomas, Ginni, 98

Thomas Merton Center, 38, 39, 41, 46

Tiger Lily (user name), 134

Tilton, Robert, 174

totalitarianism, 105, 119, 231

"Transformed Wife" (@
    godlywomanhood), 142

transgender people, 68–69, 77, 105–6,
    175–76, 215, 229

tribalism, 4

troll farms in Russia, 214–15

Trump, Donald, 145
    antidemocratic movement's predating
        of, 4
    attempted coup, 31, 32–34 (*see also*
        January 6, 2021, insurrection)
    attempt to overturn election results, 31
        (*see also* Big Lie)
    attempt to subvert certification of
        election results, 34, 116
    blame placed on, 180
    campaign for president, 161
    and Catholics, 44, 45
    considered anointed by God, 160
    considered a success, 137
    and Constitution of the US, 26

and COVID-19 conspiracies, 191
criminal indictments/convictions, 2,
    59, 99, 161, 181, 190, 192
on danger "from the people within,"
    113
drivers of support for, 23–24
and "The Flight 93 Election," 101
on gender ideology, 72
Jaffa on anarchy of, 118
and January 6, 2021, insurrection, 31
Kesler on, 146, 147
keynote address at CWA convention,
    122–23
Lopez's rhetoric on, 177
Marini on, 148
and Mueller's investigation, 54
pastors for, 11
predictors of support for, 23
and presidential election of 2016, 234
and presidential immunity, 49, 115
public confidence undermined by, 32
and ReAwaken America Tour, 189
rejection of election results, 32–33
religious leaders' defense of, 161–62
and Republican primary, 64, 72
Republicans against, 193
and rule of law, 148
and Russia, 216, 234
sexual misconduct of, 123
supporters' devotion to, 189
and Ukraine, 214
violent imagery associated with, 182
on "wokeness," 101
women's rights impacted by, 123
Trump, Eric, 183, 186
Trump administration, 84, 144–46,
    150–52
Truth & Liberty Coalition, 80, 160
Turner, Jay, 83–84

Uighur genocide, 56
Uihlein, Richard, 88–89
Ukraine, 101, 133–34, 214, 215, 216

unions, 153, 240
United in Purpose, 28, 92
United Kingdom, spread of evangelicalism
    to, 195–98, 200–205, 206–12, 221–24
United States Coalition of Apostolic
    Leaders (USCAL), 21
United States Conference of Catholic
    Bishops, 41, 44
Universal Declaration of Human Rights,
    219
universities, 128, 132
University of Florida's Hamilton Center
    for Classics and Civics Education, 131,
    132
Unmasking the Administrative State
    (Marini), 148
U.S. Coalition of Apostolic Leaders
    (USCAL), 172
U.S. Conference of Catholic Bishops
    (USCCB), 40
U.S. Constitution, 25, 26, 27, 55, 69,
    78, 236
U.S. Department of State, 145, 151
U.S. Department of the Interior, 104
U.S. Supreme Court, 38–39
    abortion rulings of, 47, 49, 51, 204, 211,
        212, 224
    and antidemocratic players, 239
    and Antonin Scalia Law School, 84
    Brown v. Board of Education, 85
    and Federalist Society, 45, 47, 82–83,
        123, 244
    and Judicial Crisis Network, 89
    on presidential immunity, 115
    reforms needed in, 237
    religious composition of, 47
    on religious liberty, 242
    and religious school funding, 78–80
    and school prayer, 65
    and Trump's attempt to subvert
        certification of election results, 116
    and women's rights, 123
    See also individual justices

vaccines, 178
Valentine, Leigh, 173–75
Valentine, Robert, 174
Values Voters Summit (now Pray, Vote, Stand), 122, 175–76
Vance, J. D., 55, 153, 238
Vaughan-Spruce, Isabel, 206–7
Vermeule, Adrian, 55–56
Verona, Italy, 1–2
victimization, 70
Victory Channel, 170–71
violence and violent rhetoric
    domestic violence, 231
    Eastman's justification of, 116
    as index of growing fears, 189
    at ReAwaken America Tour, 182, 183–84, 185, 189, 192
    spiritual warfare, 162–63, 168, 170, 178, 179, 182
    threats against political enemies, 192
    in written propaganda, 189
Virginia, 241
Virginia Project, 27
voter fraud, 27, 30, 35
voter guides, 80
voting rights, 7, 142, 237, 239
Vought, Russ, 105, 145

wages, 5, 126, 240
Wagner, C. Peter, 170
Waldo, Dwight, 148
Walker, Scott, 40
WallBuilders Presentation, 18, 27, 28, 65
Waller, Adam, 197–98, 201
Wallnau, Lance, 160–61, 170, 171, 172, 175, 176
Walton, William L., 89
Wambsganss, Leigh, 69
Ward, Charlie, 186
Ward, Vicky, 89
Warsaw, Michael, 45
Washington, George, 27–28
Watchmen on the Wall, 11, 19, 32

Watson, Mike, 115
wealthy and wealth disparity, 5, 41, 239, 240. *See also* Funders
Weaver, Robert, 162
Weiss, Melissa, 77–78
Well Versed ministry, 160–61
Western civilization, 134–35
Westmont College, 17–18
Weyrich, Paul, 22, 50, 51, 224
Whaley, Jane, 174
White, Paula, 168
white people
    claims of discrimination against, 23, 24
    white genocide conspiracy theory, 108
    white nationalists, 177–78
    and white supremacy, 23, 85–86, 124, 132
Whitlock, Jason, 142
Why Liberalism Failed (Deneen), 55
Wilks brothers, 9, 88
Willis, Fani, 185
Wilson, Jason, 134
Wilson, Teddy, 67
Wilson, Woodrow, 147–48
Winters, Michael Sean, 44
Witherspoon Institute, 45
"wokeness," 10, 70, 72, 136
    called totalitarianism, 105
    in churches, 178
    and "deconstruction of the administrative state," 144–45
    and human rights, 219
    at New College, 102–4
    New Right's hatred of, 99, 100–103
    in public education, 72, 75, 76, 84, 87
    as root of all evil, 10
    seen as public threat, 100–102
    and Ukraine's war, 214
    and "Watchman Decree" prayer, 171
    Yenor's take on, 127
    See also progressives and liberals
Wolf, Naomi, 216
Wolfe, William, 105

women
  access to power in conservative
    circles, 123
  and antidemocratic ideology, 238
  BAP's abhorrence of, 127
  "childless cat ladies," 55
  cultivated as Sergeants, 35
  and "deconstruction of the
    administrative state," 145
  employment of, 199, 221
  and equality, 198, 217, 221, 224, 231
  excluded from leadership positions, 20
  and feminism, 50, 127, 130, 217
  gender discrimination in wages, 126
  and gender dynamics in authoritarian
    movement, 6
  and gender ideology, 229
  identity and belonging of Christian,
    123
  male domination over, 199, 202
  Mansfield's perspectives on, 130
  and misogyny, 6, 108, 125–26, 134,
    142
  money spent on campaigns against,
    233
  negative impacts of progress by, 137
  as the opposition, 111
  political engagement of conservative, 61
  and religious conservatives, 50
  resentments toward, 136–37
  and Russian authoritarianism, 224
  submission/subordination expected of,
    6, 141–42, 198, 199, 202
  victims of abuse, 199
  and voting rights, 7, 142
  white men's claims of victimization by,
    124
  and Yenor, 125–27
  See also reproductive health/rights
Wommack, Andrew, 80, 171
Word of Faith Fellowship, 173–74
working people, 8, 238–39, 240
World Congress of Families (WCF), 1,
  97–98, 221, 225–26
World Economic Forum, 184
The World Over (television program), 45

Yakunin, Vladimir, 230
Yarvin, Curtis, 140, 141
  and "The Cathedral," 138–39
Yass, Jeff, 88, 89
Yenor, Scott, 125–27, 128, 129, 130, 131, 141
Youngkin, Glenn, 20, 32, 33
Youth Defense, 222

Zack, Aaron, 113–14
The Zapatero Project (Arsuaga and Santos),
  231
Zelensky, Volodymyr, 133–34
Ziegler, Bridget, 60, 69, 72, 75, 76, 205
Ziegler, Christian, 60–61, 76
Ziklag Group, 12, 92

A NOTE ON THE AUTHOR

KATHERINE STEWART writes about the intersection of faith and politics and the threat to democratic institutions. Her previous book, *The Power Worshippers: Inside the Dangerous Rise of Religious Nationalism*, won First Place for Excellence in Nonfiction Books from the Religion News Association as well as a Morris D. Forkosch Award. The book was adapted into a documentary feature, *God & Country*, produced by Rob Reiner and Michele Reiner.

Stewart's earlier book, *The Good News Club: The Christian Right's Stealth Assault on America's Children*, was an examination of the religious right and public education. She writes for the *New York Times*, the *Washington Post*, NBC, the *New Republic*, and *Religion News Service* and has been featured on MSNBC, CNN, NPR, and other broadcast media.